The

COMPLETE

LANGUAGE

of FOOD

The
COMPLETE
LANGUAGE
of FOOD

A Definitive and Illustrated History

S. Theresa Dietz

Inspiring | Educating | Creating | Entertaining

Brimming with creative inspiration, how-to projects, and useful information to enrich your everyday life, quarto.com is a favorite destination for those pursuing their interests and passions.

First published in 2022 by Wellfleet Press, an imprint of The Quarto Group,
142 West 36th Street, 4th Floor, New York, NY 10018, USA
T (212) 779-4972 F (212) 779-6058 www.Quarto.com

Wellfleet titles are also available at discount for retail, wholesale, promotional, and bulk purchase. For details, contact the Special Sales Manager by email at specialsales@quarto.com or by mail at The Quarto Group, Attn: Special Sales Manager, 100 Cummings Center Suite 265D, Beverly, MA 01915 USA.

10 9 8 7 6 5 4 3 2 1

ISBN: 978-1-57715-259-0

Library of Congress Cataloging-in-Publication Data available upon request.

Publisher: Rage Kindelsperger
Creative Director: Laura Drew
Managing Editor: Cara Donaldson
Editor: Elizabeth You
Cover and Interior Design: Verso Design

Printed in China

This book provides general information on various widely known and widely accepted images of plants, minerals, fungi, and other elements commonly used for culinary purposes. However, it should not be relied upon as recommending or promoting any specific diagnosis or method of treatment for a particular condition, and it is not intended as a substitute for medical advice or for direct diagnosis and treatment of a medical condition by a qualified physician. Readers who have questions about a particular condition, possible treatments for that condition, or possible reactions from the condition or its treatment should consult a physician or other qualified healthcare professional.

CONTENTS

INTRODUCTION

To survive in this world, we human beings require air, water, shelter, and food. Whether or not the food is delicious, we must eat or we shall die. There are foods that can sustain us from within that will energize, heal, and empower us physically. In this way, we can effectively get through our entire day and seamlessly move through to the next, from day to day to day.

In addition to sustaining physical life, foods have symbolic meanings they have acquired over time. Food can also have mystical, magical, and metaphysical powers that can coax, bend, fend off, and protect us from negative energies that swirl around us from the spirit realm. Food is one of the building blocks that can be used to erect protective shields to protect and fortify our spiritual selves. Food can also set the stage so that we can recognize love, wish for some luck or more of it, attract money to our pockets, push out negative and especially malicious energies, and invite the balanced harmonies of peace and love to enter our homes, blessing ourselves and all of those who live under the same roof.

Nearly all of us have a morning ritual that we start our days with, even if it is merely a yawn and a stretch. There is sweet magic in that. And, *possibly*, that magic is a positive power that can be utilized as a spiritual brick to construct what we have started to call our personal "wheel house." This mythological structure is located within our mind. It is where we retain our accumulated knowledge, which includes every skill we have ever acquired. The potential to utilize all that we know to empower us to begin something . . . *anything* . . . starts with the beginning of our day. From there on, we can follow through and fully accomplish the great things to which we set our mind to accomplishing.

It is empowering to believe we can do great things. Even if it *seems* mundane, it's still important. We need to believe we *can* in order to proceed *to* and *through* to the completion of virtually anything! Whether it be a day's work or a project of any kind. Belief in ourselves and in what we set out to accomplish can help. Empowerment can make that which could have, should have, and would have occurred if we had believed it could be. Since there is meaning and power in our food, what we eat can be our personal supply of positive energy. It is also the type of energy that can be planned for in advance.

Recognizing the symbolic meaning and the possible power of a specific ingredient is an interesting association to make. What we might eat on any highly significant day, for any particularly, critically important event, can be more meaningful than we realized. It can also have meaning because we planned it. For an event, an especially meaningful showpiece dish of celebration can be placed at the center of a table set for a feast. Even if not thought out in advance, there is no doubt such a dish should taste sublime and look magnificent. Is there any reason why it could not or should not also mean something positive and fitting for the occasion?

To consider the ingredients is a way to empower that special dish to be all it has the potential to be, and the most empowering way is to wish good luck for all present who partake of the celebration food. This specially made food could be as common a presentation as a birthday cake or a wedding cake, a decorated yule cake, or a towering glistening croquembouche. Or, it can be something like a savory and elaborately-presented stuffed and roasted turkey with all the favorite trimmings and associated side dishes close by.

More so now than before I started this immensely interesting study of the meanings and possible powers of foods, I recognize how my own favorite foods connect to me. This recognition provided insight into why I like them and include them in my repertoire of favorite foods. I discovered how they have connected to me in the past and why I still enjoy them so much. Or, in some cases, not at all. I noticed that my own favorite foods could actually fortify me spiritually and might have been doing so since before I even knew that possibility existed. I'm thinking that they will do so again and again, day after day.

In this book, from A–Z are the raw, naturally growing edible ingredients that have been used as food in various kinds of ways for up to thousands of years. In the second part of the book titled "Culinary Finds Around the World," there are outlines of some foods that have drifted down to us today, from a long ago time. Some dishes came from so long ago that one would think they would be completely forgotten by now. However, that is not the case. What has happened is that they have been developed, adopted, and adapted again and again into the cuisines and taste profiles of many different cultures in countries all around the world!

How to
USE THIS
BOOK

*I*f you do not know the scientific name of a plant, but you do know one of its common names, you can find that name in the Index of Common Food Names. There you will find the corresponding number that you can then refer to in the body of the book. You can also locate the number of a specific plant (or several different plants) by determining which Meaning you are researching. This is a book that specifically references food, so an effort has been made to point out the toxicity of a plant, what part or parts of the plant are toxic, and if their toxicity is eliminated with ripening or cooking. Even so, take the time to do further research of your own to determine whether something is safe to eat before you do so. The internet is a wonderful source for that kind of scientific information when it comes to food and food preparation.

From A through Z the focus is on the edible parts or the derivatives of many plants that humans consider to be food. Among them are fruits, vegetables, chilies, herbs, grains, nuts, berries, a few plants of the sea, and some choice edible forest fungi that ultimately became the base of the inexhaustible global menu that we human beings have devised.

Following that section are forty-four foods created during some time in history that eventually circled the globe to become adapted, adopted, and repeatedly prepared because, all around the world, people love to eat and they enjoy their own cuisine and that of others. Appreciation for good food can easily connect us all.

Be informed, stay safe, feel free to tap into the innate powers of trees, plants, and flowers, always let the recipients of your culinary gifts know what significant thoughts and feelings are in your heart... and please, whatever you do and whenever you do it: *do not even dare to vex the fairies!*

No. 000: (cross-reference number for searching from any index)

Specific primary scientific name

 (toxicity symbol)

 (medicinal symbol) •┄┄┄┄┄┄┄┄┄┄┄┄┄┄┄┄┄

Note: *The medicinal symbol indicates that either currently or at some time in the past, folk healers, herbalist practitioners, or traditional medicine physicians have used this ingredient or its derivative for medicinal purposes. Further research into its medicinal potential is encouraged.*

Other Known Scientific Names | Common Names

❋ **SYMBOLIC MEANING:** Come to me; I am shy; my heart aches for you; and so on.

🎨 **COLOR MEANINGS:** When applicable to particular colors of a flower or leaf.

🌱 **COMPONENT MEANINGS:** Any meanings associated with branches, leaves, seeds, or sprays of a plant.

 POSSIBLE POWERS: Healing; love; protection; and so on.

 PLEASANT DREAMING: Pleasant meanings from dreams associated with food.

 FOLKLORE AND FACTS: Tidbits of factual, fanciful, mystical, magical, or plain silly information.

No. 001

Abelmoschus esculentus

Okra
Green Okra | Ladies' Fingers | Ochro

☀ SYMBOLIC MEANING
Curse breaker.

🌀 POSSIBLE POWERS
Protection against a curse or evil; Repels negative energy.

☾ FOLKLORE AND FACTS
Okra is one of the most heat- and drought-tolerant plants in the world. The leaves, pods, and seeds of the Okra plant are edible. The leaves can be prepared and cooked like beet greens. The gooey pods will thicken soups and stews. To help reduce the Okra slime, sauté the vegetable on high heat. One way to enjoy relatively slime-free Okra is by first dredging slices in beaten egg and seasoned cornmeal, before deep-frying them until crispy. • Cajun "gumbo" would not be the same without Okra. • The seeds may be roasted, ground, then brewed into a decaffeinated substitute for Coffee.

No. 002

Acer saccharum

Sugar Maple
Hard Maple

☀ SYMBOLIC MEANINGS
Reserve; Reservation.

🌀 POSSIBLE POWERS
Air element; Earth element; Jupiter; Longevity; Love; Masculine energy; Money.

☾ FOLKLORE AND FACTS
In early spring, growers tap Sugar Maple trees to collect the flowing sap in either small buckets or by using tubing and gravity to pull the sap to a collection tank at the bottom of a hill. The sap is brought into a "sugar shack" to continually evaporate the water by boiling it out until the sap becomes a viscous syrup, or further on to become maple sugar. • Sugar Maple seed pods are unusual in that they occur connected in pairs that spin as they fall from the tree, to be known as samaras, maple keys, helicopters, whirlybirds, or poly-noses. The connected seed pods are sometimes gilded with silver or gold, then worn as jewelry. • The US Army developed a carrier based on the shape of the *Acer* tree seed that can hold up to sixty-five pounds of supplies when dropped from a plane. • Sugar Maple tree wood makes a fine first magic centering wand.

No. 003

Actinidia deliciosa

Kiwifruit
Chinese Gooseberry | Kiwi | Kiwi Fruit

☀ SYMBOLIC MEANINGS
Adventure; Adventurous.

🌀 POSSIBLE POWERS
Adventure; Relaxation.

☾ FOLKLORE AND FACTS
The pulp of a ripe, coarsely fuzzy-skinned Kiwifruit is edible and can, when mashed or juiced, be used as a meat tenderizer. That is because the natural enzyme in Kiwifruit, actinidin, will break down tough tissue without turning the meat's tissue mushy. The fruit can be mashed and mixed with olive oil and vinegar, then be used as a marinade. Or, the fleshy underside of the skin can simply be rubbed on all sides of the meat. • The first written reference to Kiwifruit was in China during the twelfth century.

No. 004

Aframomum corrorima

Korarima
Ethiopian Cardamom | False Cardamom

☀ SYMBOLIC MEANING
Familiar comfort.

🌀 POSSIBLE POWERS
Aphrodisiac; Love; Luck; Lust; Money; Wishing.

☾ FOLKLORE AND FACTS
The edible part of the Korarima tree is the dried seeds, which can also be found as an ingredient in several Ethiopian seasoning blends, such as *mitmita* and *berbere*. Korarima features in Ethiopian recipes, Middle-Eastern seasoning blends, and as a flavoring for coffee. • Make, then carry a pink and red sachet filled with Korarima seeds to entice romantic love. • Folk medicine remedies widely use Korarima for flatulence relief.

A

No. 005

Aframomum melegueta

Grains of Paradise

Alligator Pepper | Guinea Pepper | Melegueta Chili | Mbongo Spice

SYMBOLIC MEANINGS

Judge; Judgment.

POSSIBLE POWERS

Determining guilt; Divination; Fire element; Love; Luck; Lust; Mars; Masculine energy; Money; Wishing.

FOLKLORE AND FACTS

Grains of Paradise has had a resurgence of great interest for use in flavoring gin as well as in contemporary cuisine, craft beers, some pastries, and liqueurs. In Europe, between the fourteenth and fifteenth centuries, it was commonly added to wine that smelled stale. In the eighteenth century, King George III ruled that Grains of Paradise could not be used in alcoholic beverages, although it continued to be used to fortify malt liquors, cordials, and gins. • In some parts of Nigeria, Igbo traditional religious prayers and offerings always involve Grains of Paradise, along with the revered Kola Nuts. West African social meetings and baby naming ceremonies include Grains of Paradise. • The seeds, either whole or powdered, can be used to make wishes by holding the pepper in the hand to make the wish, then tossing a little of it in each of the four cardinal directions, beginning with north and ending with west.

No. 006

Agaricus bisporus

Champignon Mushroom

Baby Bella | Button Mushroom | Common Mushroom | Cremini Mushroom | Italian Brown Mushroom | Mushroom | Portabello Mushroom | Swiss Brown Mushroom | White Mushroom

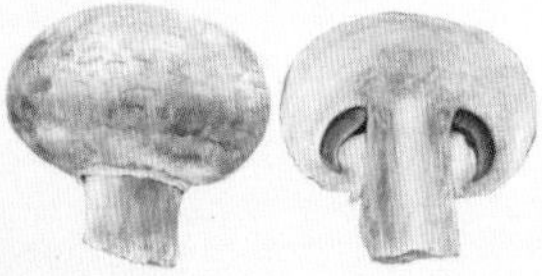

SYMBOLIC MEANINGS

Enlightenment; Good luck; Longevity; Rebirth.

POSSIBLE POWERS

Elves; Energy; Enlightenment; Fairies; Healing; Luck; Longevity; Prosperity; Rebirth; Safety; Transformation that is either good or bad.

FOLKLORE AND FACTS

Champignon Mushrooms are cultivated in at least seventy countries and are edible at its various stages between immaturely small and white, or maturely large and brown. • The small white mushrooms are most often marketed as Buttons. When larger and brown, they are Cremini Mushrooms, which are perfect for stuffing and then broiling or baking. A brown cap between four to six inches indicates a Portabello Mushroom. A large, grilled Portabello Mushroom makes a superb burger. • A word of warning is to *never* trespass into a fairy ring of these or any species of mushrooms growing wild. It is where fairies carry out their magical ceremonies and celebrations. The mushrooms are there to provide a seat for the elder fairies and those others who may be needing to sit and rest. According to both English and Celtic legends, the consequences of trespassing into that circle of sacred private fairy property can be vengefully dire.

No. 007

Agastache foeniculum

Blue Giant Hyssop

Anise Hyssop | Fragrant Giant Hyssop

SYMBOLIC MEANINGS

Clean; Cleanliness.

POSSIBLE POWERS

Plenty; Provision.

FOLKLORE AND FACTS

A North American mint, the rich aniseed flavor of the edible Blue Giant Hyssop leaves is highly favored in salads and teas. • Blue Giant Hyssop is among the most prolifically blooming plants for feeding hummingbirds, butterflies, and honeybees. Throughout summer until first frost, one acre can support one hundred beehives.

No. 008

Agave tequilana ☠ ⚗

Blue Agave

Maguey | Sentry Plant | Tequila Agave

☀ SYMBOLIC MEANINGS
Desire; Lust; Lusty;
Sensual desire.

🌀 POSSIBLE POWERS
Abundance; Fire element;
Healing; Infuses meaning; Lust;
Mars; Masculine energy.

☾ FOLKLORE AND FACTS
Any harvestable Agave plant is grown from seven to
fourteen years before extracting its toxic juice, which is
highly processed before it is edible. • Agave syrup is a
commercially made sweetener created from *Agave tequilana*
as well as some other *Agave* varieties using different methods
than in the making of tequila. Syrup produced by the Blue
Agave dissolves in both hot and cold liquids, is as sweet as
sugar, and can be used, in some recipes, as a sugar or honey
substitute. The harvesting process begins with removing the
tall stalk or "mast" to allow Agave juice to accumulate in the
hollow. This liquid is collected and then processed to make
Agave syrup. Agave syrup is not "agave nectar."

No. 009

Akebia quinata ☠ ⚗

Akebia

Chocolate Vine | Five-Leaf Akebia | Raisin Vine

☀ SYMBOLIC MEANINGS
Complete; Peacemaker;
Powerful.

🌀 POSSIBLE POWERS
Completion; Emotional
security; Finance; Planning; Power; Sharing.

☾ FOLKLORE AND FACTS
The soft sweet pulp of the Akebia fruit is a seasonal Japanese
delicacy. Its bitter rind is often treated as a vegetable that
is stuffed with ground meats before deep frying. • Akebia
vines are a favorite material among basket weavers. • The
people of Yamagata, Japan, offer Akebia fruit on the autumn
equinox because of a legend that their ancestors will return
during an autumn equinox in a ship woven from Akebia
vines. • To facilitate a positive outcome when acting as
peacemaker, carry a talisman of Akebia wood.

No. 010

Allium ampeloprasum var. ampeloprasum ⚗

Leek

Broadleaf Wild Leek | Elephant Garlic | Great-headed Garlic |
Kurrat | Ramps | Wild Leeks

☀ SYMBOLIC MEANING
Lingering presence.

🌀 POSSIBLE POWERS
Exorcism; Fire element; Love; Mars; Masculine energy;
Protection; Sun.

☾ FOLKLORE AND FACTS
Cultivated Leeks can be harvested when they are small. Or,
they can be thinned then hilled with soil, which will force
a longer white portion along the stem while it continues
to grow. The white portion of the Leek is tender, whereas
the green tops are not, although they can be tenderized
in stocks, soups, and stews. • The human man-fist-sized
Elephant Garlic is closely related to the Leek. • For many
Leek aficionados, foraging for the flavor-intense Wild Leeks
or "ramps" is a ritual of spring that lasts from when the
trees begin to bud new leaves until they fill out to become
leafy. Enormous patches of aromatic Wild Leeks will direct
an inexperienced forager right to them. • There is a saying
that Wild Leeks keep the sniffles and the neighbors away.
The sniffles? Maybe. • The Leek is believed to have been
brought into Southwest England and Wales
by Prehistoric people. • The British
one-pound coin in 1985 and 1990 both
depicted a Leek in its design as a tribute
to Wales, where it is a national symbol.
• If two people eat Leeks together,
they will fall in love. • To break
a hex and drive away evil, bite
into a Leek.

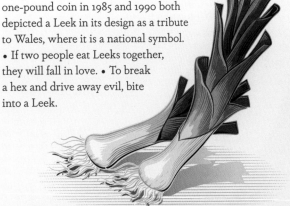

A

No. 011

Allium ascalonicum

Shallot

Eschalot | French Gray Shallot | French Red
Shallot | Persian Shallot | True Shallot

✳ SYMBOLIC MEANINGS
Land of Astolat; Unrequited
love.

✺ POSSIBLE POWERS
Cures misfortune; Fire element; Luck; Mars; Masculine
energy; Purification; Sun.

☾ FOLKLORE AND FACTS
The cloves of the Shallot plant's bulb are edible. When a
Shallot is unavailable for use in a recipe, an onion is an
acceptable substitute. • The ancient Greeks believed that the
Shallot came from an ancient city in biblical Canaan called
Ashkelon. Another land associated with the Shallot is The
Land of Astolat, which in Arthurian legend is the location
of the castle belonging to Lady Elaine, who died of a broken
heart due to her unrequited love for Sir Lancelot.

No. 012

Allium cepa

Common Onion

Egyptian Tree Onion | Red Onion | Walking Onion | White Onion | Yellow Onion

✳ SYMBOLIC MEANINGS
Emotional release; Multi-layered protection.

✺ POSSIBLE POWERS
Cleverness; Colorize; Exorcism; Fire element; Healing; Isis;
Lust; Mars; Masculine energy; Money; Prophetic dreaming;
Protection; Purification; Removes aggressive or negative
energy; Spiritual cleansing; Spirituality; Sun.

☾ FOLKLORE AND FACTS
Ancient Egyptians
worshipped the Onion
because its shape, layers, and
concentric rings symbolized
eternal life. Funerary priests
of ancient Egyptians included
Onions in their burial rituals.
• In the Middle Ages, Onions
were gifts valuable enough
to use for paying rent. • The Pilgrims brought Onions over
to America from England, to discover they were already
enjoyed by Native Americans. • The edible Egyptian Tree

Onion's leafy stalks and bulb are usually only available fresh
near to where they are grown, and are used the same as
most onions would be, including pickling. • An Onion on
the mantelpiece or hung in a room will strongly attract and
absorb negative energy and possibly even a malicious spirit,
to be removed by burying or burning the Onion after the
anxiety dissipates and the process feels as though it has been
completed. • An interesting divination for decision-making
is to scratch different possibilities on individual Onions. Put
them in a dark place, checking *once* daily. The first sprouting
Onion will provide the answer.

No. 013

Allium fistulosum

Everlasting Onion

Bunching Onion | Long Green Onion | Scallion | Spring Onion | Welsh Onion

✳ SYMBOLIC MEANINGS
Strength; You're elegant; You're perfect.

✺ POSSIBLE POWERS
Enhances psychic ability; Fire element; Prophetically dream;
Protection; Sun.

☾ FOLKLORE AND FACTS
The leaves and bulb of the Everlasting Onion are pungent
and edible. They can be sautéed, added raw to salads, or
lightly trimmed for the table to be eaten with salt. Everlasting
Onion can be sliced then dried in a low oven to keep as a
jarred herb for later use. • The Everlasting Onion stem is tall
and the flowers globular, making it possible to tuck at least
a few plants into any garden. • Sleep with a small
pouch containing Everlasting Onion under
the pillow to enhance psychic ability and
prophetic dreams.

No. 014

Allium sativum ♥

Garlic

Porcelain Garlic | Purple Stripe Garlic | Silverskin Garlic |
Soft-necked Garlic | Stinking Rose

✺ SYMBOLIC MEANINGS
Courage; Get well; Strength.

✺ POSSIBLE POWERS
Anti-theft; Aphrodisiac; Attracts
love; Exorcism; Fire element;
Healing; Lust; Mars; Masculine energy; Protection;
Protection against an evil spirit, vampire, or werewolf; Sun;
Unrequited love; Wards off evil; Wards off the evil eye;
Wards off illness; Wards off a vampire; Wards off a werewolf.

☾ FOLKLORE AND FACTS
Garlic has been continually used as an ingredient in various
international cuisines for at least 4,000 years because it
pairs well with so many different vegetables and meats.
The Garlic plant's bulb is comprised of many edible cloves
that can be pressed, chopped, then added to a recipe, or
roasted whole until it's soft, to spreading the pulp on cooked
meats, vegetables, or bread. • Carry Garlic as protection
against monsters. • A Garlic wreath on a door is there to
ward off malicious witches and psychic vampires. • For his
own protection, a superstitious matador will wear a Garlic
clove on a string around his neck before a bullfight. • For
protection against hepatitis, string thirteen cloves of Garlic
into a necklace to wear for thirteen days. In the middle of the
night on the thirteenth day, walk to the nearest intersection
and toss the Garlic necklace behind you. Don't look back.
Run all the way home.

No. 015

Allium schoenoprasum ♥

Chives

Allium Herb | Rush Leek

✺ SYMBOLIC MEANINGS
Courage; Strength; Usefulness; Why are you crying?

✺ POSSIBLE POWERS
Eternity; Everlasting; Exorcism; Fire element; Healing;
Longevity; Promotes psychic powers; Prophetic dreams;
Protection from evil; Protection from negativity and negative
energies; Psychic Power; Sun.

☾ FOLKLORE AND FACTS
The Chive plant's flowers and leaves are edible, with the
leaves generously snipped as needed, then allowed to grow
out again in order to extend the plant's usefulness. Chives can
be added to both savory and sweet dishes, like fruit salads.
Chives are considered one of French cuisine's *fines herbes*.
• Early Dutch American settlers deliberately planted Chives
in the fields that were used for grazing their dairy cows, so
they could enjoy milk naturally flavored with the distinctive
taste. • Bunches of Chives used to be hung in homes to
repel evil spirits. • Carry a sachet of Chives to push away a
clinging bad habit.

No. 016

Allium scorodoprasum ♥

Rocambole

Hard-necked Garlic | Korean Pickled-peel | Sand Leek

✺ SYMBOLIC MEANING
Patience.

✺ POSSIBLE POWERS
Flavoring; Fire element;
Healing; Protection against evil;
Strength; Sun.

☾ FOLKLORE AND FACTS
Rocambole is an edible species of
wild onion that is only occasionally cultivated
for use in cooking. It is most often found
growing wild near very old homes where,
once upon a time, it might have been grown
for the household's personal use to flavor
soups and stews.

No. 017

Allium tuberosum

Garlic Chives

Chinese Chive | Chinese Leek | Jeongguji | Jiu Cai

✹ **SYMBOLIC MEANINGS**
Courage; Strength.

🌀 **POSSIBLE POWERS**
Prophetic dreams; Protection; Psychic power.

☾ **FOLKLORE AND FACTS**
Although the edible leaves smell like Onions when they are cut or crushed, the fragrance of the Garlic Chives flower resembles that of a violet. In East Asia, Garlic Chives have been cultivated for the leaves, stalks, and unopened flower buds for hundreds of years. In China, the Garlic Chive is sometimes a substitute for Scallions in the green onion flatbread pancake that is known as *cong you bing*.

No. 018

Aloysia citrodora 🥣

Lemon Verbena

Lemon Beebrush

✹ **SYMBOLIC MEANINGS**
Attraction; Attracts the opposite sex; Love; Sexual attraction; Sexual attractiveness.

🌀 **POSSIBLE POWERS**
Air element; Art; the Arts; Attraction; Beauty; Friendship; Gifts; Harmony; Joy; Love; Masculine energy; Mercury; Pleasure; Protection; Purification; Sensuality.

☾ **FOLKLORE AND FACTS**
Lemon Verbena leaves provide a lemony flavor to beverages, alcohol, liqueurs, some fish and poultry dishes, salad dressings, marinades, jam, savory puddings, yogurt, and herbal teas. Dried leaves can be brewed as a tea. • Lemon Verbena leaves can be added to a bath to purify negative energies.

No. 019

Amaranthus cruentus 🥣

Amaranth

Amarant | *Amaranthus caudatus* | Blood Amaranth | Flower Velour | Huautli | Kiwicha | Lady Bleeding | Mexican Grain Amaranth | Prince's Feather | Purple Amaranth | Red Amaranth | Velvet Flower

✹ **SYMBOLIC MEANINGS**
Desertion; Endless love; Fidelity; Hopeless, not heartless; Hopelessness; Immortality; In waiting; Love; Never fading.

🌀 **POSSIBLE POWERS**
Artemis; Feminine energy; Fire element; Guards against evil; Healing; Healing broken hearts; Immortality; Invisibility; Magical attack; Magical protection; Protection; Protection against bullets, cooking burns, or household accidents; Saturn; Summon spirits.

☾ **FOLKLORE AND FACTS**
The edible Amaranth plants are *Amaranthus cruentus* and *Amaranthus caudatus*. The leaves and stems of these two varieties can be prepared like spinach or as a curry. Amaranth is most commonly available as a seed grain and as a flour. • Ancient Greeks believed the Amaranth was a strong symbol of immortality and would spread Amaranth flowers over graves. • Carry a sachet of dried Amaranth flowers to heal a broken heart. • Amaranth was once outlawed in Mexico by the colonial Spanish authorities because it was used in Aztec rituals. • Wearing an Amaranth wreath will supposedly give the wearer the power of invisibility. • Uprooting an Amaranth plant on a Friday with a Full Moon, making an offering, then wrapping the plant into a white cloth before binding it to one's chest will supposedly make one magically bullet-proof. Don't try it!

No. 020

Amelanchier alnifolia 🜩

Saskatoon

Alder-leaf Shadbush | Dwarf Shadbush |
Pacific Serviceberry | Saskatoon Serviceberry |
Western Juneberry | Western Serviceberry

✻ SYMBOLIC MEANING
Everywhere.

🌀 POSSIBLE POWERS
Colorize; Gathering;
Sociability; Sustain.

🌒 FOLKLORE AND FACTS
The Saskatoon berry was vital to the Indigenous Peoples of
Canada, who depended on every part of the tree in one way
or another. The fruit is eaten fresh or dried, and can be added
to dried meat for additional flavor. Dried berries are also
blended with other ingredients for a trail mix. The berries are
juiced, mixed into cider blends, brewed into wine, baked into
pies, made into jam, or candied.

No. 021

Amorphophallus paeoniifolius

Elephant Foot Yam

Telingo Potato | Whitespot Giant Arum

✻ SYMBOLIC MEANINGS
Appreciation of God; Masculinity; Power; Thanksgiving;
Wealth.

🌀 POSSIBLE POWERS
Good health; Inner strength; Prosperity; Wellbeing.

🌒 FOLKLORE AND FACTS
The Elephant Foot Yam tuber is edible when fried, mashed,
and added to other vegetables, or used in a chutney recipe.
The Elephant Foot Yam is a vital staple food in Southeast
Asia, India, and West Africa.

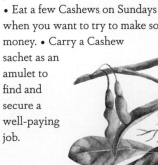

No. 022

Anacardium occidentale ☠🜩

Cashew

Cashew Apple Tree | Cashew Nut Tree | Jambu Monyet | Marañon Tree

✻ SYMBOLIC MEANING
Reward.

🌀 POSSIBLE POWERS
Fire element; Job seeking; Masculine energy; Money;
Prosperity; Sun.

🌒 FOLKLORE AND FACTS
Where the Cashew tree grows, the fruit of the tree is known
as *marañon* or "cashew apple" and is more popular than the
nut; it is available fresh as well as juiced. The seed recognized
as the Cashew "nut" will develop on the tree before the fruit
does. The ripe fruit will fall to the ground to be gathered.
The protruding seed is separated from the fruit, the fruit
is then sent to market, and the multi-step processing of the
seed begins. The seed is baked at a high temperature to burn
off the caustic outer husk before breaking open the hard
inner shell of the seed to remove the seed within it. The
next step is baking the shelled seeds at a low temperature for
twenty-four hours to soften the inner shell covering over the
kernel, which can then be easily removed to reveal the highly
processed Cashew. The kernel can be further processed to
produce Cashew "butter" and "milk."
• Eat a few Cashews on Sundays
when you want to try to make some
money. • Carry a Cashew
sachet as an
amulet to
find and
secure a
well-paying
job.

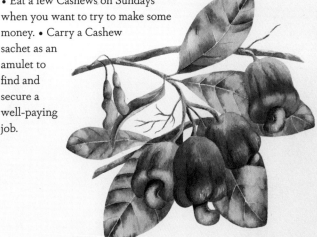

A

No. 023

Ananas comosus ☠ ⚗

Pineapple

Abacaxi | Ananá | Ananas | Piña | Pine Apple

✹ SYMBOLIC MEANINGS

Chastity; Hospitality; Joy; Perfection; You are perfect.

✺ POSSIBLE POWERS

Chastity; Fire element; Gambling luck; Good fortune; Luck; Masculine energy; Money; Perfection; Sun; Wealth.

☾ FOLKLORE AND FACTS

Pineapple is the third most popular tropical fruit in the world. It takes two years for the Pineapple plant to produce one fruit. Each section of a Pineapple is a fruit unto itself, making it a multiple fruit. • Unripe Pineapple is very toxic. A ripe Pineapple is golden yellow. Pineapple juice can tenderize meat. • Gelatin will not set properly if fresh Pineapple is added to it. • The leafy top of a fresh Pineapple can be cut off then planted to eventually produce a fruit. • Eating the fresh ripe Pineapple fruit reportedly relieves laryngitis. • Make an infusion with the core of the Pineapple fruit and distilled or filtered water to add to bathwater to encourage chastity or good luck before gambling. Spray the infusion at the front door of the home to encourage good luck and a spirit of chaste respectfulness to its inhabitants.

No. 024

Anethum graveolens ⚗

Dill

Dill Weed | Garden Dill | Sada Kuppi

✹ SYMBOLIC MEANINGS

Good cheer; Luck.

✺ POSSIBLE POWERS

Aphrodisiac; Fire element; Love; Luck; Lust; Masculine energy; Mercury; Money; Protection; Soothing; Survival; Wards off evil.

☾ FOLKLORE AND FACTS

The edible parts of the Dill plant are the seeds and the fine, tiny leaves which are known as "Dill weed." • In the Middle Ages, Dill was used in magic spells and witchcraft. • Hanging Dill at a door offers protection against harm and will keep out envious or unpleasant people. • A sprig of Dill attached to a cradle is there to protect the child in it. • Dill is said to stimulate the libido if the plant is eaten or even smelled. • Dill is always a good omen. • Dill seeds used to be given to ancient Norse babies to help them sleep.

No. 025

Angelica archangelica ☠ ⚗

Angelica

Garden Angelica | Herb of the Angels | Herb of the Holy Ghost | High Angelica | Holy Herb | Norwegian Angelica | Purple Angelica

✹ SYMBOLIC MEANINGS

Gentle melancholy; Inspiration; Inspire me; Symbol of good magic; Symbol of poetic inspiration.

✺ POSSIBLE POWERS

Courage; Eliminate the effects of intoxication; Exorcism; Fire element; Healing; Magic; Masculine energy; Protection; Removes curses, enchantments, and hexes; Removes lust; Renders witchcraft harmless; Renders the evil eye harmless; Strength; Sun; Venus; Visions; Wards off disasters; Wards off evil spirits; Wards off lightning strikes.

FOLKLORE AND FACTS

Exercise caution before even touching *Angelica archangelica* because it resembles poisonous hemlock and poisonous parsnip, two of the deadliest poisonous plants. • Dried Angelica seeds are sometimes used in cakes, cookies, confections, and liqueurs. The stems need to be cooked to be edible to then be used in the same ways as Rhubarb. They can then be candied, used in jams, pie fillings, roasted with meats, or even sautéed in butter. Angelica root is poisonous until it has been thoroughly cooked. After cooking, it has been used in some liqueurs. Angelica was the original green candied fruit bits that were found in Victorian fruit cakes. • A legend from the Middle Ages tells of a monk who dreamt of an angel who gave him a recipe for a tonic to cure any sickness. Angelica was one of the ingredients. • Some believe that angels smell exactly like Angelica. • Aromatherapists call Angelica the oil of angels because of its peacefully calming influence.

No. 026

Annona cherimola ☠⚱

Cherimoya

Chirimoya | Chirimuya | Custard Apple | Ice Cream Fruit

☀ SYMBOLIC MEANING

Rarity.

🌀 POSSIBLE POWER

Healing.

FOLKLORE AND FACTS

The Cherimoya is the fruit of the *Annona cherimola* tree, which is edible when ripe and considered by many to be the finest of all known fruits. Cherimoya seeds are inedible and poisonous if they are crushed to open them. The fruit can be halved and the pulp eaten with a spoon. Its flavor is similar to a blend of apple, banana, pineapple, papaya, peach, and strawberry. When the fruit is ripe, it is soft to the touch and the skin is a yellowish-green color. However, when the skin turns brown, it is inedible. The Cherimoya is eaten fresh as well as added as a flavoring to yogurt and ice cream. • Natural-growing Cherimoya trees rely on wind for pollination, while cultivated trees need to be pollinated by hand.

Anthriscus cerefolium ⚱

Chervil

French Parsley | Garden Chervil | Gourmet Parsley | Salad Chervil

☀ SYMBOLIC MEANINGS

Serenity; Sincerity.

🌀 POSSIBLE POWER

Sense of the higher, divine, immortal spirit.

FOLKLORE AND FACTS

Chervil has delicate, anise-like flavored stems and leaves for flavoring broths and sauces, poultry and seafood, and vegetables such as carrots. Chervil is mostly available fresh and is a part of the *fines herbes* in French cuisine. • Roman soldiers spread Chervil by planting it close to their camps across the entire Roman Empire, because they hated being without it. • Make, then carry or wear a white sachet of Chervil when attempting to make contact with a loved one on "the other side" via any method. • Chervil is in the Nine Sacred Herbs healing charm that was originally written of in the dialect of that day used in Wessex, England, around the tenth century.

No. 028

Apium graveolens var. graveolens ⚱

Celery

Chinese Celery | Leaf Celery | Pascal Celery

☀ SYMBOLIC MEANINGS

Banquet; Entertainment; Feast; Festivity; Lasting pleasures; Merriment; Rejoicing; Useful knowledge.

🌀 POSSIBLE POWERS

Aphrodisiac; Attracts love; Balance; Calm; Concentration; Fire element; Lust; Masculine energy; Mental clarity or power; Mercury; Psychic power; Sleep; Virility.

FOLKLORE AND FACTS

The Celery plant's stems, leaves, and seeds can be eaten raw or cooked. The concave cavities of the Celery stems can be tastily stuffed with seasoned or flavored soft cheeses, seasoned butter, cream cheese, or even peanut butter. Celery stems, leaves, and seeds are often added to soups. Homemade chicken soup wouldn't be the same without Celery. Along with Onion and Bell Pepper, Celery is a crucial ingredient in Louisiana cuisine's "holy trinity" of herbs, the specific mirepoix (a flavor base of carrots, celery, and onions), that is vital in Creole and Cajun dishes. • The ancient Greeks regarded Celery with the same esteem as Bay Laurel, using it in wreath making for the crowning of athletes. • Carry or wear a sachet of Celery leaves to encourage lust. • Leaf Celery's essential oil is useful for its calming effect. • Celery stalks and seeds are both believed to be aphrodisiacs. • Chewing Celery seeds before flying off on a broom will keep you aright so you will not fall off.

No. 029

Apium graveolens var. *rapaceum* 🥣

Celeriac
Celery Root | Knob Celery | Turnip-rooted Celery

☀ SYMBOLIC MEANINGS
Feast; Feasting.

🌀 POSSIBLE POWERS
Balance; Fire element; Masculine energy; Mercury.

☾ FOLKLORE AND FACTS

The edible part of the Celeriac plant is the "hypocotyl" that develops in the space between the roots and the stems, bulging half out of the ground just below the seed leaves. Celeriac can be eaten raw, or cooked by roasting or stewing. It is often served mashed as a substitute for potatoes, or added to stews and soups. To store Celeriac for up to seven months, it must be refrigerated after all the little roots are removed. The flavor weakens as the hypocotyl ages. • In the *Iliad*, horses graze on Celeriac in marshes near Troy. In the *Odyssey*, Celeriac grows outside Calypso's cave.

No. 030

Arachis hypogaea 🥣

Peanut
Goober | Groundnut | Monkey Nut

☀ SYMBOLIC MEANINGS
Many children; Prosperity; Wishing for children.

🌀 POSSIBLE POWERS
Earth element; Good fortune; Growth; Health; Jupiter; Longevity; Luck; Pleasure; Plentitude; Prosperity; Stability; Wealth.

☾ FOLKLORE AND FACTS

Evidence of the Peanut has been found in some Aztec and Incan archeological sites that date back 7,600 years. • The Peanut is a legume, not a nut. The edible part is the bean within the pod that develops underground on the roots of the plant. The Peanut oil pressed from the beans can be used for deep frying. Peanuts are also a favorite ingredient for baking and cooking, either as an addition to dishes or as the main ingredient, such as for Peanut soup. • Peanut butter was developed and marketed in Canada and the United States between 1880 and 1900 as a specialty food for the wealthy, because it was initially marketed at high-end health spas and medical rehabilitation facilities as a health food. Since that time, a Peanut butter and Concord Grape jelly sandwich has become an iconic comfort food for many Americans. • A dream about a Peanut may signify a desire to get to the root of a problem.

A

No. 031

Arctium lappa ☠ ⚗

Burdock

Beggar's Buttons | Bugloss | Burrdock | Burrseed |
Clotbur | Cockleburr | Edible Burdock | Gobo | Great
Burdock | Lappa Burdock | Thorny Burr

☀ SYMBOLIC MEANINGS

Falsehood; Importunity;
Touch me not.

✺ POSSIBLE POWERS

Feminine energy; Healing;
Protection; Venus; Water
element.

☾ FOLKLORE AND FACTS

The edible part of the Burdock plant
is the root. Burdock was a relatively
common vegetable in Europe during the
Middle Ages. Nowadays, it is gathered as an immature plant,
then cooked and consumed as a vegetable in Brazil, Portugal,
and Italy, where it is known as *bardana* or *garduna* and tastes
similar to artichoke. Burdock root is also widely enjoyed as a
vegetable in East Asian cuisine. Shredded Burdock root can
be added to soups, stews, and casseroles. Sliced thinly and
deep-fried, Burdock root has a texture and taste that is very
similar to potato chips. • Burdock root is used as flavoring
for an herbal British drink known as Dandelion and Burdock
that has been brewed and consumed since the Middle Ages.
• Velcro was inspired by an *Arctium lappa* burr. • Burdock
roots gathered during a waning moon, cut into short
lengths, strung on a red thread, then dried can be worn like
a bead necklace as protection against negativity and evil.
• Discreetly stick Burdock burrs around the home to fend off
negativity.

No. 032

Arenga pinnata ⚗

Sugar Palm

Areng Palm | Arengga Palm | Black Sugar
Palm | Feather Palm | Gomuti Palm |
Kaong Palm

☀ SYMBOLIC MEANINGS

Eternal life; Peace.

✺ POSSIBLE POWERS

Fertility; Freedom; Happiness; Healing;
Health; Love; Relationships; Resurrection;
Reward; Righteousness; Sweetening;
Triumph; Victory.

☾ FOLKLORE AND FACTS

Sugar Palm sap is collected by tree-tapping before being
converted to sugar by boiling it down much like sugar
maple sap. Then it can be used as a syrup or fermented into
wines, liqueurs, and vinegars. A tapped Sugar Palm tree
can release approximately thirty liters of sap a day. • It is
believed that a Sugar Palm responds to one tapper who will
pray for the tree, recite incantations, chant, and sing to it
while tapping once in the early morning and then again in
the late afternoon.

No. 033

Armoracia rusticana ⚗

Horseradish

Chrain | Horseradish Root | Khren | Khreyn | Stingnose

☀ SYMBOLIC MEANING

Bitterness of enslavement.

✺ POSSIBLE POWERS

Exorcism; Fire element; Mars; Masculine energy;
Purification.

𝒜

☾ FOLKLORE AND FACTS

The edible part of the Horseradish plant is the pungent, tasty, fume-flaring, nose-clearing root that is beloved by nearly all who try it. The familiar nasal sensation felt when eating Horseradish is caused by allyl isothiocyanate vapors. Without that sensation, Horseradish aficionados will turn their nose away from it. Horseradish is often added to sauces, most especially to add flavor and zing to seafood cocktail sauce. • Putting a piece of Horseradish in your pocket during New Year's Eve promises a year of adequate funds. • A mural in Pompeii, Italy, depicts a Horseradish plant. In Greek mythology the Oracle of Delphi told Apollo that Horseradish was worth its weight in gold. • To clear evil powers and dissipate negative spells cast upon a home, sprinkle dried Horseradish root around the house, on the entry steps, on every windowsill, and in every corner.

No. 034

Artemisia dracunculus ⚗

Tarragon

Dragon Herb | Dragon Wort | Estragon | French Tarragon | Fuzzy Weed | Green Dragon | Herbe Dragon | King of Herbs | Petit Dragon | Russian Tarragon | Snakesfoot | Spanish Tarragon

✳ SYMBOLIC MEANINGS

Horror; Lasting commitment, interest, or involvement; Permanence; Shocking occurrence; Terror.

✺ POSSIBLE POWERS

Dragon magic; Hunting; Love; Snakebite cure.

☾ FOLKLORE AND FACTS

Tarragon leaf is one of the four primary culinary herbs used in French cuisine, having a licorice-like flavor for use as seasoning. • Carry Tarragon for good luck when hunting.

No. 035

Artocarpus altilis

Breadfruit

Camansi | Seeded Breadfruit

✳ SYMBOLIC MEANINGS

Defensive stance; Emotional innocence.

✺ POSSIBLE POWERS

Prominence; Wealth.

☾ FOLKLORE AND FACTS

In many tropical regions, the prepared and cooked fruit of the Breadfruit tree is a staple food that can be boiled, roasted, fried, or baked. Once it has been cooked, it can then be added to other foods or as an ingredient in recipes and soups. In Sri Lanka, Breadfruit is made into a spiced curry with coconut milk. In Indonesia and Malaysia, it is very commonly made into a snack fritter sold as street food. Deep fried, finely sliced Breadfruit is often served dipped into a sugary spiced syrup. A staple of Jamaican cuisine, Breadfruit is often cooked as a side dish.

No. 036

Artocarpus heterophyllus ☠ ⚗

Jackfruit

Chakka Pazham | Jaca-Manteiga | Jack Tree | Kathal | Langka | Muttomvarikka | Nangka

✳ SYMBOLIC MEANING

A good relationship.

✺ POSSIBLE POWERS

Conception; Fertility.

☾ FOLKLORE AND FACTS

Jackfruit was once considered to be a truly exotic "wonder fruit of the East." Each section of a Jackfruit is a fruit unto itself, making it a multiple fruit. The fruit and the seeds within it are edible. The Jackfruit tree can grow up to eighty feet tall and produce up to 500 fruits in a year. Jackfruit is the largest fruit produced by any tree, growing up to thirty inches long, twenty inches in diameter, and weighing up to 120 pounds. There are two types of Jackfruit. The hard variety is crunchy, dry, and fleshier but less sweet. The soft type is moist and sweeter. Uncut, the fruit has a slightly unpleasant, musty smell. When it has been cut open, it gives off a sweet, tropical fragrance reminiscent of pineapple, banana, mango, and apple with a hint of bubblegum. Jackfruit seeds are edible after roasting. Roasted Jackfruit seeds smell like chocolate. • Archeologists have discovered evidence of Jackfruit's cultivation in India from 6,000 years ago. • During religious rituals, Hindu priests sit on seats carved from Jackfruit wood. Sculptors have carved many Buddhist statues from the wood as well. • Drinking water after eating Jackfruit can disrupt the digestion process.

No. 037
Asimina triloba ☠ ⚗

Paw-Paw
American Pawpaw | Pawpaw | Paw Paw

☀ SYMBOLIC MEANING
Abundance and scarcity.

✿ POSSIBLE POWERS
Coping with scarcity; Preparing for less. Reveling in plentitude; Seasonal great abundance.

☾ FOLKLORE AND FACTS
The fruit of the Paw-Paw tree has a sweet banana-like texture and flavor with hints of pineapple, cantaloupe, and mango. It is usually eaten raw out of hand or in a smoothie. The fruit can be frozen for later use. The seeds are poisonous. • Of all the indigenous fruits of North America, the Paw-Paw is the largest. • The first mention of Paw-Paw in writing was in Hernando de Sota's expedition journal in 1541, noting that Native Americans near to the Mississippi River were growing Paw-Paw trees.

No. 038
Aspalathus linearis ⚗

Rooibos
Bush Tea | Red Tea Bush | Redbush | Rooibosch

☀ SYMBOLIC MEANING
Natural.

✿ POSSIBLE POWERS
Fire element; Health; Mars

☾ FOLKLORE AND FACTS
A tea known as Redbush Tea is brewed from the leaves of the Rooibos plant that has been consumed in South Africa for many generations. Harvesting the needle-like leaves from the Rooibos plant required climbing mountains to cut the leaves, bundling the leaves in a burlap bag, then toting the rolled bag down the mountain tied to the back of a donkey.

No. 039
Asparagus officinalis ☠ ⚗

Asparagus
Aspar Grass | Asparag | Asparage | Asparagio | Asparago | Asparagus | Aspargo | Espárrago | Garden Asparagus | Spargel | Sparrow Grass

☀ SYMBOLIC MEANINGS
Fascination; Phallus.

✿ POSSIBLE POWERS
Aphrodisiac; Attracts love; Change; Cleansing; Dreams; Fertility; Growth; Healing; Lucid dreaming; Lust; Masculinity; Passion; Rebirth; Renewal; Reproduction; Sex; Travel.

☾ FOLKLORE AND FACTS
Since ancient times, the rise of phallic Asparagus shoots in spring have signified male sexuality, stamina, and virility. The tender young Asparagus shoots that emerge in the spring are edible and harvested as shoots before the flower heads open, when what was tender will turn woody. A "White Asparagus" is not a species variation; it's achieved with a growing process called blanching, which requires that, as the Asparagus shoots grow taller, they are immediately covered over with soil each day to prevent their exposure to sunlight. Therefore, the new growing shoots remain pale. • Asparagus is the only food that contains asparagusic acid, which is responsible for the distinctive urine smell that follows after eating Asparagus. Due to this odor of urine, Victorian wives could smell unfaithfulness on their husbands, knowing that they had consumed it as an aphrodisiac they enjoyed with others. • Asparagus still commands a premium price on the market, but the global popularity of Asparagus has made it less of a delicacy than it once was.

A

No. 040

Avena fatua 🝧

Wild Oat

Common Wild Oat

❉ **SYMBOLIC MEANINGS**

Music; Musical; the Witching soul of music.

🌀 **POSSIBLE POWERS**

Earth element; Healing; Money; Music; Venus.

🌜 **FOLKLORE AND FACTS**

Since the Iron Age, naturalized Wild Oats have been a harvested cereal grain. However, because it is highly competitive and will rapidly deplete soil resources and moisture, it only takes a few invasive Wild Oat plants to wreak major havoc on a crop of cultivated oats and other cereal grain crops. • During the Middle Ages it was believed that Wild Oats would attract a vampire, which inspired the farm practice of draping garlic garlands over doors and windows. • Wild Oat straw can be used to fashion a woven magical object such as a talisman, charm, or wand. • The saying regarding "sowing one's wild oats" means participating in a period of youthfully wild, sexually promiscuous behavior before committing to a serious monogamous relationship.

No. 041

Avena sativa 🝧

Oat

Common Oat | Groats | Joulaf

❉ **SYMBOLIC MEANINGS**

Music; Musical; the Witching soul of music.

🌀 **POSSIBLE POWERS**

Anxiety reduction; Concentration; Earth element; Endurance; Enhances mental power; Feminine energy; Fertility; Healing; Health; Inner peace; Money; Music; Rejuvenation; Stress relief; Venus.

🌜 **FOLKLORE AND FACTS**

The edible parts of the *Avena sativa* Oat plant are the seed grains. Oats are available whole grain, cut, or sliced, as a coarse meal, and with finer flour grinds used in baking. Popular for commercial cereal blends, but most especially for oatmeal and porridge, are "steel-cut oats," "old-fashioned rolled oats," "quick oats," and the even more quickly and conveniently prepared "instant oatmeal." Oat "milk" is also produced to provide a plant-based milk substitute. • To bring prosperity into one's life, eat oats during the first meal of the day.

No. 042

Averrhoa carambola ⚱

Star Fruit

Balimbing | Carambola |
Carambolo | Starfruit

☀ **SYMBOLIC MEANING**
Stars.

✺ **POSSIBLE POWERS**
Calls for spiritual forces;
Conjures a spirit.

☾ **FOLKLORE AND FACTS**
The Star Fruit has a waxy edible skin, similar to that of a new
grape, and is very juicy. Unripe Star Fruit tastes similar to
a tart green apple, while the ripe fruit has a complex flavor
of apple, grape, pear, and a touch of citrus. The fruit can be
juiced and also made into jam or a chutney-style condiment.
• Star Fruit can also be sliced and oven-dried or sun-dried to
make Star Fruit chips. • The ridges along the sides of the Star
Fruit can number five, six, or seven. When the five-ridged
whole fruit is sliced across, the individual slices are in the
shape of a star and can be used as a pentagram for magical
purposes. A six-ridged fruit can be a magical hexagram
known as the Seal of Solomon. With it, spirits or spiritual
forces can be conjured. A seven-ridged fruit will produce a
magical heptagram, which is also known as the Elven Star,
Fairy Star, and Elf-queen's Daughters. Magically, it can mean
seven directions, which is implying "North, South, East, West,
Above, Below, and Within." It can also represent the seven
days of the week. Regardless of how many star points a slice
can produce, Star Fruit is magically powerful. • Star Fruit
juice can be used to clean rust and tarnish off brass and most
other metals.

A

No. 043

Backhousia citriodora ☠ ⚗

Lemon Myrtle

Lemon Scented Backhousia | Lemon Scented
Ironwood | Lemon Scented Myrtle | Lemon Scented
Verbena | Queen of the Lemon Herbs | Sweet
Verbena Myrtle | Sweet Verbena Tree

✴ SYMBOLIC MEANING
Chaste beauty.

✿ POSSIBLE POWERS
Cleansing; Flavoring; Healing; Insect repellent; Purification;
Relaxation; Relieves anxiety; Relieves stress.

☕ FOLKLORE AND FACTS
Crushed Lemon Myrtle leaves emit a strong lemony
fragrance, are edible, and can be added as a lemony flavoring
to baked goods, pasta dishes, oil infusions, and brewed
into tea. Lemon Myrtle will not curdle milk as acidic
Lemon will, so it can be used to flavor milk-based foods
like cream, sauces, and puddings. • The essential oil of the
Lemon Myrtle is crisp and more lemony than Lemon. In
aromatherapy it is uplifting while simultaneously calming to
someone who is anxious.

No. 044

Bambusa vulgaris ☠ ⚗

Bamboo

Bambú | Common Bamboo | Giant Gray | Moso Bamboo | Sweetshoot Bamboo

✴ SYMBOLIC MEANINGS
Endurance; Flexibility; Good fortune; Longevity; Loyalty;
Luck; Protection; Rendezvous; Scientific research;
Steadfastness; Strength; Summer; Suppleness; Youth.

✿ POSSIBLE POWERS
Breaks a hex; Classical elements (Air, Earth, Fire, Water);
Luck; Masculine energy; New start; Protection; Sun; Wealth;
Wishing.

☕ FOLKLORE AND FACTS
There are several different species of Bamboo that will
produce tasty edible shoots, such as *Phyllostachys dulcis*,
Phyllostachys edulis, *Phyllostachys nigra*, and *Phyllostachys
nuda*. In every case, they all require careful preparation
and must be boiled before consuming due to the presence
of a type of cyanide called taxiphyllin. This makes Bamboo
among the most toxic of plant foods, more so than even
the highly poisonous apricot and bitter almond kernels.

However, unlike those other cyanide-deadly foods,
taxiphyllin will degrade when boiled, uncovered, in salted
water. Canned Bamboo shoots are safe. • Because Bamboo
grows to its full height and diameter in one growing season,
it serves a multitude of
commercial purposes,
including in construction,
fabrics, flooring, foods, and
furniture. • Carve a wish
on a piece of Bamboo, then
bury it in a quiet place that
is unlikely to be disturbed.
What's to be will be.
• Grown, carried, or burned,
Bamboo can help break a
hex. • *Dracaena sanderiana*,
the plant often marketed
as "lucky bamboo," isn't
Bamboo.

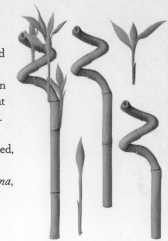

No. 045

Bertholletia excelsa ⚗

Brazil Nut

Castañas de Brasil | Castanhas-do-Pará | Nuez de Brasil

✴ SYMBOLIC MEANING
Preparing.

✿ POSSIBLE POWERS
Air element; Fire element; Love; Mars; Masculine energy;
Mercury; Moon; Water element.

☕ FOLKLORE AND FACTS
The oily kernel found within a shelled seed "nut" of the
Brazil Nut fruit is edible. The tree can grow up to 165 feet
tall and live for 700 years. It takes fourteen months for the
fruit to mature after it has been pollinated. The fruit has a
hard woody shell similar to a coconut. It is very large and
heavy, containing twelve to twenty-five Brazil Nuts within it.
When the ripened fruit falls, it drops down with a loud crash.
The nuts are arranged inside the fruit like *Citrus* segments,
having up to three whorls of nuts stacked within the fruit.
• Capuchin monkeys have been seen breaking open Brazil
Nuts with a rock. • Carry a Brazil Nut as a talisman to have
good luck in love.

B

No. 046

Beta vulgaris subsp. *vulgaris* 🏺

Beet

Acelga | Beetroot | Beet Spinach | Blood Turnip | Chard | Dinner Beet |
Garden Beet | Golden Beet | Leaf Beet | Mangel | Mangold | Perpetual Spinach |
Red Beet | Seakale Beet | Silver Beet | Spinach Beet | Sugar Beet | Sweet Beet |
Swiss Chard | Table Beet

✳ SYMBOLIC MEANINGS

Blood; Heart; Love.

🌀 POSSIBLE POWERS

Aphrodisiac; Earth element; Feminine energy; Jupiter; Love;
Saturn; Venus.

☾ FOLKLORE AND FACTS

The Beet plant was originally grown for its greens. Preparing
a fresh Beet root can be messy, but well worth the clean up.
One Pennsylvania Dutch dish is the hardboiled egg pickled
with Beets. Grated Beet mixed with grated horseradish is a
condiment from Poland and Ukraine. A slice of pickled Beet
is a topping on an Australian hamburger. A Beet and beef
broth soup known as "borscht" comes from Eastern Europe.
• Because the two are so extremely close to one another, Beet
greens and Chard greens can be cooked in the same ways,
by sautéing or boiling to be a leafy green vegetable, or added
to soups and stews. • Fresh raw Chard leaves as well as raw
young Beet leaves can be used in salads. • If you need blood
for ink, use Beet juice instead. • Until the mid-1700s, when a
method was developed that made it possible to extract sugar
from Sugar Beets that could be processed into affordable
white sugar crystals, only aristocrats could afford cane sugar.

Betula lenta ☠ 🏺

Black Birch

Cherry Birch | Mahogany Birch |
Spice Birch | Sweet Birch

✳ SYMBOLIC MEANINGS

Adaptability; Dreams; Elegance;
Grace; Gracefulness; Growth; Initiation;
Meekness; Pioneer spirit; Renewal; Stability;
Transformation.

🌀 POSSIBLE POWERS

Astral travel; Colorize; Exorcism; Feminine energy;
Protection; Protection against infertility, lightning, or the evil
eye; Purification; Thor; Venus; Water element.

☾ FOLKLORE AND FACTS

The sap of the *Betula lenta* Black Birch tree can be tapped in
the springtime like a much faster-running sugar maple sap,
thus requiring the sap to be gathered three times as often.
Boiling it down will produce a stronger-flavored syrup with
the viscosity of molasses. The syrup can be used to make the
very tasty non-alcoholic beverage known as "birch beer."
• Manufacturers used to make cradles from Black Birch to
protect the babies sleeping in them from evil. • Planting
Black Birch close to your home protects the household from
lightning, the evil eye, and infertility. • In aromatherapy,
Black Birch essential oil helps relax an overworked mind.

No. 048

Bistorta officinalis 🏺

Bistort

Common Bistort | Easter-Ledges | European Bistort |
Meadow Bistort | Snake-Root | Snakeroot | Snakeweed

✳ SYMBOLIC MEANINGS

Arrow-shaped; Barbed; Horror.

🌀 POSSIBLE POWERS

Binding; Binding spell; Clairvoyance;
Colorize; Divination; Earth element;
Feminine energy; Fertility; Health;
Protection; Psychic power; Saturn;
Trance.

☾ FOLKLORE AND FACTS

The edible parts of the Bistort plant
are the young shoots, leaves, and
root after they have been steamed or
boiled. Bistort leaves are an ingredient

in a Northern England bitter Lenten pudding that is made using oatmeal and eggs, as well as other herbs. It is also a primary ingredient in a dish from Yorkshire, England, which is known as "dock pudding" and is fried in a pan with bacon and whatever additional ingredients one chooses to include. • If carried close to the breast, Bistort is considered to be a charm to help those suffering from frenzy. • Bistort is also thought to heal an individual's unwanted desires. • It is also believed that touching Bistort grants the person special powers offered by their astrological Sun sign. • To rid a home of pesky poltergeists, make an infusion of Bistort and rainwater, natural spring water, or distilled water, then sprinkle it all around the house. • Prior to the steady emigration of people moving from England, Bistort was virtually unknown in North America until it was introduced into the newly planted English gardens in the New World.

No. 049

Bixa orellana ❂

Achiote
Annatto | Urucum

✴ SYMBOLIC MEANINGS
Blood; Masculinity; Sun.

🌀 POSSIBLE POWERS
Protects against snakebites; Wards off infection.

☾ FOLKLORE AND FACTS
The seed of the *Bixa orellana* Achiote tree is edible. However, the fruit is inedible. Achiote seed is available dried and ground into a powder or as a paste. It will transform food to a bright orange-yellow color. Achiote is a common ingredient in Latin American recipes, primarily in Mexico and Central America, as well as in Filipino cuisine. Yellow rice is commonly colored with Achiote.

No. 050

Boesenbergia rotunda ❂

Finger Root
Chinese Ginger | Chinese Keys | Fingerroot | Lesser Galangal | Temu Kunci

✴ SYMBOLIC MEANING
Keys.

🌀 POSSIBLE POWERS
Aphrodisiac; Attracts love; Calms anger; Fire element; Healing; Mars; Masculine energy; Promotes a pleasant environment.

☾ FOLKLORE AND FACTS
Finger Root is a type of edible ginger that is used in many Cambodian, Indonesian (especially Javanese), and Thai dishes. Finger Root is available fresh where it is grown, otherwise it may be found pickled. • Finger Root essential oil aromatherapy helps calm anger to promote a positive atmosphere in which to find ease. • Tuck a red Finger Root sachet under the mattress for a boost to lovemaking.

B

No. 051

Borago officinalis 🍶

Borage

Borak | Borraja | Bugloss | Burrage | Flor de Borraja |
Lesan-El-Tour | Lisan Selvi | Starflower

✳ SYMBOLIC MEANINGS
Abruptness; Bluntness; Bravery;
Rudeness.

🌀 POSSIBLE POWERS
Air element; Courage; Jupiter;
Masculine energy; Psychic power;
Sense of wellbeing.

☾ FOLKLORE AND FACTS
The leaves and blossoms of the
Borage plant are edible. The leaves
have a cucumber-like flavor and are used as garnish, brewed
as an herbal tea, batter-dipped to be fried as a fritter, added to
soups, or sautéed before using as a filling for something such
as ravioli. The blue Borage blossoms have a honey-like taste
and are used as a garnish, and even frozen into ice cubes. A
traditional British Pimm's cocktail is often garnished with
a Borage blossom. • In Poland, Borage is sometimes used
as a flavoring when pickling gherkins. • To fortify courage,
carry a Borage flower and leaf sachet. • Wear a Borage
flower when walking outdoors for protection. • Medieval
needleworkers commonly stitched the bright blue Borage
flowers into their scarf designs intended to be worn by their
knights as a symbol of their courage.

No. 052

Brassica juncea 🍶

Brown Mustard

American Mustard | Chinese Mustard | Curled Mustard | Curled-Leaf Mustard | Cut-Leaf
Mustard | Giant-Leafed Mustard | Green-in-Snow Mustard | Indian Mustard | Japanese Giant
Red Mustard | Korean Red Mustard | Large-Petiole Mustard | Leaf Mustard | Red-in-Snow
Mustard | Southern Curled Mustard | Southern Mustard | Vegetable Mustard

✳ SYMBOLIC MEANING
Faith.

🌱 COMPONENT MEANINGS
Seed: Good luck
charm; Indifference;
Visible faith.

🌀 POSSIBLE POWERS
Confidence; Fire element; Mars; Mental clarity or power;
Protection; Reassurance.

☾ FOLKLORE AND FACTS
Brown Mustard seeds can be ground to produce a creamy,
spreadable mustard as well as powdered mustard. Ancient
Romans were the first to have experimented with making
Brown Mustard to make a condiment by mixing ground
Brown Mustard seeds with grape juice. Brown Mustard
provides the "mustard" ingredient in the world-renowned
Dijon mustard. • In England, Brown Mustard appears in
a cookbook that dates back to 1390. • Hot Mustard can be
prepared at home by mixing dry powdered mustard with a
very small amount of water, wine, vinegar, milk, or beer.
• Put Brown Mustard seeds under or near the doorstep to
keep supernatural beings from entering.

No. 053

Brassica napus 🍶

Rutabaga

Kålrot | Koolraap | Neep | Steckrübe | Swede | Swedish
Turnip | Yellow Turnip

✳ SYMBOLIC MEANINGS
Charity; Indifference.

🌀 POSSIBLE POWERS
Banish negativity; Ending relationships;
Endings; Fertility; Fire element; Luck;
Mars; Mental clarity; Mental powers;
Protection; Wealth.

☾ FOLKLORE AND FACTS
Rutabaga is a root vegetable reminiscent of but much larger
than a turnip. The flavor of a Rutabaga is very mild and
similar to a sweeter-tasting potato. It is usually available fresh
and waxed to protect it from spoiling in storage. • There
was a tradition in Ireland, Scotland, and parts of England of
carving Rutabagas into small, hollowed-out lanterns lit by a
candle.

No. 054

Brassica napus subsp. *napus* ☙

Rape Kale

Colza Kale | Oilseed | Rape Kale | Rapeseed

✸ **SYMBOLIC MEANINGS**

Profit; Self-willed.

🌀 **POSSIBLE POWERS**

Fire element; Luck; Mars; Wealth.

☾ **FOLKLORE AND FACTS**

Rape Kale seed oil is extracted for use as canola vegetable oil, which is bottled and commonly available. It is also used in lubricants, some cosmetics, and vegetable fat soaps. • In addition to its edible uses, the potential of Rape Kale oil being useful as a sustainable biodiesel fuel is being explored. • Blooming Rape Kale plants are a primary foraging crop for honeybees.

No. 055

Brassica nigra ☙

Black Mustard

California Wild Mustard | Moutarde | Rai | Senafitch

✸ **SYMBOLIC MEANINGS**

Charity; Indifference.

🌱 **COMPONENT MEANINGS**

Seed: Aesculapius; Fire element; Good luck charm; Indifference; Mars; Masculine energy; Visible faith.

🌀 **POSSIBLE POWERS**

Banish negativity; Ending a relationship; Endings; Fertility; Fire element; Mars; Mental clarity or power; Protection.

☾ **FOLKLORE AND FACTS**

The small young leaves, buds, flowers, and most especially the seeds of the Black Mustard plant are edible. In India the fatty seeds are also pressed to produce *sarson ka tel*, which is a commonly used cooking oil. • Black Mustard is believed to be the type of mustard seed in the parable "having faith the size of a mustard seed" that Jesus refers to in the Christian Bible's New Testament. • Make, then carry a sachet of Black Mustard seeds to travel through the air with or without an airplane.

No. 056

Brassica oleracea var. *capitata* ☙

Cabbage

Green Cabbage | Red Cabbage | Savoy Cabbage | Spring Greens Cabbage | White Cabbage

✸ **SYMBOLIC MEANINGS**

Profit; Self-willed.

🌀 **POSSIBLE POWERS**

Feminine energy; Luck; Moon; Water element; Wealth.

☾ **FOLKLORE AND FACTS**

Cabbage can be leafy green, red, purple, or white. It can be eaten raw, sautéed, boiled, baked, roasted, and pickled to be sauerkraut. When shredded it is the primary ingredient in coleslaw salad. Cabbage is a vital ingredient in the dish known as a boiled dinner that includes either ham or corned beef along with carrots, potatoes, and onion. Corned beef and Cabbage is a similar dish that is an iconic meal on St. Patrick's Day. • The first thing that newlyweds should do to wish good luck on their marriage and on their garden is to plant Cabbage.

B

No. 057

Brassica oleracea var. *gemmifera*

Brussels Sprouts

Sprouts

✺ **SYMBOLIC MEANINGS**
Profit; Self-willed.

🌀 **POSSIBLE POWERS**
Luck; Moon; Water element; Wealth.

🌙 **FOLKLORE AND FACTS**
Brussels Sprouts are prepared whole, halved, or sliced for boiling, steaming, slow cooking, stir-frying, sautéing, roasting, or grilling. They can also be eaten raw when shredded and dressed to be a salad. • French immigrants brought Brussels Sprouts to Louisiana in the eighteenth century.

No. 058

Brassica oleracea var. *gongylodes*

Kohlrabi

Knolkhol | Navalkol | Navilkosu | Navilu Kosu

✺ **SYMBOLIC MEANINGS**
Charity; Indifference.

🌀 **POSSIBLE POWERS**
Banish negativity; Ending relationships; Endings; Fertility; Mental clarity; Mental powers; Protection.

🌙 **FOLKLORE AND FACTS**
After peeling, the bulbous stem of the Kohlrabi plant can be edible raw in salads. The leaves can be cooked as a green. Kohlrabi is a common and important ingredient in Kashmiri cuisine. • A Kohlrabi can be grown as an interesting bulbous houseplant.

No. 059

Brassica oleracea var. *italica* 🥣

Broccoli

Calabrese Broccoli | Green Sprouting Broccoli | Little Trees | Purple Broccoli | Purple Cauliflower | Sprouting Broccoli | Violet Broccoli | Violet Cauliflower

✺ **SYMBOLIC MEANINGS**
Profit; Self-willed.

🌀 **POSSIBLE POWERS**
Luck; Money; Protection; Strength; Wealth.

🌙 **FOLKLORE AND FACTS**
Broccoli originated in Italy over 2,000 years ago. It grows in shades of red, green, orange, yellow, or white and is believed to be the most nutritious of the green vegetables, being rich in vitamins C and K. The stalk, small leaves, and large flower head are edible raw or cooked. The flower head is usually pulled apart into smaller segments that resemble tiny green trees. It pairs very well with the flavors of garlic and lemon.

No. 060

Brassica oleracea var. *longata* 🥣

Wild Cabbage

Cow Cabbage | Jersey Cabbage | Jersey Kale | Tree Cabbage | True Colewort |

✺ **SYMBOLIC MEANINGS**
Destiny; Grace.

🌀 **POSSIBLE POWERS**
Calming; Cleansing; Correctness; Drives away drunkenness; Luck; Money; Psychic ability; Relaxation; Shrewdness.

🌙 **FOLKLORE AND FACTS**
Wild Cabbage can sometimes be found growing on the seaside cliffs on both sides of the English Channel. Wild Cabbage on the Channel Island of Jersey is sometimes known as Jersey Cabbage and Tree Cabbage. Its leaves are harvested throughout the year, without destroying the plant itself. • By stripping the leaves off the stalk, the stalk will grow up to ten feet tall, when it is then harvested, dried, cut

into appropriate lengths, and fashioned to be used as a sturdy Jersey walking stick. • Wild Cabbage was the only internal remedy for digestive illnesses used by the Romans for at least 600 years. • It is thought that the looming height of the Wild Cabbage stalks may have inspired the story of Jack and the Beanstalk. • In Great Britain, it was common to leave the stalk in the ground to continue growing table greens. It was an occasional practice to carve an "x" on the flat cut end of the remaining stalk to fend off garden sprites and demons.

No. 061

Brassica oleracea var. *sabellica* 🝱

Kale

Bumpy Leaf Kale | Curly Leaf Kale | Leaf Cabbage | Leaf and Spear Kale | Plain Leaf Kale | Red Russian Kale | Scots Kale

✴ SYMBOLIC MEANINGS
Profit; Self-willed.

🌀 POSSIBLE POWERS
Luck; Wealth.

🜨 FOLKLORE AND FACTS
Kale leaves are commonly sautéed or added to sausage and potato types of soups such as the Portuguese dish known as *caldo verde*. A traditional Irish dish known as *colcannon* is a mixture of kale and mashed potatoes. In Northern Germany, Kale dishes are considered to be comfort foods. • Growing Kale in the United Kingdom during WWII was widely encouraged because it was nutritious and easy to grow.

No. 062

Brassica oleracea var. *viridis* 🝱

Collard

Colewort | Couve | Haakh | Kaanyil Haakh | Mbida | Muriwo | Raštan | Raštika | Sukuma

✴ SYMBOLIC MEANINGS
Fortitude; Profit; Self-willed; Survival; Wisdom.

🌀 POSSIBLE POWERS
Banish negativity; Ending relationships; Endings; Fertility; Luck; Mental clarity; Mental powers; Protection; Wealth.

🜨 FOLKLORE AND FACTS
Collard's large leaves have been consumed for over 2,000 years. They are sautéed, steamed, boiled, added to soups or stews, or used as an ingredient in a casserole. A common dish is simmering Collard leaves with a smoked meat such as a ham hock, bacon, or smoked turkey drumstick until the leaves are tender to be eaten as leafy greens. The broth is considered "pot liquor" that is soaked up with fresh baked cornbread. Collards are commonly harvested just prior to reaching their maximum size, when the leaves are thicker and cooked differently than younger leaves. • Collard is a tenacious, nutritious plant that can sustain life through the extremes of harsh heat or cold more than any other green. • In the USA, the Collard has long represented survival, fortitude, and wisdom in African American culture. This is because during the harsh years of enslavement, slaves could harvest the plentiful but unappreciated Collard plants that grew wild in the South. They boiled Collards flavored with cast-off ingredients such as pigs' feet and ham hocks, to create a historic, iconic "soul food" dish. • Eat Collards to banish a negative relationship. • Eating Collards on New Year symbolizes good luck and prosperity for the year to come.

No. 063

Brassica rapa subsp. *pekinensis*

Napa Cabbage

Baechu | Celery Cabbage | Chinese Cabbage | Hakusai | Michihili | Nappa | Pe-Tsai | Wombok

✳ SYMBOLIC MEANINGS

Charity; Good luck charm; Indifference; Prosperity; Visible faith.

🌀 POSSIBLE POWERS

Banishes negativity; Ending relationships; Endings; Fertility; Mental clarity; Mental powers; Protection.

☾ FOLKLORE AND FACTS

Cultivation of Napa Cabbage started in fifteenth-century China. It is a common ingredient in Chinese, Japanese, and Korean cuisine. It is the traditional vital ingredient for the salted and fermented, sauerkraut-style Korean condiment and side dish known as kimchi. Napa Cabbage leaves can be eaten raw in salads and cooked in stir-fries, added to soups, and used for wraps. • During WWII, when the USA was unable to get seeds from Europe and Asia, the government heavily promoted growing fruit and vegetables to produce seed stocks. Napa Cabbage was one of the vegetables deliberately cultivated for its seeds.

No. 064

Brassica rapa var. *botrytis*

Cauliflower

Cabbage Flower | Cornish Cauliflower | Curd Plant | Fioretto Cauliflower | Green Cauliflower | Purple Cauliflower | Orange-Yellow Cauliflower | Romanesco Cauliflower | White Cauliflower

✳ SYMBOLIC MEANINGS

Charity; Good luck charm; Indifference; Visible faith.

🌀 POSSIBLE POWERS

Banish negativity; Ending relationships; Endings; Fertility; Mental clarity; Mental powers; Moon; Protection; Water element.

☾ FOLKLORE AND FACTS

The edible part of the Cauliflower plant is the white flower head, or "curd." Although it is easily recognized by the curd's white color, Cauliflower also comes in varieties that are green, orange, or purple. Cauliflower can be eaten raw as crudités or added to a salad. When cooked it is often steamed, stir-fried, roasted, batter-dipped, or deep-fried. • For additional spiritual protection, eat Cauliflower.

No. 065

Brassica rapa var. *chinensis*

Bok Choy

Chinese Cabbage | Chinese Leaf | Chinese Mustard | Pak Choi | Petsay | Pichay | Pok Choi | Tatsoi

✳ SYMBOLIC MEANINGS

Charity; Indifference.

🌀 POSSIBLE POWERS

Banishes negativity; Ending relationships; Endings; Fertility; Fire element; Luck; Mars; Mental clarity; Mental powers; Protection; Wealth.

☾ FOLKLORE AND FACTS

In Asia, Bok Choy is an important vegetable and crop that has been cultivated in China since the fifth century. The Bok Choy plant's leaves and bulb are edible. Bok Choy is often added raw to salads or sautéed, but is tastiest stir-fried. It is a substitute for Napa Cabbage when making kimchi, a Korean salted and fermented side dish and condiment. • Versatile Tatsoi is closely related to Bok Choy and used in the same ways. The tender raw leaves taste similar to Romaine. The stalks have a mildly bitter Cucumber flavor and lend themselves well to pickling.

No. 066
Brassica rapa var. *rapa* 🝫

Turnip
Common Turnip | White Turnip

✹ **SYMBOLIC MEANINGS**
Charity; Indifference.

🌀 **POSSIBLE POWERS**
Banishes negativity;
Earth element; Ending
relationships; Feminine
energy; Fertility; Good luck; Luck; Mental clarity or power;
Moon; Positive omen; Protection.

☾ **FOLKLORE AND FACTS**
Turnips are pungent ancient root vegetables that taste
milder after cooking. They can be yellow, orange, red, or the
well-known white-fleshed variety, and can grow quite large,
reaching sizes weighing two pounds, although the smaller
sizes are favored, as they can be eaten raw, greens and all.
The greens can be prepared by boiling, steaming, sautéing, or
added to soups. Boiled Turnip roots can be mashed alone or
with potatoes. Turnip roots are sweeter when roasted. • Put a
hollowed-out candlelit Turnip at the window on Halloween
night to scare away malicious spirits. • Place a Turnip in the
home to turn away every kind of negativity.

No. 067
Brassica rapa var. *ruvo*

Rapini
Broccoletti | Broccoli Raab | Broccoli Rabe | Cime di Rapa | Ruvo Kale

✹ **SYMBOLIC MEANINGS**
Charity; Indifference.

🌀 **POSSIBLE POWERS**
Banishes negativity; Ending relationships; Endings; Fertility;
Mental clarity; Mental powers; Protection.

☾ **FOLKLORE AND FACTS**
The entire stalk of the Rapini plant is edible when young,
with the base becoming increasingly fibrous as the plant
continues to grow. Rapini is greatly enjoyed
throughout Italy, Portugal, Spain, and the
USA. It is most usually sautéed in olive oil
and seasoned with garlic, tossed
with hot pasta, or added to
soup. Better known as Broccoli
Rabe in Philadelphia, it is
popular grilled with peppers and
used as a topping on a hoagie,
but most especially as a crucial
ingredient in a roast pork and
Broccoli Rabe with peppers
submarine sandwich. • Carry
Rapini seed in a red cloth pouch to
increase your mental powers.

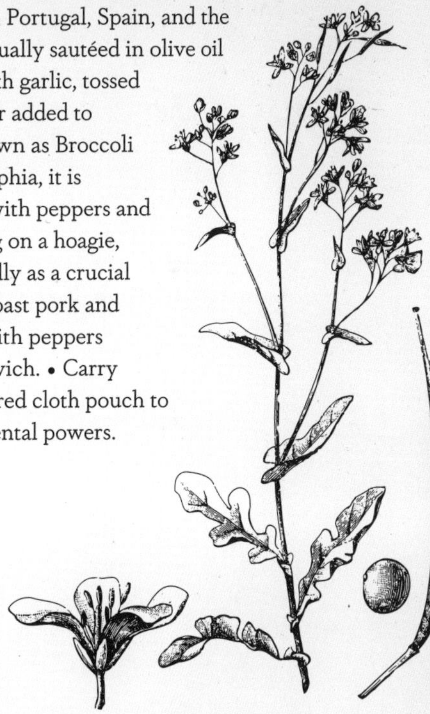

B

No. 068

Calendula officinalis 🏺

Calendula

Caléndula | Common Marigold | Pot Marigold |
Ruddles | Scotch Marigold

☀ SYMBOLIC MEANINGS

Affection; Anxiety; Constructive loss; Cruelty; Despair;
Fidelity; Grace; Grief; Health; Jealousy; Joy; Longevity; Pain;
Sacred affection; Trouble.

🌀 POSSIBLE POWERS

Amorousness; Dream magic; Evil thoughts; Fire element;
Helps with seeing fairies; Legal matters; Prediction;
Prophetic dreams; Protection; Psychic power; Rebirth;
Sleep; Sun.

☘ FOLKLORE AND FACTS

Calendula flowers are often used as a saffron substitute,
as well as added to salads or used as a garnish. The leaves
are also edible, but taste unpleasant. • The Calendula is
considered one of the most sacred herbs of ancient India. Its
flower heads were commonly strung into garlands and used
in temples and at weddings. • Carry a sachet of Calendula
petals along with a Bay Laurel leaf to quell gossip. • Burn
Calendula petals to create some smoke, then pass a prepared
Calendula amulet, talisman, or sachet through its smoke (not
the flames!) to entirely imbue it with magical powers. It may
be possible to see visions within the smoke.

No. 069

Camassia quamash 🏺

Camas

Camash | Quamash | Wild Hyacinth

☀ SYMBOLIC MEANING

Play.

🌀 POSSIBLE POWER

Playfulness.

☘ FOLKLORE AND FACTS

It takes several years for the nutritious
Camas bulb to fully mature and bloom.
It's usually fully cooked by boiling or
roasting. The indigenous people of
the Pacific Northwest would often
pit-roast the bulbs. A pit-roasted Camas
bulb looks like a sweet potato but
tastes sweeter. The Camas bulbs can

also be dried and ground into a flour used for baking or as a
thickener. • Over-eating Camas or eating undercooked bulbs
can result in a profuse bout of flatulence. • The indigenous
people of the Pacific Northwest methodically cultivated
permanently marked Camas plots, protecting, planting, and
caring for them to eventually pass on ownership via family
lineage, with multiple generations harvesting from the same
plot. • During the Lewis and Clark 1804–6 expedition, the
group ate Camas bulbs to fend off hunger. • Do not confuse
Camas with poisonous Meadow Death-Camas. It's difficult
distinguishing between these two plants that are frequently
found growing in the same area.

No. 070

Camellia sinensis 🏺

Black Tea

Assam Tea | Bird's Tongue | Ceylon | Cha | Congou | Darjeeling |
Dianhong | Jiu Qu Hong Mei | Kangra | Keemun | Kukicha | Lahijan |
Lapsang | Nepali | Nilgiri | Orange Pekoe Tea | Plant of Heaven |
Puerh Tea | Yingdehong

☀ SYMBOLIC MEANINGS

Change; Constancy; Contentment; Courage;
Fire element; Harmony; Mars; Masculine
energy; Peace; Refreshment; Rejuvenation; Riches; Spiritual
awakening, connection, or enlightenment; Steadfastness;
Strength; Sun; Young sons and daughters.

🌀 POSSIBLE POWERS

Courage; Feminine energy; Fire element; Healing; Mars;
Moon; Peace; Prosperity; Rejuvenation; Riches; Spiritual
connection; Stress relief; Water element.

☘ FOLKLORE AND FACTS

The choice edible part of any *Camellia sinensis* Black Tea
bush are the very new leaf tips, which are harvested by
hand twice a year. The second harvest is the most prized
and known as "tippy tea," because by then the tips of the
leaves are a golden shade that is considered to be a sweeter,
more flavorful leaf. Black Tea leaves are available dried
loose and also collected at an optimum amount within a
sachet for brewing a single cup. • Assam Tea is one of the
three most common black teas used to brew traditional
Chai tea. It is also blended to create "breakfast tea," such as
"English Breakfast" and "Irish Breakfast." • Wear a sachet or
pouch of Black Tea as a talisman to increase your strength
and give yourself a boost of courage. A pre-made store-
bought tea bag is not the proper kind of sachet. The dried
tea within it is acceptable, but it should be emptied out
into the handmade sachet packet. • The word "tea" in the
common names for *Camellia sinensis* Tea Shrub, *Melaleuca*

C

alternifolia Tea Tree, and *Leptospermum scoparium* New Zealand Tea Tree imply they are similar plants, but they are not.

No. 071

Campanula rapunculus

Rampion
Rampion Bellflower | Rapunzel | Rover Bellflower

✹ SYMBOLIC MEANINGS
Longing; Loyalty; Small bell.

✹ POSSIBLE POWER
Profound wisdom.

✹ FOLKLORE AND FACTS
The Rampion plant was widely grown in European home gardens for its edible spinach-like leaves and radish-like root. • An old legend tells of a young woman who pulled up the plant to find a staircase that led to a castle deep in the earth. • The fairy tale "Rapunzel" tells of a beautiful maiden with magically long hair whose mother had an insatiable food craving for the Rampion that grew in a witch's garden. When the witch caught Rapunzel's father stealing her Rampion she demanded that he give his unborn child to her. When the baby was born, the witch fetched baby Rapunzel, then locked her in a room at the top of an impenetrable tower that only the witch could enter by climbing up the girl's long-hanging hair. Eventually, an insistent prince in love rescued her. • Carry a sachet of the Rampion flower and leaf to inspire wisdom.

No. 072

Cantharellus cibarius ⚱

Chanterelle
Girolle | Golden Chanterelle

✹ SYMBOLIC MEANING
Abundantly wealthy.

✹ POSSIBLE POWERS
Abundance; Banishing; Elevates social status; Fertility; Happiness; House-warming; Increases psychic ability; Joy; Prophetic dreams; Protection; Psychic travel between worlds.

✹ FOLKLORE AND FACTS
The *Cantharellus cibarius* Chanterelle is a wild European mushroom that can be foraged from late summer through late autumn. The Chanterelle has such a distinctively wavy shape that it is easy to sort this edible fungus from those that are deadly poisonous. Chanterelles can be frozen to preserve them. They can also be air dried. The Chanterelle mushroom's superior succulence and delicate flavor make it a gourmet ingredient. They cannot be cultivated, being found only in the wild.

No. 073

Capparis spinosa ⚱

Caper
Caper Bush | Caperberry Bush | Flinders Rose

✹ SYMBOLIC MEANING
Escapade.

✹ POSSIBLE POWERS
Aphrodisiac; Attracts love; Feminine energy; Love; Lust; Potency; Venus; Water element.

✹ FOLKLORE AND FACTS
The edible parts of the Caper tree are the zingy peppery flower buds and the fruit-berries, which are salted or pickled. If you are fortunate to live in Cyprus or Greece, where Caper leaves would be available in the garden or market, these are edible too. The dried leaf is sometimes used in cheesemaking as a substitute for rennet. • A Caper is sometimes used in a martini instead of a green olive. • It was once believed by some that an impotent man needed to eat Capers to be miraculously cured. • The Caper flower is beautifully unusual and would work well when making two love and lust red sachets with each containing a Caper flower and a leaf, or just the buds if the flowers and leaves are unattainable. Tuck the sachets under the mattress with one on each side of the bed.

No. 074

Capsicum annuum ⚱

Chili Peppers

Aleppo Pepper | Ancho | Banana Pepper | Bell Pepper | Bird's Eye Chili |
Cayenne Pepper | Cherry Pepper | Chili Tepin | Chiltepin |
Cuaresmeño | Friggitello | Golden Pepperoncini Pepper |
Halaby Pepper | Haleb Biber | Hungarian Paprika |
Hungarian Wax Pepper | Jalapeño Pepper | Paprika
Pepper | Pimento | Red Cherry Pepper | Spanish
Pimiento | Sweet Italian Pepper | Syrian Chili | Thai Chili |
Turkey Pepper | Tuscan Pepper | Pimiento | Yellow
Wax Pepper

✴ SYMBOLIC MEANINGS

Beauty; Beneficial change; Consumerism; Culture;
Deception; Desire to gain freedom; Dishonesty; Fairness;
Greed; Healing; Hidden desires; Hidden feelings; Hope;
Maturity; Overview; Peace; Perseverance; Productivity;
Resilience; Selfishness; Spice in your life; Things missing
in life; Wellbeing.

🌀 POSSIBLE POWERS

Aphrodisiac; Attracts love; Banishing; Breaks a hex;
Creativity; Energy; Fidelity; Fire element; Healing; Hope;
Love; Mars; Masculine energy; Mental ability; Prosperity;
Protection; Restores things missing in life; Strength; Sun;
Wards off evil; Wards off the evil eye; Wealth.

☾ FOLKLORE AND FACTS

Capsicum annuum encompasses many different Chili
Peppers, which are all botanically berries, ranging from
the sweetest to some of the hottest varieties. • The heat of
a pepper is measured by "Scoville Heat Units," or "SHU,"
a rating that was developed by American chemist Wilbur
Scoville. • The Bell Pepper is the mildest of all, being entirely
heat-free and distinctly flavorful. The wide range of mild
sweet Bell Pepper colors are green, red, orange, yellow,
lavender, dark purple, brown, and white. They are very often
thinly sliced, chopped, or minced to add to a wide variety
of cooked foods and salads, as well as roasted, or stuffed
then baked. The hottest is the little Chiltepin Pepper, which
grows in green, yellow, orange, or red varieties. This Chili
Pepper is tiny in size, but two months after the fruit has set
on the Chiltepin Pepper plant, it is hotter than a Habanero.
Measuring around an astonishing 75,000 Scovilles, the
Chiltepin Pepper has the hottest heat level in all green fruit.
The Chiltepin's heat varies greatly one year to another, from
somewhat mild to a violently intense, unbearable heat. • In
between those two Chili Pepper extremes in hotness are a
range of other *Capsicum annuum* Chili Peppers, such as the
Banana Pepper, Paprika Pepper, Pimiento, Poblano Chili,
Cayenne, Jalapeño Pepper, and Bird's Eye Chili. • With
regards to the Aleppo pepper, people have continually
prepared this herb by hand in Aleppo, a 6,000-year-old
city in northern Syria that is one of the oldest in the world.
Aleppo Peppers are traditionally processed there by cutting
the peppers in half, then removing the seeds and inner flesh.
The flesh is wiped with a white cloth and given a light coating
of olive oil and salt, then dried on a rooftop. They are then
coarsely ground to produce a mild, peppery, flaky seasoning
with a natural touch of sweetness that is beloved and liberally
used in many Middle Eastern and Mediterranean dishes.
• A chipotle chili is a smoke-dried Jalapeño Pepper. Texans'
abiding love of and utter devotion to the Jalapeño is evident
since they will add a Jalapeño in at least one dish at every
celebration meal of every year. • Encircle a house with Bird's
Eye Chili to break the curse. • Make a red sachet using one
whole small Bird's Eye Chili to put under the mattress to
encourage spicy romance.

No. 075

Capsicum baccatum ⚱

Ají Cito Pepper

Ají Dulce Pepper | Ajicito | Ajíes | Ají Gustoso | Ají Cachucha | Quechucha Pepper

✴ SYMBOLIC MEANINGS

Enchanted; Holy; Magical.

🌀 POSSIBLE POWERS

Breaks a hex; Fidelity; Fire element; Love; Love charms;
Mars; Masculine energy; Protection against vampires;
Protection against werewolves; Sun.

☾ FOLKLORE AND FACTS

The literal translation of *Baccatum* is "berry-like." The small
Ají Cito Pepper comes in colors of green to yellow. • At
around 100,000 Scovilles, it is the hottest of the *Capsicum
baccatum* peppers.

C

No. 076

Capsicum chinense

Hot Pepper

Adjuma Pepper | Bhut Jolokia | Datil | Fatalii | Ghost Pepper |
Habanero Chili | Madame Jeanette Pepper | Scotch Bonnet |
Trinidad Scorpion Pepper | Yellow Lantern Chili

☀ SYMBOLIC MEANING

Spice in your life.

🌀 POSSIBLE POWERS

Breaks a hex; Fidelity; Fire element; Love; Mars; Masculine
energy; Sun; Wards off an evil spirit; Wards off the evil eye.

🌍 FOLKLORE AND FACTS

The *Capsicum chinense* species contains the hottest Hot
Peppers in the world! In Mexico, archeologists have found
Capsicum chinense seeds in burial sites dating to 7,000
BCE. Because a *Capsicum chinense* Hot Pepper contributes
considerable heat to food, cooks primarily use it in salsas,
sauces, and stews. The hottest part of any Hot Pepper is
found in the seeds and pith. After handling a Hot Pepper in
food preparation, the heat can remain on the skin for hours.
The burning skin sensation can be alleviated by applying
a liquid antacid to the area. When the Hot Pepper you just
ate is too hot, drink some milk to help cool the heat seething
in your mouth. Ice cream helps, too. • Due to the wide
popularity of Tex-Mex and Mexican foods, Hot Pepper
aficionados are abundant all over the world. On the internet,
there are many websites, blogs, and global discussion forums
that are entirely devoted to Hot Peppers. • With the ongoing
competition to create another new, hotter, Hot Pepper
hybrid, the Hot Pepper seems to be getting hotter and hotter.

No. 077

Capsicum frutescens var. *tabasco*

Tabasco Pepper

Tabasco Chili

☀ SYMBOLIC MEANINGS

Hidden desires or feelings;
Things missing in life.

🌀 POSSIBLE POWERS

Banishing; Creativity; Energy; Fire element; Healing;
Love; Mars; Masculine energy; Mental ability; Prosperity;
Protection; Strength; Wards off evil; Wards off the evil eye;
Wealth.

🌍 FOLKLORE AND FACTS

The Tabasco Pepper is the only chili pepper that isn't dry
inside and has a juicy fruit. They should be left on the plant
to fully ripen to red before picking them, although the end-
of-the-season green peppers can be used for cooking, added
to soups and other dishes needing some heat. The iconic
sauce made from this pepper is very spicy and pleasantly hot
enough at around 40,000 Scovilles. Tabasco hot sauce seems
to have birthed a cadre of hot sauce connoisseurs who amass
large hot pepper sauce collections to discuss and compare.

No. 078

Capsicum pubescens

Rocoto Pepper

Locoto | Manzano Pepper

☀ SYMBOLIC MEANINGS

Hidden desires or feelings;
Things missing in life.

🌀 POSSIBLE POWERS

Banishing; Creativity; Energy; Fire element; Healing;
Love; Mars; Masculine energy; Mental ability; Prosperity;
Protection; Strength; Wards off evil; Wards off the evil eye;
Wealth.

🌍 FOLKLORE AND FACTS

Unlike other *Capsicum* peppers, the Rocoto Pepper
cannot survive tropical heat. The plant requires the cool
temperature of higher elevations to thrive well enough to
fruit. • The Rocoto Pepper is a vital ingredient in many
Bolivian and Peruvian recipes.

No. 079
Cardamine hirsuta 🜚

Hairy Bittercress
Bitter Cress | Hairy Bitter Cress

✳ **SYMBOLIC MEANING**
Paternal error.

🌀 **POSSIBLE POWERS**
Fire element; Mars; Moon; Protection;
Spiritual warfare; Water element.

🌑 **FOLKLORE AND FACTS**
The edible parts of the Hairy Bittercress
plant are the leaves, which can be consumed raw, and the
stems, which can be cooked like other tender greens. • Hairy
Bittercress is one of the magical ingredients in the Nine
Herbs Charm, written in England during the tenth century.
• Soldiers in holy battle used the ancient charm to fend off
The Serpent's perceived power against them.

No. 080
Carica papaya ☠

Papaya
Caribbean Red Papaya | Pawpaw | Red Papaya | Yellow
Papaw

✳ **SYMBOLIC MEANINGS**
Bad health; Good health; Inner
peace.

🌀 **POSSIBLE POWERS**
Feminine energy; Love; Moon;
Protection; Water element; Wishing.

🌑 **FOLKLORE AND FACTS**
The edible part of the Papaya tree is the ripe fruit and the
seeds within it. Unripe green Papaya must be cooked before
it can be eaten because the latex within the fruit is poisonous.
The papain enzyme in Papaya can be used as a meat
tenderizer. Fresh Papaya will prevent gelatin from setting.
• Eating large amounts of Papaya is not recommended
because it could possibly damage the esophagus. • Though
both are called "Paw-paw," *Carica papaya* and *Asimina
triloba* are not related to each other. • Tie a ribbon around
a Papaya tree limb and visualize what you want. • A piece
of *Carica papaya* wood over the door will keep evil from
entering the home.

No. 081
Carthamus tinctorius 🜚

Safflower
American Saffron | Bastard Saffron | False Saffron

✳ **SYMBOLIC MEANINGS**
Marriage; Welcome.

🌀 **POSSIBLE POWERS**
Colorize; Transformation.

🌑 **FOLKLORE AND FACTS**
Safflower is one of the oldest crops, with archeological
evidence of cultivation dating back to 2500 BCE in
Mesopotamia. • Safflower blossom garlands were discovered
in Tutankhamun's tomb. • Since the 1960s, Safflower plants
have been cultivated for the seeds, which are pressed to
produce a vegetable oil that is most commonly used in
cooking, in salad dressings, and to make margarine.
• Safflower flowers are used as an economical substitute for
the much more expensive saffron.

No. 082
Carum carvi 🜚

Caraway
Carum | Meridian Fennel | Persian Cumin

✳ **SYMBOLIC MEANING**
Faithfulness.

🌀 **POSSIBLE POWERS**
Air element; Anti-theft; Business transactions; Caution;
Cleverness; Communication; Creativity; Faith; Faithfulness;
Health; Illumination; Initiation; Intelligence; Keeps lovers
true; Learning; Love; Lust; Masculine energy; Memory;
Mental power; Mercury; Passion; Protection; Protection
against Lilith; Prudence; Repels negativity; Science; Self-
preservation; Sound judgment; Thievery; Wisdom.

🌑 **FOLKLORE AND FACTS**
What people commonly call the seed is actually the tiny
fruit of the Caraway plant. Caraway has a slight anise-like
taste while simultaneously retaining its own identifiable
flavor. Caraway is used to flavor food such as cabbage or
pork. It's also used to top rolls and breads. Caraway is added
into *kavring*, or Swedish black bread, and is an iconic part
of Jewish rye bread. It can also be brewed into or added to
an herb tea. Caraway is available whole or ground. • In the
Middle Ages, people used Caraway seeds in love potions that
were specifically created to prevent lovers from turning and

C

wandering away from each other. • Use Caraway, along with other herbs, to increase protection. • Sprinkle some Caraway seeds amongst your most prized possessions to fend off a burglary. A thief who makes it into a house will supposedly be held magically transfixed until arrested. • Wearing an amulet of Caraway seeds is supposed to improve the memory. • Caraway has the power to consecrate magical tools. • Chew Caraway seeds as an aphrodisiac.

No. 083
Carya illinoinensis 🝋

Pecan
Hardy Pecan | Nuez de la Arruga

☀ SYMBOLIC MEANINGS
Southern hospitality; Wealth.

🌀 POSSIBLE POWERS
Air element; Employment; Masculine energy; Mercury; Money.

☾ FOLKLORE AND FACTS
Pecans are readily available as whole husked roasted nuts in shell, as well as shelled. • Pecan wood is a favorite for grilling and smoking meat. • Cultivation of Pecan trees did not commence until the 1880s. • Thomas Jefferson planted Pecan trees at his Virginia plantation, Monticello. He gifted trees to George Washington, who planted them at his own Virginia plantation, Mount Vernon. • San Saba, Texas, claims to be "The Pecan Capital of the World." A Pecan tree there dates to 1850 and is believed to be the "Mother Tree" of all the Pecan trees in Texas that followed it. • Add a Pecan to all spells concerning money and prosperity.

No. 084
Carya ovata 🝋

Shagbark Hickory
Carolina Hickory | Scalybark Hickory | Shellbark Hickory | Upland Hickory

☀ SYMBOLIC MEANING
Holding.

🌀 POSSIBLE POWERS
Legal matters; Love; Lust; Protection.

☾ FOLKLORE AND FACTS
Shagbark Hickory is closely connected to Northeastern Native American tribes who ate the seed nuts raw, although a light toasting of the nuts intensifies and elevates their flavor significantly. The nuts are usually foraged, although shelled Shagbark Hickory nuts can *sometimes* be found at a farmers' market. The nuts are extremely tedious to open, but worth the effort. The tree's wood is favored for producing high-quality charcoal for cooking and for smoking meat, most often bacon, ham, and some types of sausage. • From earliest American times until this day, the exceptionally strong wood has been useful in tool making, most especially for use as axe handles. • The Ojibway people used the wood to make archery bows. • To protect your home against legal trouble, burn a piece of the root to ashes. Mix the ashes with *Argentina anserina* Silver Cinquefoil. Put this mixture into sachets and hang them over each entrance door of the home.

No. 085
Castanea sativa 🝋

Sweet Chestnut
Chestnut | Gështenjë | Spanish Chestnut

☀ SYMBOLIC MEANINGS
Chastity; Do me justice; Independence; Injustice; Justice; Luxury.

🌀 POSSIBLE POWERS
Abundance; Air element; Energy; Enhance intuition; Fertility; Fire element; Jupiter; Justice; Longevity; Love; Masculine energy; Mental acuity; Recognizing or overcoming difficulties; Stamina; Strength; Success; Sun; Sympathy.

☾ FOLKLORE AND FACTS
The edible parts of the long-living Sweet Chestnut tree are the kernels of the seeds. • The highly versatile Sweet Chestnut has been cultivated as a source for food and for use as a flour since at least 2000 BCE. There is a Sweet Chestnut tree in Corsica that is 1,000 years old. • In 1904, Chestnut blight fungus was discovered in North America, resulting in the death of at least four billion trees. The species is still endangered in the USA and Canada. • Ancient Romans didn't particularly care for the taste of the Sweet Chestnut. • Keep Sweet Chestnuts in the house to attract positive energy. • If wanting to conceive, carry or wear a Sweet Chestnut amulet to boost fertility. • Carry a Sweet Chestnut amulet during class to help absorb and retain information. • Carry a Sweet Chestnut amulet to court to encourage justice to prevail. • Feed your heart's desire a Sweet Chestnut to inspire love. • Do not mistake inedible toxic "Horse Chestnut" for the Sweet Chestnut.

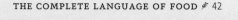

No. 086
Castanospermum australe ☠ ⚗

Black Bean Tree
Baway | Binyjaalga | Blackbean Tree | Ganyjuu | Junggurraa | Mirrayn | Morton Bay
Chestnut | Yiwurra

✳ SYMBOLIC MEANINGS
Family; Signal; Supply; Sustenance.

⟡ POSSIBLE POWERS
Gathering; Guidance; Life; Migration.

☾ FOLKLORE AND FACTS
For over 2,500 years the Australian Black Bean Tree was
known to be a gathering place for Aboriginal people during
ceremonies because of its food value. • Ancient Aboriginal
people planted the Black Bean Tree wherever they migrated
around the entire Australian continent. It is so much a part
of their culture that the tree is included in several Australian
Aboriginal "dreaming track" song cycles. • As a staple
bush food of the Aboriginal people, the seed is only edible
after several long days of processing, which requires many
different vital steps carried out by knowledgeable people to
remove its extreme toxicity. Days later, the resulting dough
is ultimately shaped and fire-baked into a patty called a
"damper" that is usually topped with honey before eating it.
• All the Black Bean Trees in New South Wales have one
tree in common that they have descended from. The tree
seeds also spread via water. • The ancient Aboriginal people
used the wood of the Black Bean Tree to fashion throwing
spears for use when hunting. • Children often use empty
Black Bean Tree seedpods as toy boats.

No. 087
Ceanothus americanus ⚗

Red Root
Jersey Tea Ceanothus | Mountain Lilac | Mountain Sweet | New Jersey Tea |
Redroot | Wild Snowball

✳ SYMBOLIC MEANING
Spiny.

⟡ POSSIBLE POWERS
Fire element; Healing; Mars; Rebellion.

☾ FOLKLORE AND FACTS
During the American Revolution, Red Root leaves were a
stimulating but caffeine-free tea substitute when imported
Black Tea was difficult to get. The leaves smell somewhat
like Wintergreen. During that time, Red Root obtained the
common name New Jersey Tea. The roots of the Red Root
plant can grow deeply and up to eight inches in diameter.

No. 088
Celosia argentea var. *cristata* ⚗

Cockscomb Celosia
Common Cockscomb | Coxcomb | Feather Cockscomb | Lagos Spinach | Velvet
Flower | Woolflower

✳ SYMBOLIC MEANINGS
Affection; Constancy; Fidelity; Foppery; Friendship; Humor;
Immortality; Love; Partnerships; Silliness; Singularity;
Warmth.

⟡ POSSIBLE POWERS
Earth element; Jupiter; Love; Partnerships.

☾ FOLKLORE AND FACTS
Cockscomb Celosia plants are the most widely consumed
vegetable plant in Benin, Nigeria, the Congo, and Indonesia,
where they are grown on small farms and home gardens. The
young stems and flowers are cooked and consumed, with the
leaves being the most favored part of the plant. The seeds can
also be consumed as a cereal grain. The flowers were once
used in Korea as a dessert garnish and as an ingredient in rice
cakes. They can also be used
to infuse alcoholic beverages.
• Cockscomb Celosia plants
are easy to grow and have
interesting-looking velvety
or fluffy plumed flowers that
encourage children to have fun
growing plants in a garden.

No. 089
Cenchrus americanus

Millet
Pearl Millet

✳ **SYMBOLIC MEANING**
Measurement.

🌀 **POSSIBLE POWERS**
Earth element; Energy; Jupiter; Money; Money energy.

🌙 **FOLKLORE AND FACTS**
Archeological research has determined that Millet was domesticated in West Africa between 2500 and 2000 BCE. The edible parts of the *Cenchrus americanus* Millet plant are the seeds. They are available as whole grain seeds and as a flour. Millet flour is used to make flatbreads. In India, Pearl Millet is boiled into a porridge called *kamban koozh*. • Millet grains were used for measurement in ancient China, with ten grains placed end-to-end equaling an inch. • An old-time German New Year's custom was to eat Millet on New Year's Day to pull in riches.

No. 090
Centaurea cyanus 🥣

Bachelor Button
Bluebottle | Boutonniere Flower | Common Cornflower | Cyani Flower | Hurtsickle

✳ **SYMBOLIC MEANINGS**
Celibacy; Clearness; Delicacy; Elegance; Endless love; Hope; Hope in love; Immortal love; Immortality; Light; Love; Patience; Refinement; Single blessedness; Single wretchedness; Unchangeable.

🌀 **POSSIBLE POWERS**
Colorize; Feminine energy; Healing; Love; Protection; Snake deterrent; Venus; Water element.

🌙 **FOLKLORE AND FACTS**
Bachelor Button flowers are edible and can be consumed raw, cooked, or dried for use in tea and as a seasoning. The flowers are primarily used in drinks and foods to add color. The dried or raw flower petals can be added to cheeses, oils, salads, cocktails, and desserts. • There was a time when men wore Bachelor Button flowers to indicate that they were in love. If the flower faded too fast it was a sign that his love would not be returned. • A wash of Bachelor Button water, also known as "cornflower water," was supposedly a treatment for the plague in the Middle Ages. • Bachelor Button flowers are sometimes used in long-lasting Hawaiian leis because they hold their shape and color after the flowers have dried. • There was a time when the sure cure for a nosebleed was to gather Bachelor Button flowers on Corpus Christi Sunday, sixty days after Easter, and hold the flowers in your hands until they were warm to the touch. By then, your nose should have stopped bleeding!

No. 091
Centella asiatica 🥣

Centella
Antanan | Asiatic Pennywort | Brahmi Booti | Ekpanni | Gotu Kola | Indian Pennywort | Luei Gong Gen | Pegaga | Pegagan | Pennywort | Takip-Kohol | Thankuni Pata

✳ **SYMBOLIC MEANINGS**
Enlightenment; Satisfaction.

🌀 **POSSIBLE POWERS**
Aphrodisiac; Attracts love; Healing; Meditation; Sexual stamina; Stamina; Youthful aging.

🌙 **FOLKLORE AND FACTS**
The edible part of the *Centella asiatica* Centella plant is the leaves, which can be used in a salad or stir-fried in Coconut oil. In Cambodia, Thailand, and Vietnam, street vendors offer health drinks and salads using the Centella greens. • According to legend, the Centella plant gave a tenth-century Sri Lankan king the sexual stamina he needed to satisfy and maintain the agreeable countenance and joy of his extensive harem.

No. 092

Ceratonia siliqua 🍵

Carob

Carob Tree | St. John's Bread

✳ SYMBOLIC MEANINGS
Affection beyond the grave;
Elegance; Love after death.

🌀 POSSIBLE POWERS
Health; Protection.

☕ FOLKLORE AND FACTS
The Carob tree's large, curled pods take a year to develop
and ripen on the tree. Carob pods are dried and used
as a chocolate substitute and as a flavoring. Carob has
a somewhat sweet taste and does not contain caffeine.
Processed Carob is used in beverages, confections, and
baked goods. In Malta and Crete, a Carob syrup known as
gulepp tal-harrub is made from the pods. Carob syrup is
also commonly enjoyed in Libya, Portugal, Turkey, Egypt,
Spain, and Sicily. Carob liqueur is also made from the syrup.
• During ancient times in the Middle East, weighing gold
and gemstones against Carob seeds was common, and is also
the source of the term "carat." • In the nineteenth century it
was believed that chewing on Carob pods was a soothing and
cleansing throat aid. Thus, it was recommended to singers
and was sold at British apothecaries. • Wear a Carob amulet
to guard against evil and maintain good health.

No. 093

Chamaemelum nobile 🍵

Chamomile

Blue Chamomile | Camomile | Camomyle | English
Chamomile | Garden Camomile | German Chamomile |
Ground Apple | Hungarian Chamomile | Lawn Chamomile |
Perennial Chamomile | Roman Chamomile | Scented
Mayweed | True Chamomile | Wild Chamomile

✳ SYMBOLIC MEANINGS
All who know you will love you; Attracts wealth; Energy in
action or adversity; Ingenuity; Initiative; Love in adversity;
May all your wishes be fulfilled; Patience; Patience in
adversity; Sleep; Sleepiness; Sleepy; Wisdom.

🌀 POSSIBLE POWERS
Abundance; Advancement; Breaks a hex or spell; Calm;
Calming; Conscious will; Deity dedication; Energy;
Friendship; Growth; Healing; Humility; Induces sleepiness;
Joy; Leadership; Life; Light; Love; Luck; Luck when
gambling; Masculine energy; Meditation; Money; Natural

power; Noble offering; Offering; Protection against lightning;
Purification; Relaxation; Sleep; Success; Sun; Tranquility;
Water element.

☕ FOLKLORE AND FACTS
The edible Chamomile flowers are available as dried
herbs for tea. German Chamomile's flower has a fragrance
similar to Apple, while Roman Chamomile's blossom is
larger. • Some gamblers would wash their hands with a
Chamomile infusion with the high hopes it would increase
their chances of winning. • A Chamomile infusion added
to a bath increases the chances of attracting love. • English
Chamomile is believed to be Mathen in the Nine Sacred
Herbs healing charm that was originally written in Wessex,
England, sometime around the tenth century. • During
the Middle Ages, on Midsummer's Eve, bonfires included
German Chamomile. Ill people would draw close to
breathe in the smoke, believing it to be healing to them,
their orchards, and their crops. • Chamomile essential oil
for aromatherapy can soothe restlessness and help promote
sleep.

No. 094

Chenopodium album ☠

Fat-Hen

Bathua | Goosefoot | Lamb's Quarters | White Goosefoot

✳ SYMBOLIC MEANINGS
Goodness; Insult.

🌀 POSSIBLE POWERS
Calls on ancestors; Earth element;
Jupiter.

☕ FOLKLORE AND FACTS
Fat-Hen is known and cultivated in North India as Bathua.
It should never be consumed raw. It should always be
cooked and eaten in moderation. The seeds are used for
making gruel, or as a substitute for Rice, as well as being
fermented into an alcoholic beverage. The young shoots,
leaves, and stems are cooked, added to soup, or made into
curries. • Napoleon supposedly depended on the Fat-Hen
seed grain to feed his troops when other food was difficult
to obtain. • Archeologists have found Fat-Hen seed grain
in the stomachs of ancient bodies uncovered from Danish
bogs. • According to ancient Sanskrit writings on art and
construction, the juice of the Fat-Hen plant is vital in the
making of wall plaster. • Fat-Hen's fragrant flowers can
repel moths.

C

No. 095

Chenopodium quinoa 🥣

Quinoa

Inca Wheat | Kinwa

✸ **SYMBOLIC MEANING**
Mother grain.

🌀 **POSSIBLE POWERS**
Air element; Earth element; Sun.

🌙 **FOLKLORE AND FACTS**
Quinoa seeds are edible when cooked.
The seeds are coated with a bitter
substance known as "saponin," which
prevents them being eaten by birds. The saponin needs to
be removed by rinsing the very tiny seeds thoroughly before
cooking to avoid a bitter taste. Quinoa can be used in all the
same ways as cooked Rice. It can be prepared either plain,
buttered and flavored with herbs as a side dish, or even as
a hot cereal. It can also be a sweet or savory dish, as well as
made into a cold or warm grain-based salad with an herb-
seasoned Olive oil and Lemon juice dressing.

No. 096

Chrysanthemum coronarium 🥣

Edible Chrysanthemum

Chop-Suey Greens | Chrysanthemum Greens | Crown Daisy | Garland Chrysanthemum

✸ **SYMBOLIC MEANINGS**
Cheerfulness; Cheerfulness and rest; Cheerfulness in
adversity; Fidelity; Happiness.

🌀 **POSSIBLE POWERS**
Cheerfulness; Fire element; Mars; Masculine energy;
Protection; Sun.

🌙 **FOLKLORE AND FACTS**
When young, the leaves and stems of Edible Chrysanthemum
have a mustard-like flavor that is enjoyed in Asian cuisine
as a vegetable and as a culinary herb in
casseroles, stews, and stir-fries.
• Any species of
Chrysanthemum is
considered a sacred flower
in Asia. • In Italy and Malta,
it is considered unlucky
to have any species of
Chrysanthemum in the house.

No. 097

Chrysanthemum leucanthemum 🥣

Oxeye Daisy

Dog Daisy | Field Daisy | Marguerite | Maudlinwort | Moon Daisy | Ox-Eye

✸ **SYMBOLIC MEANINGS**
Cheer; Disappointment; Faith; Innocence; Loyal love;
Patience; Purity; Simplicity; Token.

🌀 **POSSIBLE POWERS**
Divination; Divination for love.

🌙 **FOLKLORE AND FACTS**
The unopened flower buds of the Oxeye Daisy can be used
like Capers after they have been marinated or pickled.
• Oxeye Daisy has been used for a divination of love for
many generations, with the plucking of the petals to the
chant of "he loves me, he loves me not." The last petal
remaining is the answer to the perplexing question. • Oxeye
Daisy is depicted on many ancient ornaments, decorations,
paintings, and ceramics
in the Middle East.
• The ancient Celts
believed that Oxeye
Daisy was the spirit of a
baby who died at birth.
• If you dream about
an Oxeye Daisy in the
spring, good luck will
come to you. It's bad
luck to dream about it
in the autumn or winter.

C

No. 098
Cicer arietinum

Chickpea

Bengal Gram | Ceci Bean | Chick Pea | Egyptian Pea | Garbanzo
Bean | Kabuli Chana | Kala Chana

✳ SYMBOLIC MEANING
Hard-earned money.

🌀 POSSIBLE POWER
Money.

🜨 FOLKLORE AND FACTS
The remains of 7,500-year-old Chickpeas have been found at
archeological sites in the Middle East. The edible part of the
Chickpea plant is the seed, also known as the bean or pea.
Chickpeas need to be cooked until completely tender before
eating. Canned Chickpeas are cooked enough and need not
be cooked further. • Chickpeas can be added to salads or
even further prepared by deep-frying until crisply crunchy.
• In the late 1790s ground-roasted Chickpeas were used as
a coffee substitute in Europe that is sometimes still brewed.
• Chickpea purée is the base ingredient in any traditional
hummus recipe. The basic recipe started being passed
down and all around the world into just about everyone's
appreciative hand thanks to some clever someone in Cairo,
Egypt, who, around the thirteenth century, wrote it into an
early cookbook. • A baked, cake-like, pan-bread or flatbread
that can be served as a standalone meal can be made using
besan, which is Chickpea flour. Depending on where it is
made, the flatbread is also known as *socca*, *farinata*, *torta di
ceci*, *cecina*, or *calentita*.

No. 099
Cichorium endivia 📷

Endive

Batavian Endive | Bavarian Endive | Belgian Endive | Broad-
leaved Endive | *Cichorium endivia* var. *latifolia* | Escarole |
French Endive | Scarole

✳ SYMBOLIC MEANINGS
Frugality; Love.

🌀 POSSIBLE POWERS
Air element; Aphrodisiac; Jupiter;
Love; Lust; Masculine energy.

🜨 FOLKLORE AND FACTS
Cichorium endivia is not found
in the wild. Interestingly, after
returning from the Belgian War of

Independence in 1831, Jan Lammers discovered the Chicory
roots he had stored in his cellar for several months, thinking
they would have dried out. But while in the damp dark
space, the roots had sprouted leafy, nearly white shoots at the
top. Bravely, he tasted them, finding them pleasantly crunchy
and mildly bitter. As a result of this surprise, a new vegetable
was discovered, with Endive now commonly farmed on
shelves in dark damp rooms with the roots planted just
beneath the soil. • Endive leaves can be eaten raw as a
salad, sautéed, and added to soups. • *Cichorium endivia* var.
latifolia Escarole is the least bitter of all the Endive varieties.
Escarole can be eaten as a salad, sautéed, and added to
soups too. When eaten as a salad, Escarole is considered an
aphrodisiac. • Carry or wear a pink and red sachet of Endive
seeds to attract love. • If Endive is worn fresh as a talisman to
attract love, replace it every third day.

No. 100
Cichorium intybus 🌀

Chicory

Blue Daisy | Blue Dandelion | Blue Sailors | Blue Weed |
Bunk | Coffeeweed | Common Chicory | Cornflower | Hendibeh |
Radicchio | Ragged Sailors | Succory | Wild Succory

✳ SYMBOLIC MEANINGS
Delicacy; Economy; Endless waiting; Rigidity;
Perseverance.

🌀 POSSIBLE POWERS
Air element; Cursing; Emotional
barriers; Favors; Frigidity; Frugality;
Humor; Invisibility; Luck; Masculine energy; Optimism;
Protection; Removing obstacles; Sun.

🜨 FOLKLORE AND FACTS
Chicory root is cultivated for use as a coffee substitute that
is enjoyed after it has been roasted, ground, and brewed in
the same way as coffee. Chicory root can also be prepared
in the same manner as parsnips. • Radicchio is a spicy and
bitter cultivated form of Chicory that is also known as
Italian Chicory. It is commonly used in Italian cuisine. It
tastes better after it has been roasted or grilled. • There is
an interesting Chicory legend that supposedly transpired on
Saint James' Day, which is on July 25th. As the legend goes,
if a lock-picker held Chicory leaves and a gold knife against
a lock, it would magically open. But only if the deed was
done in total silence. If even a single word was spoken, death
would be the consequence. • Carry a sprig of Chicory to
magically remove the obstacles that stand between you and
your goals. • Carry a sprig of Chicory to promote frugality.
• It is said that if you bless yourself with Chicory juice then

C

great people will pay attention to you and offer you favors.
• During the Middle Ages, the Chicory flower was considered a protector of Christian martyrs.

Cinchona officinalis 🗲

Cinchona

Fever Tree | Jesuit's Bark Tree | Jesuit's Powder Tree | Peruvian Bark Tree | Quinine Tree | Quinquina | Red Cinchona

✳ SYMBOLIC MEANINGS
Aspiring; Fever breaker.

🌀 POSSIBLE POWERS
Boosts power to magic working; Breaks a fever; Healing; Health; Luck; Protection; Repels anger; Repels malicious energy; Resists a spell.

☾ FOLKLORE AND FACTS
The carbonated beverage known as "tonic water" has the distinctive bitter taste of quinine, which is found in Cinchona bark. Tonic water originated in British Colonial India, created by by the British who lived there. They mixed their medicinal-quality, malaria-preventative and treatment quinine into their gin. The first tonic water that was available commercially was made in 1858. It was simply quinine mixed into carbonated water, with some sugar added to help mask the bitter taste of the quinine. Nowadays, tonic water is readily available in public markets to be commonly used as a favorite mixer for cocktails. There would be no such thing as a gin and tonic without it. Tonic water still contains quinine, but not as much as it used to, and not for the same malarial preventative or treatment purposes.

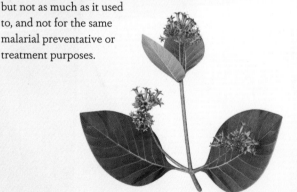

Cinnamomum verum ☠ 🗲 ☠

Cinnamon

Baker's Cinnamon | Cassia | Ceylon Cinnamon | Chinese Cassia | Chinese Cinnamon | Cinnamon Tree | Cinnamomum cassia | Sri Lanka Cinnamon | Sweet Wood | True Cinnamon

✳ SYMBOLIC MEANINGS
Beauty; Business; Forgiveness of injuries; Logic; Love; Lust; Power; Success; Sweet love; Temptress.

🌀 POSSIBLE POWERS
Abundance; Advancement; Aphrodite; Conscious will; Encourages self-worth; Energy; Fire element; Friendship; Growth; Healing; Joy; Leadership; Life; Light; Love; Luck; Lust; Masculine energy; Money; Natural power; Passion; Power; Prosperity; Protection; Psychic power; Spirituality; Strength; Success; Sun; Venus.

☾ FOLKLORE AND FACTS
The edible part of the *Cinnamomum verum* Cinnamon tree is the bark, which is used as a flavoring for candies, curries, desserts, pastries, and some meat dishes. It is available as chunked pieces of bark, slivered rolled "quills," shorter "sticks," or ground. • There is no way to discern whether "ground cinnamon" is inexpensive *Cinnamomum cassia* or the more expensive *Cinnamomum verum* unless it is properly labeled. When in stick form, *Cinnamomum cassia* is one thick, rolled, hard piece of bark. *Cinnamomum verum* is a rolled stick composed of several soft, thin layers of bark. • Cinnamon sticks can be easily ground into a fine powder using a spice or coffee grinder. • Cassia buds resemble Cloves and are sometimes used as a seasoning, as well as for brewing a tea, adding to a marinade, or pickling. • The ancient Egyptians used Cinnamon as a mummification spice. • Ancient Hebrew high priests used Cinnamon oil as a vital ingredient to a holy anointing oil. • The ancient Chinese and Egyptians used Cinnamon to purify their temples. • When Cinnamon is used as incense or in a sachet, it provides the power to increase spiritual vibrations, help heal, bring in money, stimulate psychic powers, and provide protection. • The warm fragrance of Cassia essential oil can encourage healthy feelings of self-worth.

C

No. 103

Cirsium vulgare ⚱

Common Thistle

Brushes and Combs | Bull Thistle | Flower of the Sun | Herb of the Witches | Lady's Thistle | Spear Thistle | Thistle | Thrissles

✸ SYMBOLIC MEANINGS

Aggressiveness; Austerity; Harshness; Independence; Nobility; Pain; Pride; Retaliation; Sternness.

🌱 COMPONENT MEANING

Seed head: Depart.

🌀 POSSIBLE POWERS

Assistance; Breaks a hex; Exorcism; Fertility; Fire element; Harmony; Healing; Independence; Mars; Masculine energy; Material gain; Persistence; Protection; Stability; Strength; Tenacity; Thor.

🜂 FOLKLORE AND FACTS

Common Thistle stems can be peeled to remove the spiny layer, then boiled or steamed before consuming. Before the plant has flowered, the taproot can be eaten either cooked or raw. In rural Italy, the flower petals are often dried before steeping in water to be used to curdle goat's milk at the start of the cheesemaking process. • There was a time in England when wizards would select the tallest Common Thistle they could find to use as a magic wand. • In the Bible, the Common Thistle refers to a desolate wilderness. • The Common Thistle is a top provider of nectar for pollinating bees, butterflies, and some small birds. • Grow Common Thistle in your garden to fend off thieves. • Wear or carry a Common Thistle blossom to get rid of melancholic feelings. • Put a vase of freshly cut flowered Common Thistle stems in a room to renew the vitality of everyone in the room.
• Carry or wear a Common Thistle on a white cotton cord around your neck as a protection amulet to fend off witches and witchery.
• A man can carry a Common Thistle blossom to improve his lovemaking skills.

No. 104

Citrullus lanatus ⚱

Watermelon

Afghan Melon | Bastard Melon | Camel Melon | Water-Melon

✸ SYMBOLIC MEANINGS

Bulkiness; Freedom; Peace; Tenacity.

🌀 POSSIBLE POWERS

Aphrodisiac; Clears energy blockages; Healing; Helps spirits move onward; Inspires peace; Lust; Moon; Overcomes oppression; Releases overwhelming emotions; Rises above when pushed below; Set; Water element.

🜂 FOLKLORE AND FACTS

The edible part of the *Citrullus lanatus* Watermelon vine is the ripe melon, which is botanically a berry. A Watermelon will stop ripening as soon as it is cut from the vine. The thick-rind seeded varieties of Watermelon are considered, by nearly all Watermelon aficionados, to have a *much* sweeter pulp and juice than the nearly flavorless thin-rind seedless varieties that cannot provide enough white mesocarp to pickle. The smaller varieties of Watermelon are known as icebox melons. The "Carolina Cross Watermelon" holds the world record for being the heaviest melon to weigh in, at 351 pounds. When fortunate enough to encounter a seeded Watermelon that you especially favor the flavor of, save and then replant the seeds. • 5,000-year-old Watermelon seeds were discovered at a prehistoric archeological site in Libya.
• *Citrullus lanatus* was considered to be sacred in ancient Egypt. • Watermelon seeds were found in Tutankhamen's tomb.

C

No. 105

Citrus × aurantiifolia

Key Lime

Bartender's Lime | Dayap | Mexican Lime |
Omani Lime | West Indian Lime

✷ SYMBOLIC MEANINGS
Fidelity; Love; Justice.

✺ POSSIBLE POWERS
Fire element; Love; Luck; Marital affection
or love; Marriage; Matrimony; Sun.

☾ FOLKLORE AND FACTS
The Key Lime originated in Malaysia and is believed to have
been carried to the Caribbean, where it became naturalized
by the Spanish around 1500. Long before there were other
cultivated *Citrus* varieties being raised in South Florida, the
Key Lime tree's fruit fulfilled the need for something that was
"tart, but not too tart" in cooking. A ripened-to-yellow Key
Lime is still tart but sweeter than a Persian Lime. Key Lime
is the key ingredient in the iconic Key Lime pie. Key Lime
was also used for the same flavor in beverages. This balanced
tartness shines in the zingy, thirst-quenching Lime Rickey
cocktail that became a South Florida favorite among the
upper-crust elite in the late 1800s. The rind is also edible, raw
or cooked. • Hot Key Lime tea with honey is a worthy home
remedy for the sniffles.

No. 106

Citrus × aurantium

Bitter Orange

Bigarade Orange | Daidai | Laraha | Marmalade Orange | Neroli Oil Orange | Seville Orange |
Sour Orange

✷ SYMBOLIC MEANING
Sensual love.

✺ POSSIBLE POWERS
Aphrodisiac; Attracts love; Cleansing; Fire element;
Freshening; Sun.

☾ FOLKLORE AND FACTS
Bitter Orange is considered a sacred spiritual tree. The fruit
is not usually eaten raw. It can be juiced. In Iraq the Bitter
Orange is often juiced to drink as a beverage known as *aseer
raranj*. The juice of a ripe Bitter Orange can also be used
in a salad dressing or marinade as a substitute for vinegar.
Bitter Orange is most often used as a flavoring in liqueurs
and cooking. The zest can be added to tea. Dried, powdered
Bitter Orange peel is also known as Curaçao orange peel.

• In Great Britain the Seville Orange is preferred for
marmalade because it has a thicker rind and a high level of
pectin. The earliest recipe for marmalade was for "marmelat
of oranges" that dates back to 1677. • Belgian *witbier* is often
spiced with Bitter Orange peel. • The blossoms can be made
into a fragrant Persian jam known as *moraba bahar-narenj*.
• The wood from a Bitter Orange tree is often made into
Cuban baseball bats. • Bitter Orange essential oil is useful
in deodorizing. • Bitter Orange fruit and leaves can lather
enough to be used like a soap. • Bitter Orange health-food
supplements are believed to have been linked to serious
cardiovascular side-effects.

No. 107

Citrus bergamia

Bergamot Orange

Bergamot | Orange Bergamot | Orange Mint

✷ SYMBOLIC MEANINGS
Enchantment; Irresistibility.

✺ POSSIBLE POWERS
Air element; Eliminating interference;
Improved memory; Irresistible;
Masculine energy; Mercury;
Money; Prosperity; Protection
from evil or illness; Restful sleep;
Success.

☾ FOLKLORE AND FACTS
The edible part of the Bergamot
Orange is the juice of the fruit which
is very sour and used as a flavoring. A small amount of the
essence that is extracted from its peel is used to lend its
distinctive flavor to Earl Grey tea, Lady Grey tea, and the
sweet known as "Turkish Delight." In Turkey, Bergamot
Orange is also used to make a marmalade. • Rub Bergamot
Orange leaves on money before spending it to ensure that
it comes back to you. • Put a few Bergamot Orange leaves
wherever you carry your money, preferably within a wallet,
to attract more money to that location. • Carry a good luck
sachet of Bergamot Orange leaves or rind to attract money
while gambling at a casino. • Bergamot Orange should not
be confused with *Monarda didyma* Bee Balm, which is also
known as Bergamot. • In aromatherapy, Bergamot Orange
essential oil is helpful in lightening a dark mood, especially in
times of grief or sadness.

C

No. 108

Citrus cavaleriei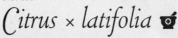

Ichang Papeda

Ichang Lemon | Shangjuan

☀ SYMBOLIC MEANING
Cold will not hinder.

✿ POSSIBLE POWERS
Unusual traits; Withstands cold.

☾ FOLKLORE AND FACTS
The Ichang Papeda tree is cold hardy, which is an extremely unusual trait for any variety of *Citrus*. The fragrant, bumpy skinned fruit's juice and zest is used as an herb seasoning. Some fruits are so entirely full of seeds that no juice can be extracted from the fruit at all.

No. 109

Citrus hystrix ☙

Makrut Lime

Leech Lime | Mauritius Papeda | Thai Lime

☀ SYMBOLIC MEANING
Prosperity.

✿ POSSIBLE POWERS
Leech repellent; Water element.

☾ FOLKLORE AND FACTS
The Makrut Lime tree's hourglass-shaped leaves and the zest of its fruit's extremely bumpy rind are frequently used as culinary herbs in Asian cuisine whenever acidity is needed. • The Makrut Lime's intensely fragrant rind produces an essential oil that is extensively used in perfumery. • There are texts from Sri Lanka dating back to 1868 that indicate the Makrut Lime's juice was often used as a leech repellent by rubbing it on a person's legs.

No. 110

Citrus × latifolia ☙

Persian Lime

Bearss Lime | Tahiti Lime

☀ SYMBOLIC MEANING
Fornication.

✿ POSSIBLE POWERS
Aphrodisiac; Attracts love; Fire element; Healing; Immortality; Love; Luck; Lust; Protection; Refreshes; Refreshment; Sun.

☾ FOLKLORE AND FACTS
Persian Lime will turn yellow as it ripens on the tree, but it is harvested and sold as fresh produce while still dark green. The juice and grated rind make it a favorite culinary herb and flavoring ingredient in a variety of foods and beverages. The rind is edible raw or cooked. Limeade is the Persian Lime's version of lemonade. • The Persian Lime's leaf and flower can be used in a love spell. • A folk cure for a sore throat was to wrap and tie a string around a whole Persian Lime then wear it as a necklace. • Carve a good luck charm out of Persian Lime tree wood. • Citrusy Persian Lime essential oil is used as aromatherapy for invigoration and to uplift a broody mood.

No. 111
Citrus × limon 🥣

Lemon

Bonnie Brae Lemon | *Citrus × meyeri* | Eureka Lemon | Lemon Tree | Lisbon Lemon | Meyer Lemon | Ponderosa Lemon | Yen Ben Lemon

☀ SYMBOLIC MEANINGS
Long-suffering; Patience; Pleasant thoughts; Zest.

🌱 COMPONENT MEANINGS
Blossom: Discretion; Fidelity; Fidelity in love; I promise to be true; Prudence.

🌀 POSSIBLE POWERS
Feminine energy; Friendship; Longevity; Love; Moon; Protection; Purification; Refresh; Refreshment; Uplift; Water element.

☾ FOLKLORE AND FACTS
The bright yellow Lemon fruit's juice, zest, and outer peel is edible raw or cooked, while the leaf can be used in recipes like a Bay Leaf. Meyer Lemons have a sweeter and floral lemony flavor than other Lemons, making them a special favorite for use in baking. The juice can be used to tenderize meat and as a common substitute for vinegar in recipes. The zest of the rind is frequently used in baking and cooking rice dishes, puddings, and soups. The leaves of the Meyer Lemon tree can be used in a tea or added to roast meat dishes to elevate and brighten the flavor. • During a Full Moon, Lemon juice can be added to the bath for purification. • Lemon essential oil has been used for centuries to uplift, energize, and refresh a slumped mood. • Secret messages can be written in Lemon juice on paper to later be revealed using heat.

No. 112
Citrus × limonia 🥣

Rangpur

Lemandarin | Mandarin Lime | Rangpur Lime

☀ SYMBOLIC MEANING
Sturdy foundation.

🌀 POSSIBLE POWERSa
Air element; Fire element; Happiness; Healing; Health; Longevity; Magical energy; Money; Moon; Physical energy; Protection; Purification; Refreshment; Rejuvenation; Stability; Sun.

☾ FOLKLORE AND FACTS
Rangpur fruit is a cross between the Citron and the Mandarin orange, which results in an intensely sour, Mandarin-looking fruit that is a perfectly suitable tart substitute for any recipe, cocktail, or beverage that calls for Lemon or Lime. Rangpur is a common *Citrus* used in Indian cuisine.

No. 113
Citrus maxima 🥣

Pomelo

Jambola | Pomélo | Pommelo | Pumelo | Pummelo | Shaddock

☀ SYMBOLIC MEANINGS
Biggest; Largest.

🌀 POSSIBLE POWERS
Abundance; Family; Good health; Healing; Healthy; Prosperity; Refresh; Unity; Uplifting.

☾ FOLKLORE AND FACTS
The Pomelo is the largest Citrus fruit and is very much like a sweet Grapefruit. • Considered to be one of the Moon Goddess' favorite foods, the Pomelo is a favorite fruit to serve at Chinese Moon Festival celebrations. • You don't eat the Pomelo membrane along with its juicy segments like you do when you eat a Grapefruit or Orange. The Pomelo's very large size does not particularly affect the acidity of the juice, but it certainly does provide much more of it. • Pomelo essential oil is helpful in aromatherapy for soothing the flustered mind, relieving stress, and alleviating depression. • Like a Grapefruit, the Pomelo can affect medication absorption. • One Pomelo can provide several days' worth of vitamin C.

No. 114

Citrus medica 🏺

Citron

Buddha's Hand | *Citrus medica var. sarcodactylis* | Ertog |
Fingered Citron | Main de Bouddha | Quả Phật Thủ

✳ SYMBOLIC MEANINGS
Estrangement; Ill-natured beauty;
Tradition.

🌀 POSSIBLE POWERS
Air element; Healing; Masculine
energy; Psychic power; Sun.

🌙 FOLKLORE AND FACTS
Citron is an original species of three *Citrus* trees from which
all other *Citrus* was eventually developed. The others are the
Pomelo and the Mandarin Orange. The pulp of the Citron
is minimal and relatively dry but edible. Citron is primarily
used as a flavoring. The outer skin is used as a zest. The thick
inner rind or pith is often candied. In the United States,
pieces of candied Citron are a prime ingredient in a holiday
fruitcake. • Citron is one of the fruits required for rituals
during the Jewish Feast of Tabernacles, or Sukkot.

No. 115

Citrus × paradisi 🏺

Grapefruit

Aranja | Grapefrugt | Grapefrukt | Greibipuu | Greip-Frout | Greipfrut | Greipfrūts | Greippi |
Grejp | Grejpfrut | Grenivka | Grep | Grepfrut | Grépfrút | Greyfurt | Toranja | Toronja

✳ SYMBOLIC MEANINGS
Bitterness; Mental problems; Successful independence.

🌀 POSSIBLE POWERS
Independence from a person or thing; Moon; Refresh;
Refreshment; Sun; Uplifting; Water element.

🌙 FOLKLORE AND FACTS
Grapefruit grows in white, pink, or red varieties. They are
often eaten from a whole fresh Grapefruit that has been
halved, sprinkled over with granulated sugar or drizzled
with honey, and the segments scooped out,
one by one, with a special serrated
"grapefruit spoon." • In Costa
Rica, Grapefruit is cooked
to reduce its sourness
to the degree that they
become confection-like.
Grapefruit rind is edible
raw or cooked.

• In 1750, Griffith Hughes, a Welsh reverend, first referenced
a Grapefruit hybrid called "forbidden fruit" in his book
about Barbados. • The fragrance of Grapefruit essential oil
in aromatherapy is uplifting. • Grapefruit juice is known to
adversely affect the proper absorption of some medications
by increasing or decreasing its effect within the body.

No. 116

Citrus × reticulata 🏺

Mandarin Orange

Clementine | Mandarine

✳ SYMBOLIC MEANINGS
Abundance; Gold; Good
fortune; Life; New
beginning; Potential for
better experiences; Prayers;
Wishes for good fortune.

🌀 POSSIBLE POWERS
Abundance; Cheer; Fire element; Good fortune;
Improvement; Prosperity; Sun; Warmth.

🌙 FOLKLORE AND FACTS
The Mandarin Orange tree has been cultivated in China
for over 3,000 years and is a sacred plant in China. • The
Mandarin Orange's dried peel is used in traditional Chinese
medicine to regulate the flow of qi, or vital energy. The fruit
is eaten raw or cooked. The rind can also be eaten raw or
cooked. The dried peel of the Mandarin Orange is also used
as a seasoning called *chenpi*. • Mandarin Oranges from Japan
have become a traditional Christmastime gift in America,
Great Britain, Canada, and Russia. • It became a tradition
to put three Mandarin Oranges in a Christmas stocking
instead of the earlier tradition of three gold coins. • In China
during Lunar New Year celebrations, Mandarin Oranges
are traditional decorations and gifts. • Mandarin Orange
essential oil can be used for aromatherapy to help reduce
nervousness and clear the mind.

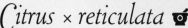

No. 117
Citrus × sinensis 🝓
Sweet Orange
Blood Orange | Cara Cara | Juice Orange | Navel Orange | Red-fleshed Navel | Valencia Orange

☀ SYMBOLIC MEANINGS
Eternal love; Generosity; Innocence; Virginity.

🌱 COMPONENT MEANINGS
Blossom: Bridal festivities; Brings wisdom; Chastity; Eternal love; Fruitfulness; Good fortune; Innocence; Marriage; Your purity equals your loveliness.

🌀 POSSIBLE POWERS
Assertiveness; Divination; Fire element; Good fortune; Heal; Healthy; Love; Luck; Masculine energy; Money; Protection; Rids depression; Sun; Wealth.

☾ FOLKLORE AND FACTS
Chinese writings dating to 314 BCE referenced the Sweet Orange. • The Sweet Orange tree was never wild, and it is widely grown in sunny climates around the world. • The Spanish explorers introduced Sweet Oranges to North America. In Spain, the fallen Sweet Orange blossoms are gathered, dried, and brewed as a tea, as can be done with the leaves. Fresh, ripe Sweet Orange fruit is eaten peeled out of hand, or halved to be eaten or squeeze-juiced. The rind can be eaten raw or cooked. The tarty-sweet flavor of orange is present in nearly all cuisines in recipes for nearly every type of food, starting from fresh fruit and moving out in all directions. Oranges or an orange flavor is present in frozen confections, hard or jellied candies that are plain, chocolate-covered, or sugar-coated. It is in beverages, baked goods, casseroles, marinades, sweet and savory sauces, as well as wines, liqueurs and liquors. A Sweet Orange-flavored something or another is everywhere, making it one of the flavors that discerning palates will easily distinguish as being deliciously natural, or unpleasantly artificial-tasting. Even the wood can be used for smoking and grilling. • During the Victorian era, brides carried or wore veil wreaths of fresh Sweet Orange blossoms whenever possible. • Louis XIV of France had potted Sweet Orange trees growing indoors throughout the entire Château de Versailles.

No. 118
Citrus sphaerocarpa 🝓
Kabosu Papeda
Papeda Kabosu

☀ SYMBOLIC MEANING
Coveted.

🌀 POSSIBLE POWERS
Fire element; Flavoring; Sun.

☾ FOLKLORE AND FACTS
Kabosu Papeda is an evergreen *Citrus* with fruit that was brought into Japan at least 300 years ago. It has extensive acidic herbal use in Japanese cuisine for its juicy sourness. There are some 200-year-old trees that are still producing fruit. • Some farm-raised fish-food meal has Kabosu Papeda mixed into it.

No. 119
Citrus sudachi 🝓
Sudachi
Sudashi

☀ SYMBOLIC MEANING
Vinegar citrus.

🌀 POSSIBLE POWERS
Fire element; Flavor; Sun.

☾ FOLKLORE AND FACTS
The Sudachi fruit is green like a Lime and just as tart. Sudachi fruit has been considered an indispensable Japanese condiment for hundreds of years.

No. 120

Citrus × tamurana ⚱

Hyuganatsu

New Summer Orange | Tosakonatsu

✳ **SYMBOLIC MEANING**

Happy surprise.

🌀 **POSSIBLE POWERS**

Fire element; Sun; Uplifting.

🜨 **FOLKLORE AND FACTS**

Hyuganatsu was first found in a Japanese garden in the 1820s. The surprising hybrid seems to have occurred naturally between a Yuzu and a Pomelo. Hyuganatsu is usually eaten cut up with the pith left intact and then sprinkled with sugar. • The meaning of Hyuganatsu is a combination of *Hyūga*, which is the ancient name of the place where the tree was discovered, and *natsu*, which is a word for summer.

No. 121

Citrus × tangelo ⚱

Tangelo

Honeybell Tangelo | Minneola Tangelo | Orlando Tangelo

✳ **SYMBOLIC MEANING**

Uniquely rare.

🌀 **POSSIBLE POWERS**

Fire element; Good fortune; Health; Healthy; Love; Luck; Masculine energy; Money; Protection; Sun.

🜨 **FOLKLORE AND FACTS**

The juicy, easy-to-peel Tangelo looks like a large Mandarin Orange with a characteristic protruding nipple. Although a Tangelo is a cross between a Mandarin and a Grapefruit, there has been no evidence that the Tangelo affects medications in the same way as Grapefruit does.

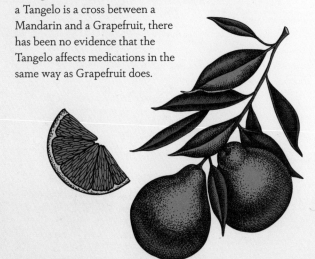

No. 122

Citrus tangerina ⚱

Tangerine

Kid Glove Orange | Mandarin | Zipper Skin Dancy

✳ **SYMBOLIC MEANINGS**

Abundant happiness; Life; New beginning; Potential for better experiences; Prayers; Wishes for good fortune.

🌀 **POSSIBLE POWERS**

Air element; Calms nervousness; Cheer; Fire element; Improvement; Luck; Prosperity; Sun; Warmth.

🜨 **FOLKLORE AND FACTS**

The Tangerine has been cultivated in China for over 3,000 years. The child-friendly, easy-to-peel sweet Tangerine is very closely related to the Mandarin Orange, although the Tangerine has more of a squat shape and a peel that is looser and comes away with less fuss. Because the Mandarin Orange and Tangerine are so closely related it seems that the Mandarin is the most available in nearly every market these days. Older people, who as children commonly ate Tangerines, can easily differentiate between the two fruits. • Tangerine essential oil is helpful when used in aromatherapy to help calm nervousness and clear the mind of cluttered, nerve-wracking thoughts.

No. 123

Claytonia perfoliata ⚱

Miner's Lettuce

Claytonia | Spring Beauty | Winter Purslane

✳ **SYMBOLIC MEANINGS**

New beginning; Survival.

🌀 **POSSIBLE POWERS**

Feminine energy; Happiness; Heal; Love; Luck; Mercury; Moon; Protection; Sleep; Soothe; Water element.

🜨 **FOLKLORE AND FACTS**

Miner's Lettuce easily takes over an area where the ground has been broken. • It was knowledge that came down from the Native Americans that saved the ailing and too often nearly starving miners who had flocked to the hills of California. The miners discovered that to fend off scurvy and hunger they should eat the Miner's Lettuce that prolifically covered so much ground nearby their camps during the

California Gold Rush. The high levels of vitamin C in the plants greatly improved their health and staved off their growling hunger.

No. 124
Clinopodium menthifolium
Calamint
Ascending Wild Basil | *Calamintha grandiflora* | Common Calamint | Large-flowered Calamint | Showy Calamint | Wood Calamint | Woodland Calamint

✳ SYMBOLIC MEANINGS
Joy; More joy.

🌀 POSSIBLE POWERS
Drives off the basilisk; Earth element; Eases emotional pain; Fire element; Flavoring; Increases joy; Mercury; Recovery from emotional suffering; Restores optimism; Soothes sorrow.

☘ FOLKLORE AND FACTS
The Calamint plant leaves are edible and are used fresh or dried as a minty flavoring in herbal teas. It is also a necessary ingredient in the popular Middle Eastern seasoning blend known as za'atar, which has traditionally been a mixture of Calamint, salt, and a select variety of other herbs, such as Oregano and Sumac. • Fresh Calamint is said to heal bruises after being in a fight. • Calamint in a warm bath can do much to soothe sorrows brought on by emotional pain. • According to legends, Calamint drives away a snake if it is burned or scattered. If that fails, the next legend is that it could heal a snake bite. It seems best to avoid the snake. • Carry a sachet of Calamint or Large-flowered Calamint to boost a feeling of joy from good to better to best.

No. 125
Coccoloba uvifera 🧉
Sea Grape
Bay Grape | Baygrape

✳ SYMBOLIC MEANING
Grape bearer of the shore.

🌀 POSSIBLE POWERS
Sea magic; Wishing.

☘ FOLKLORE AND FACTS
The edible parts of the Sea Grape are the grape-like clusters of green berries that slowly ripen to a purplish color when they can be eaten raw, made into jelly or jam, or into wine. • The highly salt- and wind-tolerant Sea Grape can withstand the trials and tribulations of an extreme seaside existence in South Florida. However, it can barely tolerate more than a shiver of frost, since the plant cannot survive below 35.6°F (2°C). • The male and the female Sea Grape flowers are on completely separate trees. Pollination is achieved with the help of bees. • On a day when the sea is calm, wishes can be scratched onto the Sea Grape leaves and floated off into the ocean. The wishing leaves can also be sent out from off a boat. • Sea Grape plant sap has been used in leather tanning and dying.

No. 126
Cocos nucifera 🧉
Coconut Palm
Côca | Coco | Cocoanut | Indian Nut | Maypan Coconut | Niyog

✳ SYMBOLIC MEANING
Chastity.

🌀 POSSIBLE POWERS
Chastity; Feminine energy; Moon; Protection; Purification; Togetherness; Water element.

☘ FOLKLORE AND FACTS
The Coconut Palm tree is the global iconic image that symbolizes the tropics and sparks the compelling urge to take a get-away vacation to a sunny beach. It is the only living species of the *Cocos* genus. • The Coconut fruit is not a huge nut at all. It is a nutritious drupe, like a peach or a plum. The outer husk of the Coconut fruit is very difficult to remove, whether it is green or dried brown. Some who are well-practiced at removing it can make it look theatrically entertaining and easy. It's not. At any rate, the husk must be removed entirely or halved with a sharp machete in the hands of someone who can deftly wield it to reach the hard nut within, which also needs to be opened to reach the edible kernel of the fruit, where the Coconut water and pulp are found. The pulp can be shaved or shredded and used in cooking a wide variety of dishes, cakes, cookies, confections, beverages, wine, liqueurs, syrup, and flavorings. The oil, "milk," and "butter" pressed from it are also used in cooking. • The Coconut Palm tree is often considered to be The Tree of Life, because for thousands of years it has contributed so much to human civilization, such as food, fuel, building materials for housing, fiber, medicine, liquid, oil, and so much more.

No. 127

Coffea arabica

Arabica Coffee

Arabian Coffee | Charrier Coffee | *Coffea canephora* |
Coffea charrieriana | *Coffea liberica* | Coffee Bean Tree |
Liberica Coffee | Robusta Coffee

✵ SYMBOLIC MEANINGS

Alertness; Camaraderie;
Friendship; Sociability.

🌀 POSSIBLE POWERS

Change; Clearing; Courage; Dispels negative thinking;
Fluctuation; Grounding; Helps keep away a nightmare;
Liberation; Make a new friend; Mercy; Overcomes a thought
blockade; Peace of mind; Sociability; Victory.

☾ FOLKLORE AND FACTS

The most gourmet and expensive Coffee beans are almost
always of the Arabica variety. *Coffee arabica* is believed to
be the first species of Coffee ever cultivated. • In the twelfth
century, Coffee was discovered in Yemen, where scholars
wrote of how it was made into a beverage brewed from
roasted Coffee beans, and that drinking the beverage helped
them work longer. From there, Coffee was introduced to
Egypt and Turkey, then all around the world. • The small
trees are pruned to be no more than around sixteen feet high,
to keep them at a shrub-like size to facilitate an unhindered
management and harvest of the berries. Between two and
four years after planting, Coffee trees will flower. The
blossoms are very sweet-smelling and resemble those of
jasmine. • When the Coffee berries ripen they are colored
a deep glossy red, and then they are ready to pick by hand.
These are called the "cherries." The berries do not ripen all
at the same time. From then onward, the processing begins,
as the interior of the berries, which are the "seeds" or
"beans," are specifically roasted to attain the desired end
result. • Coffee beans are made into a confection by coating
them in chocolate. • A method of immediately clearing a
scent from the nose is to sniff whole beans or ground Coffee.
• When feeling under the weather, the fragrance of Coffee
essential oil can be uplifting.

No. 128

Coix lacryma-jobi

Job's Tears

Adlay | Coix Seed | Coixseed | Croix Seed | Hatomugi | Tear Grass

✵ SYMBOLIC MEANING

Survived great suffering.

🌀 POSSIBLE POWERS

Healing; Luck; Wishing.

☾ FOLKLORE AND FACTS

The Job's Tears plant is a wild grass with seeds that are
perfect beads, as they have natural holes and so can be
easily strung and worn as jewelry. Throughout Asia the
seeds are dried and cooked as a cereal grain to make
porridges and gruels, as well as being used as an ingredient
in desserts, teas, and other beverages. In Korea and China,
powdered Job's Tears are the primary ingredient in drinks
called *yulmu-cha* and *yi ren jiang*. Sweet dessert soups in
China are called *tong sui* and *ching bo leung*. In Vietnam it
is known as *sâm bổ lượng*. • In Korea, Job's Tears is distilled
with Rice to be a liquor called *okroju*. • In some areas in
southeast Asia and northeast India the grain is used for
brewing beers. • Job's Tears can be used inside hollow, dried
gourds to create shaker instruments. • To make a wish,
concentrate on your wish while counting out seven Job's
Tears seeds, then carry them with you everywhere for seven
days. At the end of the seven days, make your wish once
more, then throw the seven seeds into naturally running
water, such as a river or stream.

C

No. 129

Cola acuminata 🥣

Kola Nut

Bissy Nut | Cola Nut | Kola

✴ SYMBOLIC MEANINGS

Hospitality; Friendship;
Respect.

🌀 POSSIBLE POWERS

Alertness; Diminishes fatigue;
Increases stamina.

☙ FOLKLORE AND FACTS

The Kola Nut is not a true nut, but the seed removed from
the center of the Kola fruit. The Kola Nut can produce a
caffeinated extract that is used as a natural food flavoring
for some soft drinks and energy beverages. • The seed nut
is sacred to the Igbo people of southeastern Nigeria. The
Kola Nut forms an integral part in important Igbo social
events, such as weddings, baby naming ceremonies, and
funerals. These events always include the important plate of
Kola Nuts, where visitors receive a nut that is blessed with
a charm spell. The nut is broken open and the number of
the seed's pieces reveal the level of prosperity in the charm.
However, if the nut breaks into two pieces, something
sinister will happen. • Kola seeds originally gave Coca-
Cola its unique flavor and caffeine kick.

No. 130

Coleus amboinicus

Indian Mint

Country Borage | Cuban Oregano | French Thyme | Indian Borage | Mexican Mint | Soup Mint |
Spanish Thyme

✴ SYMBOLIC MEANING

Soothing.

🌀 POSSIBLE POWERS

Courage; Good luck; Protection; Psychic power; Sense of
wellbeing; Venus; Water element.

☙ FOLKLORE AND FACTS

The leaves of the Indian Mint plant are very strongly
flavored and most often used as an Oregano substitute to
mask the strong flavors and odors of goat, fish, and mutton.
• An infusion of fresh Indian Mint in water can be used as an
herbal rinse to add fragrance to hair. • To impart a sense of
well-being, pin a sprig of Indian Mint on the lapel of a jacket.

No. 131

Colocasia esculenta ☠🥣

Taro

Dasheen

✴ SYMBOLIC MEANINGS

Abundance; Community; Sustenance.

🌀 POSSIBLE POWERS

Health; Healthy; Nurture; Satisfy hunger.

☙ FOLKLORE AND FACTS

The properly prepared and cooked Taro corm tubers have
been a staple food in South Asian, West African, Middle
Eastern, and Oceanic cuisines for thousands of years,
considering that Taro is one of the earliest cultivated plants
in the world. • Uncooked, all parts of the Taro plant are
toxic. Properly prepared and then roasted, baked, or boiled,
the starchy cooked Taro has a sweet, nutty flavor that is
easily digestible at any age. Mashed Taro is a common baby
food. • In Fiji, Taro's centuries-long importance to the
culture is celebrated on Taro Day. In Hawaii, Taro is served
like a Potato or as the iconic and traditional paste known as
"poi." Taro has been included as an ingredient in nearly all
the cuisines around the world by, at the very least, adding it
to soups. In Greece, Taro grows on the island of Icaria, where
the islanders boil it, then serve it as a salad, crediting the
availability of the vegetable growing on their island as the
food that saved them from starvation during WWII.

No. 132

Cordyline fruticosa ☠

Ti

Good Luck Plant | Lauti | Ti Pore

❋ SYMBOLIC MEANINGS

Knowledge; Tree of life.

✿ POSSIBLE POWERS

Fire element; Healing; Jupiter; Lono;
Masculine energy; Pele; Protection.

☙ FOLKLORE AND FACTS

In the Polynesian islands the leaves of the green-leaf Ti plant are used to wrap food and line pit ovens. The roots are dug and processed into a pulp confection that is sweet and as thick as molasses. In Hawaii, the roots are mixed with water before fermenting into an alcoholic drink that is known as *okolehao*. • Between 1806 and 1807 the Taro plants on Maui died, which caused a famine. It was at that time that the taboo against consuming Ti was finally lifted to save the people from starvation. • In ancient Hawaii, the red variety of Ti plant leaves are believed to have great spiritual power and only the high priests and chiefs were permitted to wear the red leaves around their necks during rituals. The red variety of Ti plant is sacred to Pele, the goddess of volcanos and fire, who is revered as the creator of Hawaii. It is very bad luck for a homeowner if the red Ti plant is planted near a home in an effort to provide themselves with protection, as they do not have the divine privilege to use red Ti plant in this way at all. To ignore the warning of Pele is to invite trouble to come. • To grow the red variety of Ti plant in a pot in the home is considered to be extremely unlucky.

No. 133

Coriandrum sativum ⚱

Coriander

Chinese Parsley | Cilantro | Cilentro | Coriandre | Koriadnon

❋ SYMBOLIC MEANINGS

Good cheer; Hidden merit or worth; Luck;
Peace between those who don't get along; Romance.

🌱 COMPONENT MEANING

Seed: Peace between those who don't get along.

✿ POSSIBLE POWERS

Air element; Aphrodisiac; Attracts love; Fire element; Healing; Health; Helps to find romance; Immortality; Intelligence; Love; Lust; Mars; Masculine energy; Mercury; Money; Protection; Protects gardeners and their households; Romance; Soothing; Survival; Virility; Wards off evil.

☙ FOLKLORE AND FACTS

As a dried seed or as a ground herb, the most common name used for *Coriandrum sativum* is its proper name, Coriander. As a green herb it is best known in Central, South, and North America by its Spanish name, Cilantro, due to its extensive use in Mexican cooking. • In the Middle Ages, Coriander was frequently used in magic spells and witchcraft. • A sprinkle of dry powdered Coriander in a glass of warm wine may make an inspiring aphrodisiac. • The hard, sweet confection known as a "jawbreaker," "sugar ball," or "comfit" used to have a tasty Coriander seed at its center. • Hanging Cilantro or a pouch filled with Coriander seed on a door offers protections against harm and will keep out anyone who is envious or unpleasant.

C

No. 134
Corylus avellana

Hazel

Common Hazel | *Corylus maxima* | Filbert Tree | Hazelnut Tree

☀ SYMBOLIC MEANINGS

Communication; Creative inspiration; Epiphanies; Reconciliation.

✺ POSSIBLE POWERS

Air element; Anti-lightning; Artemis; Divination; Fertility; Heightened awareness; Luck; Masculine energy; Meditation; Mercury; Protection; Sun visions; Thor; Wisdom; Wishing.

☾ FOLKLORE AND FACTS

The edible part of the Hazel tree is the ripe kernel of the round nut or "cobnut." The difference between a Hazelnut and a Filbert is that the Hazelnut is round and the Filbert's cobnut is longer. The kernels of each can be eaten raw, but they are more often roasted to enhance the flavor. The kernels can also be ground into a smooth paste or distilled into an extract for baking or flavoring syrup and beverages such as coffee. • Give a Hazelnut to a bride to wish her good fortune, fertility, and wisdom. • Make, then wear a wishing crown by weaving Hazel tree twigs together. • A forked Hazel tree branch is the diviner's dowsing rod of first choice. • Eat one Hazelnut before attempting a divination. • For the most opportune effect to be imbued into a brand-new divining rod, the cutting must be done after the sun sets on one of the following nights: on the eve of a New Moon, on the first night of a New Moon, Good Friday, Shrove Tuesday, Epiphany, or Saint John's Day. The one who is severing the branch from the tree should be the intended diviner, who would best be the seventh son of a seventh son. He must face east to cut the first branch, which will be the one to catch the very first rays of the morning sunlight. In this way the divining rod would be prepared to perform particularly well for the magically destined operator.

No. 135
Crataegus laevigata

English Hawthorn

Glastonbury Thorn | Hawberry Tree | Haweater Tree | Hawthorn | May Blossom | Mayblossom | May-tree | Midland Hawthorn | Thornapple Tree

☀ SYMBOLIC MEANINGS

Chastity; Contradictions; Duality; Fairy tree; Hope; Male energy; Spring; Sweet hope; Union of opposites.

✺ POSSIBLE POWERS

Caution; Chastity; Fairies; Fends off negative energies; Fends off negative magic; Fends off witches and witchcraft; Fertility; Fire element; Fishing magic; Flora; Happiness; Love; Mars; Masculine energy; Relaxation.

☾ FOLKLORE AND FACTS

The English Hawthorn is the most common small tree or shrub in the British Isles and also one of the most sacred trees on Earth. The Glastonbury Hawthorn in Glastonbury, England, is the most revered tree in the country. • The edible parts of the *Crataegus laevigata* and *Crataegus monogyna* Hawthorn trees are the early spring flower petals and the tender new leaves that can be used raw in salads. However, it is the berries that are most desired. The seeds of the berries are not edible. • There are long sharp thorns on every branch of the Hawthorn tree. Protective leather gloves must be worn when the ripe berries are harvested by hand in the autumn. • Once gathered, they are commonly made into jams, jellies, syrups, wine, and are also very often used to flavor brandy. • An English Hawthorn stake was considered a highly effective instrument to use to impale a vampire. • The English Hawthorn is also a fairy tree, with the fairies of the area living under it as its guardians, who are dedicated to treating the tree with love, respect, and care, as all mortal humans should do too. It is believed that one will be able to see fairies where the English Hawthorn, oak, and ash trees are growing together in a cluster.

No. 136

Crithmum maritimum 🥣

Sea Fennel

Crest Marine | Rock Samphire | Samphire

❊ SYMBOLIC MEANING

Down to earth.

✺ POSSIBLE POWERS

Grounding; Healing;
Regeneration; Renewing;
Seasoning.

❦ FOLKLORE AND FACTS

Sea Fennel abides on sea-sprayed, slippery, rocky coastal
spots. It grows in the clefts of rocks, which makes gathering
Sea Fennel a treacherous endeavor. Because of its sea-
saltiness, in coastal areas where it grows, the dried herb is
often used to add a salty, carroty-lemony aspect to some foods.
Due to over-harvesting, wild Sea Fennel has become rare in
its natural environment. Any effort to domestically cultivate
the herb is highly encouraged. • It was believed by some that
Sea Fennel essential oil supposedly has skin regenerative
properties that combat the issues plaguing aging skin.

No. 137

Crocus sativus

Saffron

Kashmiri Saffron | Kesar Saffron |
Saffron Crocus | Spanish Saffron

❊ SYMBOLIC MEANINGS

Ancient symbol of the Sun; Beware of
excess; Cheerfulness; Do not abuse;
Excess is dangerous; Happiness; Mirth.

✺ POSSIBLE POWERS

Abuse; Aphrodisiac; Attracts love; Eros;
Euphoria; Fire element; Happiness; Healing; Laughter; Love;
Lust; Magic; Masculine energy; Psychic power; Raises up a
spirit; Singing; Spirituality; Strength; Sun; Uplifting; Wind-
raising.

❦ FOLKLORE AND FACTS

The visible difference between the Saffron crocus, *Crocus
sativus*, and the deadly poisonous *Colchicum autumnale*,
which is *also* known as Autumn Crocus or Meadow Saffron,
is that the Saffron *Crocus sativus* flower blossom *never* has
any more than three stigmas. The vivid red-orange-colored
stigma of the *Crocus sativus* Saffron crocus flower is the
flavorful edible part of the plant. It is used as a seasoning

and golden-coloring herb for many international cuisines
and baked goods. • The stamens have no flavor, but more
times than not they are harvested and added in with the
stigmas to add weight to the extremely expensive herb. By
weight, Saffron is worth more than gold. This is due to the
fact it takes approximately a football field's worth of flowers
to produce one pound of Saffron stigmas. • The fragrance
of Saffron is especially exotic while harvesting. It is also
somewhat mood-altering, due to its natural anti-depressant
properties. After a while of harvesting the blossoms' stigmas,
medieval nuns would break into song, being somewhat
euphoric under the stimulating influence of Saffron. • In
India, Saffron flowers are often scattered on the marriage
bed of newlyweds.

No. 138

Cucumis melo subsp. *cantalupo*

Cantaloupe

Muskmelon | North American Cantaloupe | Rock Melon | Spanspek Sweet Melon

❊ SYMBOLIC MEANINGS

Chastity; Criticism; Long life.

✺ POSSIBLE POWERS

Chastity; Fertility; Good health; Healing; Longevity; Moon;
Water element.

❦ FOLKLORE AND FACTS

The edible part of the Cantaloupe vine is the juicy flavorful
flesh within the rough netted rind of the round melon that is
most usually eaten fresh alone, in a salad, or as an ingredient
on an antipasto platter with a very thin slice of prosciutto
wrapped around it. Cantaloupe seeds can be rinsed, then
toasted or dried to be eaten salted as a snack. The flesh
can be puréed to be used in frozen sorbets or sherbets. A
Cantaloupe will continue ripening after it has been cut from
the vine. Underripe Cantaloupe will have no fragrance, but
overripe Cantaloupe will have an alcoholic aroma or worse.
Optimum ripeness is achieved naturally in a garden, or for
one or two days at room temperature indoors. • In 1943,
there was a worldwide search for a particular strain of mold
to produce much-needed penicillin,
which was *finally* discovered
in a Peoria, Illinois, market
in the form of a moldy
Cantaloupe.

C

No. 139
Cucumis melo var. inodorus
Honeydew
Bailan | Chindire | Green Flesh Honeydew Melon | Hmzail | Hualaishi | Lanzhou | Melón Tuna | Orange Flesh Honeydew Melon | Te'e | Wallace | Yellow Rind Honeydew Melon

✹ SYMBOLIC MEANINGS
Chastity; Criticism; Long life.

✺ POSSIBLE POWERS
Chastity; Fertility; Good health; Healing; Longevity; Moon; Water element.

☾ FOLKLORE AND FACTS
The fruit of the Honeydew melon vine has been unfairly maligned as being called a "filler" and a "garbage fruit" in inexpensive fresh fruit salads. This negative innuendo seems to have emerged because the melon was over- or underripe. Optimum ripeness is achieved naturally in a garden, or for one or two days at room temperature indoors. A ripe Honeydew should feel a bit heavy for its size and have a smooth, waxy surface rather than the somewhat fuzzy surface of an unripe melon.

No. 140
Cucumis melo 'Yubari King'
Yubari King Melon
Yūbari Melon

✹ SYMBOLIC MEANINGS
King of melons; Royalty; Valuable.

✺ POSSIBLE POWERS
Moon; Perfection; Water element.

☾ FOLKLORE AND FACTS
The Yubari King Melon is so exalted, it is actually a status symbol to give or receive one as a gift. This is because it is *the most* expensive melon in the world. The Yubari King melon is handled with care from the time it is cut from the vine using scissors, leaving a characteristic length of stem attached to the utterly perfect melon. In 2019, two melons were auctioned for $45,000.

No. 141
Cucumis sativus ⚗
Cucumber
Baby Pickle | Belt Alpha Cucumber | Cuke | East Asian Cucumber | European Cucumber | Gherkin | Kheera Cucumber | Lebanese Cucumber | Persian Cucumber | Telegraph Cucumber

✹ SYMBOLIC MEANINGS
Chastity; Criticism.

✺ POSSIBLE POWERS
Chastity; Feminine energy; Fertility; Healing; Moon; Water element.

☾ FOLKLORE AND FACTS
The edible part of the sprawling Cucumber plant is the fruit, which is consumed as a vegetable. Cucumber varieties are known as being either a "slicer," "pickler," "burpless," or "gherkin," the last of which is also known as a "cornichon" and "baby pickle." A Cucumber will stop ripening as soon as it is cut from the vine. Cucumbers are available fresh or pickled. The small Gherkins are always pickled whole. Cucumbers are also chopped or minced and pickled as a relish that is used in salads, sauces, and as a condiment to dress hotdogs on a bun. • Roman midwives would carry a Cucumber then throw it away when they delivered a baby. • Roman wives, desiring a baby, would wear a Cucumber tied around the waist as a talisman. • Roman households would use a Cucumber to frighten away mice that would enter their homes.

No. 142
Cucurbita maxima ⚗
Hubbard Squash
Boston Marrow | Buttercup | French Turban Squash | Gray-Skinned Pumpkin | Jarrahdale Pumpkin | Kabocha Squash | Lakota Squash | Nanticoke Squash | Turban Squash

✹ SYMBOLIC MEANINGS
Abundance; Greatness.

✺ POSSIBLE POWERS
Decision-making; Recognizing options; Water element.

☾ FOLKLORE AND FACTS
Cucurbita maxima squash originated 4,000 years ago in South America. The Hubbard Squash is one of the more popular varieties, of which the flesh, seeds, and flowers of each can be fried, baked, roasted, steamed, stuffed, and used

in a variety of dishes, soups, and stews. • Nearly all the giant "pumpkins" that are entered in extreme weight competitions are of the *Cucurbita maxima* species.

No. 143
Cucurbita moschata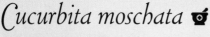

Butternut Squash
Aehobak | Al Hachi | Dickinson Pumpkin | Korean Zucchini | Musquée de Provence | Seminole Pumpkin | Tromboncino | Zucchetta

✳ SYMBOLIC MEANING
Happiness.

🌀 POSSIBLE POWERS
Crone magic; Healing; Prosperity; Water element.

☙ FOLKLORE AND FACTS
The most commonly enjoyed *Cucurbita moschata* squash is the Butternut. Its flesh, flowers, and seeds are edible when fried, baked, roasted, steamed, stuffed, and are used in a variety of dishes, soups, and stews. The Dickinson Pumpkin is used to produce canned pumpkin pie fillings.

No. 144
Cucurbita pepo

Pumpkin
Field Pumpkin | Pompion | Pumpkin Squash | Winter Squash

✳ SYMBOLIC MEANINGS
Bounty; Coarseness; Grossness; Plenty.

☘ COMPONENT MEANING
Carved: Protection.

🌀 POSSIBLE POWERS
Abundance; Banishing; Divination; Earth element; Enchantment; Fertility; Good luck; Grants a wish; Health; Love; Moon; Prosperity; Protection; Successful children; Sustenance; Water element; Wealth.

☙ FOLKLORE AND FACTS
The iconic Halloween jack-o'-lantern never seems quite the same unless it has been carved using a Pumpkin. The Pumpkin's interior flesh, flowers, and seeds are edible. The seeds are often toasted as a treat. The interior flesh is cooked to be used in pies, baked goods, casseroles, soups, stews, hot beverages, jams, and liqueurs. • In the USA, just as the end of summer teases the coming of autumn, the Pumpkin-loving people impatiently await the return of Pumpkin anything because they love the flavor of Pumpkin so much. • Jack-o'-lanterns originally were made in Ireland to put out on the front step to scare away the Devil and any other sinister spirits that may come near. • On October 31st, illuminate a carved, hollowed-out Pumpkin using a white candle for additional protection from intrusive or pesky negative spirits.

No. 145
Cucurbita pepo subsp. *pepo*

Summer Squash
Baby Marrow | Courgette | Crookneck | Golden Zucchini | Green Summer Squash | Pattypan | Round Zucchini | Spaghetti Squash | Straightneck Squash | Vegetable Spaghetti | Zucchini

✳ SYMBOLIC MEANING
Enthusiasm for newness.

🌀 POSSIBLE POWERS
Enthusiasm; Water element.

☙ FOLKLORE AND FACTS
The summer squashes are botanically berries that are eaten as vegetables. • The green, smooth, edible, thin-skinned fruit of the Zucchini plant is a berry. Zucchini can be eaten raw or cooked. Zucchini flowers are edible and can be batter-dipped and deep-fried. The first references to Zucchini in the United States were in the 1920s when seeds were planted by Italian immigrants. There is rarely a summer that goes by without someone trying to gift an enormous Zucchini to a friend with the cheerful suggestion, "You can make Zucchini bread with it!" • Crookneck Squash and Straightneck Squash are yellow and bumpy with a slightly thicker edible skin with a flavor quite similar to but slightly less watery than the Zucchini. • Pattypan Squash is fairly small and saucer-shaped with a scalloped edge. The edible skin and firmer flesh can be prepared and eaten in all the same ways, such as sautéing, broiling, roasting, baking, and grilling. • Spaghetti Squash is prepared differently, in that the seeds are scooped out prior to cooking, but after the squash has been cooked, a fork is used to shred the cooked pulp into noodle-like strands.

No. 146

Cucurbita pepo var. *turbinata* 🜍

Acorn Squash

Des Moines Squash | Pepper Squash

✴ **SYMBOLIC MEANING**
Announcement.

🌀 **POSSIBLE POWERS**
Enthusiasm; Health; Water element.

☽ **FOLKLORE AND FACTS**
Acorn Squash is a deeply ridged, hard winter squash that has edible flesh, seeds, and flowers. It is usually halved, seasoned, then baked, although it can be microwaved. The seeded cavity is sometimes filled with sausage, rice, or vegetables, and is also used in soups, stews, and casseroles. In the Philippines, the very top leaves that are closest to the squash are cooked and eaten as a leafy green vegetable. • Although the Acorn Squash is a winter squash, it is in the same family as summer squash. • Acorn Squash does not store well.

No. 147

Cuminum cyminum 🜍

Cumin

Cummin | Geerah

✴ **SYMBOLIC MEANINGS**
Faithfulness; Fidelity.

🌀 **POSSIBLE POWERS**
Anti-theft; Cleansing; Constancy in love; Exorcism; Fidelity; Fire element; Mars; Masculine energy; Memory; Peace of mind; Protection; Retention.

☽ **FOLKLORE AND FACTS**
The edible part of the Cumin plant is the seeds, with each one found within a fruit. The seeds are dried and used whole or ground into a fine powder. The seasoning has a distinctive fragrance and taste that is liberally used in Mexican, Indian, and South Asian cuisine. • Cumin can supposedly prevent the theft of anything that it is on or in it. • Mixed with salt and scattered on the floor, Cumin will supposedly drive out evil. • A sprig of the Cumin plant is sometimes worn by a bride to keep any negativity away from her on her wedding day. • To gain peace of mind when it is needed the most, make, then carry or wear a Cumin sachet using a sprig of the plant or ground Cumin from a spice bottle. • Cumin's ability to possess the power of retention has given it a rightful place

in love potions and charms to help maintain love as constant and faithful.

No. 148

Curcuma longa 🜍

Turmeric

Haldi | Indian Saffron

✴ **SYMBOLIC MEANINGS**
Fertility; Luck; Sun.

🌀 **POSSIBLE POWERS**
Air element; Luck; Mercury; Power; Purification.

☽ **FOLKLORE AND FACTS**
The edible part of the Turmeric plant is the root, which can be used fresh or boiled in water before drying and then grinding it into a fine powder. Turmeric has a flavor that is somewhat like Black Pepper and an aroma that is mustard-like. It can colorize food to be a golden yellow-orange. It is commonly used in curries. • In every part of India, Turmeric is considered to be very lucky and has been used in weddings and religious ceremonies for thousands of years. • Occasionally in Hawaii, for the purpose of purification, powdered Turmeric is mixed with salt and water to be sprinkled with a Ti leaf over the affected area. • Traces of Turmeric have been identified in an Israeli tomb that dates back to 2600 BCE. • Turmeric is believed to be greatly beneficial in reducing inflammation.

No. 149

Curcuma zedoaria 🜍

Zedoary

White Turmeric

✴ **SYMBOLIC MEANING**
Confidence.

🌀 **POSSIBLE POWERS**
Air element; Aphrodisiac; Attracts love; Confidence; Courage; Healing; Magic; Mercury; Passion; Protection; Purification; Spell-breaking; Stimulation; Strength.

☽ **FOLKLORE AND FACTS**
Zedoary is an ancient plant that was consumed by the ancient Austronesian people as both a food and a seasoning. The edible white root of the plant has the aroma of a Mango and the flavor of Ginger with a bitter aftertaste. • In India, Zedoary is used fresh in some dishes and for use in pickling. In Thailand, the root is occasionally thinly slivered for use

in salad. In Indonesia, the root is dried, ground finely, then used to make a white curry paste. • Since the Zedoary plant is very showy, it is sometimes a houseplant. • The essential oil of the fragrant Zedoary rhizome is used in soap-making and perfumery.

No. 150

Cydonia oblonga ☠ ⚗

Quince

Apple Quince | Aromatnaya Quince | Jumbo Quince | Le Bourgeaut | Pineapple Quince | Smyrna Quince

☀ SYMBOLIC MEANINGS
Excellence; Fairies' fire; Fertility; Fidelity; Happiness; Life; Love; Scornful beauty; Temptation.

🌀 POSSIBLE POWERS
Earth element; Happiness; Love; Protection; Protection from evil; Saturn; Venus.

☾ FOLKLORE AND FACTS
Quince fruit is edible and looks very much like a plump Pear. Although some varieties of Quince produce fruit that when ripe can be eaten raw, most Quince varieties produce fruit that is too hard and tart to be eaten raw. It is usually peeled, then cooked or roasted for use in dishes, or used to make jelly, jam, pudding, or marmalade. It can even be made into a wine or liqueur. Because the aroma and flavor of Quince is strong, small amounts of it can be used as a flavor enhancer in an applesauce, apple jelly, or pie recipe. • Art seen in the excavated remains of Pompeii has revealed images of bears carrying Quince fruit in their paws. • To carry even one Quince seed is supposed to provide protection against accidents, evil, and harm to the body. • The Quince is sacredly associated with the goddesses Aphrodite and Venus. • The Quince is yet another fruit considered to be The Forbidden Fruit found in the Garden of Eden.

No. 151

Cymbopogon citratus ☠ ⚗

Lemongrass

Lemon Grass | Tanglad | West Indian Lemon Grass

☀ SYMBOLIC MEANING
Open communication.

🌀 POSSIBLE POWERS
Air element; Aphrodisiac; Attracts love; Communication; Fosters openness; Lust; Masculine energy; Mercury; Psychic cleansing; Psychic opening; Psychic power; Repels insects; Repels a snake.

☾ FOLKLORE AND FACTS
The fragrance of Lemongrass is lemony, with its fresh or dried leaves used as a flavoring herb in Thai and other Asian dishes. The tough top of the Lemongrass stalk can be used to flavor soup. • Lemongrass planted around the home is believed to repel snakes. • Lemongrass is good for psychic cleansing and opening, which allows for the development of one's psychic ability. • Lemongrass essential oil can be used for aromatherapy to uplift a sagging spirit.

No. 152

Cynara cardunculus var. scolymus ⚗

Globe Artichoke

French Artichoke | Green Artichoke

☀ SYMBOLIC MEANINGS
Courage; Hope; Peace; Prosperity; Strength.

🌀 POSSIBLE POWERS
Aphrodisiac; Armor; Attracts love; Layers of protection; Protection.

☾ FOLKLORE AND FACTS
The edible part of the Artichoke plant is the budding flower head. The "hearts" of the flower head are available frozen, canned, and marinated in jars. The whole fresh flowers are commonly boiled, steamed, stuffed, roasted, and fried. The Artichoke hearts are made into dips, hors d'oeuvres, added to salads, or served on extravagantly created charcuterie board presentations. In addition, Artichokes can be made into liqueurs as well as brewed as a tea. • The dried stalk of the Globe Artichoke will make a fine magic wand. • Over time, it has been implied that "the one who carries the Artichoke is the better lover." The saying is where the idea of it being an aphrodisiac was passed along. • The Globe Artichoke is enormous and represents strength and courage in the face of adversity.

C

No. 153
Daucus carota subsp. *sativus* ⚗

Carrot
Common Carrot | Garden Carrot

✺ SYMBOLIC MEANINGS
Do not refuse me; Fantasy; Good character; Haven; Sanctuary.

✺ POSSIBLE POWERS
Aphrodisiac; Attracts love; Fertility; Fire element; Good luck; Lift worry; Lust; Mars; Masculine energy; Relaxation.

☾ FOLKLORE AND FACTS
Although the orange-colored root vegetable is iconic and the most commonly available, there are easily obtained Carrot seeds for growing yellow, white, red, purple, and even black taproots. • What are known as "baby carrots" or "mini carrots" are *not* new little Carrots. They are peeled Carrots that are machine-cut into uniform shapes, then bagged to be marketed as a snack food. • Carrot essential oil is useful in aromatherapy for relieving worry and helping to promote relaxation prior to sleep.

No. 154
Digitaria exilis

Fonio
Black Fonio | Digitaria iburua | Hungry Rice | White Fonio

✺ SYMBOLIC MEANINGS
Satisfaction; Value.

✺ POSSIBLE POWERS
Air element; Healthy; Sun.

☾ FOLKLORE AND FACTS
White Fonio and Black Fonio are also called Hungry Rice, a cereal that has been cultivated in very dry parts of the world. Fonio is a nutritious high-protein grain that has multiple uses in breads, porridges, couscous, and beer-making.

No. 155
Diospyros kaki ⚗

Oriental Persimmon
Fruit of the Gods | Japanese Persimmon | Kaki Persimmon | Khormaloo | Lilac Persimmon | Sharon Fruit

✺ SYMBOLIC MEANINGS
Bury me amid nature's beauties; Deliciousness; Hypocrisy; Resistance.

✺ POSSIBLE POWERS
Feminine energy; Fertility; Healing; Luck; Lust; Potency; Power; Protection; Resistance; Venus; Water element.

☾ FOLKLORE AND FACTS
The Oriental Persimmon has been cultivated in China for over 2,000 years. The edible ripe fruit is dark orange and very closely resembles a tomato. Although the skin is often removed beforehand, it can be eaten. When ripe, the pulp is soft and often cut into pieces and sprinkled over with sugar before eating. • In Korea, the fruit is often dried to eat over the winter as a special treat that children enjoy. Persimmon vinegar can also be made from the fruit. If kept in a cool, dry, dark place the fruit can be stored for several months. • A magic wand made from the wood of any *Diospyros* can provide undiluted pure power. • Bury a green Persimmon fruit near to the entrance of the home for good luck. • It is believed that to be rid of the chills and fend them off from returning, you should tie one string to an Oriental Persimmon tree for each chill that was experienced.

No. 156
Durio zibethinus

Durian
King of Fruits | Mao Shan Wang | Musang King | Red Prawn Durian | Stinky Fruit

✺ SYMBOLIC MEANING
Mystique.

✺ POSSIBLE POWER
Aphrodisiac.

☾ FOLKLORE AND FACTS
The large fruit of the Durian tree did not get tagged with the common name of Stinky Fruit for no good reason. Many describe the smell as a disgusting stench that reeks of sewage mixed with decaying onions, dirty socks, and rotten eggs with a splash of turpentine thrown into the stink of it, all of which can linger behind, for days and days. On the other hand, people who do not find the Durian to be repugnantly odorous seem to favor eating it, considering it to be delectable. The texture of the Durian is often described as being like a smooth, cheesecake-like, yellow custard, with the taste being somewhat of a sweet banana, almond, vanilla, hazelnut, apricot, and caramel combination of flavors. It is usually eaten fresh or used to flavor milkshakes, baked goods, sweets, added to sauces and soups, and also deep-fried.

D

No. 157

Eleocharis dulcis

Water Chestnut

Chinese Water-Chestnut | Water-Chestnut

☀ **SYMBOLIC MEANING**
Surprise healer.

🌀 **POSSIBLE POWERS**
Healing; Hopeless healings; Unity.

☗ **FOLKLORE AND FACTS**
The crisp white-fleshed corms of the aquatic Water Chestnut that grow on the roots of the plant can be eaten raw. These are more often boiled, grilled, or pickled. They are most often purchased canned, still retaining their crispness after cooking and needing only to be rinsed to eat from the can as is or used in recipes for casseroles and dips. The Water Chestnut is a favorite vegetable in Chinese cuisine. • Many Chinese people believe that eating a Water Chestnut will instantly cure food poisoning and any infection. • To dream about a Water Chestnut is a revelation advising to eat it to heal an underlying condition.

No. 158

Elettaria cardamomum ⚗

Cardamom

Cardamon | Ceylon Cardamom | Elaichi | Green Cardamom | True Cardamom

☀ **SYMBOLIC MEANING**
Brings peaceful thoughts.

🌀 **POSSIBLE POWERS**
Aphrodisiac; Attracts love; Feminine energy; Love; Lust; Venus; Water element.

☗ **FOLKLORE AND FACTS**
Cardamom seed is one of the oldest spices, having been used since the fourth century BCE. It is said to be the "Queen of Spice," having a unique taste and fragrance, and is considered the third most expensive spice in the world. • Use Cardamom to add an exotic flavor to coffee and tea. • In the Middle East, Coffee and Cardamom are frequently ground together prior to brewing. It is also used as an ingredient in bitters, as well as a flavoring for gin. Cardamom is best stored in the pod, since after grinding the seeds will lose some of their flavor. Cardamom is commonly included in seasoning blends. Individual seeds are sometimes chewed

like gum. Cardamom is commonly used in Indian, Middle Eastern, and Thai recipes for sweet as well as savory dishes such as curries. Cardamom is also a common ingredient in Nordic baked good recipes, such as *kardemmabullar, pulla,* and *julekake.* • The fragrance of Cardamom essential oil in aromatherapy supposedly improves the body's ability to utilize oxygen during exercise. • Add Cardamom seed powder to warm wine as an aphrodisiac.

No. 159

Elsholtzia ciliata ⚗

Xiang Ru

Kinh Giới | Vietnamese Balm | Vietnamese Lemon Balm | Vietnamese Lemon Mint

☀ **SYMBOLIC MEANING**
Crested.

🌀 **POSSIBLE POWERS**
Flavoring; Healing; Soothes.

☗ **FOLKLORE AND FACTS**
The leaves are the most commonly used edible part of the Xiang Ru plant. It is often used in Vietnamese cuisine to imbue a lemony flavor to meats, salads, and soups. Sometimes the seeds are dried, then powdered for use as a flavoring. Where there are large Vietnamese communities, Xiang Ru citrus-scented mint herb is available fresh in markets nearby.

No. 160

Eragrostis teff

Teff

Annual Bunch Grass | Williams Lovegrass

☀ **SYMBOLIC MEANING**
Connection.

🌀 **POSSIBLE POWERS**
Honor the unknown that is between death and rebirth; Reconnect with the joy of our youth.

☗ **FOLKLORE AND FACTS**
The edible parts of the Teff plant are the cooked grain seeds that have been harvested as one of the earliest cultivated plants. Teff dates back to Ethiopia around 4000 BCE. It is most widely used to make a nutritious flatbread staple known as Ethiopian *injera*, which is eaten at nearly every meal. It is also used for porridges, baby food, and beer-making.

No. 161

Eriobotrya japonica

Loquat

Chinese Plum

✳ **SYMBOLIC MEANINGS**
Gold; Wealth.

🌀 **POSSIBLE POWERS**
Healing; Health; Luck;
Richness; Wealth.

☾ **FOLKLORE AND FACTS**
Tiny and tartly sweet when ripe, the Loquat fruit has been a trusted favorite in Chinese gardens for several thousand years. The flavor of the Loquat is slightly like that of peach and apricot. After the large seeds are removed and discarded, the Loquat fruit is often mixed with other fresh fruits in a fruit salad. It is also used in Asian-inspired jams, pies, pastries, sweet confections, and chutney. It is added to smoothies, too. The fruit can be used to make homemade wine. • The Loquat is a favorite in folk medicine, being a trusted thinner and dissolver of lung phlegm, as well as an expectorant. • If your birthday should be on a Sunday, there is a way to increase your good luck on that day that must be carried out *before* sunset. First, tuck a Loquat leaf into your wallet before going to the casino. Preferably go to the one nearest to where you were when you woke up that morning. When you enter the casino, look for a game or a table that shows something gold *on it* or *very near to it*. Intend to gamble no more than your age on that day. Not one penny more. See what comes of it. It's worth a Loquat leaf, a reasonable amount of money to wager, some genuine high hopes, and a birthday wish to find out.

No. 162

Eruca vesicaria

Arugula

Eruca | *Eruca sativa* | Garden Rocket | Rocket | Rocket Leaf | Rocket Salad | Roquette | Ruchetta | Rucola | Rughetta | Rugola | Rugula | Rukola

✳ **SYMBOLIC MEANING**
Rivalry.

🌀 **POSSIBLE POWERS**
Aphrodisiac; Attracts love.

☾ **FOLKLORE AND FACTS**
The edible parts of the Arugula plant are the leaf, stem, mature seed, flower, and young seed pod. Arugula is most commonly available as raw leaf, which can be added to salads, cooked in soups, or added to sauces. Because Arugula is high in vitamin K, which is important in the blood-clotting process, it can interfere with blood-thinning medication. • In ancient Rome, Arugula was considered an effective aphrodisiac for both men and women. For that reason alone, during the early Middle Ages, Arugula was absolutely forbidden to be grown in any monastery garden. In 802, the Holy Roman Emperor, Charlemagne, changed his mind and lifted the ban. • Because Arugula was thought to be so erotically stimulating, it was mixed with Lettuce to supposedly keep one's sexuality under some kind of control at the dinner table. Hence, the "mixed salad" was invented.

No. 163

Euterpe oleracea

Açaí

Açaï | Açaí Berry Tree | Açaí Palm |
Amazon Acai Berry

✸ SYMBOLIC MEANING
Sad cries.

❀ POSSIBLE POWER
Sorrow memorialized.

☾ FOLKLORE AND FACTS
The edible parts of the Açaí palm
are the berry fruits known as the Açaí berry. In North
America, Açaí berries are used a topping for oatmeal
or tapioca along with nuts and sweeteners. • Since its
introduction to the food market in the early 2000s, Açaí has
been central in many internet falsehoods attributing Açaí
berries or juice to such miracle scams as the cure for cancer,
a cure for diabetes, and the only surefire way of improving
the size and stamina of a penis. None of these particular
claims are even remotely true. • A legend among the people
along the Amazon River is that Iaçá, the daughter of chief
Itaqui, gave birth to a child who was sacrificed along with
all other newborns during a terrible famine, by order of her
father. Iaçá's sorrow caused her death. Where she died, a tree
grew. The tree provided food for Chief Itaqui's people. Out
of gratitude for their survival, the tribe named the tree Açaí,
as it was the chief's daughter's name spelled backwards.

No. 164
Fagopyrum esculentum

Buckwheat
Beechwheat | Bitter Buckwheat | Common Buckwheat | French Wheat

✳ SYMBOLIC MEANINGS
Peace of mind; Psychological peace.

❋ POSSIBLE POWERS
Earth element; Feminine energy; Money; Peacefulness; Protection; Venus.

☾ FOLKLORE AND FACTS
Buckwheat pollen dating back to 4000 BCE was found in Japan. • Buckwheat is not related to wheat. • Buckwheat was among the very first seed crops planted in North America by European colonists in the 1600s. • The edible part of the Buckwheat plant is the processed grain seed which is actually the fruit of the plant. After harvesting, the grain may be used as a whole grain "groat" for roasting, cooked with a liquid such as broth, or transformed into a tasty filling for Cabbage rolls. The grain may also have the seed coating or "hull" removed before being milled into a coarse or finer flour for use in making noodles, such as the plump soba noodles enjoyed in Japan. Some breads and pastas are also made using Buckwheat flour. • Buckwheat pancakes, with their pleasant earthy flavor that is reminiscent of mushrooms, have global variations to the basic recipe, starting with the simple style that early American pioneers favored. In Russia, Buckwheat pancakes are commonly known as "blinis." In the Netherlands they are called *poffertjes*. The crepe-like *galettes bretonnes* are the favorite in France, and *kuttu ki puri* in India. • Sprinkle Buckwheat flour around the entire perimeter outside your house to keep evil from it.

No. 165
Ferula assa-foetida

Asafoetida
Asafetida | Asant | Devil's Dung | Hilteet | Hing | Ingua | Perungayam | Stinking Gum

✳ SYMBOLIC MEANINGS
Chase away evil; Chase away the Devil; Luck; Positive energy; Stink.

❋ POSSIBLE POWERS
Avoiding spirits; Banishes negativity; Curses; Evokes demonic forces and binds them; Exorcism; Fire element; Fish bait; Mars; Masculine energy; Protection; Protection from demonic forces or illness; Purification; Repels spirits; Wolf bait.

☾ FOLKLORE AND FACTS
The edible part of the Asafoetida plant is the resinous gum that is extracted from the stem and roots of the plant. • Asafoetida didn't get the name Devil's Dung for nothing. It has one of the most horrible odors of all herbs. Merely the scent of it is known to induce vomiting. It is one herb that must be stored in an airtight container so the smell does not permeate herbs and spices near it. • In India, it is one of the most commonly used herbs for culinary and medicinal purposes, where the religious Brahmins and Jains substitute Asafoetida for Onion and Garlic, which are forbidden by their beliefs. • Asafoetida is a very powerful herb that was believed to have the ability to destroy all manifestations of spirits.

No. 166
Ficus carica

Fig
Common Fig

✳ SYMBOLIC MEANINGS
Argument; Desire; Kiss; A kiss; Longevity; Long-lived; Prolific.

❋ POSSIBLE POWERS
Aphrodisiac; Attracts love; Divination; Fertility; Fire element; Hera; Isis; Juno; Jupiter; Love; Love charm; Masculine energy.

☾ FOLKLORE AND FACTS
Figs can be eaten fresh, although they are most often available dried because they do not hold up well once picked. • Figs are a common ingredient in many baked goods, cookies, desserts, jams, beverages, wine, and liqueur. • The Fig tree has been cultivated since ancient times. In the Jewish text known as the Aggadah, the Forbidden Fruit grown on the Tree of Knowledge in the Garden of Eden was a Fig. Fig leaves from a Fig tree in the Garden of Eden were what Adam and Eve supposedly clothed themselves with in the Christian Bible's Book of Genesis. As a consequence, Fig leaves were often used to modestly cover the genitals of many other nude figures in artworks throughout the ages. • For a yes-or-no divination, write a question on a Fig leaf. If the leaf dries quickly the answer is *no*. If it dries slowly, then the answer is *yes*. • To increase the fertility of, as well as overcome any sexual impotency for both men and women, whittle a small phallic carving from *Ficus carica* wood. Then tuck it under the mattress and leave it there.

F

No. 167

Ficus sycomorus ⚗

Sycamore Fig

Fig-Mulberry | Mugumo Tree | Sycamore Tree

✸ SYMBOLIC MEANINGS
Curiosity; Grief.

🌀 POSSIBLE POWERS
Divination; Fertility; Love; Luck; Prosperity; Protection.

☾ FOLKLORE AND FACTS
Sycamore Fig trees were as sacred to ancient Egyptians and nomadic tribes as the oak was to ancient Druids. The ancient Egyptians considered the Sycamore Fig to be the Tree of Life. • The fruit of the Sycamore Fig is large, fragrant, and sweet. It has a different flavor than a common Fig and is edible fresh. Sycamore Figs can be found in Israeli produce markets. • The Sycamore is one of the few trees mentioned in the Bible. It is referred to seven times in the Old Testament, and once in the New Testament. • To protect the Sycamore trees, King David commissioned a careful watch over them. • Legend tells that Joseph and Mary rested under the shade of a Sycamore tree when they were fleeing to Egypt from Bethlehem with baby Jesus. • The Sycamore Fig is a sacred tree to the Kikuyu people who live in the highlands near Mount Kenya. So much so, that a Sycamore Fig tree falling was a very bad omen requiring rituals to fend off the trouble that was coming. • Some Egyptian mummy caskets were made from Sycamore Fig wood.

No. 168

Foeniculum vulgare ⚗

Sweet Fennel

Fennel | Finocchio | Florence Fennel

✸ SYMBOLIC MEANINGS
Courage; Deceit; Endurance; Flattery; Force; Grief; Merit; Worthy of all praise.

🌀 POSSIBLE POWERS
Charm ingredient; Courage; Dionysus; Exorcism; Fire element; Healing; Immortality; Longevity; Masculine energy; Mercury; Prometheus; Protection; Purification; Repels a ghost; Repels an evil spirit; Strength; Virility.

☾ FOLKLORE AND FACTS
The bulb, leaves, fruit "seeds," and flowers of aromatic Sweet Fennel are edible and will impart a flavor to food that tastes much like anise. The most potently flavorful part of the plant is the flowers, which are hard to find and much more expensive. The green fruits are more flavorful for cooking than those that have been dried. The dried Sweet Fennel fruits are a brown color and marketed as "seeds" that will turn grayish as they age. The Sweet Fennel fruits are one of the most important spices used in Italian sweet sausage, Kashmiri dishes, and those of African, Indian, Middle Eastern, and Chinese cuisine. The leaves look very much like Dill leaves, have a delicate flavor and can be used in the same ways as dill to add flavor to salads, sauces, puddings, and soups, as well as being used as a garnish. The greens can also be prepared as a vegetable on their own or added to others. The Sweet Fennel bulb is firm and crunchy. It can be eaten raw like celery, or cooked by braising, grilling, sautéing, or stewing. • Sweet Fennel essential oil for aromatherapy can ease worries and impart a feeling of inner calm without sleepiness because it is also uplifting. • Sweet Fennel is in the Nine Sacred Herbs healing charm that was originally written in Wessex, England around the tenth century.

F

No. 169
Fortunella japonica

Kumquat
Kinkan | Marumi Kumquat | Meiwa Kumquat | Morgani Kumquat | Nagami Kumquat | Round Kumquat

✹ **SYMBOLIC MEANINGS**
Fortunate; Good luck; Good luck of the best kind; Prosperity; Prosperous good luck; What glitters may not be gold.

🌀 **POSSIBLE POWERS**
Air element; Prosperity; Sun; Wealth.

🌙 **FOLKLORE AND FACTS**
Kumquat fruit has an appealing, edible, sweet peel with a very tart interior. The fruit is mostly eaten fresh, although it can be cooked to make jelly and marmalade. • The Kumquat's combination of sweet and sour could imply, "that which appears golden may not truly be gold." • Kumquats are referenced in Imperial Chinese literature dating back to the twelfth century. • Kumquats and Kumquat trees are often given as much-appreciated gifts during the Lunar New Year celebration in Asian countries. • There is one particular variety of the Kumquat that is found growing wild in Southern China. It is also known as the *Fortunella hindsii* Hong Kong Kumquat. The fruit is not much larger than pea-size, has large seeds with very little pulp, and tastes very bitter. It is grown more as an attractive ornamental tree. But what is most interesting about it is that it is the most primitive of all the Kumquat varieties, the one that is considered the most primitive of all *Citrus*, and the source from which all *Citrus* has evolved.

No. 170
Fragaria × ananassa

Strawberry
Alpine Strawberry | Carpathian Strawberry | Common Strawberry | European Strawberry | *Fragaria vesca* | Fraises des Bois | Garden Strawberry | Surecrop Strawberry | Tristar Strawberry | Wild European Strawberry | Wild Strawberry | Wood Strawberry | Woodland Strawberry |

✹ **SYMBOLIC MEANINGS**
Delight; Fertility; Intoxication; Perfect excellence; Perfect goodness; Perfection; Righteousness.

🌀 **POSSIBLE POWERS**
Aphrodisiac; Attracts love; Feminine energy; Freya; Love; Luck; Lust; Venus; Water element.

🌙 **FOLKLORE AND FACTS**
The fruit of the Strawberry plant is beloved by so many people all around the world that the flavor of Strawberry is part of nearly everyone's memory. There are Strawberry juices, ice pops, ice cream, yogurt, confections, pastries, and just about anything else that has fruit in it will most likely also include Strawberry. • Fresh Strawberries should be refrigerated with their caps left on and they should not be removed until preparing the berries for a recipe. Chocolate-covered fresh Strawberries present a double dose of love and the possible power of an aphrodisiac. • There have been archeological indications that Wild Strawberry fruit has been a delight to find since the Stone Age. • Cultivated Strawberries were grown in the late eighteenth century in Brittany, France. • In England, the popular treat of Strawberries served with cream was originated for the eating pleasure of Henry VIII in the sixteenth century, and then for everyone who followed thereafter. • Carry Strawberry leaves in a sachet for good luck.

F

No. 171
Garcinia indica ⚗

Kokum
Kundong

⚹ **SYMBOLIC MEANING**
Love for one another.

🌀 **POSSIBLE POWERS**
Cooling; Healing; Love; Protection from all worldly diseases.

☾ **FOLKLORE AND FACTS**
The outer covering of the *Garcinia indica* Kokum fruit is sun-dried to be used as a seasoning as well as a substitute for the sour-tasting Tamarind fruit, particularly in some curries. The fruit pulp is sweetened with sugar and diluted with water to make sherbet desserts and a beverage that is popular in parts of India. A fatty, butter-like extract called "kokum butter" is obtained from the seeds and is used in the making of chocolate confections.

No. 172
Garcinia mangostana

Mangosteen
Mang-Chi-Shih | Purple Mangosteen | The Queen of Fruit

⚹ **SYMBOLIC MEANING**
Honesty.

🌀 **POSSIBLE POWERS**
Honesty; Truth.

☾ **FOLKLORE AND FACTS**
Mangosteen is cultivated in Southeast Asia and is considered to be the most deliciously luscious of all fruits. During the ten week-long Mangosteen season, wherever the fruit is grown you'll find it sold fresh from roadside fruit stands. • There is an undocumented rumor that Queen Victoria offered a hefty reward of a knighthood to anyone who could bring her a fresh Mangosteen fruit. There is no record that she ever received one. • Once a Mangosteen tree has established itself in a consistently warm climate and has matured to fruiting, which takes between six to twelve years, it can live and produce fruit for at least one hundred years.

No. 173
Gardenia jasminoides ⚗

Gardenia
Cape Jasmine | Cape Jessamine | Common Gardenia

⚹ **SYMBOLIC MEANINGS**
Ecstasy; Emotional support; Exhilarating emotions; Good luck; Healing; I am too happy; I love you in secret; Joy; Love; Peace; Purification; Purity; Refinement; Secret love; Spirituality; Sweet love; Transient joy; Transport; Transport of joy; You're lovely.

🌀 **POSSIBLE POWERS**
Aphrodisiac; Attracts love; Feminine energy; Healing; Love; Moon; Peace; Seduction; Spirituality; Water element.

☾ **FOLKLORE AND FACTS**
Gardenia flower petals are used to brew a fragrant tea in China. They can also be eaten raw, preserved in honey, or pickled. • The exotic perfume of the Gardenia flower is irresistibly intoxicating and has an extremely high spiritual vibration. Used as aromatherapy, the fragrance of just one freshly picked Gardenia blossom floating in a bowl of clean water will promote a sense of extreme inner peacefulness and increased spirituality. • There is a legend that the Gardenia was a gift from a sea goddess to her earthly lover. • The fragrance of the Gardenia is believed to have the ability to attract angels that offer spiritual guidance. • It was once believed that engaged young women who died before they were married are very upset, viciously lusty, wandering ghosts looking for love, leaving the scent of Gardenia behind wherever they go. They even seduce living men who would lust after the ghosts in their sleep. The men would wake up exhausted and sore with the vague recollection of a very weird dream. Most difficult for them to make sense of was a lingering scent of Gardenia in their bed.

No. 174

Gaultheria procumbens ⚕

American Wintergreen

American Mountain Tea | American Wintergreen | Boxberry |
Brossaea procumbens | Canada Tea | Canterberry |
Checkerberry | Eastern Teaberry | *Gaultheria humilis* |
Gaultheria repens | *Gautiera procumbens* |
Ground Berry | Spicy Wintergreen | Wintergreen

✺ **SYMBOLIC MEANING**
Harmony.

🌀 **POSSIBLE POWERS**
Breaks a hex; Feminine energy;
Fire element; Harmony; Healing; Mars; Moon; Protection.

☾ **FOLKLORE AND FACTS**
The fruits of the American Wintergreen plant are the berries that are used to create the Teaberry extract that flavors candy, chewing gum, and even ice cream. • It is believed Wintergreen essential oil is useful in aromatherapy to uplift the spirit and promote positive thinking.

No. 175

Gentiana lutea ⚕

Yellow Gentian

Great Yellow Gentian | Yellow Mountain Gentian

✺ **SYMBOLIC MEANING**
Loveliness.

🌀 **POSSIBLE POWERS**
Applying knowledge;
Astral plane; Breaks a hex;
Controlling lower principles;
Finding lost objects; Love;
Overcoming evil; Power;
Regeneration; Removes
depression; Sensuality;
Uncovering secrets; Victory.

☾ **FOLKLORE AND FACTS**
The root of the Yellow Gentian plant is used to make an extract that is included in a variety of bitters and bitter liqueurs. Yellow Gentian requires ten years to mature before flowering. If the plant is permitted to grow, it will do so for up to fifty years. • When seeking something that was lost and needs to be found, carry a sachet of a Yellow Gentian flower and leaf to help find it. • When trying to uncover a secret, carry or wear a sachet of a Yellow Gentian flower and leaf to help reveal the truth.

No. 176

Geum urbanum ⚕

Wood Avens

Colewort | Herb Bennet | St. Benedict's Herb

✺ **SYMBOLIC MEANING**
Work as a prayer.

🌀 **POSSIBLE POWERS**
Drives away an evil spirit; Exorcism;
Fire element; Jupiter; Love;
Masculine energy; Meaningful work;
Purification.

☾ **FOLKLORE AND FACTS**
Wood Avens root has been used to flavor some ales and soups. • If worn as an amulet, Wood Avens protects against attacks by wild beasts, dogs, and venomous snakes. • Since the leaves grow in threes and the petals in fives, the Wood Avens has been associated with Christianity's Holy Trinity and the five wounds that Jesus suffered during His crucifixion.

No. 177

Ginkgo biloba ☠ ⚕

Ginkgo

Gingko Ginnan | Maidenhair Tree

✺ **SYMBOLIC MEANINGS**
Age; Old age; Remembering;
Survival; Thoughtfulness;
True Tree of Life.

🌀 **POSSIBLE POWERS**
Aphrodisiac; Attracts love; Fertility;
Healing; Hope for wealth; Intense concentration; Longevity;
Love; Mental acuity; Survival under the most extreme of all circumstances.

☾ **FOLKLORE AND FACTS**
The cooked kernels of Ginkgo seeds are valued in Asia and used as an ingredient in special-occasion foods such as those served at weddings and for a dish known as "Buddha's delight," which has been traditionally prepared for the Lunar New Year. Ginkgo seed kernels should not be consumed in large quantities or over a long period of time. • *Ginkgo biloba* is considered a living fossil because it is the only member of its genus, which is also the only genus in its family, which is also the only family in its order, which is also the only order in its subclass. • Gingko dates from *before* the time that dinosaurs roamed the Earth.

G

No. 178

Glechoma hederacea ☠ ⚱

Ground Ivy

Alehoof | Creeping Charlie | Creeping Jenny | Field Balm | Gill-over-the-Ground | Runaway Robin

✳ SYMBOLIC MEANINGS
Assertiveness; Attachment; Persistence.

✇ POSSIBLE POWERS
Divination; Enduring friendship; Loving friendship.

☾ FOLKLORE AND FACTS
Sprawling, invasive Ground Ivy leaves were used by the Vikings to clarify, flavor, and help preserve their brewed ales. The use of Ground Ivy for ale brewing was later adopted by the English for the same purposes until the late fifteenth century, when hops changed the methodology and the process from brewing ale into beer. Ground Ivy has been used as a substitute for animal rennet in cheese-making. • There was a time when Ground Ivy was planted on a grave as a symbol of love and friendship. • European settlers eventually and successfully carried seeds and cuttings of Ground Ivy all around the world. • To find out who is working against you using negative magic, starting on a Tuesday, encircle a yellow candle with Ground Ivy and then light the candle. The knowledge of who it is will come to mind.

No. 179

Glycine max ☠ ⚱

Soybean

Curd Bean | Soy | Soya | Soya Bean

✳ SYMBOLIC MEANING
Salty sweetness.

✇ POSSIBLE POWERS
Earth element; Moon; Sustain.

☾ FOLKLORE AND FACTS
The edible part of the Soybean plant is the bean, which is considered a sacred plant in China, where it has been cultivated for more than 5,000 years. Raw Soybeans are toxic and must be cooked with wet heat to make them safe to consume. Soybeans are sometimes referred to as being *magic beans* due to the diversity of their use, which includes being a very popular edible legume known as "edamame." Soybeans are also used to make diverse derivative unfermented foods, such as tofu and soy milk, and fermented foods, such as soy sauce and tempeh. Soybean oil is transformed into popular non-dairy margarines, hot beverage creamers, and even yogurts. The key ingredient in the salty-sweet "hoisin sauce" is fermented Soybean paste. • The first Soybean crop grown in North America was on Skidaway Island, Georgia, in 1765. • In 1908 bottled soy sauce production began in Hawaii. • Soybean oil is used in the manufacture of some cleaning products, for illumination as candles, as a biodiesel fuel, and as an effective solvent to help remove industrial oil spills from shorelines.

G

No. 180

Glycyrrhiza glabra ⚗

Licorice

Licourice | Liquorice | Zoethout

✴ SYMBOLIC MEANINGS

Domination; Love; Rejuvenation.

🌀 POSSIBLE POWERS

Business transactions; Caution; Cleverness; Communication; Creativity; Faith; Feminine energy; Fidelity; Illumination; Initiation; Intelligence; Learning; Love; Lust; Memory; Prudence; Science; Self-preservation; Sound judgment; Thievery; Venus; Water element; Wisdom.

☾ FOLKLORE AND FACTS

The edible part of the Licorice plant is the root, from which an extract is obtained for use in a very popular flavoring that is included in a wide variety of confections as well as liqueurs. • In candy, the flavor is often supported by the inclusion of anise extract in the recipes, with only a small amount of Licorice extract used. An early sweet candy drop type of confection that was a mix of sugar with Licorice was devised in Yorkshire, England, where it came to be known as a *Pontefract cake*. In Italy, pure Licorice extract is used to make a confection that is sold in small pieces, and also to flavor liqueurs. Chewing on a plain dried Licorice root stick releases its flavor and intense sweetness, and is a favorite confection in the Netherlands. The sticks are also known as *zoethout*. In Egypt and Syria, a popular Licorice-flavored beverage is sold by street vendors. • In Italy and France, Licorice is a popular breath-freshener. • Carry a piece of Licorice root to attract love.
• A long, dried, woody stem of the Licorice plant is believed to make a good magic wand.

No. 181

Gnetum gnemon ⚗

Melinjo

Belinjo | Gnemon Tree | Gnetum | Melinjo Nut | Paddy Oats

✴ SYMBOLIC MEANING

Intuitive.

🌀 POSSIBLE POWERS

Earth element; Health; Intuition; Jupiter; Shade; Sustenance.

☾ FOLKLORE AND FACTS

The Melinjo tree grows throughout Indonesia, and among its virtues it provides much-needed shade as a pleasant comfort in the extreme heat of the tropics. • The nuts are edible raw, boiled, or roasted. The cooked new leaves, flowers, outer flesh of the fruit, and seeds are commonly used for a sour flavoring in curries, soups, and stews in Indonesia, New Guinea, Thailand, the Philippines, Fiji, and the Solomon Islands. • A natural resveratrol, which acts somewhat like an antioxidant, is extracted from Melinjo seeds.

G

No. 182

Gossypium hirsutum ☠ ⚗

Cotton

Gossypium herbaceum | Levant Cotton | Mexican Cotton | Upland Cotton

✳ SYMBOLIC MEANINGS
I feel my obligations; Obligations.

❂ POSSIBLE POWERS
Earth element; Feminine energy; Fishing;
Fulfill obligations; Healing; Luck;
Moon; Protection; Rain.

☾ FOLKLORE AND FACTS
Cotton has been cultivated since ancient
times. It is now grown in most countries
around the world. The *Gossypium
hirsutum* and *Gossypium herbaceum* Cotton
species are the primary sources of the cottonseed
oil extracted from the seeds and processed for
edible consumption as a salad oil used in salad
dressings and mayonnaise. • Cottonseed oil is
higher in fat than other vegetable oils, which
has made it useful in soap and candle-making, as well as in
laundry detergents, insecticides, and even rubber. • Cotton
that is either scattered or planted on your property will keep
ghosts away. • Cotton cloth should be your first choice when
you require cloth for magical purposes. • Burning a piece of
Cotton supposedly will bring rain. • A piece of Cotton in the
sugar bowl brings good luck.

No. 183
Helianthus annuus

Sunflower
Common Sunflower | Corona Sunflower

✹ SYMBOLIC MEANINGS
Ambition; Constancy; Devotion; False appearance; False riches; Fire element; Flexibility; Good luck; A good year; Haughtiness; Have a good year; Healing; Homage; Inspiration; Intellectual greatness; Lofty thoughts; Loyalty; Masculine energy; Misery; Nourishment; Opportunity; Power; Pride; Pure; Pure and lofty thoughts; Spiritual attainment; Splendid; Splendor; Strength; Unhappy love; Vitality; Warmth; Wealth.

🌀 POSSIBLE POWERS
Constancy; Deep loyalty; Energy; Fertility; Fire element; Happiness; Health; Longevity; Loyalty; Nourishment; Power; Protection; Sun; Sustenance; Warmth; Wisdom; Wish magic; Wishing.

☾ FOLKLORE AND FACTS
The Sunflower's seed kernels are edible. Sunflower oil is extracted from the kernels to be commonly used for frying. The kernels are also processed to produce a creamy spread. • In the early 1800s, it was believed that a powerful amulet could be made from parts of a Sunflower plant's leaf, petal, seed, stem, and root collected during August while under the sign of Leo the Lion, to then be wrapped together with Bay Laurel leaves and a wolf's tooth. The resulting amulet would be extremely powerful, so much so that whoever carried it would never be treated in any manner other than peacefully and kindly. In addition to that benefit, should someone ever steal anything, sleeping with the amulet under the pillow would reveal the full identity of the thief in a dream.

No. 184
Helianthus tuberosus

Jerusalem Artichoke
Earth Apple | Sunchoke | Sunroot | Topinambour

✹ SYMBOLIC MEANING
Sunny outlook on life.

🌀 POSSIBLE POWER
Healing.

☾ FOLKLORE AND FACTS
The Jerusalem Artichoke tuber is edible raw and can be sliced thin for addition to a salad, but it can be cooked or pickled as well. When cooking, the texture is better when it is steamed. Jerusalem Artichoke has been used as the primary ingredient for distilling Jerusalem Artichoke brandy.

No. 185
Hemerocallis fulva ☠ ⚗

Orange Daylily
Corn Lily | Ditch Lily | Fulvous Daylily | Outhouse Lily | Railroad Daylily | Roadside Daylily | Tawny Daylily | Tiger Daylily | Washhouse Lily

✹ SYMBOLIC MEANINGS
Coquetry; Diversity; Tenacity.

🌀 POSSIBLE POWERS
Indifference; Jupiter; Moon; Nonchalance; Purity; St. Joseph; Tenderness.

☾ FOLKLORE AND FACTS
The petals and unopened flower buds of the Orange Daylily flower can be found in several Chinese dishes. The best known can be found in Chinese restaurants everywhere, called "Moo Shu Pork." • The Orange Daylily is not a true lily, but a member of the *Asphodelus* family. • Introduced to North America by European immigrants, the Orange Daylily originated in China and Korea. Because the *Hemerocallis fulva* bulb can survive for weeks unplanted, Orange Daylily bulbs were carried across the sea and all the way across North America by wagon trains, to now bloom wild along roadsides and railroad tracks where they still prolifically grow. • Orange Daylily flowers last for one day.

H

No. 186
Hibiscus rosa-sinensis ⚗

Hibiscus
Bunga Raya | Chinese Hibiscus | Gumamela |
Shoe Flower | Shoeflower

✹ SYMBOLIC MEANINGS
Beauty; Delicate;
Delicate beauty;
Peace and Happiness;
Rare beauty.

🌀 POSSIBLE POWERS
Ambition; Attitude;
Celebration of the simplest joy;
Clear thinking; Divination; Enjoying each
step of life's journey; Feminine energy; Higher
understanding; Logic; Love; Lust; Manifestation in material
form; Outward expression of happiness or joy; Seeing hidden
and obvious beauty; Spiritual concepts; Thought processes;
Venus; Water element.

☾ FOLKLORE AND FACTS
In Polynesia, the raw petals of the Hibiscus flower are
sometimes used in a salad. The dried petals are brewed as
a tea. • The Hibiscus is called Shoe Flower because the
crushed petals can be used to shine shoes. • In the Pacific
Islands, a red Hibiscus flower is worn by women as a sign
of their interest. If worn behind the left ear, it signals that
she desires a lover. If behind the right ear, she already has a
lover. If a Hibiscus is worn behind both ears it signals that
she has one lover but would welcome another one. • In
parts of India, the Hibiscus flower is used to venerate the
Hindu goddess, Kali. • A Hibiscus flower will bloom to live
for only one day.

No. 187
Hibiscus sabdariffa ⚗

Roselle
Ambadi | Amile | Amlamadhur | Anthur Sen | Belchanda |
Cây Bụp Giấm | Cây Bụt Giấm | Cây Quế Mẫu | Chin Baung |
Dachang | Datchang | Flor de Jamaica | Gal Da | Gongura |
Hmiakhu Saipa | Hanserong | Hoilfa | Isapa | Karkadeh | Khata
Palanga | Kraceíyb | Krachiap | Lakher Anthur | Luoshen
Hua | Matu Hmiakhu | Mwita | Okhreo | Pulicha Keerai |
Pundi Palle | Pundi Soppu | Rosella | Rosella Fruit | Saril |
Sillo Sougri | Tengamora | Yakuwa | Ya Pung

✹ SYMBOLIC MEANINGS
Femininity; Joy; Kindness.

🌀 POSSIBLE POWERS
Aphrodisiac; Beauty; Courage; Divination; Freedom;
Harmony; Independence; Lord Ganesha; Increases passion;
Love; Love spells; Lucid dreams; Lust; Passion; Prophetic
dreams; Psychic work; Sun.

☾ FOLKLORE AND FACTS
In Northeast India, almost every home has a Roselle plant
growing near it for its use as an ingredient in vegetable and
fish dishes, soups, stews, and sauces. The fresh green leaves
of the Roselle bush are prepared by steaming, boiling, or
sautéing them like Spinach and eating them as leafy green
vegetables. The red petal is a flavoring for chutney. The fruit
and flowers of the plant are dried and used in teas, beverages,
and cocktails in the Caribbean and the subtropical southern
United States, as well as in jams and jellies. • Tuck a sachet
of a Roselle leaf and flower under the pillow to encourage a
prophetic dream.

No. 188
Hierochloe odorata ☠⚗

Sweetgrass
Bison Grass | Buffalo Grass | Holy Grass | Manna Grass | Mary's Grass | Seneca Grass |
Sweet Grass | Vanilla Grass

✹ SYMBOLIC MEANINGS
Healing; Mother Earth's hair; Peace; Poor but happy;
Spirituality.

🌀 POSSIBLE POWERS
Calling in good spirits; God; Healing; Jesus; Meditation;
Peace; Protection; Purification; Repels negative energy;
Venus; Virgin Mary; Water element.

FOLKLORE AND FACTS

In Poland, Russia, and France, Sweetgrass extract has been used to flavor some soft drinks, confections, and liqueurs. • The Native Americans consider Sweetgrass to be the oldest of all plants and the hair of Mother Earth. It is considered a sacred plant that still holds significant importance to Native Americans, who burn it as incense. The Native American Plains tribes believe Sweetgrass attracts positive energy and good spirits. It is also considered to be one of the four sacred medicines, symbolizing healing and peace. It is often used for smudging to purify and protect the body, mind, spirit, and living environment, as well as repel all forms of negative energy. Sweetgrass is often braided or left in bundles at burial sites and other sacred sites as an offering. The three braid sections represent body, mind, and soul. They also represent honesty, kindness, and love. • In parts of Europe, Sweetgrass extract has been used as a fragrance that is added to perfumes.

No. 189

Hippophae rhamnoides

Sea Buckthorn

Sallow Thorn

SYMBOLIC MEANINGS

Glowing mane; Horse shiner.

POSSIBLE POWERS

Beauty; Healing.

FOLKLORE AND FACTS

The edible Sea Buckthorn berries need to be *pulled* from the thorny branches of the plant by hand, which makes them very time-consuming to harvest. However, the fruit contains a much higher level of vitamin C than that present in oranges, lemons, or limes. • Sea Buckthorn berries are also used in some cosmetics, Russian and Asian folk medicine, and as a food for livestock.

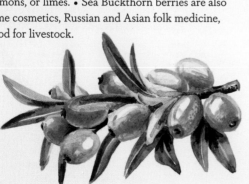

No. 190

Hordeum vulgare

Barley

Hulless Barley | Jt | Naked Barley

SYMBOLIC MEANINGS

Love; Grain of life.

POSSIBLE POWERS

Demeter; Earth element; Feminine energy; Fertility; Harvest; Healing; Love; Love spell; Male sexual potency; Money; Pain relief; Protection; Sex; Venus.

FOLKLORE AND FACTS

Barley is one of the oldest cultivated crops on Earth. The seed grain of the Barley plant has been harvested for use as food as far back as approximately 8500 BCE. Ancient growers domesticated Barley between 1500 and 891 BCE. Whole Barley grain and ground flour are used in a wide range of cuisines around the world, in soups, stews, side dishes, desserts, gruels, breads, and alcoholic beverages such as beer. It is also commonly made into "malt," which is used in beer, beverages, confections, and baked goods. • Barley held important significance in the religious rituals of various Middle Eastern, Egyptian, and Greek cultures in antiquity. • In the Middle Ages, one type of divination, called alphitomancy, used Barley cakes to determine guilt or innocence. Suspected criminals ate the Barley bread or cake. The first person to get indigestion was guilty.

H

No. 191
Hovenia dulcis 🝆

Japanese Raisin Tree

✹ **SYMBOLIC MEANING**
Fisted hand.

🌀 **POSSIBLE POWER**
Healing.

☾ **FOLKLORE AND FACTS**
The flowers of the Japanese Raisin Tree are fleshy and look like raisins when they are dried. They are sweet, fragrant, and edible both raw and cooked. The flowers can also be brewed as a tea. Extract that is taken from the leaves, stem, and seeds is very sweet and used as a substitute for honey in confections and winemaking.

No. 192
Humulus lupulus

Hop

Beer Flower | Common Hop | European Hop

✹ **SYMBOLIC MEANINGS**
Injustice; Mirth; Passion; Pride.

🌀 **POSSIBLE POWERS**
Air element; Colorize; Healing; Mars; Masculine energy; Sleep.

☾ **FOLKLORE AND FACTS**
Ingesting Hop fruit in any other way than using it in beer brewing is definitely not recommended. In the brewing of beer, the female cone-shaped Hop fruits have been used to add an aromatic bitter note and act as a natural preservative. • Sleep on a pillow that has been stuffed with dried Hops for improved rest.

No. 193
Hydrangea serrata

Mountain Hydrangea

Seven Barks | Tea of Heaven

✹ **SYMBOLIC MEANINGS**
Appreciation; Boaster; Carelessness; Coldness; Coolness; Devotion; False pride; Frigidity; Frigidness; Gratefulness; Heartfelt praise; Heartlessness; Pride; Remember; Ruthlessness; Thank you for understanding; Uncrossing; Vain glory; You are cold.

🌀 **POSSIBLE POWERS**
Attracts love; Breaks a hex; Creates one's own destiny; Draws straying lovers to return; Fidelity; Fire element; Helps identify and repel a psychic attack; Helps identify karmic patterns; Helps rebuild protective energy fields; Helps redirect a curse; Intuition; Mars; Protects boundaries; Psychic awareness.

☾ **FOLKLORE AND FACTS**
In Japan, Mountain Hydrangea leaves are used to make a tea that is brewed to celebrate the Buddha's birth. • The Hydrangea has the ability to inspire the active creation of one's own destiny in such a way that steps are taken to commence onward, rather than make excuses that avoid proceeding on one's destined path. • Make, then carry a sachet of petals and leaves to encourage goodness to come forward from without and within.

No. 194
Hylotelephium telephium 🝆

Orpine Stonecrop

Frog's-Stomach | Harping Johnny | Life-Everlasting | Live-Forever | Livelong | Orphan John | Orphine | Witch's Moneybags

✹ **SYMBOLIC MEANINGS**
Constancy; I think of you; Never-ceasing memory; Never-ceasing remembrance; Perpetual remembrances; Unceasing remembrance.

🌀 **POSSIBLE POWERS**
Air element; Earth element; Feminine energy; Healing; Health; Longevity; Memory recall; Prevents illness; Promotes longevity; Protection; Remembering; Sun; Venus; Vivid dreams; Wards off sickness; Wisdom.

H

FOLKLORE AND FACTS

Orpine Stonecrop can be found growing on old thatched rooftops, from pockets in stone walls, on beach dunes, within thickets, and in pastures. Because the plant has the ability to retain water it was given the name of Livelong. Very young leaves can be eaten raw or cooked. The tubers can also be cooked. • Carry a sachet of Orpine Stonecrop flowers and leaves to improve the ability to remember something significant, especially when it will be important to recall the memory of it with as much detail as possible. • Orpine Stonecrop can be burned in an incense blend when attempting to contact deceased loved ones. • An interesting love divination is to take two stems of Orpine Stonecrop and hang them close together in the room of someone who is engaged. If the stems grow together, that is a positive sign that the couple is a good match and there will be happiness. If the stems grow but do not join together, the match is not meant to be. If one or both stems die, that is a very negative omen.

No. 195

Hymenaea courbaril ⚗

West Indian Locust

Amami-Gum | Brazilian Cherry | Brazilian Copal | Courbaril | Flour Tree | Guapinol | Stink Toe | Stinking Toe

✳ SYMBOLIC MEANING
Marriage.

✴ POSSIBLE POWERS
Crafts; Fire element; Healing; Incense; Love; Marriage; Masculine energy; Perfumery; Sun.

FOLKLORE AND FACTS

The West Indian Locust tree primarily grows in South America. It has a massively wide, umbrella-like canopy. The tree produces large, unpleasantly smelling pods that are at least four inches long. • Its legumes are used to make custards, ice creams, liqueur, and a tea. They are also dried and made into a powder that can be added into soups and baked goods. If the legume's pulp is eaten raw it will cling unpleasantly inside the mouth. Because of its exceptionally high levels of proteins and starches, it is known to be one of the richest vegetable foods on Earth, one that has sustained many South American indigenous peoples for millennia. • The genus for the West Indian Locust is *Hymenaea*, named after the Greek god of marriage, Hymen, making it useful to add to love amulets and in incense for weddings.

Hyssopus officinalis ⚗

Hyssop

Herb Hyssop | Holy Herb | Hyssop Herb | Yssop

✳ SYMBOLIC MEANINGS
Cleanliness; Holiness.

✴ POSSIBLE POWERS
Fire element; Healing; Jupiter; Masculine energy; Protection; Purification; Spiritual cleansing; Venus; Wards off an evil spirit; Water element.

FOLKLORE AND FACTS

Referred to frequently in the Bible and used since ancient times, Hyssop is a mint that is considered to be especially sacred and is the herb that is most often used for holy purification. • It is included in the popular Middle Eastern seasoning blend known as za'atar. It is also used to flavor some liqueurs, with it being part of the official recipe for the distilling of chartreuse as well as absinthe. • Hang Hyssop in the home to force out evil and negativity. • The sponge, wet with vinegar, that was brought to Jesus to drink from when He was suffering on the cross, was held up to His mouth on a Hyssop branch. • Hyssop essential oil can be used for aromatherapy to help stimulate creativity and aid concentration when meditating.

No. 197

Ilex paraguariensis

Yerba Mate
Erva Mate | Mate | Paraguay Tea | Yerba | Yerba Maté | Yerva Mate

✹ SYMBOLIC MEANINGS
Love; Mate; Romance.

✺ POSSIBLE POWERS
Binding; Building; Death; Fidelity;
Fire element; History; Knowledge;
Limitations; Love; Lust; Mars;
Masculine energy; Obstacles; Time.

☕ FOLKLORE AND FACTS
A popular tea-like caffeinated infusion
known as "mate" is brewed with water and the
leaves of the Yerba Mate plant. Mate was first consumed by
the early indigenous Guaranì people of Paraguay, spreading
far and wide from there. The drinking of mate is popular
in Paraguay and Uruguay, where it is a social experience.
People are commonly seen carrying the mate around in
containers that are or at least resemble a hollowed-out
Calabash gourd. • Wear a sprig of Yerba Mate to attract the
opposite sex. • Spill an infusion of Yerba Mate to break off
what was once a romantic relationship.

No. 198

Illicium verum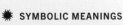

Star Anise
Badian | Badiane | Chinese Anise |
Chinese Star Anise | Eight-Horn |
Star Aniseed | Staranise

✹ SYMBOLIC MEANINGS
Good luck; Luck.

✺ POSSIBLE POWERS
Air element; Divination; Good luck charm; Healing; Jupiter;
Masculine energy; Psychic ability; Psychic awareness;
Psychic power.

☕ FOLKLORE AND FACTS
It is the firm, seed-holding, six-pointed pod from the Star
Anise tree that is harvested and dried for use as a seasoning.
Fragrant and anise-flavored, Star Anise is often used to
flavor baked goods, roast meats, liqueurs, and wine. Star
Anise is widely used in Chinese, Indian, Indonesian,
Malaysian, and Vietnamese cuisine. • Star Anise is one of
the spices used in the seasoning blend known as traditional
Chinese "five-spice powder." • The pods can be added to a
cup of hot coffee to flavor it while it steeps. A pod can be
used this way many times over. • Star Anise is included in
masala chai. • Wear a Star Anise necklace to increase your
psychic power. • In aromatherapy, Star Anise essential
oil may help calm unexplainable feelings and sensations
resulting from stress. • A Star Anise seed can be burned like
incense to increase one's psychic awareness. • An enormous
percentage of the world's crops of the *Illicium verum* Star
Anise plant has been dedicated to making the urgent anti-
viral medication oseltamivir, which is more commonly
known as Tamiflu.

No. 199

Ipomoea batatas

Sweet Potato
Kūmara | Sweetpotato | Yam

✹ SYMBOLIC MEANINGS
Attachment; Hard times; I attach
myself to you.

✺ POSSIBLE POWERS
Friendship; Grounding; Harmony; Nurturing; Sensuality;
Venus; Water element.

☕ FOLKLORE AND FACTS
Although frequently referred to as a "yam," botanically the
Sweet Potato is quite distinctly unrelated to yams. • Sweet
Potato was cultivated in Central America at least 5,000 years
ago. Although the very young leaves are sometimes boiled
or sautéed, it is the orange tuber of the Sweet Potato plant
that is most enjoyed. In some parts of the world it's a staple
crop. • Sweet Potato can be eaten raw, as it was consumed
that way by the early American colonists. Digestibility is
improved with cooking, as is the absorption of the tuber's
nutrients. • Whether Sweet Potatoes have been baked,
boiled, steamed, roasted, deep-fried, mashed, transformed
into a soup, or dried and ground into flour, there are many
world cuisines that elevate the Sweet Potato. The Sweet
Potato is the primary ingredient in beloved iconic holiday
foods served on dinner tables in the USA such as "sweet
potato pie," "candied sweet potatoes," and "sweet potato
casserole." • According to New Zealand legend, when the
Sweet Potato tuber is in the ground, it is so powerful that an
enemy can be driven mad and will simply run away from it.

I

No. 200
Juglans nigra ☠

Black Walnut
Eastern American Black Walnut

✸ **SYMBOLIC MEANINGS**
Infertility; Intellect; Presentiment; Stratagem.

🌀 **POSSIBLE POWERS**
Accesses divine energy; Brings forth blessings; Colorizes; Fertility; Fire element; Health; Infertility; Masculine energy; Mental clarity or power; Strong mental power; Sun; Wishing.

🜄 **FOLKLORE AND FACTS**
The edible part of the Black Walnut tree is the roasted kernel of the corrugated seed or "nut." Once the fruit ripens and drops to the ground, and the husk is removed, the nut's kernel is laboriously taken out and roasted. Black Walnut is used in pastries, confections, vegetables, meats, and pasta dishes. • In the spring, the trees can be tapped to collect the sap, which can be drunk, cooked down to a syrup, or distilled into a distinctively flavored liqueur.

No. 201
Juglans regia ☠ 🜨

English Walnut
Allegheny Walnut | Broadview Walnut | Carpathian Walnut | Circassian Walnut | Common Walnut Tree | European Walnut | Gewone Walnoot | Nut Fit for a God | Persian Nut | Persian Walnut | Walnoot | Walnuss

✸ **SYMBOLIC MEANINGS**
Infertility; Intellect; Presentiment; Stratagem.

🌀 **POSSIBLE POWERS**
Attracts lightning; Colorize; Family happiness; Fertility; Fire element; Health; Infertility; Mental clarity or power; Strong mental power; Sun; Wishing.

🜄 **FOLKLORE AND FACTS**
The edible part of the English Walnut tree is the extracted kernel of the seed or "nut." English Walnuts are eaten raw or roasted. They are also an ingredient in a wide variety of recipes, such as those for pastries, baked goods, and salads. They can be made into syrup or fermented into a liquor, or even pickled to be either sweet or savory. • Walnut oil is used in salads. • All wishes will be granted if someone is luckily gifted a bag of English Walnuts. • If suffering infertility issues, make four sachets by tucking either English

or Black Walnut leaves into small white cotton pouches that you, yourself, have made. In your best handwriting, write out your array of prayers, hopes, and dreams for a child on four pieces of paper. Fold each note small enough to tuck into each of the sachets. Hang the first over the head of the bed. Tuck the second under the foot of the mattress. Tuck the remaining two on each side of the mattress. Relax.

No. 202
Juniperus communis 🜨

Juniper
Gin Berry | Gin Plant | Juniper Berry

✸ **SYMBOLIC MEANINGS**
Cleanse; Bless; Protect.

🌀 **POSSIBLE POWERS**
Abundance; Advancement; Anti-theft; Aphrodisiac; Binding; Blessing; Breaks a hex; Building; Cleanses; Conscious will; Curse breaking; Death; Drives off snakes; Energy; Exorcism; Fire element; Friendship; Growth; Healing; Health; History; Joy; Knowledge; Leadership; Life; Light; Limitations; Male sexual potency; Masculine energy; Natural power; Obstacles; Protection; Psychic power; Purification; Success; Sun; Time.

🜄 **FOLKLORE AND FACTS**
The dried berries from the Juniper bush are used in several Scandinavian and Northern European dishes, most particularly as a flavoring for wild game and wild birds. Juniper is also used to flavor gin and some other beverages. Take care which type of Juniper berries you eat. Some species of Juniper will produce inedible, toxic berries. • Juniper berries can be strung together and hung over a door to help protect the home from evil forces, evil people, intruding ghosts, sickness, snakes, and theft. • Men can make, then carry or wear a red sachet or amulet of a Juniper sprig to hopefully increase their sexual potency. • Juniper berries can enhance psychic power. • Juniper essential oil can create a peaceful atmosphere for aromatherapy.

No. 203
Kaempferia galanga
Resurrection Lily
Aromatic Ginger | Galangal | Kencur |
Sand Ginger

✴ **SYMBOLIC MEANING**
Relive.

🌀 **POSSIBLE POWERS**
Aphrodisiac; Attracts love;
Awareness; Breaks a hex;
Clarity of thought; Creates internal peacefulness; Euphoria;
Healing; Health; Hex breaking; Insecticide; Legal aid; Lust;
Money; Mosquito preventative; Overcomes exhaustion;
Prophetic dreams; Protection; Psychic powers; Seasoning.

☾ **FOLKLORE AND FACTS**
Kaempferia galanga is an aromatic herb that has been used
to flavor vodka and liqueurs. The common name of the
Resurrection Lily plant comes from the fact that, even after
the root has been used to brew a tea, it can be removed and
allowed to dry, then be reused several more times. It is also
used in Southeast Asian recipes in a similar way to common
Ginger. However, the Resurrection Lily is uniquely different
from common Ginger and the other *galangal* plants. Its
leaves are used in the Malaysian rice dish that is known as
nasi ulam. • Chewing on a piece of *Kaempferia galanga*
root while thinking of one's heart's desire is supposed to be
undertaken until the piece is reduced to a mush. Spitting it
out while fully determined that the wish is to come true will
make it so.

No. 204
Kigelia africana ☠ 🥣
Sausage Tree
Cucumber Tree | Worsboom

✴ **SYMBOLIC MEANINGS**
A lost loved one; Ingenuity.

🌀 **POSSIBLE POWERS**
Handicrafts; Healing; Hide tanning; Portability; Usefulness.

☾ **FOLKLORE AND FACTS**
The sacred *Kigelia africana* Sausage Tree flowers are
huge, deep-dark red, trumpet-shaped, and dripping with
nectar. The unusual fruits of the Sausage Tree look like long
sausages hanging all over it. The fresh fruit is highly toxic.
The ripe fruit requires drying and roasting to make it edible.
It is then covered over with honey and fermented to make
an alcoholic sweet beer known in Central Kenya as both
muratina and *kaluvu*. The huge woody fruit of the Sausage
Tree can grow to be up to thirty-nine inches long, eight
inches around, and can weigh between eleven and twenty-
six pounds. Considering the size and overall weight of the
Sausage Tree fruit, it is easy to imagine the extent of damage
that the fruit can cause to vehicles and people who may
happen to be under a tree when
a dangling "sausage" falls. • The
Sausage Tree fruit can be dried,
hollowed out, and converted into
sturdy containers, cups, ladles, and
even mouse traps. • The Luo and
Luhya people in Kenya will bury a
Sausage Tree fruit as a proxy body
for someone who has been missing
and is believed dead.

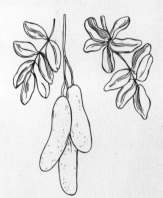

K

No. 205
Lablab purpureus ☠ ⚗

Lablab Bean
Australian Pea | Bonavist Bean | Dolichos Bean | Egyptian Kidney
Bean | Hyacinth-Bean | Indian Bean | Seim Bean

✸ SYMBOLIC MEANING
Vividly lovely.

⟳ POSSIBLE POWER
Attractiveness.

☾ FOLKLORE AND FACTS
Although the colorful Lablab Bean plant
leaves and flowers can be eaten raw or cooked in a curry
or steamed like spinach, the magenta fruit pods and beans
are highly toxic until they have been thoroughly boiled,
changing out the water several times. The root needs to be
boiled or baked before eating.

No. 206
Lactuca sativa

Lettuce
Bibb Lettuce | Boston Lettuce | Bunching Lettuce |
Butterhead | Cos | Crisphead Lettuce | Cutting Lettuce |
Garden Lettuce | Head Lettuce | Iceberg Lettuce |
Leaf Lettuce | Romaine

✸ SYMBOLIC MEANINGS
Chastity; Cold-hearted;
Cold-heartedness; Coldness.

⟳ POSSIBLE POWERS
Aphrodisiac; Attracts love; Childbearing; Contraception;
Divination; Feminine energy; Fertility; Hope for a child
soon; Love; Love divination; Moon; Protection; Sleep; Water
element.

☾ FOLKLORE AND FACTS
Lettuce is native to the Mediterranean area and is one of
the oldest-known plants on Earth. There are basically three
types of Lettuce: leaf, head, and cos. The most popular
Lettuce in the USA is Iceberg Head Lettuce. Romaine
Lettuce is also a widely popular cos type and favored for
Caesar salad. Loose-leaf Lettuce is the most widely planted
variety for home gardens. Lettuce leaves are often used
to wrap sandwich fillings instead of bread. Lettuce leaves
can also be sautéed or stir-fried as well as added to soups.
• It was once believed in England that if too much Lettuce
was growing in the garden, it would cause sterility in the
household. • A love divination using Lettuce is to write
your love interest's name in the soil then plant the name
with Lettuce seeds. If the seeds sprout then love will grow
between you and your love interest.

No. 207
Lactuca sativa
var. augustana ⚗

Celtuce
Asparagus Lettuce | Celery Lettuce | Chinese Lettuce | Qingsun | Stem Lettuce | Wosun

✸ SYMBOLIC MEANINGS
Chastity; Cold-hearted; Cold-heartedness; Coldness.

⟳ POSSIBLE POWERS
Aphrodisiac; Attracts love; Childbearing; Contraception;
Divination; Fire element; Love; Love divination; Masculine
energy; Mercury; Protection; Sleep.

☾ FOLKLORE AND FACTS
Experts believed that Celtuce originated in the
Mediterranean and made its way to China between 600 and
900 CE. Celtuce is a popular vegetable in China, where it
is grown for its nutritious thick stem more than for its
leaves. The tender new leaves
can be eaten raw, while the
older leaves can be cooked as
a leafy green vegetable. The
stems can be stir-fried, roasted,
grilled, and pickled. Although
there have been several attempts
since the 1890s to introduce
Celtuce to the United States, it is
barely known. Fresh Celtuce can be
found in most Chinese markets.

L

No. 208
Laurus nobilis 🏺

Bay Laurel
Bay Tree | Grecian Laurel | Laurel Tree | Sweet Bay

✳ SYMBOLIC MEANINGS
Fadeless affection; Fame; Glory; Health; I change but in death; Immortality; Love; No change till death; Notability; Poets; Praise; Prosperity; Renown; Resurrection of Christ; Strength; Success; Victory.

⚘ COMPONENT MEANINGS
Leaf: I change but in death.
Wreath: Fame; Glory; Reward of merit.

꩜ POSSIBLE POWERS
Abundance; Advancement; Apollo; Asclepius; Attracts romance; Ceres; Clairvoyance; Cleansing; Conscious will; Energy; Eros; Fire element; Friendship; Good fortune; Good luck; Growth; Healing; Induces prophetic dreams; Joy; Leadership; Life; Light; Masculine energy; Natural power; Physical and moral cleansing; Prosperity; Protection; Protection against black magic; Protection against evil spirits; Protection during an electrical storm; Psychic power; Purification; Ritual purification; Strength; Success; Sun; Wards off evil; Wards off evil magic; Wards off lightning; Wards off negativity; Wisdom.

☾ FOLKLORE AND FACTS
The edible parts of the Bay Laurel tree are the berry-like fruit and the leaf. The fruit is harvested, dried or pressed, then marketed as the seasonings called "Laurel Berry" and "Laurel Oil." It is the "Bay Leaf" that is used in many dishes, especially in Mediterranean cuisine, to flavor soups, stews, and sauces. It is typically added as a whole leaf during cooking and removed before serving. The wood is sometimes used for smoking foods. • In ancient Greece, the poets, heroes, winning athletes, and esteemed leaders were crowned with wreaths made from Bay Laurel leaves. • Wishes written on Bay Laurel leaves then buried in a sunny spot or burned will help make them come true. • Bay Laurel leaves placed under a pillow can induce prophetic dreams.

No. 209
Lavandula angustifolia 🏺

English Lavender
Common Lavender | Official Lavender | True Lavender

✳ SYMBOLIC MEANINGS
Constancy; Devotion; Distrust; Faith; Faithful; Humility; Love; Mistrust; Silence.

꩜ POSSIBLE POWERS
Air element; Aphrodisiac; Attracts love; Business; Business transactions; Calls in Good Spirits; Caution; Charms against the Evil Eye; Chastity; Cleverness; Communication; Creativity; Deodorize; Expansion; Faith; Happiness; Healing; Honor; Illumination; Induces sleep; Initiation; Inner sight; Intelligence; Leadership; Learning; Longevity; Love; Magic; Masculine energy; Memory; Mercury; Peace; Politics; Power; Protection; Prudence; Public acclaim; Purification; Responsibility; Royalty; Science; Self-preservation; Sleep; Sound judgment; Success; Thievery; Wealth; Wisdom.

☾ FOLKLORE AND FACTS
Not all varieties of Lavender are edible. *Lavandula angustifolia* English Lavender is the variety cultivated for culinary use. English Lavender has a sweet fragrance with lemony notes that is often used in teas, salads, salad dressings, desserts, pastries, cheeses, custards, sorbets, flans, wine, and liqueurs. It can also flavor granulated sugar and honey. English Lavender buds become more intense when dried. It is one of the herbs in the seasoning blend called *herbes de Provence*. English Lavender buds can be candied and used as decorations on baked goods and other sweet confections. For culinary purposes, a little English Lavender goes a long way. Too much will impart a soapy taste. • English Lavender essential oil for aromatherapy brings forth a calm, tranquil, and peaceful environment for relaxation, meditation, and restful sleep. The essential oil is absolutely *never* intended for ingestion of any kind. • English Lavender can bring peacefulness into the home. • Dried English Lavender buds can be floral confetti to toss toward newlyweds.

L

No. 210

Lentinula edodes 🜇

Shiitake Mushroom

Black Mushroom | Black Forest Mushroom |
Golden Oak Mushroom | Sawtooth Oak Mushroom

✳ SYMBOLIC MEANINGS
Long life; Youthfulness.

🌀 POSSIBLE POWERS
Aphrodisiac; Activates the Life Force; Boosts the immune
system; Heals; Health; Increases energy; Longevity;
Provides nourishment; Virility.

☾ FOLKLORE AND FACTS
In Japan and China, the Shiitake Mushroom has been
revered for its medicinal uses as well as for its culinary value
for thousands of years. It grows wild, but it is cultivated in
Asia as well as in the United States, where the mushrooms
are grown on dead oak logs. The Shiitake Mushroom is
widely used in East Asian cuisine, and is very often added
to miso soup, or used as an ingredient in various rice or
vegetable dishes, as well as for flavoring. • In China during
the Ming dynasty, the Shiitake Mushroom was considered
the elixir of life.

No. 211

Lepidium meyenii

Maca

Ayak Willku | Maca-Maca | Peruvian Ginseng

✳ SYMBOLIC MEANING
Endure.

🌀 POSSIBLE POWERS
Adapts to stress; Anti-depressant; Aphrodisiac; Attracts
love; Copes with a challenge or stress; Endurance; Energy;
Fertility; Health; Improves stamina; Increases libido;
Longevity; Memory booster; Sex magic; Sexual performance.

☾ FOLKLORE AND FACTS
The overall shape of the Maca plant's taproot is inconsistent:
large, small, flattened, rectangular, triangular, or an overall
surprise when it is uprooted. Attached at the top of the
root is the celery-like "hypocotyl," which may be green,
cream-colored, golden, red,
purple, black, or even
blue. The hypocotyl
is traditionally
pit-roasted. The
boiled and mashed

roots are used in soups, fillings, and jams. The primary use
of the Maca root is to dry it, then grind it into a flour called
harina de maca, which can be used for baking and included
in porridge, but mostly for producing a beer-like beverage
known as *chicha de maca*, which has been brewed in the
Andes for more than 3,000 years. • Maca root powder can
produce too much testosterone in the body, causing voice
deepening, excessive body hair growth, and a resistance to
insulin.

No. 212

Lepidium sativum 🜇

Cress

Garden Cress | Garden Pepper Cress | Mustard and Cress |
Pepper Cress | Pepper Grass | Pepperwort |
Poor Man's Pepper

✳ SYMBOLIC MEANINGS
Always reliable; Power; Roving;
Stability.

🌀 POSSIBLE POWERS
Aphrodisiac; Attracts love; Courage; Daring; Fire element;
Invisibility; Mars; Moon; Power; Saturn; Water element.

☾ FOLKLORE AND FACTS
Garden Cress seeds are sometimes used in salads and stir-fries.
The tangy, peppery, green leaves are also added to sandwiches
and soups. Young shoots are cut up and often used in hard-
boiled-egg dishes. • Because of its speedy germination and
growth, *Lepidium sativum* seeds are sometimes used in
schools to study the stages of plant growth.

No. 213

Lens culinaris ☠

Lentil

Pulse

✳ SYMBOLIC MEANING
Good luck in the New Year.

🌀 POSSIBLE POWERS
Expansion; Money; Moon; Luck; Peace; Prosperity; Water
element.

☾ FOLKLORE AND FACTS
Archeological traces of Lentils dating back to 11,000 BCE
were found in the Franchthi Cave in Greece. The edible
part of the Lentil plant is the cooked seed, which is a legume
that is also known as a "pulse." Like all other legumes, raw
and undercooked Lentils are toxic. Unlike other legumes,

L

Lentils do not need to be soaked prior to being thoroughly cooked. Canned Lentils are already sufficiently cooked. When cooked, hulled Lentils will disintegrate in the same way green or yellow split-peas will when cooked in a soup. Those Lentils that have not had the hull removed will retain much of their shape. • Lentils can be in a range of earth-tone colors from light green to black. Some of the small green Lentils have a peppery taste. Red Lentils have the outer hulls removed before polishing and splitting the beans. • Lentils are a common ingredient in many international dishes such as soups, stews, and casseroles that are most often cooked with Rice or served as a thick stew-like sauce topping. Lentil dishes are most often vegetarian, although they may also include chicken or pork. One of the first solid foods an Ethiopian mother will feed her baby is mashed Lentils. • Eat Lentils for peace.

No. 214
Levisticum officinale 🥣

Lovage
Chinese Lovage | Liebstöckel | Lovage Leaf

✹ SYMBOLIC MEANINGS
Brings love; Love.

🌀 POSSIBLE POWERS
Air element; Aphrodisiac; Attraction; Attracts trustworthy friends; Courage in love; Love; Mercury; Permanent love; Protection against negative spirits; Removes sexual blockages; Sexual love; Success; Wealth.

☾ FOLKLORE AND FACTS
Lovage has a somewhat distinctive Celery and Parsley-like fragrance and flavor. It has been cultivated for the leaves, roots, and seeds, which are often used in European cuisine. The leaves can be used in salads or added to soups as a seasoning potherb. The root can be added to soups or it can be pickled. Lovage seeds are used as a seasoning that is added to pickled Cabbage or Cucumbers. The seeds are also added to flavor brandy. • People are believed to fall in love with someone who has been made magically attractive with Lovage. Due to that particular magical property, Lovage has been used in love potions and charms for hundreds of years. • During medieval times, a bride would sometimes tuck a sprig of Lovage in her hair. • It is believed that adding Lovage to the bath water before going out to meet new people will increase one's attractiveness.

No. 215
Ligusticum scothicum

Scots Lovage
Scottish Licorice-Root

✹ SYMBOLIC MEANING
Inspired love.

🌀 POSSIBLE POWERS
Air element; Enhances attractiveness; Fire element; Flavoring; Healing; Health; Love; Masculine energy; Mercury; Prophetic dreams; Psychic cleansing; Purification; Romance; Sun.

☾ FOLKLORE AND FACTS
Scots Lovage leaves and stalks are edible before the flowers appear. The taste is similar to Celery or Parsley, while the seeds taste similar to Cumin or Fenugreek. Young shoots are sometimes candied. • Scots Lovage is commonly found growing on cliff tops and in the crevices between rocks. • A sachet to attract love is all the more effective with an herb that has the word "love" in its name, as Scots Lovage does. • Make, carry, or wear a pink and red sachet of Scots Lovage to attract romance and love.

No. 216
Lilium auratum ☠ 🥣

Goldband Lily
Goldenband Lily | Golden-Rayed Lily | Mountain Lily | Yamayuri

✹ SYMBOLIC MEANING
Pure of heart.

🌀 POSSIBLE POWERS
Repels a malicious spirit; Repels any malicious entity; Repels dark magic; Repels negative energy; Resists negative influences.

☾ FOLKLORE AND FACTS
The Goldband Lily is one of the true lilies, strongly scented and considered to be most abundantly blooming, and also the tallest, reaching up to eight feet. In China and Japan, the Goldband Lily bulbs are grown until they are large enough to cook. • By simply planting it in the garden, the Goldband Lily exudes positive energy that can protect the garden, the property, the home, and all who reside in it against dark magic, negative energy, malicious spirits, and unpleasant entities, as well as help resist pestering negative influences.

L

No. 217
Limnophila aromatica

Rice Paddy Herb
Ngò Om

☀ SYMBOLIC MEANING

Submerged.

✿ POSSIBLE POWERS

Fertility; Water element; Water magic.

☾ FOLKLORE AND FACTS

Rice Paddy Herb is aquatic and often cultivated and harvested for use in fish aquariums. It is harvested during the dry season following the Rice harvest. After drying it on the rooftop, Rice Paddy Herb is saved for use as a lemony, cumin-like flavored condiment for seafood or for use in Thai, Cambodian, and Vietnamese soups.

No. 218
Lindera benzoin 🝆

Spicebush
Benjamin Bush | Common Spicebush | Northern Spicebush | Wild Allspice

☀ SYMBOLIC MEANINGS

Arable land; Growth potential.

✿ POSSIBLE POWERS

Air element; Crop worthy; Masculine energy; Success in the field; Sun.

☾ FOLKLORE AND FACTS

A tea can be made from the buds and leaves of the Spicebush. The fruits are dried for use like Allspice. • During the pioneer years in North America, land surveyors used Spicebush as a sign that the land could sustain cultivated crops. • The *Papilio troilus* butterfly favors the Spicebush so much as a host plant to feed its developing caterpillars that one of its common names is Spicebush Swallowtail.

No. 219
Linum usitatissimum 🝆

Flax
Common Flax

☀ SYMBOLIC MEANINGS

Beauty; Benefactor; Domestic industry; Fate; Genius; Healing; I feel your benefits; I feel your kindness; Kindness; Money.

✿ POSSIBLE POWERS

Beauty; Cloth; Clothe; Draws in money; Fends off poverty; Fire element; Healing; Health; Luck; Masculine energy; Mercury; Money; Polishing; Preserves wood; Protection; Protection against sorcery; Psychic power; Purification.

☾ FOLKLORE AND FACTS

Dyed wild Flax fibers found in the prehistoric Dzudzuana Cave were scientifically determined to be at least 34,000 years old. • The seed of the *Linum usitatissimum* Flax plant is edible. Whole Flax seed will keep well for a long time if refrigerated. Once Flax seeds are ground, they can become rancid in less than a week if exposed to air. An airtight container combined with refrigeration can extend the usability of ground Flax for up to twenty months. Ground Flax seed is often used in breads and cereals. • Mix Flax seeds with crushed Red Pepper to keep in a small wooden box. Place the box in a position of honor in the home for luck and protection. • Carry a Flax seed sachet for protection from sorcery.

L

No. 220

Lippia abyssinica 🥣

Koseret

African Verbena | Brégué Balenté | Butter Clarifying Herb | Dutmutzuri | Gambia Tea Bush | Kusaayee | Kusaye | Lemon Herb | Mousso et Mâle | Quereret | Verveine d'Afrique

✸ SYMBOLIC MEANING
Stay.

🌀 POSSIBLE POWERS
Fire element; Longevity; Mars; Preservation; Protection.

☾ FOLKLORE AND FACTS
The leaves of the Koseret plant are used as a minty oregano-like potherb, seasoning, or tea in Ethiopian cuisine as well as in Congolese, Gambian, and other West African dishes. But Koseret's most notable and incredible use is as a preservative in oil and butter that can resist spoilage for as long as fifteen years.

No. 221

Litchi chinensis subsp. *chinensis* ☠ 🥣

Lychee

Cây Vai | Lichee | Litchi

✸ SYMBOLIC MEANINGS
Beauty; Close family; Good fortune; Good luck; Happiness; Love; Romance; Summer; Wishing for children.

🌀 POSSIBLE POWERS
Family ties; Love; Luck; Romance; Wishing.

☾ FOLKLORE AND FACTS
The cultivation of the Lychee tree in China dates back to 1059. The Lychee tree's fruit is edible and was favored by ancient Chinese emperors and empresses as a delicacy. Although some species of Lychee grow wild in tropical areas of the world, the only commercialized Lychee is *Litchi chinensis* subsp. *chinensis*. • The edible part of the Lychee tree is the interior flesh of the rough, pink-red fruit that is a favorite dessert. Only ripe Lychee should be eaten. Fresh Lychee is available in season from late spring until early fall. Canned Lychee is available year round.
• Lychee tree wood is supposedly indestructible.

No. 222

Litsea garciae 🥣

Engkala

Borneo Avocado | Beva' Mali | Bua Talal | Engkala | Kalangkala | Kangkala | Kayu Mali | Kelima | Kelimah | Kelime | Kelimie | Lan Yu Mu | Malei | Pangalaban | Pong Labon | Tebulus | Wi Lahal | Wuru Lilin

✸ SYMBOLIC MEANING
Interested.

🌀 POSSIBLE POWERS
Healing; Renewal.

☾ FOLKLORE AND FACTS
Although it is cultivated more for its medicinal uses, the fruit of the *Litsea garciae* Engkala tree has an avocado-like flavor and is edible raw, cooked, or pickled. • The oil extracted from the Engkala fruit seeds is used for making soaps and candles.

No. 223

Luffa cylindrica 🥣

Smooth Loofah

Dishrag Gourd | Egyptian Cucumber | Rag Gourd | Sponge Gourd | Vegetable Sponge | Vietnamese Luffa

✸ SYMBOLIC MEANING
Wash to clean.

🌀 POSSIBLE POWERS
Cleanliness; Scrubber.

☾ FOLKLORE AND FACTS
In parts of Asia, the Smooth Loofah is specifically grown for use as a cooked vegetable that is harvested when the fruit is very young, before it becomes fibrous and inedible.
• Using the dried and processed Smooth Loofah gourd fiber as a bath sponge is as common now as it was during the late Roman Empire.

No. 224

Lupinus mutabilis ☠

Tarwi

Andean Lupin | Pearl Lupin | Peruvian Field
Lupin | South American Lupin

✳ SYMBOLIC MEANINGS
Dejection; Forgiveness;
Imagination; Self-sacrifice;
Survival; Voraciousness.

✺ POSSIBLE POWERS
Inner strength to
overcome trauma of any
origin; Psychic vision.

☾ FOLKLORE AND FACTS
It is the bitter-tasting white seeds of the *Lupinus mutabilis*
Tarwi plant that are edible and have been used in salads,
soups, and stews by Andean people since ancient times.
Before they can be cooked for eating, the seeds *must* be
soaked over a period of several days with multiple changes
of water throughout that time. • To contemplate upon a
wild *Lupinus* flower is believed by some to present a portal
to the fairy world.

No. 225

Lycium barbarum ⚗

Goji Berry

Barbary Matrimony Vine | Chinese Wolfberry | Duke of Argyll's Tea Tree |
Himalayan Goji | Matrimony Vine | Mede Berry | Red Medlar

✳ SYMBOLIC MEANING
Ghost thorn.

✺ POSSIBLE POWERS
Attracts love; Beauty; Fire element; Mars; Sexual attraction.

☾ FOLKLORE AND FACTS
The Goji Berry shrub is a member of the deadly nightshade
family and has been used in England as a hedging plant since
the 1700s. Fully ripe Goji Berry
fruit is edible and has a
slight licorice flavor. In
China, it is sometimes
added to soups.

L

No. 226
Macadamia integrifolia ☠

Macadamia
Bauple Nut | Prickly Macadamia | Queensland Nut

✷ SYMBOLIC MEANING
Ingenuity.

❂ POSSIBLE POWERS
Aphrodisiac; Attracts love;
Earth element; Fertility; Jupiter.

☾ FOLKLORE AND FACTS
Low in protein but high in monounsaturated fat, the
Macadamia nut is native to Australia and was introduced to
Hawaii in 1882. The kernel of the seed is edible raw, but not
every variety of Macadamia is edible. After growing for ten
years, the Macadamia tree can produce seeds for more than
one hundred years. • Macadamia oil is also extracted for use
in salad dressings and frying. • The nuts have extremely hard
shells that must be cracked with a hammer or notched with
a saw, then popped open with a tool that looks like a steel
guitar pick and functions like a key. • The hyacinth macaw is
one of the very few birds capable of shelling the Macadamia
nut, using only its powerful beak.

No. 227
Mahonia aquifolium ☠ ⚗

Oregon Grape
California Barberry | Mountain Grape |
Oregon Grape Root | Oregon Grape-Holly |
Oregon Holly-Grape | Oregongrape |
Rocky Mountain Grape | Trailing Grape |
Wild Oregon Grape

✷ SYMBOLIC MEANING
Sharp-tempered beauty.

❂ POSSIBLE POWERS
Earth element; Feminine energy; Money; Prosperity.

☾ FOLKLORE AND FACTS
After there has been a frost, the tart, purple-black Oregon
Grape berries can be gathered and eaten raw, or they can
be brewed into a folk-style wine using the same methods
employed to make barberry wine. • Make, then carry an
Oregon Grape sachet to attract popularity and money
and ensure financial security. • The Oregon Grape leaves
resemble holly and are very often used by florists for
greenery in Christmas-themed arrangements.

No. 228
Malpighia emarginata ⚗

Acerola Cherry
Barbados Cherry

✷ SYMBOLIC MEANINGS
Fertility; Innocence;
Love; Youthfulness.

❂ POSSIBLE POWERS
Fertility; Love;
Love energy.

☾ FOLKLORE AND FACTS
The edible part of the Acerola
Cherry shrub is the fruit-berry. It's considered to be a high
source of natural vitamin C. • It is believed that the Acerola
Cherry was spread from one island to the next in the West
Indies by birds. It was introduced to Florida from Cuba in the
late nineteenth century. • The Spanish explorers named the
fruit *cereza*, which is the Spanish word for cherry, because it
reminded them of the cherries they remembered from their
homeland.

No. 229
Malus domestica ☠ ⚗

Apple
Apple Tree | Fruit of the Gods | Fruit of the Underworld | Orchard Apple | Silver Bough |
Silver Branch | Tree of Love

✷ SYMBOLIC MEANINGS
Art; Breasts; Death; Fall of man; Immortality; Joy;
Knowledge; Lingering love; Love;
Luxury; Motherhood; Peace-
loving; Perpetual concord;
Perpetual peaceful
agreement; Poetry;
Presence of love; Purity;
Self-control; Sexuality;
Sin; the Soul; Temperance;
Temptation; Transformation;
Virtue; Vulva; Wisdom.

❂ POSSIBLE POWERS
Adam; Aphrodite; Apollo; Attracts love; Eve; Feminine
energy; Fertility; Friendship; Garden blessing; Garden magic;
Healing; Hera; Immortality; Longevity; Love; Love magic;
Mutual happiness; Pomona; Sensuality; Transformation;
Venus; Water element; Zeus.

M

FOLKLORE AND FACTS

The edible parts of a *Malus domestica* Apple tree is the fleshy fruit and skin. Apples are available fresh, dried, juiced, as cider, liqueur, and wine, added as an ingredient in baked goods, or cooked down to be "apple butter" and "applesauce," as well as fermented to be "apple cider vinegar." • An Apple is an excellent source of pectin for jelly and jellied confections. • A cider Apple is always used to make cider. Cider apple varieties have been sorted into the definitive categories of a "cooker" or an "eater," which is good enough for dessert. Or it will be a "spitter" if it is deemed to be good for nothing else but adding to the cider-making blend. • Apple cider vinegar has been used as a home remedy for a wide variety of ailments for hundreds of years. • Before eating an Apple, rub it to remove any evil spirit that might be hiding within it. • An Apple appears in the writings of many religions, most often as a forbidden fruit, although up until the 1600s, the word "apple" was a term used to describe all fruits other than berries. • Druids fancied magic wands they had cut for themselves from an Apple tree, because they knew these would positively respond to them magically.

No. 230

Malus sylvestris ☠ ⚗

Crabapple

Crab Apple | Crabtree | European Crabapple | Forest Apple | Wild Apple | Wild Crab Apple

SYMBOLIC MEANINGS

Beguiling; Crabby; Ill nature; Ill-tempered.

POSSIBLE POWERS

Colorize; Healing.

FOLKLORE AND FACTS

A Crabapple tree that is fully wild will have thorns. Wild Crabapple trees can live and continue to produce fruit for one hundred years. The Crabapple tree is the only ancient apple tree in Britain that is indigenous. Crabapples can be made into jelly but are most often added into the mix with *Malus domestica* apples of all varieties when making apple cider. • Crabapple features in the Nine Sacred Herbs healing charm from Wessex, England, written in the tenth century. • In the spring, before a Crabapple tree will leaf out, it is covered over with a spectacular

mass of blossoms. There are also some varieties that will flower fully with blossoms that are a bright rosy pink, which very slowly lighten daily until the flowers are the palest pinkish-white, turning whiter before the petals flutter off the tree. • When you cut across a Crabapple, the same symbolic star shape of the core and seeds, as with any other apple, can be seen.

No. 231

Malva sylvestris ⚗

Common Mallow

Blue Mallow | Chinese Cluster Mallow | High Mallow | Mallow | *Malva moschata* | *Malva verticillata* | Musk Mallow | Rödmalva | Sléz Lesní

SYMBOLIC MEANINGS

Childishness; Consumed by love; Consumed love; Immaturity; Maternal tenderness; Persuasion; Weakness.

POSSIBLE POWERS

Beltane; Comfort; Communication; Exorcism; Fertility; Healing; Love; Lust; Moon; Protection; Softens a hard heart; Softens inflexible thinking; Soothes; Venus; Water element.

FOLKLORE AND FACTS

The edible part of the *Malva sylvestris* Mallow and *Malva moschata* Musk Mallow are the flower petals that can be eaten raw and the young leaves, which can be steamed or boiled. *Malva verticillata* Chinese Cluster Mallow has been consumed raw or cooked as a leafy vegetable in China for thousands of years. • Since medieval times, Mallow flowers have been woven into garlands and wreaths for celebrating May Day on May 1st. • Mallow was virtually unknown in North America until it was introduced into the newly planted English gardens. • Mallow can be used to consecrate ritual implements. • Graves in ancient Greece were often planted with Musk Mallow. • Make, then carry a Musk Mallow sachet using the flower and leaves to expand one's thinking to better tolerate those persons who have been somewhat intolerable.

No. 232
Mangifera indica ☠🏺✴

Mango
Common Mango | Indian Mango | King of Fruits

✴ **SYMBOLIC MEANINGS**
Happiness; Life.

🌀 **POSSIBLE POWERS**
Conversion; Fire element; Grant a wish; Happiness; Love;
Romance; Sensual romance.

🌙 **FOLKLORE AND FACTS**
The Mango was introduced to Asia around 500 BCE. • Nearly
all varieties of Mango are sweet, although some are soft and
juicy while others are firm and fibrous. Juicy, sweet ripe
Mangoes can be cut up and eaten fresh, juiced, or dried,
or used in curries, jelly, smoothies, milkshakes, sauces, and
pastries. Unripe and sour Mangoes can be used to make
jam, chutney, daal, confections, and Mango pickles. In the
Philippines, dried Mango strips are combined with Tamarind
to make a very popular treat known as mangorind. A popular
spicy street treat in Mexico is a peeled Mango on a stick
cut to appear as a pinecone, which is seasoned with fresh-
squeezed lime juice and hot pepper. • A mixture of Mango
and sweetened condensed milk can be used as a topping
for cake, ice cream, and shaved ice. • Cutting a Mango can
be a challenging effort. The large, flat seed or stone clings
tenaciously to the *very* slippery fruit flesh. The easiest way
to cut and remove the fruit is by using a cross-cutting grid
method. • Mango tree wood is frequently used to craft
ukuleles, fine furniture, and wood flooring. • A pink Mango
blossom sachet, made then carried, can attract romance.

No. 233
Manihot esculenta ☠🏺✴

Sweet Cassava
Mandioca | Manioc | Maniok | Tapioca | Yuca

✴ **SYMBOLIC MEANING**
There is life.

🌀 **POSSIBLE POWER**
Possible survival.

🌙 **FOLKLORE AND FACTS**
Cassava, like the Almond, has a "sweet"
and "bitter" variety. In the case of *Manihot esculenta* Cassava,
one is edible with proper preparation and thorough cooking.
In the other case, it is so deadly dangerous that even if it is
processed properly and cooked, one *might* possibly survive
Cassava's deadly toxin *if* particularly lucky, because cooking
it is absolutely not safe enough. And yet, even with its
dangerously iffy safety concern, most especially when one
doesn't undoubtedly know the tuber's true nature of toxicity
at all by simply looking at it, Cassava is the third-largest
carbohydrate source in many tropical countries, behind Rice
and Corn. The starchy root is also transformed into a flour
that is used for cooking and baking, and most popularly
when making tapioca pearls for puddings and as a novelty
ingredient in bubble tea beverages. • One use for Cassava that
endangers no one is as a laundry starch to stiffen shirt collars.

No. 234
Manilkara zapota 🏺

Sapodilla
Chikoo | Sapota | Sapoti

✴ **SYMBOLIC MEANING**
Fortitude.

🌀 **POSSIBLE POWERS**
Fertility; Peace.

🌙 **FOLKLORE AND FACTS**
The edible and nutritious ripe fruit
of the Sapodilla tree is brown-colored with a rough, fuzzy
feeling, but soft when pressed with the fingers. It is also
sweet and juicy with a flavor similar to that of a Pear. The
unripe fruit is unpleasant to touch. The tree bark contains
chicle, which has a texture similar to latex that is used to
make a natural chewing gum.

M

Maranta arundinacea

Arrowroot

Araruta | Maranta | Obedience Plant | West Indian Arrowroot

✴ SYMBOLIC MEANINGS
Good life; Obedience; Prayer.

✺ POSSIBLE POWERS
Energy cleansing;
Energy healing;
Good fortune;
Graveyard dust;
Luck; Opportunities;
Petition; Protection;
Purification.

☕ FOLKLORE AND FACTS
Arrowroot has been cultivated by
indigenous cultures around the world
for over 8,000 years. • Arrowroot starch is obtained by
processing the edible roots of the *Maranta arundinacea*
Arrowroot plant, then grinding them into a powder for use
as a digestible thickener for acidic stews and soups. However,
do not use it when preparing a dairy sauce, because it
will make it slimy. • Arrowroot can be frozen and thawed
without changing its composition; nor does it have a starchy
taste or mouth feel. Powdered Arrowroot is often used as a
substitute for cornstarch in thickening sauces. • Dust hands
with powdered Arrowroot before choosing specific lottery
numbers. • Sprinkle Arrowroot at the doors of the home to
help keep unwanted people's negative energy from crossing
over the threshold. • Sprinkle a little Arrowroot at the
doorways and along the windowsills to keep positive energy
inside the home. • When in need of graveyard dust for a
spell, Arrowroot powder makes an acceptable substitute.
• Sprinkle Arrowroot powder around a child's room to help
protect them from harm.

Marrubium vulgare ⚗

Horehound

Common Horehound | Hoarhound | Marrubium | White Horehound

✴ SYMBOLIC MEANING
Imitation.

✺ POSSIBLE POWERS
Air element; Balance; Exorcism;
Fire element; Healing; Health;
Mars; Masculine energy; Mental
clarity or power; Mercury;
Protection; Purification.

☕ FOLKLORE AND FACTS
The extract of the Horehound
plant leaves is used to flavor
a hard candy drop that is
somewhat more medicinal
than a confection.
• Horehound leaf is used to
brew a tea, as well as a beer that
is somewhat like root beer. It provides
a necessary ingredient in a "Rock and Rye" cocktail. • Carry
Horehound to protect yourself against magical fascination
and sorcery. • Horehound was thought to be struck by
Donar, the Germanic god of thunder and lightning, which
made Horehound incredibly powerful. • Elves, pixies, and
fairies are believed to be obsessed with Horehound flowers.

Medicago sativa ⚗

Alfalfa

Buffalo Herb | Lucerne | Lucerne Grass | Purple Medic

✴ SYMBOLIC MEANINGS
Existence; Life.

✺ POSSIBLE POWERS
Abundance; Anti-hunger; Brings
in money; Earth element;
Feminine energy; Money;
Prosperity; Protects
against financial
misfortune; Venus.

☕ FOLKLORE AND FACTS
Alfalfa plant seeds are edible
after they sprout. Sprouted
Alfalfa sprouts are a common

ingredient in South Indian cuisine, offered in most American salad bars, and can be added to sandwiches. • Alfalfa seeds can be easily sprouted using only water, a jar, and frequent rinsing for three or four days. A tablespoon of Alfalfa seeds can produce approximately three cups of sprouts. However, there is much controversy over the food safety of raw sprouts. This is due to a question regarding bacterial safety on the seeds, even if sprouting them at home. Cooking will kill the bacteria, but few people cook sprouts, although they should. • Place a small jar of Alfalfa seeds in a corner on your pantry shelf to keep the pantry from going empty. • Scatter Alfalfa ashes around the house to protect those who live there from poverty and hunger.

No. 238

Mel

Honey

Acacia Honey | Avocado Honey | Blueberry Blossom Honey | Buckwheat Honey | Clover Honey | Dandelion Honey | Eucalyptus Honey | Fireweed Honey | Heather Honey | Lavender Honey | Linden Honey | Macadamia Nut Honey | Mānuka Honey | Orange Blossom Honey | Palmetto Honey | Pine Honey | Rosemary Honey | Sage Honey | Sourwood Honey | Thyme Honey | Tupelo Honey | Wildflower Honey

☀ SYMBOLIC MEANINGS
Abundance; Blessing; Divinity; Ecstasy; Endearment; Golden wealth; Immortality; Industry; Plenty; Poetry; Richness; Spiritual wisdom; Sweetness.

🌀 POSSIBLE POWERS
Air element; Aphrodite; Brigid; Fends off evil; Fertility; Happiness; Health; Healing; Holds two things together; Kindness; Longevity; Love; Mellona; Mother Earth; Prosperity; Protection from evil; Purification; Ra; Romance; Sensuality; Sex; Spirituality; Sun; Sweetness; Vishnu; Wisdom; Youth.

◎ ADDITIONAL POWERS
Acacia Honey: Banishes negative energy; Restores vital energy.
Eucalyptus Honey: Healing and protection spells.
Wildflower Honey: Magic relating to beauty, happiness, and love.
Lavender Honey: Grants additional magical powers.
Mānuka Honey: Connects oneself to the divine; Healing.
Pine Honey: Protection; Psychic rejuvenation.

Rosemary Honey: Beauty and love; Healing one's own self; Seeking prophetic revelations.
Thyme Honey: Instilling confidence; Protection.

☾ FOLKLORE AND FACTS
Nearly all fruit- and vegetable-bearing plants are pollinated by bees, the precious flying insects that have been diligently ensuring the growth and ongoing propagation of the food plants that have sustained the people of Earth for many thousands of years. • Honey can be whipped to a creamy consistency and used as a spreadable topping or added to warmed beverages. • If Honey has crystallized in the jar, soften it by putting the jar into a bowl of hot tap water. • Mead, the sweet and inebriating wine made from Honey, dates back 9,000 years and is possibly the oldest fermented beverage. • According to Egyptian mythology, the Sun god, Ra, wept tears that turned into bees that made the first Honey. A honeybee was one of the royal symbols for the pharaohs. Offerings of Honey were made to Min, the Egyptian god of fertility. Jars of perfectly edible honey were found in Tutankhamen's tomb, proving that Honey in a sealed container will not spoil, even after 1,000 years. • In Bangladesh, Honey is given to the Buddhist monks in honor of the Buddha during the Madhu Purnima festival. • On Ikaria island, in the Aegean Sea, most of the elderly residents aged over ninety attribute their longevity to the natural vitamins and minerals from the Ikarian honey they consume by the teaspoon daily. • Honey is one of the five ingredients in the Hindu elixir of immortality. • The ancient Greeks used Honey on their faces for beautification. Many home-facial recipes include other ingredients mixed into Honey. All one really needs to use is the Honey. • The first days after a marriage are called the "honeymoon" because it once followed the sharing of Honey mead between the newlywed couple for one full lunar month. This act was a symbol of love and wisdom that protected the marriage from evil. • To bring two separated things, people, or groups together, write the name of each on two separate pieces of paper and coat the written sides of the papers with Honey, pressing them together with positive thoughts for a successful union. Put the papers on a saucer and place a lit candle on top, allowing the flame to burn until it extinguishes on its own. • Honey is medicinal, used both internally to soothe sore throats and to help calm a cough, especially a nighttime cough. It is also used topically to soften skin or provide an anti-bacterial ointment for a wound. It can be employed as a rooting hormone for plant propagation, by simply dipping the raw end of a stem cutting into the honey just before putting it into the soil. • The Biblical Old Testament's first mention of Honey was in reference to the Promised Land as the "land that flowed with milk and honey."

M

No. 239
Melicoccus bijugatus ⚗

Guinep

Kenèp | Kinnip | Limoncillo | Mamoncillo | Quenepa | Spanish Lime

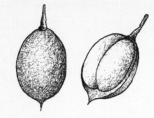

✳ SYMBOLIC MEANING
Soothing calm.

✺ POSSIBLE POWERS
Calming; Sleep.

☾ FOLKLORE AND FACTS
The fruit of the Guinep tree is bittersweet, juicy, and edible. The pulp is often prepared for use in both non-alcoholic and alcoholic beverages. The seed can be roasted and eaten. • The wood of the Guinep tree is used for fine indoor cabinetmaking.

No. 240
Melissa officinalis ⚗

Lemon Balm

Balm Mint | Sweet Melissa

✳ SYMBOLIC MEANINGS
Brings love; Cure; Joke; Pleasantry; Regeneration; Social intercourse; Sympathy; Wishes will be fulfilled.

✺ POSSIBLE POWERS
Feminine energy; Healing; Love; Moon; Success; Water.

☾ FOLKLORE AND FACTS
The fragrant leaves of the Lemon Balm plant are used to brew a pleasantly comforting herbal tea. They can also be used as a flavoring for ice cream, fruit dishes, candies, fish, pasta, and even pickles. Lemon Balm is most usually grown in home gardens. • Elizabethan Londoners would often carry posies of Lemon Balm to sniff throughout the day to mask the stench of unsanitary filth in the streets.

No. 241
Mentha × piperita ⚗

Peppermint

American Mint | Brandy Mint | Vilayati Pudina

✳ SYMBOLIC MEANINGS
Affability; Cordiality; Love; Warmth of feeling.

✺ POSSIBLE POWERS
Air element; Aphrodisiac; Attracts love; Fire element; Healing; Love; Masculine energy; Mercury; Prophetic dreaming; Psychic power; Purification; Sleep.

☾ FOLKLORE AND FACTS
The leaves of the Peppermint plant are edible and can be used fresh or dried. The flowering tops can be used and dried if collected before the blossoms open. Peppermint is brewed as a tea or added to a blend of other herbs. Peppermint extract can be used in baked goods and confections, as well as to flavor alcoholic beverages, flavoring syrup, and chewing gum. Peppermint is the iconic flavor of the red-and-white-striped Christmas candy cane. • Sniff fresh Peppermint leaves to help sleep. • Put Peppermint leaves under the pillow to promote prophetic dreaming. • Peppermint in any area will increase its positive vibrations. • A Peppermint leaf in the wallet encourages money to come to it. • Peppermint essential oil aromatherapy will invigorate the senses. • Tuck Peppermint leaves all over the house to help rid it of negative energy.

M

Mentha spicata ⚱

Spearmint

Common Mint | Garden Mint | Green Mint | Lamb Mint | Lammit | Mackerel Mint |
Our Lady's Mint | Spear Mint | Spire Mint

☀ SYMBOLIC MEANINGS

Burning love; Warm feelings; Warm sentiment;
Warmth of sentiment.

✹ POSSIBLE POWERS

Air element; Aphrodisiac; Attracts love; Enhances sexuality;
Feminine energy; Healing; Humble virtue; Love; Masculine
energy; Mental clarity or power; Mercury; Passion; Venus;
Virtue; Water element.

☾ FOLKLORE AND FACTS

The most flavorful and diverse of
all the mints is *Mentha spicata*
Spearmint. Its fragrance and
flavor are almost sweet.
Spearmint leaves can be used
fresh or dried. To keep the
leaves' aromatic strength
from diminishing,
pinch the flower buds
as soon as they start to
develop. Spearmint leaves can be
dried, candied, frozen in ice, preserved in
oil, sugar syrup, sugar, salt, vodka, or rum,
used in cocktails or sweet tea, placed on a platter or atop a
beverage as a garnish, or rubbed on the wrists and temples
as a natural minty skin fragrance. • Smelling Spearmint is
supposed to sharpen mental power. • Spearmint essential oil
can be helpful as aromatherapy to help alleviate emotional
agitation, sluggish concentration, and tension. • In ancient
Rome and Greece, Spearmint was thought to increase the
desire for lovemaking.

Monarda didyma ⚱

Bee Balm

Bergamot | Crimson Beebalm | Oswego Tea |
Scarlet Bee Balm | Scarlet Beebalm |
Scarlet Monarda | Wild Bergamot

☀ SYMBOLIC MEANINGS

You change your mind
too much; Your whims are
unbearable.

✹ POSSIBLE POWERS

Air element; Feminine energy;
Fire element; Healing; Love;
Mars; Psychic development;
Spiritual development; Success.

☾ FOLKLORE AND FACTS

The edible parts of the Bee Balm plant
are the leaves, which can be brewed for a tea. • After
the rebellious Boston Tea Party, colonists resorted to and
popularized Bee Balm tea as a patriotic substitute for
imported teas. • Bee Balm is believed to bring clarity to
unclear situations and working order to disorderly situations.
• Bee Balm in a love charm will attract romance. • Bee Balm
works well in spells focused on healing disorders of the mind.
• Don't confuse Bee Balm's other common name of Bergamot
with the Bergamot Orange; the only similarity between the
two is their fragrance.

No. 244
Monstera deliciosa ☠

Swiss-Cheese Plant

Balazo | Ceriman | Cheese Plant | Costela de Adão | Costilla de Adán | Fruit Salad Plant | Mexican Breadfruit | Monster Fruit | Monsterio Delicio | Penglai Banana | Piñanona | Plante Gruyère | Split-Leaf Philodendron | Windowleaf

☀ **SYMBOLIC MEANINGS**
Long life; Mates; Monster; Mystery; Suffocation.

✺ **POSSIBLE POWERS**
Feeds on chaotic energy; Harmony; Mental activity; Protection; Self-organization.

☾ **FOLKLORE AND FACTS**
The ripe fruit of the Swiss-Cheese Plant is edible. Its ripened fragrance has been compared to a combination of Pineapple and Banana. • The common names Costilla de Adán and Costela de Adão compare the Swiss-Cheese Plant to the ribs of the first man, Adam, who had a rib taken by God to use in the creation of the first woman, Eve. • The aerial roots of the Swiss-Cheese Plant have been used for basketry in Mexico and rope-making in Peru. • It was believed by some that the Swiss-Cheese Plant's "monster" feeds on chaos and chaotic energy in the household, thereby harmonizing it by removing it entirely.

Morchella esculenta ⚗

True Morel

Common Morel | Morel Mushroom | Sponge Morel | Yellow Morel

☀ **SYMBOLIC MEANING**
Spring.

✺ **POSSIBLE POWERS**
Banishing; Breaks curses; Communicates with the dead; Communicates with fairies; Elevates social status; Increases psychic ability; Prophetic dreams; Protection; Psychic travel between worlds.

☾ **FOLKLORE AND FACTS**
The True Morel, whose surface looks pock-marked, is a prized culinary mushroom that is only edible after it has been cooked by blanching, boiling, sautéing, or baking. True Morels can also be dried in the sun. • There are some who believe that certain fairies will take up residence in the holes of the True Morel mushroom.

No. 246
Moringa oleifera ☠ ⚗

Moringa Tree

Ben Oil Tree | Benzolive Tree | Drumstick Tree | Horseradish Tree | Oil of Ben Tree

☀ **SYMBOLIC MEANING**
Cadence.

✺ **POSSIBLE POWERS**
Health; Nourishment.

☾ **FOLKLORE AND FACTS**
Several parts of the Moringa Tree are edible and commonly consumed in Southeast Asia, such as the flowers, leaves,

immature seed pods, the seeds, and the clear odorless oil that also resists rancidity. The tree's young fruit is shaped like a drumstick with an outer skin that is tough and fibrous. The fruit is usually cut up, then stewed until tender, and has a flavor similar to a sweeter asparagus. The seeds are often fried and eaten as a snack, added to sauces, or used as a condiment. They are also processed for drying and grinding to a nutritional fortifying powder that is added to wheat flour. The leaves are also dried and powdered to make a nutritious dietary supplement that is added to soups, smoothies, sauces, yogurt, soft cheeses, bread, and pastries. • An ancient Egyptian perfume known as *kyphi* included the Moringa Tree's scent-free essential oil. • Moringa Tree oil can be used to help purify water by way of the chemical process that is known as flocculation.

No. 247

Morus nigra ☠ ⚗

Black Mulberry

Black Berry Tree | China Mulberry | *Morus alba* | *Morus rubra* | Red Mulberry | Russian Mulberry | Shahtoot | Silkworm Mulberry | White Mulberry

☀ SYMBOLIC MEANINGS
Devotedness; I shall not survive you; Kindness; Prudence; Strength; Wisdom.

🌀 POSSIBLE POWERS
Air element; Masculine energy; Mercury; Protection.

☾ FOLKLORE AND FACTS
In ancient times, a forest area that was thick with White Mulberry trees was considered the most sacred of all places. Its careful cultivation began in China more than 4,000 years ago, for the specific intention of using the leaves as the preferred food for raising healthy, productive silkworms. • It is the fruit of the Black Mulberry that is the most consumed and used for jam-making, pastry fillings, and sherbets when ripe. Red Mulberry trees are edible raw when they're ripe and used in pastry fillings. The Black, Red, and White Mulberries are all commonly fermented into wine. • Black Mulberry will supposedly protect your property from lightning. • Since Black Mulberry wood is powerfully protective against evil, it makes an excellent wood for a magic wand.

No. 248

Murraya koenigii

Curry Leaf Tree

Curry Bush | Curry Leaves | Curry Tree | Sweet Neem

☀ SYMBOLIC MEANING
Pungent.

🌀 POSSIBLE POWERS
Fire element; Flavor; Health; Healthy; Mars; Masculine energy; Protection.

☾ FOLKLORE AND FACTS
The fresh leaves of the Curry Leaf Tree are edible and are commonly known as "curry leaves," which are a fundamental ingredient in Indian cuisine. They are often used in curries, fried with onions, added to soups, or stewed in sauces.

M

Musa acuminata 'Cavendish' ⚗

Banana

Cavendish Banana | Dessert Banana | Dwarf Cavendish | Manzano Banana | Mysore Banana

✳ SYMBOLIC MEANING
Goodness.

🌀 POSSIBLE POWERS
Brilliance; Education; Feminine energy; Fertility; Money;
Potency; Prosperity; Venus; Water element.

☙ FOLKLORE AND FACTS
The Cavendish Banana is the most commonly cultivated
Banana found in markets around the world. The edible parts
are the fruit as well as the Banana flower or "heart," which
tastes similar to an Artichoke when it is prepared and eaten
as a vegetable. Banana fruit grows in massive heavy clusters
that hang from the top of the plant. A Banana will continue
to ripen after it has been harvested. Banana varieties other
than Cavendish may be yellow, red, purple, or brown. The
ripe fruit is most often eaten freshly peeled out of the hand.
• Sweet dessert Bananas can be used as ingredients in baked
goods, pastries, casseroles, confections, dried and ground to
make a flour, or juiced and fermented for an aromatic liqueur.
The small-fruited Mysore Banana is the most popular in
India. The Manzano Banana is the favorite in Latin America.
• The large Banana leaf is often used much in the same
way that parchment paper or aluminum foil is used for
steaming, grilling, or poaching food. • To be married beneath
any Banana tree is lucky. • Until 1819, in Hawaii certain
species of Banana were so strictly forbidden to women that
the punishment for violating this taboo was death. • In
ceremonial sacrifices to the gods by Tahitians and Hawaiians,
a Banana stalk would be used as a proxy for a human being.
• The leaves, flowers, and
fruit of the Banana tree
are used in money and
prosperity spells because
the Banana tree is such a
fruitful plant and the fruit
turns a golden color.

Musa × paradisiaca ⚗

Plantain Banana

Cooking Banana | Edible Banana | French Banana

✳ SYMBOLIC MEANINGS
Energy; Fertility; Goodness.

🌀 POSSIBLE POWERS
Energy; Fertility; Money;
Potency; Prosperity.

☙ FOLKLORE AND FACTS
The Plantain is a starchy
cooking banana that has a
thicker, tougher skin than any
dessert banana. A Plantain is best
used when it is at its ripest, as indicated
by a very dark peel. At that point it will be sweet
like a banana, but without the characteristic banana-like
flavor of one. • The ripe Plantain can be sliced and deep-
fried, used as an ingredient in casseroles, boiled, broiled,
dried, or ground to make a flour. • There are some scholars
who believe that the Biblical Tree of Life in the Garden of
Eden could have been *Musa × paradisiaca.*

Muscari comosum ⚗

Tassel Hyacinth

Grape Hyacinth | Purse Tassel Hyacinth

✳ SYMBOLIC MEANING
Romantic.

🌀 POSSIBLE POWERS
Flirtation; Romance.

☙ FOLKLORE AND FACTS
In ancient Rome, the bulbs of the Tassel Hyacinth were
cooked and served with olive oil, vinegar, and the fermented
fish sauce known as *garum*. The bulb of the Tassel Hyacinth
is still eaten in Greece and Crete, where it is considered a
delicacy that is prepared by cleaning the bulbs and then
boiling them, changing out the cooking water several
times before discarding the water and pickling the bulbs
by submerging them in olive oil. • Make, then carry a pink
sachet of Tassel Hyacinth to encourage romance. • The bulb
of the Tassel Hyacinth is mentioned as *bulbūsīn* in Hebrew
literature.

No. 252
Myosotis sylvatica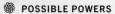

Forget-Me-Not
Mouse Ears | Scorpion-Grass | Woodland Forget-Me-Not

✸ SYMBOLIC MEANINGS
Clinging to the past; Do not forget
me; Faithful love; Faithfulness;
Human desire for loyalty; Humility;
Links to the past; Memories;
Remembering; Remembrances; Shared
secrets; True love.

✿ POSSIBLE POWERS
Healing; Remembrance; Secrecy.

☾ FOLKLORE AND FACTS
The Forget-Me-Not is a symbol of the human desire
for loyalty and shared secrets. • Because of the flower's
resemblance to a mouse's ear, the Forget-Me-Not plant's
genus was given the name *Myosotis*. The flower is edible and
is most often sugar-candied like Violet blossoms are. The
flowers are used as decorations on cakes and pastries.

No. 253
Myrica gale ☠

Sweetgale
Bog Myrtle | Sweet Gale

✸ SYMBOLIC MEANINGS
Discipline; Instruction.

✿ POSSIBLE POWERS
Good fortune; Healing;
Insecticide; Love; Luck;
Money; Stress relief; Venus;
Water element;
Youthfulness.

☾ FOLKLORE AND FACTS
During the Middle Ages and through
to the sixteenth century, Sweetgale
leaves were commonly used in beer making until Hops
began to be preferred. It can also be used as an herbal
additive while fermenting. Sweetgale leaves and nutlets can
be dried and used as a seasoning for flavoring soup. The
leaves can be dried and used to make a tea. • Sweetgale is
completely unsafe for pregnant women. • Carry a small piece
of Sweetgale wood or place it in an amulet to promote a
youthful presence and demeanor. • Make a cap of Sweetgale
leaves to wear upon one's own head while preparing an

important love charm. • Queen Victoria planted a sprig of
Sweetgale at her palace on the Isle of Wight. Years later,
it became a tradition to add a few sprigs from that plant to
royal bridal bouquets. • Sweetgale leaves can be brought
inside a camper's tent for use as an insect repellent.
• Sprinkle crushed Sweetgale bark onto a white candle, then
burn it for good fortune with money.

No. 254
Myrica rubra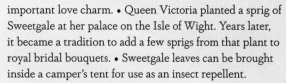

Yangmei
Chinese Bayberry | Japanese Bayberry | Red Bayberry | Yamamomo | Yumberry

✸ SYMBOLIC MEANING
Slow to age.

✿ POSSIBLE POWERS
Anti-aging; Earth element;
Good fortune; Jupiter;
Healing; Health; Luck;
Protection; Yang.

☾ FOLKLORE AND FACTS
The succulent fruit of the
Chinese *Myrica rubra* Yangmei tree is most often eaten
fresh, but it is very often used to make different types of
alcoholic beverages, as well as jam. The fruit can also be
dried and added to recipes. • Yangmei berries are often
soaked in an alcoholic beverage known as *baijiu*. An infusion
of the berries in the *baijiu* is also consumed for medicinal
purposes.

M

No. 255

Myristica fragrans ☠ ⚗

Nutmeg
Mace

☀ **SYMBOLIC MEANING**
Clarity of thought.

🌀 **POSSIBLE POWERS**
Air element; Aphrodisiac; Attracts love; Breaks a hex; Earth element; Fidelity; Fire element; Health; Increases clarity of thought; Intellect; Jupiter; Luck; Masculine energy; Mental power; Mercury; Money; Protection; Psychic power; Purification; Sun.

🌙 **FOLKLORE AND FACTS**
It is the grated or ground seed that is used as a seasoning and is one of the edible parts of the Nutmeg tree. The reddish covering of the seed tastes similar, but is the more delicately flavored seasoning known as Mace. The whole Nutmeg is grated or ground to a powder. Nutmeg and Mace are both used as seasonings to flavor baked goods, pastries, meats, fish, vegetables, fruits, and beverages. • Mace can be burned like incense to purify and consecrate a ritual area, as well as increase one's psychic powers. • Make, then carry a Mace sachet to improve one's intelligence prior to taking exams. • Sprinkle Nutmeg on a lottery ticket for good luck. • Make an amulet of a whole Nutmeg to carry as a good luck charm and to increase clarity of thought. • If you want a lover to be faithful, cut a whole Nutmeg into four pieces. Bury one piece. Burn one piece. Toss one piece off a cliff. Then boil the last piece in water. Drink one very small sip of the water, then carry that boiled quarter piece of Nutmeg with you wherever you go, putting it under your pillow when you sleep.

No. 256

Myroxylon balsamum var. pereirae ☠ ⚗

Balsam of Peru
Balsam Tree | Peru Balsam | Santos Mahogany

☀ **SYMBOLIC MEANING**
Calm.

🌀 **POSSIBLE POWERS**
Aromatic; Healing; Relaxation; Shade.

🌙 **FOLKLORE AND FACTS**
The Balsam of Peru resin is obtained by stripping the bark off the *Myroxylon balsamum* var. *pereirae* tree and wrapping rags around the wounded trunk to soak up the resin. The resin is extracted when the rags are boiled and the fragrant, oily, brown balsam resin sinks to the bottom of the vessel, where it is collected. • One of its many uses is for flavoring a wide range of beverages and foods that include but are not limited to: barbecue sauce, beer, candy, chewing gum, chili sauce, chocolate, vanilla, citrus fruit peel, coffee, cola, flavored teas, gin, ice cream, juice, liqueurs and apéritifs, marmalade, pickled fruits and vegetables, puddings, soft drinks, tomato products, and wine. Needless to say, Balsam of Peru is extremely versatile and immensely useful. • Balsam of Peru's sweet fragrance smells like vanilla with a hint of cinnamon, and it is useful in aromatherapy to calm nervous tension and help promote a tranquil environment in which to relax.

M

No. 257

Myrrhis odorata &

Sweet Cicely

Cicely | Garden Cicely Garden Myrrh

✺ SYMBOLIC MEANING
Gladness.

✾ POSSIBLE POWERS
Abundance; Advancement;
Protection; Psychic vision;
Second sight.

☙ FOLKLORE AND FACTS
The edible leaves of Sweet
Cicely have a flavor that is
similar to Anise and are used
raw or cooked to season food.
The leaves are also used to
flavor liqueur. • Because of its
unsettling similarity between a
few other plants that are deadly
poisonous it should never be
gathered in the wild. To be on
the safe side, if you intend to use
Sweet Cicely, plant this herb in
your own garden. • In Finland,
Sweet Cicely was believed to
offer protection against suddenly
painful invisible arrows aimed
at a human or animal, let loose by a malicious elf or a witch
attacking with foul intent. • Sweet Cicely was once believed
to offer a glimpse of Álfheimr, which is the home of the elves.
Álfheimr is better known as Fairyland. • Make, then wear
a Sweet Cicely sachet to improve the quality and clarity of
psychic visions.

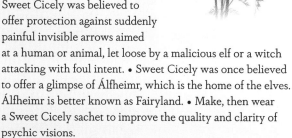

No. 258

Myrtus communis ☠ &

True Myrtle

Common Myrtle | Corsican Pepper |
Myrtus | Sweet Myrtle

✺ SYMBOLIC MEANINGS
Beauty; Chastity; Commitment;
Friendship; Generosity;
Good deeds; Happiness;
Heartfelt love; Honor; Hope;
Immortality; Joy; Justice; Love;
Marriage; Memory of the Garden
of Eden; Mirth; Modest worth;
Money; Peace; Prosperity;
Sacred love; Scent of the
Garden of Eden; Souvenir
of the Garden of Eden; Symbol
of the Garden of Eden;
Weddings; Youth.

✾ POSSIBLE POWERS
Aphrodite; Artemis; Assistance;
Commitment; Feminine energy; Fertility;
Fond memories; Friendship; Harmony;
Hathor; Independence; Love; Material gain; Money;
Peace; Peace of mind; Persistence; Purification; Recovery;
Restoration; Romance; Stability; Strength; Tenacity; Venus;
Water element; Youth.

☙ FOLKLORE AND FACTS
True Myrtle is a sacred plant that symbolizes the Garden of
Eden and its fragrance. Its fruit and leaves are aromatic and
have been used to flavor some Middle Eastern dishes.
• The berries can be a milder-flavored substitute for Juniper
berries. In Sardinia and Corsica, the ripe berries are used to
make a popular liqueur. • According to Arabian traditions,
when Adam was forced to leave the Garden of Eden, he took
with him three plants, one of them being the True Myrtle
so that he could replant it, as it is considered the foremost of
all sweetly scented flowers. • A sprig of True Myrtle from
Queen Victoria's bridal bouquet was planted on the Isle of
Wight. Sprigs from that plant have been included in royal
bridal bouquets up to the present day. • True Myrtle flowers
are used to make an "angel water" cologne. • According to
the Talmudic Jewish tradition, a leafy bough of True Myrtle
is one of the four species of plants tied together to be waved
in the festival of Sukkot. • Sleep on a True Myrtle-filled
pillow to attain peace of mind.

M

No. 259
Nasturtium officinale ⚗

Watercress
Stime | Yellowcress

✺ SYMBOLIC MEANING
Cure of cures.

❂ POSSIBLE POWERS
Aphrodisiac; Attracts love; Fertility; Fire element; Healing; Mars; Mind activity; Moon; Moon magic; Sex magic; Strengthens the conscious mind; Water element.

❀ FOLKLORE AND FACTS
Peppery tasting Watercress is one of the oldest-known, leafy, herbal vegetables in the world. The plant has hollow stems that buoyantly float the plant in water. It is more widely available fresh or packaged by the bunch in grocery stores. The Watercress leaves, stems, and fruit can all be eaten raw. • The ancient Romans believed that Watercress had the power to cure mental illnesses. • Hippocrates is believed to have built the first hospital in Kos, Greece, deliberately near water to grow Watercress for use as a remedy for his patients. • The first commercial cultivation of Watercress intended to be used for consumption was undertaken in 1808 along the River Ebbsfleet in Kent, England. • Watercress was once known as Stime and is one of the Nine Sacred Herbs, written in Wessex, England, around the tenth century, that was often referred to as the "Cure of Cures."

No. 260
Nigella sativa ☠ ⚗

Black Cumin
Black Caraway | Black Onion Seed | Kalonjis

✺ SYMBOLIC MEANING
Listen.

❂ POSSIBLE POWER
Aphrodisiac.

❀ FOLKLORE AND FACTS
The edible part of the Black Cumin plant is the black seeds, which are dry roasted and used as a seasoning in Middle Eastern and Indian cuisine for curries, poultry, vegetables, fruit, breads, cheeses, and mixed spices. • In what is now Turkey, archeologists discovered Black Cumin seeds dating

to the Bronze Age that were inside an ancient Hittite wine flask. Archeologists also found the seeds in the tomb of Pharaoh Tutankhamun.

No. 261
Nymphaea nelumbo ☠ ⚗

Sacred Lotus Root
Indian Lotus | Lotus Lily | Lotus Root | *Nelumbo nucifera*

✺ SYMBOLIC MEANINGS
Beauty; Chastity; Divine female fertility; Eloquence; Enlightened one in a world of ignorant beings; Estranged love; Estrangement; Evolution; Far from the one who is loved; Forgetful of the past; Mere display; Potential; Purity; Resurrection; Spiritual promises; Truth; Virtuous.

❂ POSSIBLE POWERS
Feminine energy; Fertility; Lock-opening; Longevity; Money; Moon; Offspring; Protection; Purity; Sons; Spirituality; Water element.

❀ FOLKLORE AND FACTS
The Sacred Lotus is a sacred plant in Egypt, India, Greece, and Japan, and is considered to be the mystical symbol of life, spirituality, and the center of the universe. Its seeds are edible, as is the rhizome that is crunchy and can be sautéed, stir-fried, deep-fried, pickled, curried, cooked into soups, and fermented into wine. Petals can be brewed as a tea. • In 1995, research biologist Jane Shen-Miller successfully germinated Sacred Lotus seeds that were approximately 1,288 years old. • Several deities of Asian religions are shown sitting upon a Sacred Lotus flower or lotus throne, such as Vishnu, Lakshmi, Brahma, Saraswati, Lakshmi, and Kubera. • The Sacred Lotus is believed to have the power to cultivate people's thoughts, words, and deeds by way of meditation. It is also believed that anyone who breathes in the fragrance of its flower will benefit from the flower's inherent blessings and protection.

N

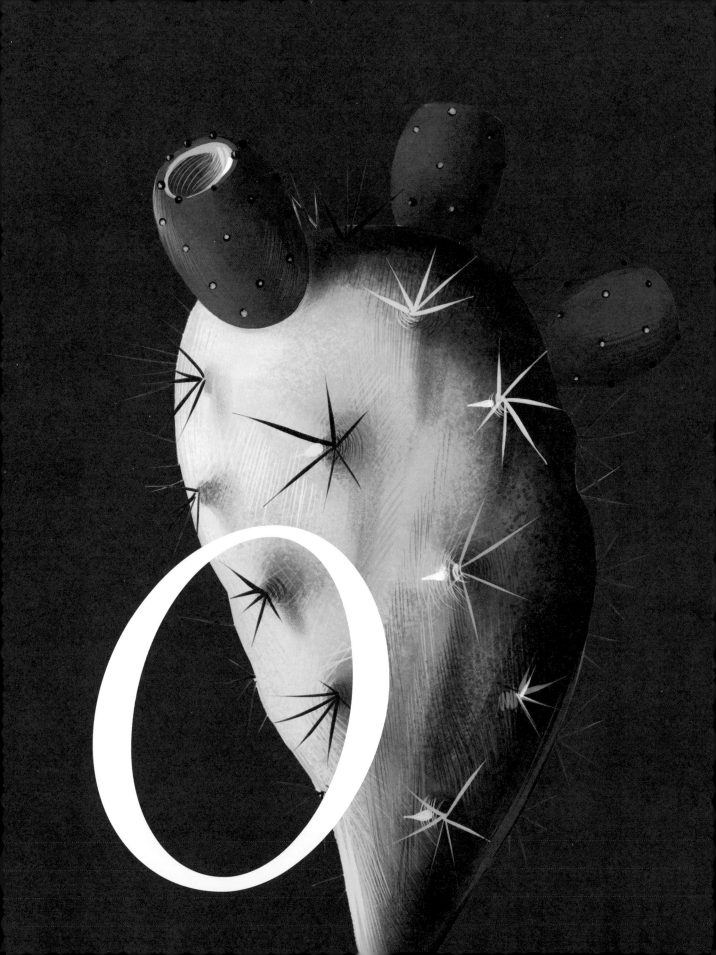

No. 262

Ocimum basilicum ⚗

Basil

Albahaca | Common Basil | Garden Basil | Genovese Basil |
Globe Basil | Great Basil | Herb of Kings | Herbe Royale | Holy Basil |
Ocimum tenuiflorum | Our Herb | Purple Ruffles |
St. Joseph's Wort | Sweet Basil | Sweet Bazil | Tulsi

✸ SYMBOLIC MEANINGS

Best wishes; Give me your
good wishes; Good luck; Good
wishes; Hatred; Hatred of the
other; Kingly; Poverty; Romance;
Royal; Sacred; Wealth.

🌀 POSSIBLE POWERS

Accidents; Aggression;
Anger; Aphrodisiac;
Carnal desire; Clears the
mind; Conflict; Exorcism; Fire element;
Flying; Love; Lust; Machinery; Mars; Masculine energy;
Prosperity; Protection; Relaxation; Rock music; Strength;
Struggle; Vishnu; War; Wealth; Witch flight.

☾ FOLKLORE AND FACTS

Basil is an essential flavoring herb in Mediterranean cuisine.
The edible part of the Basil plant is the leaf, which is used
both fresh and dry, crumbled or ground. Cooking weakens
the intensity of Basil's flavor. Sprigs of fresh Basil can be
kept in a small amount of water that is changed daily. • The
ancient Greeks considered Basil to be a strong symbol of
hate, misfortune, and poverty. • Carry a Basil leaf in one's
pocket to bring in money. • In several parts of the world,
Basil is placed around shops, in cash registers, and under
computers to attract customers. • In Italy, Basil is a symbol
and token of love. • Giving a sprig of Basil to a man means,
"Be wary, for someone is plotting against you." • In Spain,
a pot of Basil on a windowsill indicated a house of ill repute.
• The fragrance of Basil can soothe mutual hot tempers.
• Sprinkle Basil at the front of the building before
entering for a job interview. • Basil essential oil is useful
in aromatherapy to clear groggy dull feelings and sluggish
reasoning, and for relaxing the mind at the end of a long,
stressful, chaotic day. • In India, *Ocimum tenuiflorum* Basil is
sacred and is known as Tulsi and Holy Basil.

No. 263

Ocimum basilicum var. *thyrsiflora* ⚗

Thai Basil

Cinnamon Basil

✸ SYMBOLIC MEANINGS

Best wishes; Give me your good wishes; Good luck; Good
wishes; Hatred; Hatred of the other; Kingly; Poverty;
Romance; Royal; Sacred; Wealth.

🌀 POSSIBLE POWERS

Accidents; Aggression; Anger; Aphrodisiac; Carnal desire;
Clears the mind; Conflict; Exorcism; Flying; Love; Lust;
Machinery; Money; Prosperity; Protection; Relaxation; Rock
music; Strength; Struggle; War; Wealth; Witch Flight.

☾ FOLKLORE AND FACTS

The fragrant, cinnamon-licorice-anise flavor of fresh Thai
Basil leaf is enough to make it a staple used in Thai curries,
seafood, pork, and chicken dishes. • It is believed by some
that if a sprig of Thai Basil is placed in a prospective lover's
hand and it immediately withers, it is a sign of promiscuity.

No. 264

Oenothera biennis ☠ ⚗

Evening Primrose

Common Evening Primrose |
German Rampion | Weedy Evening Primrose

✸ SYMBOLIC MEANINGS

Eternal love; Happy love;
Inconstancy; Love; Memory;
Silent love; Youth.

🌀 POSSIBLE POWERS

Attracts fairies; Attracts love; Earth element;
Feminine energy; Increases desirability;
Reveals one's inner beauty; Venus.

☾ FOLKLORE AND FACTS

The leaves of the Evening Primrose can be eaten raw in
a salad, added to soups, or cooked like spinach. The roots
can be prepared like a potato and cooked by soaking and
boiling. The stems can be peeled and sautéed. However,
it is the flower buds that are a delicacy, picked then either
eaten raw, added to salads or soups, sautéed, or pickled. A
flower blossom can be used as a garnish. • The Evening
Primrose will bloom just after the sun sets, filling the air
with its vanilla-like fragrance. • The blooming of Evening
Primrose flowers was such a pleasant spectacle that, during

the Renaissance, evening revelers and theater-goers would hesitate to leave their gardens to attend their events until after the flowers in their own gardens had bloomed for the night. • Plant Evening Primrose to attract fairies.

No. 265

Olea europaea 🪔

Olive
Common Olive

🟐 **SYMBOLIC MEANINGS**
Abundance; Fertility; Friendship; Glory; Holiness; Peace; Power; Purity; Sacredness; Wisdom.

🌱 **COMPONENT MEANING**
Leaf: Peace.

🌀 **POSSIBLE POWERS**
Abundance; Air element; Apollo; Benediction; Bond friendship; Fertility; Fire element; Healing; Irene; Lust; Masculine energy; Peace; Potency; Protection; Purification; Ra; Sun.

🌑 **FOLKLORE AND FACTS**
The Olive tree is one of the first plants mentioned in the Bible's Book of Genesis. • The Quran mentions the Olive tree and its oil seven times. • In the countries around the Mediterranean Sea, there are some 3,500-year-old trees still producing fruit. • In Mediterranean cuisine, the Olive is used for its fragrant oil, green, semi-ripe Olives, and ripe table Olives. • Raw unprocessed Olives are inedible but not toxic. • The color of the Olive indicates its ripeness when it was picked, turning from green to black. Most canned "ripe olives" found on grocery store shelves are not ripe, having been chemically cured to turn the skins shiny black. • Some traditional methods of extracting Olive oil dates back thousands of years. • The first cold pressing is "extra virgin," which is preferred for sautéing and for salads or other foods that can be consumed cold. • The flavors of different Olive oils vary, and are thoughtfully evaluated like wine. • Olive leaves can be dried and powdered, and also brewed as a tea. • Olive oil is used in the sacred rituals of several religions, anointing blessings and healings, as well as consecrating monarchs. • According to Jewish law, the Olive is one of the Seven Species that requires a blessing before eating. • The eternal flame at the original Olympic Games in Greece was fed by Olive oil. • Scatter Olive leaves to create a vibration of peace.

No. 266

Ophrys apifera 🪔

Bee Orchid
Bee Orphrys | Bumblebee Flower | Bumblebee Ophrys | Bumblebee Orchid | Eyebrow Orchid | Fly Ophrys | Fly Orchid | *Ophrys bombyliflora* | *Ophrys insectifera*

🟐 **SYMBOLIC MEANINGS**
Error; Hard work; Industry; Mistake.

🌀 **POSSIBLE POWERS**
Aphrodisiac; Attracts love; Decoy; Energy; Feminine energy; Healing; Health; Mimicry; Sustenance; Venus; Water element.

🌑 **FOLKLORE AND FACTS**
The roots of the Bee Orchid, the Bumblebee Orchid, and the Fly Orchid are sources of "salep," which is a fine, whitish powder that is made by grinding these dried orchid tubers. One part salep to fifty parts water will make a jelly. It is believed that one ounce of the powdered salep jelly can sustain and energize a person for a full day.

No. 267

Opuntia ficus-indica

Prickly Pear
Barbary Fig | Cactus Pear | Fig Opuntia | Indian Fig Opuntia | Nopales | Paddle Cactus

🟐 **SYMBOLIC MEANINGS**
Did not forget; I burn; Satire.

🌀 **POSSIBLE POWERS**
Colorize; Fire element; Healing; Mars; Repair; Softening; Transformation.

🌑 **FOLKLORE AND FACTS**
The raw fruit of the Prickly Pear has one of the highest concentrations of vitamin C. The paddles are skinned or left unskinned, cut into strips, then cooked as a dish known as *nopalitos*. Cooked strips of Prickly Pear, along with the fruit, can be blended into smoothies, prepared with chicken, or added to tacos. The fruit is also made into jams and jellies. In Mexico the fruits are made into a type of wine known as *colonche*. • To protect the home, plant four Prickly Pear plants outside to face each of the four cardinal directions. • A Prickly Pear spine can be used as a stylus for writing magical words or symbols on wax as well as upon vegetables, fruits, or herbs, such as on an onion or an apple. • There is ongoing research into the possibility of using Prickly Pear as a biodegradable substitute for plastic.

No. 268

Origanum majorana

Marjoram

Knotted Marjoram | Sweet Marjoram

✹ SYMBOLIC MEANINGS

Blushes; Comfort; Consolation; Happiness; Joy; Love.

🌀 POSSIBLE POWERS

Air element; Aphrodite; Happiness; Health; Longevity; Love; Masculine energy; Mercury; Money; Protection; Soothes anxiety; Soothes grief; Venus.

☾ FOLKLORE AND FACTS

Although Marjoram spread throughout the British Isles after seeds were believed to have been brought there during the Middle Ages, the herb was not used very much in the USA until after WWII. By then, Marjoram leaves were beginning to be added to herbal tea as well as into soups, stews, sauces, and salad dressings. • It is thought that if someone rubs Marjoram on themselves before falling asleep, he or she will dream of their future spouse. • Ancient Greeks believed Marjoram grew over the grave of a dead person who was happy. • Ancient Greeks and Romans would make Marjoram crowns for marrying couples to wear as symbols of love, happiness, and honor. • When feeling under the weather, Marjoram essential oil may provide comforting aromatherapy and relaxation to facilitate sleep.

No. 269

Origanum vulgare

Oregano

Wild Marjoram

✹ SYMBOLIC MEANINGS

Brilliant joy of the mountain; Good luck; Happiness; Joy; Soothing; Will banish sadness.

🌀 POSSIBLE POWERS

Air element; Good health; Good luck; Happiness; Joy; Mercury; Prophetic dreaming; Protection; Protection against poison; Purification; Repels evil; Reveals the mystical secrets for using black magic.

☾ FOLKLORE AND FACTS

Oregano is considered to be the herb of all herbs, liberally added to Mediterranean and Middle Eastern cuisine via soups, stews, sauces, and salad dressings. The top-note aroma that perfumes an Italian restaurant is that of Oregano. • The ancient Greeks believed that the goddess Aphrodite created and grew Oregano in her garden atop Mount Olympus. • Ancient Greeks would sometimes wear an Oregano crown while they slept for psychic purposes and with the hope of having prophetic dreams. • Put Oregano under the pillow to encourage pleasant dreams. • Place a nosegay of Oregano at a grave as a wish for the peaceful journey of the deceased spirit while transitioning to the afterlife. • Oregano essential oil is not intended for use in food, but it can be used for household cleaning.

No. 270

Oryza sativa

Rice

Asian Rice | Brown Rice | Indica Rice | Japonica Rice | *Oryza sativa* subsp. *indica* | *Oryza sativa* subsp. *japonica* | Sinica Rice

✹ SYMBOLIC MEANINGS

Fertility; Remembrance.

🌀 POSSIBLE POWERS

Air element; Close family; Family; Fertility; Fidelity; Link between Earth and Heaven; Luck; Masculine energy; Money; Prosperity; Protection; Rain; Sun; Wealth.

☾ FOLKLORE AND FACTS

The edible part of the Rice plant is the seed grain. Rice is available as whole grain unhulled Brown Rice or as processed White Rice. The short-grained, sticky variety of Rice is Japonica, while the long-grained, non-sticky variety is Indica. Rice can be boiled, steamed, or baked with liquid to absorb and expand the grain. • Rice used to be tossed at a newly married couple to increase their fertility. • Toss Rice onto the roof to protect a house against misfortune. • A few grains of Rice in a saltshaker will keep the salt from clumping. • One way to wish for money is, before adding the water to cook whole grain Brown Rice, use your finger to draw a dollar sign in the Rice first.

O

No. 271

Pachyrhizus erosus ☠🥣

Jicama
Mexican Potato | Mexican Turnip |
Spanish Jicama | Yam Bean

✴ SYMBOLIC MEANING
Thick.

🌀 POSSIBLE POWERS
Assumes challenges; Emotional
connection; Intuition; Love; Sense of
connection to the universe.

☘ FOLKLORE AND FACTS
Evidence of Jicama has been found at several Peruvian
archeological sites that date back to 3000 BCE. • All parts of
the Jicama plant are poisonous except for the tuber root,
which is crunchy with a starchy texture and a sweet, zingy
flavor that is somewhat like an Apple. It can be eaten raw or
cooked by sautéing, stir-frying, adding it to soups, or grated
and added as an ingredient in savory vegetable or meat pies.
• Jicama tubers can be as large as six feet long and weigh up
to forty-four pounds. In 2010, the largest Jicama root was dug
up in the Philippines and was revealed to weigh just over
fifty pounds.

No. 272

Palmaria palmata 🥣

Dulse
Dillisk | Dilsk | Red Dulse | *Rhodymenia palmata* |
Sea Lettuce Flakes | Söl

✴ SYMBOLIC MEANINGS
Harmonious; Lustfulness;
Two coming together.

🌀 POSSIBLE POWERS
Harmony; Lust; Moon; Moon
magic; Sea magic; Water
element; Water magic.

☘ FOLKLORE AND FACTS
On Iona, in Scotland, early Christian monks harvested
the red algae known as Dulse 1,500 years ago. • Dulse is a
favorite food in Iceland, where it is called *söl* and has been
eaten with butter for hundreds of years. It is also added
to soups and stews, and is an ingredient in breadmaking,
casseroles, salads, fish and meat dishes, sandwiches,
flatbreads, pasta, and snacks. • Throw Dulse into the waves
as an offering when working sea magic rituals.

No. 273

Panax quinquefolius ☠🥣

Ginseng
American Ginseng | Asian Ginseng | Chinese Ginseng | Ginseng | Korean Ginseng

✴ SYMBOLIC MEANINGS
Immortality; Strength.

🌀 POSSIBLE POWERS
Aphrodisiac; Attracts love; Beauty;
Fire element; Healing; Longevity;
Love; Lust; Masculine energy;
Protection; Sexual healing;
Sexual potency; Wishing;
Yang stimulation (Asian
Ginseng); Yin (American
Ginseng).

☘ FOLKLORE AND FACTS
Freshly slivered, grated, or dried then powdered Ginseng
root can be added to teas, soups, stir-fries, and baked goods.
• Most of the American Ginseng harvested in North America
is exported to Asia, where it is considered to be of the quality
sought, as it is appreciated for its use in traditional Chinese
and other folk medicine treatments. • Both American
Ginseng and Asian Ginseng will bring beauty, love, money,
sexuality, and health to all who carry it. • An interesting way
to make a wish is to carve it into a Ginseng root, then throw
it into running water, which will carry the wish to where it
needs to go.

No. 274

Pandanus edulis

Bakong
Knob-Fruited Screwpine

✴ SYMBOLIC MEANINGS
Comfort; Devotion.

🌀 POSSIBLE POWERS
Protection; Protection from the elements.

☘ FOLKLORE AND FACTS
The fruit of the Bakong tree looks like a perfectly round
Pineapple fruit hanging prettily from a fancy palm tree. In
Guam and the Philippines, the flesh of the fruit is cooked
and eaten. • The seeds can be eaten and taste like coconut.
• The leaves of the Bakong are commonly harvested for use
in making handicrafts and weaving mats. The root fibers are
made into twine. • Fold, then tuck a Bakong leaf into a sachet
to wear or carry for personal protection.

No. 275

Papaver somniferum ☠ ⚗

Opium Poppy

Breadseed Poppy | Poppyseed

✺ SYMBOLIC MEANINGS

Avoidance of problems;
Consolation; Ephemeral charms;
Eternal rest; Eternal sleep; Fun-
loving; Good and evil; Imagination;
Life and death; Light and darkness;
Love; Oblivion; Pleasure;
Remembrance.

✺ POSSIBLE POWERS

Ambition; Attitude; Clear thinking;
Fertility; Fruitfulness; Harmony; Higher understanding;
Invisibility; Logic; Love; Luck; Magic; Manifestation in
material form; Money; Moon; Sleep; Spiritual concepts;
Thought processes; Water element.

☾ FOLKLORE AND FACTS

The same poppyseeds that are readily sold in grocery stores
and are used on bread and other baked goods come from
the *Papaver somniferum* Opium Poppy. • Up to ninety
percent of the morphine content is removed from the Opium
Poppy seeds when they are processed in the United States.
However, a residue might possibly be left on the seeds when
they are processed in other countries. • The ancient Romans
believed that Opium Poppy seeds could heal wounds
inflicted by hurtful love. • Write a question on a piece of
paper. Fold it and tuck it into a sachet with Opium Poppy
seeds, then sleep with it under the pillow to dream an answer
to the question.

No. 276

Passiflora edulis ☠ ⚗

Passionflower

Golden Passionfruit | Guavadilla | Maracujá | Maypop | Parcha | *Passiflora incarnata* | Passion
Vine | Purple Passionflower | Purple Passionfruit | True Passionflower | Wild Apricot

✺ SYMBOLIC MEANINGS

Faith; Faith and suffering; I have no claims; Piety; Primeval
nature; Unpretentious; Yearning for a long-lost paradise; You
have no claims.

✺ POSSIBLE POWERS

Calm anxiety; Feminine energy; Friendships' prosperity;
Increases libido; Moon; Peace; Peacefulness; Sleep; Venus;
Water element.

☾ FOLKLORE AND FACTS

Passionflower fruit is a botanical berry that is cultivated
for its sweet fruit that needs to be fully ripe before eating
fresh, scooping out the gelatinous seedy pulp with a spoon
or preparing the pulp for use as a beverage, jam, tea, or
pastry filling. • The Passionflower has its own legend and
was used as an early visual teaching aid to explain the
Christian gospel and Christ's suffering before there were any
printed materials. • Use a small, clear, glass bowl to float a
Passionflower blossom in water for a blessing of peace and to
promote some peacefulness
in your life. • Put a
Passionflower leaf
under the pillow
for restful sleep.

No. 277

Pastinaca sativa

Parsnip

All-American Parsnip | Harris Model Parsnip |
Hollow Crown Parsnip | Kral Russian Parsnip |
Parsnip Herb | Parsnip Root

✸ SYMBOLIC MEANING
Life's energy.

✱ POSSIBLE POWERS
Aphrodisiac; Attraction; Energizing.

☾ FOLKLORE AND FACTS
The carrot-like, mildly lemony-tasting edible taproot of the
Parsnip plant will become sweeter after a winter frost. The
Parsnip can be enjoyed raw or cooked, so prepare, use, and
cook Parsnip by adding to soups or stews, baking, boiling,
puréeing, roasting, frying, grilling, steaming, mashing,
fermenting it into a wine, or using it as an ingredient in
other dishes. • It was once believed that eating Parsnips will
awaken the sleeping libido. • If you did not plant Parsnips
from seed in your own garden or buy Parsnips at the grocer,
do not be tempted to harvest "wild parsnip," which is better
known as the "poison parsnip plant," "water hemlock," or
"cowbane."

No. 278

Paullinia cupana ☠ ⚗

Guaraná

Brazilian Cocoa

✸ SYMBOLIC MEANING
Eyes of the gods.

✱ POSSIBLE POWERS
Aphrodisiac; Stimulation.

☾ FOLKLORE AND FACTS
The seeds of the *Paullinia cupana* Guaraná plant have been
processed in Brazil since 1905 and are the basis for flavoring
highly caffeinated beverages that are frequently consumed
like coffee. • According to a legend originating with the
indigenous people of Brazil, a deity had killed a child whom
all the villagers loved. The villagers were inconsolable, so a
kinder deity plucked out the deceased child's left eye then
planted it deep within the center of the jungle to grow wild
Guaraná. He planted the right eye in the village where
everyone could see it, to grow domesticated Guaraná. • Put a
dried Guaraná seed or powder in a pouch and keep it on the
desk to keep the eyes and the mind on the task at hand.

No. 279

Pelargonium graveolens ☠ ⚗

Rose-Scented Geranium

Apple Geranium | Apple Pelargonium | Old Fashion
Rose Geranium | *Pelargonium odoratissimum* |
Pelargonium radens | Rasp-Leaf Pelargonium |
Rose-scent Geranium | Scented Geranium | Storksbill

✸ SYMBOLIC MEANINGS
Balance; Calm; Folly; Gentility;
Happiness; I prefer you;
Preference; Present preference;
Spiritual happiness; Stork.

✱ POSSIBLE POWERS
Acceptance; Alleviates the negativity that stress instigates;
Balances opposing energies within; Balances the mind; Calm;
Eases anxiety; Feminine energy; Fertility; Happiness; Health;
Love; Moves past indecision; Opens the chakras; Prosperity;
Protection; Purification; Restores balance; Smoothing
coarseness; Venus; Water element.

☾ FOLKLORE AND FACTS
The fragrant leaves of the Rose-Scented Geranium, Apple
Geranium, and Rasp-Leaf Pelargonium are edible and can be
used as a flavoring in fruit jellies and herbal teas. The flowers
can be used to flavor vodka. • Rose-Scented Geranium
essential oil for aromatherapy is spiritually uplifting in times
of stress, agitation, aggravation, and sadness. • The Apple
Geranium's essential oil has an apple-scented fragrance
helpful in alleviating some effects of anxiety and depression.
• When life has issues that feel too rough to handle, the
Rasp-Leaf Pelargonium can help smooth them out enough to
manage.

No. 280

Perilla frutescens var. crispa ☠ ⚱

Shiso

Beefsteak Plant | Chinese Basil |
Japanese Basil | Perilla Mint | Perilla
Sesame | Purple Perilla | Red Shiso |
Red-Leaf Shiso | Tía Tô

✴ SYMBOLIC MEANING

Meaning of meaning.

✺ POSSIBLE POWERS

Fire element; Healing; Perfumery;
Reawakens courage; Reconnects to life; Sun.

☙ FOLKLORE AND FACTS

The first mention of Shiso in writing was around 500 CE.
Smooth or ruffled, green, red, or bi-colored, the Shiso
plant's leaf is a common ingredient, seasoning herb, and
condiment in Japanese cooking of all kinds. This includes
the use of either fresh leaves or dried and pulverized flakes
in beverages, pickling, sushi, and tempura. Shiso buds and
blossoms are also pickled as well as used as a garnish.

No. 281

Persea americana ☠

Avocado

Abacate | Alligator Pear | Butter Fruit | Butter Pear |
Haas Avocado | Persea Testicle Tree

✴ SYMBOLIC MEANINGS

Love; Relationship; Romance;
Sexual romance.

✺ POSSIBLE POWERS

Aphrodisiac; Attracts
love; Beauty; Feminine
energy; Fertility;
Love; Lust; Sex
magic; Sexual vigor;
Venus; Water element.

☙ FOLKLORE AND FACTS

An Avocado seed dating from between 9,000 and 10,000
years ago was discovered in the Coxcatlan Cave in Puebla,
Mexico. The first time the word "avocado" was recorded
in English was in an index of Jamaican plants written in
1696. The fruit-like berry Avocado is edible and will not
ripen until after it has been removed from the tree. It is
better to purchase a hard underripe Avocado and ripen

it to the desired softness at home, than to buy a softer
Avocado and wait another day to eat it. • Avocado oil and
olive oil have similar monounsaturated fat profiles. Both
unrefined and refined Avocado oil can be safely heated for
high-heat cooking that includes stir-frying. • To grow an
Avocado plant in the house from the seed of a fruit that you
have consumed will bring love into the home. • A magic
wand made from Avocado tree wood is believed to be very
powerful for any reason.

No. 282

Petroselinum crispum

⚱

Parsley

Curly Leaf Parsley | Flat-leaf Parsley | French Parsley |
Garden Parsley | Hamburger Parsley | Italian Parsley |
Leaf Parsley | Rock Parsley | Root Parsley

✴ SYMBOLIC MEANINGS

Bring love; Death; Evil; Festivity;
Fickleness; Love.

✺ POSSIBLE POWERS

Air element; Aphrodisiac; Attracts love; Attraction;
Business transactions; Caution; Cleverness; Communication;
Creativity; Faith; Illumination; Initiation; Intelligence;
Learning; Love; Lust; Masculine energy; Memory; Mercury;
Persephone; Protection; Purification; Science; Self-
preservation; Sound judgment; Thievery; Wisdom.

☙ FOLKLORE AND FACTS

Parsley has been cultivated since 300 BCE. It is widely used
in American, Mediterranean, Middle Eastern, and Brazilian
cuisine where it is added to pasta, rice, fish, poultry, meat,
casseroles, stews, soups, salads, fillings, stuffings, vegetable
dishes, fruit salads, and anything else someone can think
of adding Parsley to, either fresh or dried. • Parsley was
valuable to witches because it was believed that it went to
the Underworld nine times and back again before sprouting.
• In medieval times, it was believed that to pluck a sprig of
Parsley while speaking an enemy's name had the power to
kill. • Ancient Romans were leery of Parsley because they
considered it evil, although they still hid a sprig on or under
their clothing daily for protection against evil. • The ancient
Greeks used Parsley in their funeral rituals commonly
enough that an impending death was spoken of as having a
need for Parsley.

No. 283

Phaseolus coccineus

Scarlet Runner Bean

Runner Bean

SYMBOLIC MEANING

Pretty red bean.

POSSIBLE POWERS

Death and rebirth; Foolishness; Poverty; Saturn; Sexuality; Souls of the dead; Venus.

FOLKLORE AND FACTS

Most commonly red-flowered with multicolored seeds as well as attractively ornamental, the Scarlet Runner Bean plant is perennial in all but the colder zones, where it is grown as an annual. It is believed to have been originally cultivated in Mexico in 2000 BCE. The seeds are edible after they have been soaked overnight then thoroughly cooked until they are tender. Scarlet Runner Beans are used in many cuisines as both a side dish and as an ingredient in soups, stews, and casseroles. After cooking, the young pods are edible. The variety with white flowers and white beans is protected in Greece, where it is an important ingredient in Greek cuisine. • The scarlet flowers are a favorite of hummingbirds.

No. 284

Phaseolus lunatus ☠

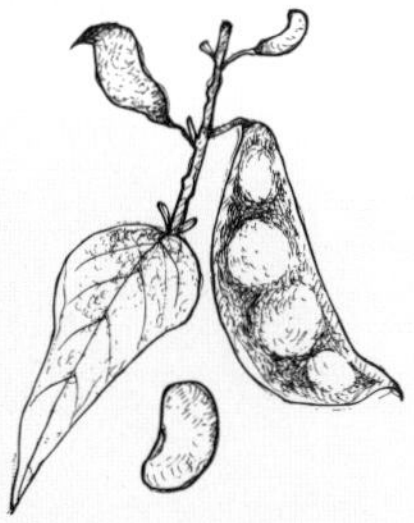

Lima Bean

Sieva Bean | Madagascar Bean

SYMBOLIC MEANINGS

Messengers; Warriors.

POSSIBLE POWERS

Conflict; Messages; Power.

FOLKLORE AND FACTS

The Lima Bean is one of the oldest beans, dating back in both North and South America to around 6000 BCE. In ancient Peru, the Lima Bean was a food reserved for the rulers of their culture. • The raw or undercooked Lima Bean seeds are toxic until they have been thoroughly cooked to tender before eating. After soaking dried Lima Beans overnight to the point that the skins soften so much they can be slipped off, the Lima Beans will cook faster and disintegrate into creamy silkiness that can be used in a favorite recipe for soup, sauce, or even a dessert. • To resolve differences that resulted in an argument, for two days a couple should carry around three Lima Beans that have been strung on a silk thread.

No. 285

Phaseolus vulgaris ☠

Beans

Anasazi Bean | Appaloosa Bean | Black Turtle Bean | Borlotti Bean | Boston Bean | Calypso Bean | Canary Bean | Cannellini Bean | Cranberry Bean | Dragon Tongue Bean | Flageolet Bean | French Bean | Haricot Bean | Kidney Bean | Navy Bean | Pea Bean | Pearl Haricot Bean | Pink Bean | Pinto Bean | White Bean | White Kidney Bean | White Pea Bean

SYMBOLIC MEANINGS

Determination; Healing; Love; Phallic; Reincarnation; Resurrection; Strength; Wisdom.

POSSIBLE POWERS

Deters evil; Divination; Exorcism; Love; Potency; Protection; Reconciliation; Wart charming.

FOLKLORE AND FACTS

All varieties of *Phaseolus vulgaris* plant seeds or "beans" are toxic when raw, dried, or undercooked. The seeds can be made edible after they have been thoroughly soaked, with the water replaced before cooking, then cooked until completely tender. Beans are used in individual dishes, added to soups and stews, and can also be used as an ingredient in casseroles. • Particularly in the Far East, scattered Bean flowers are thought to appease demons. • English tradition associates Beans with death if one bean in a pod is white instead of green. • A common European divination that was done with Beans is to hide three pods: one untouched for wealth, one half-peeled for comfort, and one fully peeled for poverty. Whichever pod the inquirer finds first foretells their future. • Red Beans are indigenous to the Americas, with each tribe having their own names and folk stories for them. The Native Americans used Red Beans as goods worthy of meaningful trade. • In the Middle Ages, a witch's powers were nullified if one were to spit a mouthful of Beans at the witch's face. • Carry a dried Bean as an amulet against evil magic and negativity.

No. 286

Phoenix dactylifera 🝕

Date

Date Palm | Deġlet Noor | Halawy | Medjool | Thoory

☀ **SYMBOLIC MEANINGS**

Prosperity; Triumph; Victory.

🌀 **POSSIBLE POWERS**

Air element; Apollo;
Artemis; Fertility;
Isis; Masculine
energy; Potency;
Ra; Spirituality;
Strength; Sun.

🌛 **FOLKLORE AND FACTS**

The Date tree's fruit will
continue ripening after it
has been picked. Dates can
be dried, ground, and even
brewed like coffee. Dates are
eaten out of hand, stuffed, added to a wide variety of sweet
and savory dishes, made into a paste, pressed and turned into
syrup, dried and powdered into "date sugar," juiced, made
into wine and liqueur, and also transformed into vinegar.
• In some parts of the world, the Date palm has been grown
for over 48,000 years. • In ancient Mesopotamia, date wine
and syrup were both considered to be sacred foods. • A
2,000-year-old *Phoenix dactylifera* Date palm seed, found
in Israel during the excavation of Masada in the mid-1960s,
successfully sprouted after being planted. • Carry a Date
seed to regain waning or lost virility.

No. 287

Phragmites australis ☠ 🝕

Reed Grass

Common Reed

☀ **SYMBOLIC MEANINGS**

Folly; Indiscretion; Music;
Musical voice; Single
blessedness.

🌀 **POSSIBLE POWERS**

Creativity; Inspiration;
Music.

🌛 **FOLKLORE AND FACTS**

The new young shoots of the
Phragmites australis Reed Grass

plant can be eaten raw or cooked. The seeds can be cooked
with water and berries to make a gruel. Reed Grass roots
are prepared and cooked in the same way as cattail root
would be. • The hollow stems of Reed Grass can be made
into a drinking straw. • Reed Grass is a useful herb for
thatching a roof that can last for one hundred years. • At
one time, inexpensive pens for writing and drawing on
parchment paper were cut from Reed Grass stems.

No. 288

Phyllanthus emblica ☠ 🝕

Amla

Amalaki | India Gooseberry | Indian Gooseberry | Malacca Tree | Myrobalan Plum

☀ **SYMBOLIC MEANINGS**

Enlightenment; Sustainer.

🌀 **POSSIBLE POWERS**

Abundance; Enlightenment; Healing; Powerful healing;
Prosperity.

🌛 **FOLKLORE AND FACTS**

The fruit of the Amla tree is edible and can be eaten raw,
cooked, or added into other dishes such as daal. • One
dish, called *amle ka murabbah*, is a sweet dessert made by
soaking the Amla berries in a sugary syrup, candying them.
• The Amla fruit is referenced in the *Ashokavadana*, where,
according to legend, half of an Amla fruit was the last gift by
the emperor, Ashoka the Great, to a Buddhist community
of religious devotees, monks, and nuns. • The Amla tree's
bark can be peeled off into thin flakes and used to make an
amulet or a sachet that can be carried to heal any malady
of body, mind, or spirit. • Tie together a small bundle of
Amla leafy twigs using a gold string or ribbon. Put
this talisman in a place of honor near
the center of the house to radiate
beneficial physical, mental,
and spiritual energy to all
within the home.

No. 289

Physalis philadelphica ⚱

Tomatillo

Jitomate | Large-flowered Tomatillo | Mexican Groundcherry | Mexican Husk Tomato

✸ **SYMBOLIC MEANING**

Little tomato.

✺ **POSSIBLE POWERS**

Aphrodite; Feminine energy; Hera; Love; Romance; Venus.

☾ **FOLKLORE AND FACTS**

The papery husk around a tart green Tomatillo fruit is inedible, although the fruit itself can be eaten either raw or cooked. • The Tomatillo is very often used to make a green sauce known as *salsa verde*. The varieties that will ripen to purple or red are sweeter for use in jams. • Whole or sliced Tomatillos can be frozen. They can be used in salads, stir-fried, cooked with meats, made into desserts, and added to soups, stews, and curries.
• The Tomatillo and the tomato are not related.

No. 290

Pimenta dioica

Allspice

Clove Pepper | Jamaica Pepper | Jamaican Pepper | Myrtle Pepper | Newspice

✸ **SYMBOLIC MEANINGS**

Compassion; Languishing; Love; Luck.

✺ **POSSIBLE POWERS**

Accidents; Aggression; Anger; Carnal desire; Conflict; Finding treasure; Fire element; Healing; Looking for hidden treasure; Love; Luck; Lust; Machinery; Mars; Masculine energy; Money; Rock music; Strength; Struggle; Treasure hunting; War.

☾ **FOLKLORE AND FACTS**

The unripe dried fruit of the *Pimenta dioica* tree is Allspice. The edible parts of the tree are the fruit berry and the leaf, which can be used in the same way as Bay Laurel leaf. Allspice received its name around 1621 because the berry tastes like a combination of clove, cinnamon, and nutmeg, which were all the important spices in those days. Allspice is used in both sweet and savory dishes and is a common ingredient in Caribbean, Mexican, North American, European, and Middle Eastern savory and sweet recipes. In areas where *Pimenta dioica* trees grow, the wood is used for smoking meat. • Christopher Columbus encountered *Pimenta dioica* trees on his second New World voyage.
• When searching for treasure, wear an Allspice sachet as an amulet to assist in the hunt.
• Allspice essential oil is often added to a light carrier oil to give it an exotic warm fragrance when used for massage.

No. 291

Pimpinella anisum ⚲

Anise

Aniseed | Anix | Pimpinella

☀ SYMBOLIC MEANINGS

Restoration of youth;
Spiritual restoration of
youthful exuberance and
confidence.

🌀 POSSIBLE POWERS

Air element;
Aphrodisiac; Attracts
love; Business; Business
transactions; Calls on
good spirits; Caution; Cleverness;
Communication; Creativity; Expansion;
Faith; Honor; Illumination; Initiation; Intelligence; Jupiter;
Leadership; Learning; Masculine energy; Memory; Politics;
Power; Protection; Prudence; Psychic ability; Public acclaim;
Purification; Repels evil; Responsibility; Royalty; Science;
Self-preservation; Sleep; Sound judgment; Success; Thievery;
Wards off the evil eye; Wealth; Wisdom.

☾ FOLKLORE AND FACTS

The Anise plant has been a crop in Egypt for at least 4,000
years. The edible parts are the seeds, which taste and smell
like licorice. • Anise is most often used in baked goods and
confections. Anise is a favorite flavor for treats around the
world such as rounded German *pfeffernüsse* cookies, the
waffle-like pressed Italian *pizzelle* cookies, and Australian
confections known as humbugs, to name just a few. Anise-
flavored cakes called *mustaceoe* were served at the end of
ancient Roman feasts to help diners digest their huge meal.
• Anise gives a distinctive flavor to some liqueurs. • Fresh
Anise leaves will repel evil and are often used around a
magic circle to force evil spirits away from the practitioner
within it. • Tuck a sachet filled with Anise seeds under a
pillow to help prevent unpleasant dreams.

No. 292

Pinus pinea ⚲

Italian Stone Pine

Parasol Pine | Stone Pine | Umbrella Pine

☀ SYMBOLIC MEANING

Prosperity in life.

🌀 POSSIBLE POWERS

Air element; Enlightenment; Mars;
Regeneration; Resurrection.

☾ FOLKLORE AND FACTS

Since prehistoric times, the *Pinus pinea* Italian Stone Pine
has been deliberately cultivated with the sole purpose of
harvesting the edible seeds from its cones. The seeds are
better known as pine nuts. • The Italian Stone Pine's
pine nuts have been coveted trade items for more than
6,000 years.

No. 293

Piper cubeba ⚲

Cubeb

Java Pepper | Tailed Pepper

☀ SYMBOLIC MEANINGS

Fidelity; Hex breaking; Love.

🌀 POSSIBLE POWERS

Aphrodisiac; Attracts love;
Elemental fire; Exorcism;
Fire element; Love; Lust; Mars;
Masculine energy; Repels evil;
Repulses demons; Sex; Wards
off incubi.

☾ FOLKLORE AND FACTS

Tasting a bit like a cross between Black Pepper and Allspice,
the dried berries of the *Piper cubeba* Cubeb are used as a
seasoning. • Make two red sachets with Cubeb berries, then
place them under the mattress on each side of the bed to
encourage sexual love. • Cubeb is mentioned in *The Travels
of Marco Polo,* with Java being a producer along with other
precious spices. • Cubeb berry can be used when needing
to add fire to a spell. • The people of both China and Italy
considered Cubeb to be repulsive to demons. An Italian
Catholic priest in the seventeenth century mentions it as an
important element in exorcisms to ward off incubi. • Cubeb
essential oil is used in aromatherapy for calming and
uplifting without being overstimulating.

No. 294
Piper nigrum 🥣
Black Pepper
Black Peppercorn | Pepper

❋ **SYMBOLIC MEANINGS**
Fidelity, Hex breaking, Love.

🌀 **POSSIBLE POWERS**
Banishes the evil eye; Energy;
Exorcism; Fire element; Mars;
Masculine energy; Protection.

☾ **FOLKLORE AND FACTS**
In the Middle Ages, Black Pepper
was very expensive and usually found only
in the homes of royals and aristocrats. It was
also considered a valid form of currency.
• The edible part of the Black Pepper plant is
the drupe fruit, peppercorn, which is dried and used whole
or ground as a seasoning in nearly every cuisine in the
world. Immature Green Peppercorns are usually pickled
or brined. White Peppercorn is actually black with the
husks removed. • Burn a pinch of Black Pepper to clear
away negative energy. • Combine equal amounts of Black
Pepper with natural sea salt to scatter around the entire
perimeter of the property to rid it of evil and to protect it
should bad spirits return. • For a purpose unknown, Black
Peppercorns were found stuffed into the mummified nose
of Ramesses II. • Make, then carry a sachet filled with Black
Pepper to banish the evil eye as well as provide protection
from having persistent envious thoughts. • Black Pepper
essential oil is used in aromatherapy for reducing stress and
anxiety and to help restore balance to emotions and lift a
dark and heavy mood.

No. 295
Pistacia lentiscus 🥣
Mastic
Chios Tears | Gum Mastic | Mastic Tree | Masticke

❋ **SYMBOLIC MEANINGS**
Chew; Gnashing of teeth.

🌀 **POSSIBLE POWERS**
Abundance; Advancement; Air element;
Conscious will; Energy; Friendship;
Growth; Healing; Joy; Leadership; Life;
Light; Lust; Masculine energy; Natural or
psychic power; Success; Sun.

☾ **FOLKLORE AND FACTS**
Mastic has been collected and used as
a chewing gum for over 2,000 years. It
is also used as a flavoring for cakes and pastries in Middle
Eastern cuisine, as well as an ingredient in Greek cuisine.
• Ivory-colored, aromatic Mastic is obtained from the resin
of the *Pistacia lentiscus* tree. The resin
is collected on the ground, dripping
from slashes made in the bark to
bleed the tree of sap. • Mastic
is a vital ingredient in *myron*,
the sacred holy oil used in
the church rituals of some
orthodox religions.

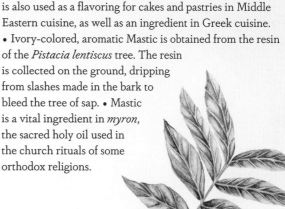

P

No. 296

Pistacia vera ☠ ⚗

Pistachio

Pistacchio | Pistacia

✳ SYMBOLIC MEANINGS
Good fortune; Happiness;
Health.

🌀 POSSIBLE POWERS
Air element; Breaking love
spells; Masculine energy;
Mercury.

☾ FOLKLORE AND FACTS
Around 700 BCE, Pistachio trees
were supposedly included among the
other plants showcased in ancient Babylon's
Hanging Gardens. Pistachios were brought to Europe by
the Romans in the first century. Pistachio trees will grow for
approximately ten years before producing a crop, after which
they can produce fruit for several hundred years. One year,
the Pistachio tree may produce a bountiful crop, while the
following year it may not. Pistachio fruits grow in clusters
like grapes. • When Pistachio fruits ripen on the tree, the
shell will change from green to a natural yellowish-red and
will suddenly split partly open with an audible popping
sound. The ripened fruit surrounding the Pistachio nut
needs to be removed and the shells dried within twenty-
four hours of their harvest to prevent them from becoming
moldy. Unprocessed Pistachios are toxic. The shell of a
Pistachio is so hard that to bite on it can hurt one's teeth.
Dyeing Pistachio nut shells red was for the purpose of hiding
blemishes on the shell. • To bring a zombie out of its trance
and allow it to pass into death, give it Pistachio nuts that
have been dyed red.

No. 297

Pisum sativum ⚗

Garden Pea

English Pea | Green Pea | Snow Pea | Sugar Snap Pea | Sweet Peas

✳ SYMBOLIC MEANINGS
Appointed meeting; Respect.

🌀 POSSIBLE POWERS
Abundance; Beauty; Earth element; Feminine energy;
Friendship; Health; Love; Money; Peace; Prosperity;
Protection; Venus; Water element; Wealth.

☾ FOLKLORE AND FACTS
During the Middle Ages, field Garden Peas were referenced
many times as the life-saving crop that fended off famine.
In 1696, Peas were still considered a delicacy in France.
The tender, sweet, new pods that appear before the seeds
within are fully developed are edible. Once the seeds
develop, Garden Peas need to be shelled. • Unlike most other
legumes, Garden Peas can be eaten raw, blanched, or cooked
through by boiling, steaming, or sautéing them. They can
be prepared alone or used as an ingredient in soups, stews,
and other dishes such as casseroles. Peas are usually green
but can also be yellow. Dried or fresh Garden Peas were
used in the "pease porridge" soup that was a favorite as far
back as the Middle Ages. A popular cooked dish made with
dried, green, split Peas that originated in northern England is
called "mushy peas." Blanched or thawed frozen Garden Peas
can be added to salads. • The skins of Peas are indigestible.
The entire pod of Snow Peas and Sugar Snap Peas can be
eaten whole either raw or cooked by sautéing or stir-frying.
• Bring fortune and profit to a business by shelling Garden
Peas. • One interesting love divination for an unmarried
woman is to find a Garden Pea pod with exactly nine seeds
within it. When this is done, if she hangs the pod over a door,
the first single man who walks beneath it will be her future
husband.

P

No. 298

Plantago major 🥣

White Man's Foot

Broadleaf Plantain | Broad-leaved Plantain | Greater Plantago | Greater Plantain | Plantain | Waybread | Wegbrade | Weybrode

✴ **SYMBOLIC MEANING**

Never despair.

🌀 **POSSIBLE POWERS**

Blessings; Earth element; Feminine energy; Heals headache; Lifts weariness; Protection from an evil spirit; Protection from snakes or snakebites; Venus.

☾ **FOLKLORE AND FACTS**

When North America was first colonized, the Native Americans noticed a new plant cropping up seemingly everywhere. They began referring to it as "white man's footprint" and "Englishman's foot" because, to them, it seemed as if the plant would grow wherever white men went. This phenomenon occurred because *Plantago major* seeds were commonly mixed into the seed bags of the cereal crops that colonists brought with them to the New World. Where settlers would plant cereal crops, which would be near where they lived, White Man's Foot would grow and ultimately naturalize. The leaves of White Man's Foot took on the distinction of being a leafy green vegetable that was easy for anyone to find, harvest, and enjoy from the start of spring to the first frost. The leaves of the White Man's Foot plant are edible raw when young or cooked in soups when they are older and stringier. • Hang a pouch with some White Man's Foot in the car to keep evil from entering. • White Man's Foot is in the Nine Sacred Herbs healing charm that was originally written in Wessex, England, around the time of the tenth century—though it was known as "Weybrode" at that time.

No. 299

Pouteria campechiana 🥣

Canistel

Cây Trứng Gà | Chicken Egg Plant | Cupcake Fruit | Danhuang Guo | Eggfruit | Egg Yolk Fruit | Khmer Peach | Peach of the Immortals | Sawo Mentega | Yolk Fruit

✴ **SYMBOLIC MEANING**

Family comes first.

🌀 **POSSIBLE POWERS**

Harmonious home life; Love; Love of family.

☾ **FOLKLORE AND FACTS**

The ripe fruit of the Canistel tree is edible when it is bright orange-yellow. Its texture is similar to hard-boiled egg yolk with a flavor reminiscent of egg custard. It can be eaten raw, made into jam and confections, blended into smoothies, milkshakes, and custards for pies, puddings, and ice cream. • The wood of any *Pouteria* tree is so hard that even power tools have difficulty cutting into it

No. 300

Primula veris ☠

Cowslip

Common Cowslip | Cowslip Primrose | English Cowslip | Key Flower | Saint Peter's Herb

✴ **SYMBOLIC MEANINGS**

Adventure; Birth; Contentment; Death; Doom; Eternal love; Frivolity; Happiness; Mischief; Modest worth; Pleasure; Satisfaction; Thoughtlessness; Wantonness.

🌀 **POSSIBLE POWERS**

Feminine energy; Finding treasure; Healing; Love; Protection; Venus; Water element.

☾ **FOLKLORE AND FACTS**

Cowslip leaves are a common ingredient in Spanish cuisine when used young and fresh as salad greens. In England, Cowslip flowers have been added to salads and used to flavor vinegar and homemade wines. • Carry a Cowslip flower to attract love. • Carry a Cowslip flower to cure madness. • If you dare to touch a rock with a nosegay of Cowslip flowers with the intention of splitting it open to find hidden fairy gold, touching it the wrong number of times could initiate doom. If done correctly, it could open the door to fairyland, fairy gifts, and fairy gold. • When fairies are frightened they will hide in a Cowslip. • On Whitsunday, when Cowslips were in bloom near Somerset, England, children would tie flower heads together with the stems pointing towards the middles to make ball-like "tisty-tosties." With one tied on a thin twig, the Cowslips were tossed about to the chant, "Tisty-tosty tell me true, Who shall I be married to?" The names of every boy or girl they knew were also called out as part of the chant. When the ball fell, that was whom they would supposedly marry.

No. 301
Primula vulgaris ☠ ⚗

Primrose
Common Primrose | Fairy Cup | Key Flower | Key of Heaven | Lady's Key | Our Lady's Keys | Paigle | Plumrocks

☀ SYMBOLIC MEANINGS
Birth; Consummation; Death; Most excellent; Wantonness; Women.

🌀 POSSIBLE POWERS
Earth element; Emotional rebirth; Feminine energy; Find treasure; Healing; Love spells; Transformation; Venus; Youth.

☾ FOLKLORE AND FACTS
Fairies love and protect the Primrose. When it rains, fairies hurry to be under the protection of Primrose leaves. • The Primrose is considered to be *extremely* sacred and connected to emotional rebirth. Although the flavors of the leaves and flowers of the Primrose plant are somewhat strong, they are edible. They can be added to soups but are best used along with other vegetables. Young Primrose flowers can be made into a wine. The leaves can be brewed as a tea. • Primrose flowers are considered fairy flowers in Ireland and Wales, and like the cowslip, it is thought that touching a fairy rock with a Primrose nosegay will open an invisible door into Fairyland. However, if there are not the proper number of flowers in the nosegay, there will be certain doom. The problem is that no one knows for sure what the required proper number of flowers actually is. It is also believed that the Primrose helps children find hidden treasures, most particularly fairy gold. • If you do not want visitors, put a sprig of Primrose on the front porch. • Wear or carry Primrose to preserve or restore your youth. • The phrase "to walk along the Primrose path" means following a life that is pleasurable and self-indulgent.

No. 302
Prunella vulgaris ☠ ⚗

All-Heal
Heal-All | Heart of the Earth | Self-Heal

☀ SYMBOLIC MEANINGS
Hope; Immortality; Strength.

🌀 POSSIBLE POWERS
Healing; Hope; Observation; Protection; Protection from the Devil; Repels the Devil.

☾ FOLKLORE AND FACTS
People once openly declared that God sent the people of Earth All-Heal to cure them of anything and everything that ailed them. • All-Heal is still considered by many people to be a sacred holy herb. The young leaves and stems of the *Prunella vulgaris* All-Heal plant can be eaten raw in salads or cooked in soups, stews, or as a leafy green vegetable. • Wearing or carrying All-Heal will hopefully bring beauty, love, money, sexuality, and health. • It was believed that All-Heal can drive away the actual Devil, which inspired some witches to plant All-Heal hidden in their gardens in a concerted effort to fend off the Devil. • There was a time when the Native American Ojibway tribes' hunters used All-Heal root with the intent of sharpening their skills of observation before they went off to hunt.

No. 303
Prunus armeniaca ☠ ⚗

Apricot
Abrecock | Abricot | Ansu Apricot | Apricot Tree | Armenian Plum

☀ SYMBOLIC MEANINGS
Beautiful woman; Beauty; Gold; Good fortune; Spring; Timid love.

🌀 POSSIBLE POWERS
Aphrodisiac; Attracts love; Feminine energy; Love; Venus; Water element; Wealth.

☾ FOLKLORE AND FACTS
The Apricot has been cultivated in Armenia since Prehistoric times, as indicated by seeds found at a Chalcolithic-era excavation site at Garni, Armenia. The Apricot may have been domesticated in China, whereas others believe that the Apricot was first cultivated in India around 3000 BCE.

• The edible part of the *Prunus armeniaca* Apricot is the ripe, fleshy drupe fruit. The Apricot is eaten fresh, juiced, made into preserves and jams, and dried. It is also added to or made entirely into liqueurs and wine. Dried Apricot is a common ingredient in Middle Eastern and Mediterranean cuisine. • Put Apricot leaves and flowers in a pouch that is made to attract love to someone who is shy. • It is supposedly lucky for an Apricot to appear in a dream. • There are some who think it is possible that the forbidden fruit in the Garden of Eden may have been an Apricot. • The seed kernels of any variety of Apricot are considered highly toxic due to the presence of a poisonous compound call "amygdalin." Apricot kernels are an especially real threat for children. There have been several disconcerting cases of extreme illness and death of children who ingested Apricot pit kernels. If there is an Apricot tree growing in the neighborhood where children play, be aware of this, especially around the time when the luscious fruit is ripening. Children will be children.

No. 304

Prunus avium ☠ ⚗

Sweet Cherry

Cherry | Gean | Mazzard | Red Cherry | Wild Cherry

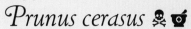

✴ SYMBOLIC MEANINGS
Ascetic beauty; Education; Faith; Feminine beauty; Gentle; Good education; Honor of graceful resignation; Immortality; Insincerity; Intelligence; Kind; Love; Peace; Power; Sexuality; Spiritual beauty; Transience of life.

🌀 POSSIBLE POWERS
The Arts; Attraction; Beauty; Deception; Divination; Education; Feminine energy; Friendship; Gifts; Harmony; Immortality; Joy; Love; Pleasure; Sensuality; Venus; Water element.

☾ FOLKLORE AND FACTS
The Sweet Cherry is considered to be a sacred tree. The edible part is the ripe fruit, which grow in pairs. • Sweet Cherry fruit can be eaten fresh or cooked. It can also be puréed, juiced, candied, made into jam, jelly, and syrup, dried, baked into an iconic pie as well as a wide assortment of other baked goods and pastries. Lastly, it can be made into wine and liqueur. The kernel of the seed is toxic. • To find love, tie one strand of your own hair to a Sweet Cherry tree that is in blossom. • One particularly macabre divination is that when a Sweet Cherry tree is full of ripe fruit, run around the tree and shake it hard. Count the number of cherries

that fall to the ground. That is how many years you will live. • Sweet Cherry tree wood is coveted by cabinetmakers all around the world because it is reddish-brown and the grain is straight. • The Sweet Cherry has flavored some medicinal syrups for many generations. • An old English superstition is that the singing cuckoo in the Sweet Cherry tree must eat three meals of cherries before it can stop singing.

No. 305

Prunus cerasus ☠ ⚗

Sour Cherry

Amarelle Cherry | Dwarf Cherry | Morello Cherry | Tart Cherry

✴ SYMBOLIC MEANINGS
Kindness; New beginnings; Revival; Youth.

🌀 POSSIBLE POWERS
Beginnings; Kindness; Love; Youthfulness.

☾ FOLKLORE AND FACTS
The tart ripe fruit of the Sour Cherry tree was more popular before WWII, whereas nowadays it is usually the generic Morello variety that is most often planted and harvested. Dried Sour Cherries are added to soups and pork dishes, made into confections, jams, pies, syrups, beers, and wines. • The seed kernel is toxic. • Unlike other *Prunus* cherry trees, *Prunus cerasus* is self-reproductive, requiring only bees to move pollen from flower to flower. • Make, then carry dried Sour Cherries in a sachet when starting something over.

No. 306

Prunus domestica ☠ ⚗

Plum

Common Plum | Damson | European Plum | Greengage

☀ SYMBOLIC MEANINGS

Beauty; Fidelity; Genius; Keep your promises; Longevity; Promise.

⚙ POSSIBLE POWERS

Colorize; Love; Protection; Venus; Water element.

☾ FOLKLORE AND FACTS

The drupe of the *Prunus domestica* Plum tree is edible when ripe. A Plum will continue ripening after it has been picked from the tree. • Plums are eaten fresh or made into jam and confections. They can be partially dried to a sticky softness—at which point they are called prunes—which are used in pastry fillings, as well as juiced. • The kernel of the Plum seed is toxic. • The pit of the Damson Plum clings to the pulp so tenaciously that when using it for jam-making, it is usually cooked with the pit intact, then removed after cooking, and before adding the sugar. Damson Plums are sometimes pickled.
• Hang a Plum branch over the home's doors and windows to protect it from evil entering.

No. 307

Prunus dulcis var. *dulcis* ⚗

Sweet Almond

Almendra Dulce | Almond

☀ SYMBOLIC MEANINGS

Fruitfulness; Giddiness; Heedlessness; Hope; Indiscretion; Promise; Prosperity; Stupidity; Thoughtlessness; Union; Virginity; Wisdom.

⚙ POSSIBLE POWERS

Abundance; Air element; Ambition; Attis; Attitude; Clear thinking; Fruitfulness; Harmony; Hermes; Higher understanding; Logic; Luck; Manifestation in material form; Masculine energy; Mercury; Money; Overcoming alcohol dependency; Prosperity; Spiritual concepts; Success in business ventures; Thoth; Thought processes; Wisdom.

☾ FOLKLORE AND FACTS

Sweet Almond is among the earliest trees to be grown domestically, dating back to the Bronze Age. The edible part of the *Prunus dulcis* var. *dulcis* Sweet Almond tree is the seed of the fruit, which is actually a drupe. The seed within that fruit is what we know to be the part that we refer to as the nut, even though it is not a nut at all. The kernel of the seed is what is edible. Domesticated Sweet Almond trees are not toxic. If you are not *absolutely certain* whether an Almond tree is the edible safe Sweet Almond or the deadly poisonous Bitter Almond, do not eat any of the nuts. • When you go out on a job hunt, carry a Sweet Almond in your pocket for good luck. • Cultivation of the Sweet Almond tree commenced when the sweet variety was able to be determined apart from the toxic bitter variety. From that time on, growing only Sweet Almond trees became a concerted effort, since the tree will grow best from a seed. • It was believed that one can guarantee a successful business venture by climbing a Sweet Almond tree. • Magic wands made from Sweet Almond wood are highly valued for the wood's correspondence to elemental Air. • Hold a Sweet Almond when calling upon divine healing energy. • Carry or wear a Sweet Almond amulet when attempting to overcome any type of addiction, whether physical or emotional.

No. 308

Prunus persica ☠

Peach

Fuzzless Peach | Nectarine | *Prunus persica* var. *nectarina* | Shaved Peach | Smooth-skinned Peach | Velvety Skinned Peach

☀ SYMBOLIC MEANINGS

Bridal hope; Divine fruit of the gods; Generosity; Gentleness; Happiness; Honors; Long life; Peace; Riches; Young brides; Your qualities and charms are unequaled.

✺ POSSIBLE POWERS

Exorcism; Feminine energy; Fertility; Health; Immortality; Longevity; Love; Protection against invisible evil; Repels a spirit; Tranquility; Venus; Vitality; Water element; Wishing.

☾ FOLKLORE AND FACTS

A Peach and a Nectarine will continue to ripen after being picked from the tree. A Peach can be white or yellow, "clingstone" or "freestone." Peach seeds can grow into trees that produce Nectarines. Velvety skinned Peach seeds can grow into trees that produce smooth Nectarines. A smooth Nectarine seed can grow into a tree that can produce either smooth Nectarines or velvety Peaches. There is no way of knowing what kind of tree the seeds of either will produce. Because of this anomaly, a Nectarine cutting, known as a "scion," is grafted onto Peach tree rootstock to guarantee Nectarine fruit. • Peaches and Nectarines are eaten fresh or juiced, as well as made into jams, jellies, confections, fillings for pies and pastries, wine, and liqueur. The kernels of Peach and Nectarine pits contain cyanogenic glycosides which metabolizes into cyanide poison. • The first written English reference of the Nectarine was in 1616. • The Chinese sacred Tree of Immortality is the Peach tree, from which every 3,000 years an immortal fruit, once ripened, is believed to have the power to allow people to remain young forever. The event is celebrated by an ethereal banquet attended by the Eight Immortals of Taoism. • It is also believed that to carry a small piece of Peach tree wood will lengthen a person's life and might even make them immortal. • Because Peach blossoms will appear before the leaves, the Chinese consider that the Peach tree exhibits more vitality than other fruit trees. • Peach wood wands are used for the purpose of exorcisms in China. Peach wood magic wands are cut personally by whoever intends to use them, on the night before the first New Moon after the winter solstice. • Because Peaches are believed to repel spirits, they are never put on tables arranged to revere the spirits of the ancestors. • Ancient Chinese rulers who ventured beyond familiar territory to attend a funeral would be led by sorcerers carrying Peach tree magic wands to fend off malicious spirits. Every so often, archers would shoot arrows in every direction using Peach wood bows and arrows for the same purpose. • Wear a Peach pit as an amulet for all forms of personal protection. • In Japan, Peach tree branches have been used as divining rods.

No. 309

Prunus serotina ☠

Black Cherry

Rum Cherry | Wild Black Cherry

☀ SYMBOLIC MEANING

Tenacious black beauty.

✺ POSSIBLE POWERS

Danger; Longevity.

☾ FOLKLORE AND FACTS

The only edible part of the *Prunus serotina* Black Cherry tree is the ripe, pitted berry that can be eaten raw, made into jelly, juiced, and fermented to be a wine, or it can be a flavoring that is added to brandy or rum, ice cream, and carbonated soda, as well as used to make jam, jelly, and wine. The berries are also used as an ingredient in recipes and go especially well with pork. Due to its unique flavor, Black Cherry is used as a seasoning. All other parts of the tree are highly poisonous. • High-quality Black Cherry lumber is used in the finest cabinetry.

P

No. 310

Prunus spinosa ☠ ⚗

Blackthorn

Sloe

✴ SYMBOLIC MEANINGS

Austerity; Blessing after a challenge; Challenges ahead;
Colorize; Constraint; Difficulty; Inevitability; Preparation;
Strife.

🌀 POSSIBLE POWERS

Banishes negative energy or entities; Colorize; Exorcism;
Protection.

☾ FOLKLORE AND FACTS

The edible part of the Blackthorn Tree is the hard, grainy,
astringently tart sloe berry. These qualities can be reduced if
collected within a few days after the first frost. This can also
be accomplished by freezing the sloes after they have been
picked, which will alleviate the arduous task of pricking each
berry before adding to gin to make homemade "sloe gin"
or "sloe vodka." By freezing the berries first, they will split
perfectly for the infusion process. Sloes can also be preserved
in vinegar or added to chutneys and jams. • The kernel of the
Blackthorn seed is toxic. • Hang Blackthorn over doorways
to ward off evil, calamity, negative vibrations, and to banish
demons from the home. • A forked branch of Blackthorn
will make an effective divining rod or wishing rod
if it is cut in the spring by the individual
who intends to use it. • Blackthorn wood
will make a good magic wand for fending
off malicious fairies. • Blackthorn wood
is very hard and takes a high polish,
so it was a favorite for walking sticks
and clubs. • Blackthorn walking
sticks and shillelaghs are carried
by officers of the Royal Irish
Regiment. The shillelagh was
originally used as a
sturdy weapon for
self-defense.

No. 311

Prunus virginiana ☠ ⚗

Chokecherry

Bitter-berry | Black Chokeberry | Virginia Bird Cherry

✴ SYMBOLIC MEANING

Better days to come.

🌀 POSSIBLE POWERS

Calm; Healing; Venus; Water
element.

☾ FOLKLORE AND FACTS

For many Native American tribes of
the Northern Plains, the *Prunus virginiana* Chokecherry
berries are an important part of a traditional, nutritious,
high-energy staple food called pemmican. It is a combination
of dried meats and particular tallow fats mixed with dried
Chokecherries, and perhaps other dried berries and varied
ingredients. The knowledge of the different ways to make
it has been passed down from generation to generation,
although there is no official recipe.

No. 312

Psidium guajava ⚗

Guava

Apple Guava | Common Guava | Guayaba | Lemon Guava | Strawberry Guava | Yellow Guava |
Yellow-fruited Cherry Guava

✴ SYMBOLIC MEANINGS

Fruit of success; Reap rewards of hard work.

🌀 POSSIBLE POWERS

Success; Venus; Water element.

☾ FOLKLORE AND FACTS

The Guava tree was cultivated in Peru for its fruit as far back
as 2500 BCE. The ripe fruit of the small bushy Guava tree is
edible raw or cooked. • Guava is often made into jams or
cooked in sauces used in condiments for pork,
chicken, or fish. It is also enjoyed
juiced and more often blended
in with other fruit juices. • A
delectable, very thick, jellied
Guava paste known as
guayabate or *goiabada*
was widely popular
in Colombia before it
became increasingly
enjoyed in other parts
of South America and the

USA. • In most places, a Guava is cut into quarters and eaten like an apple, either plain or sprinkled over with a pinch of salt, sugar, masala seasoning blend, or ground cayenne pepper. Guava wood and leaves are often used for meat smoking. • Guava wood is resistant to fungus and insects, and is strong enough to be used as roof trusses in Nigeria. • A rinse made of boiled, cooled, and strained Guava leaves in water is believed to help thwart hair loss and aid new growth.

No. 313

Pteridium aquilinum ☠ ⚱

Bracken Fern
Bracken | Common Bracken

✳ SYMBOLIC MEANINGS
Confidence; Confusion; Protection; Rain; Wealth.

🌀 POSSIBLE POWERS
Air element; Colorize; Fertility; Healing; Health; Invisibility; Luck; Magical powers or qualities; Masculine energy; Mercury; Prophetic dreams; Protection; Rain magic; Riches; Stress relief.

☾ FOLKLORE AND FACTS
The young shoots of the *Pteridium aquilinum* Bracken Fern are widely eaten as a vegetable in parts of China, Japan, and Russia. They are often steamed or added to soups, and sometimes preserved in miso, sake, or salt, as well as used to make a home-brewed beer. The rhizome can be dried and then ground into flour. • Place a frond of Bracken Fern under the pillow to dream of the solution to a perplexing problem and help release and eliminate negativity. • Bracken Fern's magic power can supposedly prevent witchcraft because it is potent enough for a witch to fear its presence nearby. • To discover who one's true love may be, slice open the stem of a Bracken Fern, then try to discern what letter or letters can be seen within it. • It was once believed that after stepping upon Bracken Fern, a traveler would become disoriented to the point of losing direction. • It was believed that Bracken seed would provide magic powers, such as invisibility, but only if it is carried around in a pocket.

No. 314

Punica granatum

Pomegranate
Carthaginian Apple | Jnhm

✳ SYMBOLIC MEANINGS
Abundance; Ambition; Compassion; Conceit; Conceited; Elegance; Fertility; Foolishness; Foppery; Fruitfulness; Fullness; Good luck; Good things; Housewarming gift; Kabbalah; Marriage; Mysteriousness; Mystical experience; Offspring; Paradise; Prosperity; Resurrection; Righteousness; Suffering; Suffering and resurrection; Summer; Sweetness of the heavenly kingdom.

🌀 POSSIBLE POWERS
Abundance; Aphrodisiac; Attracts love; Binding; Ceres; Creative power; Divination; Elegance; Fertility; Fire element; Immortality; Incarceration; Intellectual ability; Love; Luck; Many children; Masculine energy; Mature elegance; Mercury; Passion; Persephone; Sensuous love; Unreciprocated love magic; Venus; Wealth; Wishing.

☾ FOLKLORE AND FACTS
Pomegranates have been cultivated in the Mediterranean region for thousands of years. The fleshy, juicy, membrane-encased, finger-staining seeds of the Pomegranate fruit are edible fresh or juiced, and are often added to smoothies, and made into wines and liqueur. Both fresh and dried Pomegranate seeds are widely used in Middle Eastern cuisine as both an ingredient and as a seasoning. As a seasoning, ground dried Pomegranates seeds are known as *anar dana*. • Grenadine syrup, popular for use in several different cocktails, and Pomegranate molasses are both made from Pomegranates. • Make, then carry a sachet filled with bits of Pomegranate husk to increase fertility. • Use a forked branch of Pomegranate as a divining rod to search for and find hidden wealth. • Pomegranates symbolize the Kabbalah as the mystical entryway into the Garden of Pomegranates. • It is traditional to eat Pomegranate seeds on Rosh Hashanah because the many seeds represent fruitfulness. • In Greece, it is customary to give a Pomegranate as a housewarming gift, which is placed on or

under the home's altar as a blessing of abundance, good luck, and fertility. • In the Book of Exodus, the robe worn by the Hebrew high priest had decorative Pomegranates embroidered all around the bottom near the hem. • According to Jewish law, the Pomegranate is one of the Seven Species that requires a blessing before it is eaten.

No. 315
Pyropia tenera 🥣

Nori

Bara Lafwr | Bara Lawr | Coldwater Seaweed | Gim | Korean Edible Seaweed | Laverbread | *Porphyra umbilicalis*

✹ SYMBOLIC MEANING
Delicate.

🌀 POSSIBLE POWERS
Moon; Moon magic; Sea magic; Water element; Water magic.

☾ FOLKLORE AND FACTS
Since ancient times, the edible sea red algae *Pyropia tenera* that is known as Nori has been used for food. Nori grows in both the Pacific and Indian Oceans. • In Wales it is known as Laver and has been used as an ingredient in traditional Welsh cuisine since the seventeenth century. Laver bread is a highly nutritious, traditional Welsh delicacy that is made by boiling the Laver until it is a soft purée to be coated over with oatmeal before frying it to eat with breakfast, as a salad, or as a condiment or side dish to lamb, fish, or cockles. It can also be used in soup.

No. 316
Pyrus communis ☠

Pear

Common Pear | European Pear

✹ SYMBOLIC MEANINGS
Affection; Health; Hope.

🌀 POSSIBLE POWERS
Colorize; Comfort; Feminine energy; Long life; Love; Lust; Venus; Water element.

☾ FOLKLORE AND FACTS
There is archeological evidence of Pears in several European Neolithic and Bronze Age sites. A Pear will continue ripening after it has been picked from the tree. Pear fruit is eaten fresh and can be cooked by poaching, or as an ingredient for baking and pastries. • Like Apple seeds, Pear seeds are also toxic. • An iconic Pear tree is included in the Christmas song, "The Twelve Days of Christmas," as the tree with the perched partridge. • Pear wood is desirable for constructing a magic wand. • Pear wood is one of the woods favored for use in the construction of higher-quality woodwind instruments. • Make, then carry a sachet of Pear blossom and leaf to encourage a long, loving, comfortable life.

No. 317

Pyrus pyrifolia 🝷

Asian Pear

Apple Pear | Chinese Pear | Chinese White Pear |
Japanese Pear | Korean Pear | Nashi Pear |
Papple | Pearple | Sand Pear

✵ SYMBOLIC MEANINGS
Gracefully special; Noble.

✺ POSSIBLE POWERS
Fertility; Health; Love; Luck;
Sex; Specialness; Water
element.

☾ FOLKLORE AND FACTS
Unlike other Pears, the ripe,
fragrant, and juicy sweet
Asian Pear is usually eaten
raw. Grated Asian Pears are
frequently used as a substitute
for sugar when sweetening.
Asian Pears are used in marinades,
sauces, and as a tenderizer for meat. • The Asian Pear is not
recommended for jam-making or pies because the juice is
watery. • Asian Pears bruise easily and require wrapping
to protect them in transit and storage. When stored and
wrapped in a dry, cool place, the fresh fruits can last for
several weeks. • Asian Pears are very often treated as special
gifts with decorative wrapping and ribbon. It is also special
enough to be appreciated by guests when served, or enjoyed
eaten as a family.

No. 318

Quassia amara ☠ ⚱

Quassia

Bitter Quassia | Hombre Grande | Quassia Bark | Quassia Wood

✴ SYMBOLIC MEANINGS
Bitter; Bitterness.

🌀 POSSIBLE POWERS
Healing; Health.

☾ FOLKLORE AND FACTS
The bitterness extracted
from Quassia bark is used in
the making of bitters. • In beer
making, it is possible to substitute Quassia bark
extract for hops.

No. 319

Quercus alba ☠ ⚱

White Oak

Celestial Tree | Common Oak | English Oak | European Oak | King of the Forest |
Pedunculate Oak | *Quercus robur*

✴ SYMBOLIC MEANINGS
Endurance; Hospitality; Liberty; Noble presence; Personal
finances; Regal power; Wealth.

🌾 COMPONENT MEANINGS
Acorn: Fruition of long, hard labor; Good luck; Immortality;
Life; Patience.

🌀 POSSIBLE POWERS
Abundance; Advancement; Air element; Aphrodisiac;
Attracts love; Autumn; Business; Conscious will; Earth
element; Energy; Expansion; Female energy; Fertility; Fire
element; Friendship; the Four Winds; Growth; Healing;
Health; Honor; Immortality; Insight; Joy; Leadership; Life;
Light; Longevity; Love; Luck; Masculine energy; Money;
Natural power; Politics; Potency; Power; Protection against
illness; Public acclaim; Responsibility; Relieves aches and
pains; Royalty; Spring; Success; Summer; Water element;
Wealth; Winter.

☾ FOLKLORE AND FACTS
Although there were many other Oak trees, the Druids
would perform rituals *only* under a White Oak tree, most
particularly if there was mistletoe growing on its branches.
• The White and the English Oak trees have been revered,
even worshipped, since prehistoric times. • The only part of
the *Quercus alba* English Oak and *Quercus robur* English
Oak trees that is edible are the acorns after they have been

processed by roasting or by boiling and drying. At that point,
they are best used ground into a flour. • A magic wand that
has been lovingly fashioned by its intended user from a
length of White Oak or English Oak wood, then properly
charged before putting it into service, will provide powerful
magic that offers tremendous protection supported by
strength, endurance, great luck, and fending off evil.
• A very powerful protector against evil is a cross whittled
from equal lengths of English Oak wood that are tied
together in the center with red thread and hung in the house.
The resulting cross predates Christianity and represents the
Earth, male and female, the four winds, the four seasons,
and the four elements. • Carry a small piece of English Oak
wood as protection from harm and as a good luck charm.
• Wearing an acorn as an amulet can encourage the relief
of aches and pains, protect against illnesses, encourage
longevity and even immortality, improve sexual powers, and
increase fertility. • If in autumn you happen to catch a falling
Oak leaf, the divination is that you will not have a cold for all
of winter.

Raphanus sativus subsp. *longipinnatus*

Daikon Radish

Japanese Radish | Long White Radish | Mooli | Oriental Radish | White Radish | Winter Radish

✸ SYMBOLIC MEANING

High status.

✿ POSSIBLE POWERS

Lust; Protection.

☕ FOLKLORE AND FACTS

In Japan the Daikon Radish is a common root vegetable that is pickled. It is also a popular ingredient in stir-fry dishes. • The raw flowers and cooked leaves are as edible as the Daikon Radish root. • The Daikon Radish is grown as a fallow crop in North America, to leave unharvested to prevent compaction of the soil. Its root is long, reaching from six to ten inches, so after the crop is tilled, a crop of Potatoes can be planted that will grow to their full potential in the improved density of the soil. • Daikon Radish offers protection against the evil eye.

Reynoutria japonica 🝕

Japanese Knotweed

Mexican Bamboo

✸ SYMBOLIC MEANING

Tiger stick.

✿ POSSIBLE POWERS

Earth element; Healing; Removes pain; Venus.

☕ FOLKLORE AND FACTS

The Japanese Knotweed plant is a highly invasive plant—by all rights a highly destructive weed—that is actually quite edible. It is reported to taste somewhat like Rhubarb and it has been pickled, sautéed, added to soups, and even used in desserts. • As an important source of nectar, the Japanese Knotweed is especially valued by Japanese beekeepers.

Raphanus raphanistrum subsp. *sativus* 🝕

Radish

Common Radish | Green Radish | Icicle Radish | *Raphanus raphanistrum* | Roseheart Radish | Shinrimei | Watermelon Radish | Wild Radish

✸ SYMBOLIC MEANINGS

High status; Spicy romance; Value the less-important things in life.

✿ POSSIBLE POWERS

Change of luck from bad to good; Fire element; Health; Lust; Mars; Masculine energy; Protection; Romance.

☕ FOLKLORE AND FACTS

The Radish is grown all over the world so people everywhere can enjoy the little white and magenta-colored, pungently sharp, crisp, and crunchy roots freshly raw with a little touch of salt. • There was a time in Germany when a Radish would be carried to seek out the location of sorcerers.

R

No. 323

Rheum rhabarbarum ☠

Garden Rhubarb

Culinary Rhubarb | Pie Plant

✹ SYMBOLIC MEANING
Advice.

✺ POSSIBLE POWERS
Earth element; Feminine energy; Fidelity; Health; Protection; Venus.

☾ FOLKLORE AND FACTS
The Rhubarb plant's leaves are toxic, but the stalks have a strongly tart flavor with the texture and crunch of celery when occasionally eaten raw. • Although Rhubarb is a vegetable, it is more often treated as a fruit and used for jams, jellies, and pie fillings, or added into recipes that include other fruit, like strawberries. Rhubarb stems can also be pickled. • In Marco Polo's time, Rhubarb was traded in the same manner as other precious herbs, spices, and even jewels. • Make, then wear a sachet of Rhubarb for protection against stomach pain.

No. 324

Rhododendron groenlandicum ☠ ⚗

Ledum

Bog Labrador Tea | Hudson's Bay Tea | Indian Plant Tea | Labrador Tea | Muskeg Tea | Swamp Tea

✹ SYMBOLIC MEANING
Harmony.

✺ POSSIBLE POWERS
Balance; Calms nervousness; Cleansing; Energy flow; Fire element; Harmony; Healing; Mars; Sleep.

☾ FOLKLORE AND FACTS
Native American tribes often used Ledum leaves to brew teas as beverages and for medicinal purposes. • When Ledum essential oil is used for aromatherapy, it may help the flow of energy that allows an ease of relaxation that promotes sleep and alleviates nervousness.

No. 325

Rhus coriaria ☠ ⚗

Sumac

Sicilian Sumac | Sumak | Tanner's Sumach

✹ SYMBOLIC MEANINGS
Intellectual excellence; Splendid; Splendor.

✺ POSSIBLE POWERS
Addresses difficulty; Elemental fire energy; Energy of wild nature; Facilitates harmony among people; Intellect; Life; Movement.

☾ FOLKLORE AND FACTS
Tangy ripe Sumac fruit, which is dried, crushed, then used as a seasoning, was introduced to Europeans long before the Lemon was. • Nine Sumac berries in the pocket will help get a lighter sentence if found guilty in a court trial. • A three-foot-long branch of Sumac wood that is approximately one and a half inches thick with a puff of downy eagle feathers attached on one end, will suffice as a suitable Navajo shamanistic healing wand called a *nahikàï*. • Since ancient times, the toxic Sumac leaves have been used to tan leather.

No. 326

Ribes nigrum 🍶

Blackcurrant

Black Currant | True Blackcurrant

✳ **SYMBOLIC MEANINGS**
Thankfulness; You please me;
Your disapproval will kill me;
Your frown will kill me; Your
unhappiness will kill me.

🌀 **POSSIBLE POWERS**
Disbursement; Improved
health; Pleasure to the giver.

☾ **FOLKLORE AND FACTS**
The ripe fruit of the *Ribes nigrum* Blackcurrant is edible
fresh or dried and used in the making of jams, baked goods,
pastry fillings, and liqueurs. The closely related *Ribes rubrum*
Redcurrant is used much in the same way.

No. 327

Ribes rubrum

Redcurrant

Red Currant | True Redcurrant

✳ **SYMBOLIC MEANINGS**
Thankfulness; You please me;
Your disapproval will kill me;
Your frown will kill me; Your
unhappiness will kill me.

🌱 **COMPONENT MEANINGS**
Branch: You please all.

🌀 **POSSIBLE POWERS**
Disbursement; Improved health; Pleasure to the giver.

☾ **FOLKLORE AND FACTS**
The ripe fruit of the *Ribes rubrum* Redcurrant is edible
fresh or dried and used in the making of jams, baked goods,
pastry fillings, and liqueurs. The closely related *Ribes nigrum*
Blackcurrant is used much in the same way.

No. 328

Ribes uva-crispa ☠

Gooseberry

European Gooseberry | Goosegogs

✳ **SYMBOLIC MEANINGS**
Anticipation; Regret.

🌀 **POSSIBLE POWERS**
Disbursement; Improved health; Pleasure to the giver.

☾ **FOLKLORE AND FACTS**
The ripe fruit of the Gooseberry is edible
while the unripe berries and the leaves
are toxic. Ripe Gooseberries are
commonly cooked to make into jams,
pies, and syrups • The European
Gooseberry bushes are where it is
still believed that fairies go to hide
from danger. • The nineteenth-
century slang for pubic hair was
"Gooseberry bush."

R

No. 329
Rosa rugosa ☙

Rugged Rose
Apothecary's Rose | Damascus Rose | Dog Rose | Eglantine Rose | Gallic Rose | Mundi Rose |
Prickly Rose | Provence Rose | Sweetbriar

✷ SYMBOLIC MEANINGS
Bashful love; Beauty is not your only attraction; Brilliant complexion; Close friendship; Divine love; Ferocity; Freshness; Grace; Healing a wound; Honesty; Ingratitude; Innermost temple; Inspiration for love; Pain and pleasure; a Poetic person; Poetry; Refreshing love; Simplicity; Spring; Sympathy; Variety; You are merry.

🎨 COLOR MEANINGS
Blush: If you love me, you will discover it; If you love me, you will find me out.
Dark pink: Thank you.
Light pink: Admiration.
Pink: Confidence; Desire; Elegance; Energy; Everlasting joy; Gentility; Grace; Gratitude; Happiness; Indecision; Joy; Joy of life; Love; Passion; Perfect happiness; Perfection; Please believe me; Pure; Pure and lovely; Romance; Romantic love; Secret love; Sweetness; Thank you; Thankfulness; Trust; You are young and beautiful; You're so loved; Youth.
Red: Beauty; Congratulations; Courage; Desire; Healing; I love you; Job well done; Love; Passion; Protection; Respect; Romance; Well done.
Striped or variegated: Immediate affection; Love at first sight; Warmth of heart.
White: Charm; Eternal love; Exorcism; Girlhood; a Heart ignorant of love; the Heart that knows not love; Heavenly; Humility; I am worthy of you; I would be single; Innocence; Purity; Reverence; Secrecy; Silence; Too young to love; Too young to marry; Virtue; Wistfulness; Worthiness; You're heavenly; Youthfulness.

🌀 POSSIBLE POWERS
Adonis; Aurora; Beauty; Cupid; Cure depression; Demeter; Divination; Domestic happiness; Domestic peace; Endurance; Eros; Feminine energy; Fertility; Fortitude; Hathor; Healing; Heart as the temple; Hippocrates; Introspection; Isis; Long-lasting relationship; Longevity; Love; Marriage; Meaningful words from the heart; Options; Peace; Potential invisibility; Protection; Protection of loved ones; Psychic power; Purification; Romance; Strength; Tenacity; True and lasting love; Unexpected travel; Venus; Water element.

☾ FOLKLORE AND FACTS
The petals of any fragrant Rose can be used in cooking to lend its sweet flavor and fragrance to a dish. Rose petals are used for culinary purposes such as rose-infused beverages, syrups, sugars, and candied petals. They can be added to salads or granola, creamed into butter, infused with water, or sugared for use as decoration or garnish. Rose petals or entire rose blossoms can be carefully frozen into ice cubes to look outstanding. They can be selected according to the meanings of their colors and then floated in a punch bowl. • The fruit, which is better known as a "rose hip," is not edible in every variety of *Rosa*. But for those that do have an edible rose hip, they are very nutritious. The thorny Rugged Rose is the source of the best-quality, edible, vitamin-C–rich rose hips, as are the Eglantine and Dog Roses. Rose hips can be made into tea, added to soups and stews, and used as an ingredient in pies and other dishes. One cup of rose hip tea will provide an adult with their daily requirement of vitamin C. • It was the Persian physician Avicenna, who, sometime just before 1037 invented Rose water using Gallic Rose essential oil and pure rainwater. Rose water is sometimes added to teas and flavored waters or lemonade, as well as milk and rice dishes, such as rice pudding, sweet foods, and confections. In the USA and Europe, before vanilla became popular to use in baking, Rose water was a very popular flavoring for cream fillings. • Many Middle Eastern dishes include Rose as an exotic flavoring in baked goods, pastries, desserts, ice cream, jam, and the confection known as Turkish delight. Roses are also used to flavor rice pudding, yogurt, teas, and other beverages. They are also a necessary ingredient in a Moroccan seasoning mixture known as *ras el hanout*. • The Damascus Rose is an ancient sacred plant with a large, beautiful, fragrant flower that originated in Iran and is revered in the Middle East. • The fragrance of the Damascus Rose can attract angels. • The Damascus Rose is the source of a pure essential oil that is used in some religious ceremonies. It is also pleasant in aromatherapy for relaxation and peace of mind. • Gallic Rose essential oil has been used for aromatherapy to help induce a sense of calm to alleviate depression. • It is believed that a

R

fairy is supposedly able to render itself invisible by eating a Prickly Rose hip, then turning counterclockwise three times. To become visible again, the fairy would need to eat another Prickly Rose hip then turn clockwise three times.

No. 330
Rubus chamaemorus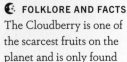

Cloudberry

Aqpik | Bakeapple Bush | Low-Bush Salmonberry | Nordic Berry

☀ SYMBOLIC MEANING
Royal gift.

✿ POSSIBLE POWERS
Good news; Love; Profit; Recognition; Respect; Venus; Water element.

☾ FOLKLORE AND FACTS
The Cloudberry is one of the scarcest fruits on the planet and is only found wild in damp marshy areas in subarctic northern climates for a few weeks in July. The ripe, fresh, pale, peachy-amber-orange colored fruit of the Cloudberry plant is nutritionally very high in vitamin C, a little tart with a flavor all its own, and very juicy. It is eaten fresh, used as an ingredient in creamy desserts, cakes, or cooked into jam, pie and pastry fillings, or juiced. Cloudberry can also provide flavoring to ice cream and cake, or be used as a cheese topping, flavoring, or liqueur. Lastly, it can be brewed into tea. • Where the Cloudberries grow is often guarded secret information handed down from generation to generation. • An image of a Cloudberry is on a Finnish euro coin. • In Norway it is illegal to pick unripe Cloudberries. • Cloudberry extract is used in some cosmetics.

No. 331
Rubus fruticosus

Blackberry

Allegheny Blackberry | Common Blackberry | European Blackberry

☀ SYMBOLIC MEANINGS
Envy; Injustice; Lowliness; Remorse; Scornful; Temptation.

✿ POSSIBLE POWERS
Aphrodisiac; Attracts love; Brigid; Colorize; Feminine energy; Happiness; Healing; Love; Money; Prosperity; Protection; Venus; Visions; Water element.

☾ FOLKLORE AND FACTS
The Blackberry was one of the earliest foods known to be eaten on Earth by a human. The edible part of the Blackberry plant is its berries. They can be used to make jam, jelly, and filling for pies and other pastries, and wine. The berries will stop ripening as soon as they are picked.
• There was a time when, after a death had occurred, prickly Blackberry branches were placed at all the windows and exterior doors to prevent the spirit of the dead individual from re-entering the home and taking up permanent residence there in the form of a haunting ghost. Brambles were planted on a grave in an effort to bind it down and keep the dead from leaving their resting places as ghosts.
• In England it was considered bad luck to pick the Blackberry fruit after October 11th.

No. 332

Rubus idaeus

Raspberry

American Raspberry | American Red
Raspberry | European Raspberry |
European Red Raspberry | Framboise |
Red Raspberry

✳ **SYMBOLIC MEANINGS**
Scornful beauty; Temptation.

🌀 **POSSIBLE POWERS**
Aphrodisiac; Attracts love;
Feminine energy; Happiness;
Healing; Love; Money; Prosperity;
Protection; Venus; Visions;
Water element.

🌙 **FOLKLORE AND FACTS**
The edible part of the Raspberry plant is the berries. They
can be used to make jam, jelly, filling for pies and other
pastries, and wine. The berries will stop ripening as soon
as they are picked. • There was a time when, following a
death in the house, branches of Raspberry brambles were
hung over all the windows and doors of the home to prevent
the spirit of the dead from coming back into it. • Raspberry
brambles were once routinely planted on a grave in an effort
to bind it down and keep the spirit of the deceased within it.
• Carry a sachet of a dried Raspberry fruit and a leaf during
pregnancy to offer protection.

No. 333

Rubus × loganobaccus

Loganberry

Tayberry

✳ **SYMBOLIC MEANING**
Happy accident.

🌀 **POSSIBLE POWERS**
Accidental good fortune;
Luck; Refresh.

🌙 **FOLKLORE AND FACTS**
High in vitamin C, the edible fruit of the Loganberry
bramble is the positive result of accidental berry breeding
by a Californian judge and amateur botanist in 1881.
Loganberries are eaten fresh, used as an ingredient in
desserts, made into jams and pie fillings, brewed into
homemade wine, and cooked down into a syrup that is used
as a beverage and milkshake flavoring.

No. 334

Rubus ursinus × idaeus

Boysenberry

Boysenmarja

✳ **SYMBOLIC MEANINGS**
Bonding; Mystery; Royalty; Thoughtful.

🌀 **POSSIBLE POWERS**
Creativity; Fairy food; Feminine energy; Healing; Intellect;
Love; Magic; Money; Protection; Stamina; Vigor.

🌙 **FOLKLORE AND FACTS**
First cultivated in California during the early 1900s by
crossing the Blackberry with the Raspberry, the edible fruit
of the Boysenberry bramble can be eaten fresh as well as
used to make jam, pie fillings, syrup, juice, and flavoring for
ice cream and beverages.

No. 335

Rumex acetosa ☠ ⚗

Common Sorrel

Garden Sorrel | Little Vinegar Plant | Sorrel | Spinach Dock | Wild Sorrel

✳ **SYMBOLIC MEANINGS**
Affection; Ill-timed wit;
Parental affection; Refreshes
the spirit; Wit.

🌀 **POSSIBLE POWERS**
Earth element; Heals
heartbreak; Healing; Health; Joy;
Jupiter; Luck; Maternal tenderness;
Protection; See a fairy;
Spiritual healing.

🌙 **FOLKLORE AND FACTS**
The sour-tasting Common Sorrel has been cultivated for
centuries to be used in soups, stews, and to be batter-dipped
and then deep-fried. The lemony French Sorrel leaves are
edible for use in salads as well as in soups, stews, and sauces.
• Make, then carry a Common Sorrel sachet to refresh the
inner spirit. • Make, then carry a dried Sheep Sorrel leaf
sachet for good luck. • Make, then carry a sachet of French
Sorrel leaves to heal the wearer from heartbreak, and to
possibly be able to see a fairy.

No. 336

Rumex crispus ☠ ⚱

Yellow Dock

Curled Dock | Curly Dock | Narrow Dock | Sour Dock

✸ SYMBOLIC MEANINGS

Curled; Curls; Curly; Patience; Religious
superstition; Shrewdness.

✇ POSSIBLE POWERS

Air element; Colorize; Earth element;
Fertility; Healing; Jupiter; Masculine
energy; Money; Venus.

☾ FOLKLORE AND FACTS

The Yellow Dock plant can grow to
be quite large, having leaves that are
long, narrow, hairless and edible. The
seeds are also edible, and are best dried
before grinding into a flour. • To help a
woman conceive a child, place a small
amount of Yellow Dock seeds in a small
cotton pouch and tie it to her left arm.

No. 337

Rumex patientia

Patience Dock

Dock | Garden Patience | Herb Patience | Monk's Rhubarb

✸ SYMBOLIC MEANINGS

Patience; Religious superstition; Shrewdness.

✇ POSSIBLE POWERS

Colorize; Fertility; Healing; Money.

☾ FOLKLORE AND FACTS

Patience Dock is a favorite herb
in Romanian cuisine for use in
soups, stews, and ground-pork-
stuffed leaf rolls called *sarmale*.
• Make an infusion of rainwater,
natural spring water, or distilled
water and Patience Dock to
sprinkle around a place of
business and especially at
the entry door to attract
customers who will be
eager to spend money.

No. 338

Rumex scutatus ☠ ⚱

French Sorrel

Shield-Leaf Sorrel

✸ SYMBOLIC MEANINGS

Affection; Ill-timed wit;
Parental affection; Refreshes
the spirit; Wit.

✇ POSSIBLE POWERS

Affection; Heals heartbreak;
Healing; Health; Joy; Luck;
Maternal tenderness;
Protection; See a fairy;
Spiritual healing.

☾ FOLKLORE AND FACTS

The lemony French Sorrel leaves are edible for use in salads
as well as for soups, stews, and sauces. Make, then carry or
wear a sachet of French sorrel leaves to heal the wearer from
heartbreak. • Carrying or wearing French sorrel is believed
to make it possible to see a fairy.

R

No. 339

Saccharomyces cerevisiae

Baker's Yeast

Yeast | Brewer's Yeast

☀ SYMBOLIC MEANINGS
False teaching; Sin.

✺ POSSIBLE POWERS
Expansion; Fullness;
Growth.

☾ FOLKLORE AND FACTS
Available dried powdered or dried compressed,
Saccharomyces cerevisiae yeast is the strain grown and used
for both Baker's Yeast and Brewer's Yeast. Yeast is used to
convert sugar and starch into alcohol and carbon dioxide,
making it useful as a leavening agent for baking and wine-
making. There are a few different recipes offering methods
for growing the *Saccharomyces cerevisiae* strain of yeast for
baking or wine-brewing by using fruits or fruit derivatives
such as raisins, potatoes, flour, or fruit juice, mixed with
measured amounts of warm water, then left in a warm place
to work its magic while being monitored for readiness. • In
the Bible's Book of Leviticus, attention was paid to every bit
of leavening during Passover, requiring that it was all thrown
out "to leave sin behind." After Passover, when leavening was
once again permitted, it was a fresh start, starting over anew.

No. 340

Saccharum officinarum ☙

Sugar Cane

Sugar | Sugarcane

☀ SYMBOLIC MEANINGS
Sweet love; Sweeten; Sweetest love;
Sweets for celebration.

✺ POSSIBLE POWERS
Aphrodisiac; Attracts love;
Celebration; Feminine energy;
Love; Lust; Stimulant; Venus;
Water element.

☾ FOLKLORE AND FACTS
Sometime around 800 BCE,
Saccharum officinarum Sugar
Cane was first cultivated in
New Guinea. • Sugar Cane was
once considered to be a spice.
• Processed first to be molasses, from
which Rum is distilled, it is further
processed to be "brown sugar" used in
baking, as well as "white refined sugar,"
which is a granulated table sugar also used in baking. The
granulated white sugar can be processed in different forms
for different uses in cooking, beverages, and cocktails. • An
extremely fine "powdered" sugar that is also known as
"confectioner's sugar" is intended to be used for a powdery
coating on baked goods and is the primary ingredient in
frosting recipes. Some commercial confectioner's sugars
include varying quantities of cornstarch. If it barely tastes
sweet, if at all, it contains more cornstarch than cane sugar.
• Sugar Cane was carried to North America on Christopher
Columbus's second journey in 1493. • A paste of granulated
brown pure cane sugar mixed with water and some freshly
squeezed lemon juice goes back to the ancient Egyptians,
who used it to remove hair in a process known as "sugaring."
• To instill lust where it may seem to be waning, mix
granulated or brown sugar and some coconut oil together to
make a coarse paste, then use it in the shower as a body scrub
that will smooth and sweetly fragrance the skin.

No. 341

Salicornia europaea ☠ ⚗

Glasswort

Common Glasswort | Marsh Samphire | Pickle Weed | Saltwort | Sea Asparagus | Sea Pickle

✹ SYMBOLIC MEANING

Salt horn.

✺ POSSIBLE POWERS

Grounding; Healing; Regeneration; Renewing; Seasoning.

☾ FOLKLORE AND FACTS

The Glasswort plant is an edible, salt-tolerant, flowering annual succulent that can be found in some salt marshes, among the mangroves, and on sandy beach dunes. It can be eaten raw or cooked by steaming or microwaving in water without added salt to be used in soups and as an ingredient in seafood dishes. • The salty Glasswort was utilized for a very long time as a source of soda ash that was instrumental in glass-making up until the beginning of the nineteenth century.

No. 342

Salvia officinalis ☠ ⚗

Sage

Bee Sage | Broadleaf Sage | Common Sage | Culinary Sage | Dalmatian Sage | Extrakta | Garden Sage | Golden Sage | Kitchen Sage | Purple Sage | Red Sage | Sacred Sage | *Salvia apiana* | True Sage | White Sage

✹ SYMBOLIC MEANINGS

Agelessness; Alleviates grief; Domestic virtue; Esteem; Good health; Holiness; Holy; Immortality; Long life; Sacred; Virtuous industry; Wisdom.

✺ POSSIBLE POWERS

Air element; Artistic ability; Banishes evil or negativity; Business; Cleanses the aura; Consecration; Expansion; Female fidelity; Great respect; Healing; Holiness; Honor; Immortality; Jupiter; Leadership; Longevity; Masculine energy; Memory; Politics; Power; Prosperity; Protection; Public acclaim; Purification; Responsibility; Royalty; Snakebite; Snakes; Success; Wards off evil; Wealth; Wisdom; Wishing.

☾ FOLKLORE AND FACTS

The ancient Romans believed that Sage was holy and powerful enough to create immortal life. The leaf of the Sage plant is as much an essential culinary herb now as it has been for thousands of years. Sage is counted on to season dishes made using fish, squash, chicken, pork, sausages, and cheeses. • Sage was often planted in cemeteries because it was believed that it would easily thrive on neglect and therefore live and grow forever. • Sage was a major ingredient in a medieval magical medicinal concoction called Four-Thieves Vinegar, which was supposedly used to ward off the plague. • For a chance at immortality, eat Sage daily throughout the month of May. • If you write a wish on a Sage leaf, put it under your pillow, then sleep upon it for three consecutive nights. If you dream of the wish coming true, it will come true. If you do not dream of that wish coming true, you must take that leaf and bury it immediately so that it brings you no harm. • Smudging with Sacred Sage will purify an area by removing negativity, spiritual impurities, and banishing evil, thus consecrating the area and providing protection. • Before entering a courtroom with the hopes of settling a lawsuit, write the names of the Christian Twelve Apostles on Sacred Sage leaves. Put them all into the defendant's shoes and enter the courtroom with confidence of gaining a positive outcome.

No. 343

Salvia rosmarinus ☠ ⚗

Rosemary

Dew of the Sea | Romarin | Severn Sea Rosemary | Sissinghurst Blue

✹ SYMBOLIC MEANINGS

Affectionate remembrance; Attraction of love; Constancy; Death; Fidelity; Fire element; Friendship; Love; Loyalty; Memory; Power of rekindling extinct energy; Remembrance; Restores balance of domestic power; Sun; Vitality; Wedding herb.

✺ POSSIBLE POWERS

Abundance; Advancement; Conscious will; Divination; Emotions; Energy; Exorcism; Fertility; Fire element; Friendship; Generation; Growth; Healing; Inspiration; Intuition; Joy; Leadership; Life; Light; Love; Love charm; Lust; Masculine energy; Mental clarity or power; Natural power; Protection; Protection from illness; Psychic ability; Purification; Repels a witch; Repels nightmares; Sea; Sleep; Subconscious mind; Success; Sun; Tides; Travel by water; Youth.

FOLKLORE AND FACTS

Rosemary was first mentioned on a stone tablet in cuneiform glyphs that date back to 5000 BCE. Native to the Mediterranean, the Rosemary bush can grow large enough to prune into topiary forms. It has needle-like leaves and blue, pink, purple, or white flowers, and is extremely fragrant when you simply brush past it. The leaves are edible and pliable when fresh, and have a deliciously strong flavor for use in cooking, baking, roasting, or simmered in soup. However, unless the dried leaves have been ground to be used as a powder, whole dried Rosemary is difficult to use without grinding it first. • In the Middle Ages, to fragrance the house during the holidays, Rosemary was commonly strewn upon the floor. • It is believed that anyone who smells the aroma of Rosemary on Christmas Eve will have happiness throughout the coming year. • Students in ancient Greece tucked sprigs of Rosemary behind an ear or in their hair to enhance their memories during academic exams. • Rosemary was thought to encourage the bridal couple to remember and stay true to their marriage vows. • It was believed one would fall in love if touched on the finger by a sprig of Rosemary. • Rosemary under the pillow is supposed to be a remedy for nightmares. • In Australia, Rosemary is worn on Anzac Day in remembrance of those who died during wartime. • During the Middle Ages, newlyweds would plant a branch of Rosemary. If the branch did not thrive, it was a bad omen for the marriage and the family. • A Rosemary plant on each side of an entry door to a home is said to repel witches. • Rosemary essential oil for aromatherapy can be helpful for remembering and for remaining alert. • To preserve youth, make a box from Rosemary wood to open and smell from time to time. • Plant Rosemary in a garden that is intended to please the fairies.

No. 344

Sambucus canadensis ☠ ⚗

Common Elder

American Black Elderberry | Black Elder | Canada Elderberry | Elder | Elder Bush | Elderberry Tree | European Black Elderberry | European Elder | European Elderberry | Rob Elder | Sweet Elder

✴ SYMBOLIC MEANINGS

Compassion; Creativity; Cycles; Death; Endings; Humility; Kindness; Protection against evil dangers; Rebirth; Regeneration; Renewal; Transformation; Zeal; Zealousness.

🌀 POSSIBLE POWERS

Aphrodisiac; Attracts love; Colorize; Death; Exorcism; Feminine energy; Good luck; Healing; Kills a serpent; Magic; Prosperity; Protection; Protection against a witch or evil spirit; Sends away a thief; Sleep; Venus; Water element.

FOLKLORE AND FACTS

The cooked Elder berries are edible and can be used to make jam, jelly, pie filling, marmalade, and wine. A sweet kitchen-brewed mix of Elderberries, cane sugar, and water simmered down to a basic syrup can be made to save and use throughout the autumn and winter as a folk medicine remedy for colds and coughs. If the sugar is not added, the syrup, called elder rob, is simply reduced using the natural sugars present in the berries. • Elder is associated with witches. • When the dead were once buried, Elder branches were planted with the body to protect them from evil spirits. • Stone Age arrowheads were shaped to look like Elder leaves. • A cross made of Elder wood then attached to stables is supposed to keep evil away from the animals. • Cradles were never to be made of Elder wood because it was believed the baby would either fall out of it, not be able to sleep, or be pinched by fairies. • The English believe that burning Elder wood logs will bring the Devil into the house. • Before pruning an Elder tree, one must ask the tree's permission, then spit three times before making the first cut. • Elder leaves gathered on April 30th can be attached to doors and windows to keep witches from entering the home. • An amulet made from a piece of Elder wood on which the Sun has never directly shone is tied inside a small pouch that is held between two knots to be worn around the neck as a pendant to protect against evil. • Elder essential oil aromatherapy might be able to help alleviate anxiety and calm irritability. It may even help lift one up from the kind of depression that one may be suffering.

S

No. 345

Sanguisorba minor 🜨

Burnet

Garden Burnet | Salad Burnet | Small Burnet

✳ SYMBOLIC MEANING

A merry heart.

🌀 POSSIBLE POWERS

Consecration of ritual accoutrements; Countering magic; Lifts depressive feelings; Penetrates despondency; Protection.

☾ FOLKLORE AND FACTS

The edible part of the Burnet plant is the young leaves, which are reported to have a flavor that is hotly spicy with a touch of tartness, while also cucumber-like. The young and new leaves can be added to salads, to beverages as a flavoring, and as an ingredient in sauces. • Because at the beginning of summer the Burnet plants will flower early, the blossoms are cut and used in spiritually and psychologically uplifting floral arrangements for the home, while the leaves are encouraged to grow on for culinary and other magical uses. When flowering, Burnet is at its best vibration yet at its briefest window of opportunity, so be sure to place cut Burnet flowers to use in the rooms of those who may be in great need of having the weight of depression lifted off of them. • Burnet can be used to counter an unwanted magical effect. • Burnet can be used to consecrate magical tools when prepared as an infusion in rainwater or natural spring water.

No. 346

Sassafras albidum ☠ 🜨

White Sassafras

Gumbo Filé | Red Sassafras | Sassafras | Silky Sassafras

✳ SYMBOLIC MEANING

Lucky wood.

🌀 POSSIBLE POWERS

Fire element; Healing; Health; Jupiter; Masculine energy; Money.

☾ FOLKLORE AND FACTS

Cajun cuisine's filé powder is made from the tiny, newly growing leaves of the *Sassafras albidum* White Sassafras tree, which are dried and ground into a fine powder. Filé powder was first devised by the Choctaw Native Americans, who used it to thicken stews. • Make a White Sassafras sachet of a leaf or a few pinches of filé powder, then carry it in the purse or wallet to attract money.

No. 347

Satureja hortensis 🜨

Summer Savory

Cimbru | Cząber | Garden Savory | Santoreggia

✳ SYMBOLIC MEANING

Interest.

🌀 POSSIBLE POWERS

Air element; Anti-flatulent; Antiseptic; Aphrodisiac; the Arts; Attracts love; Attraction; Beauty; Diminishes sexual desire; Friendship; Gifts; Harmony; Joy; Love; Love charm; Mental clarity; Mental power; Mercury; Pleasure; Seasoning herb; Sensuality; Sex magic; Sexuality; Strength.

☾ FOLKLORE AND FACTS

The flavors of the annual herb *Satureja hortensis* Summer Savory and the perennial herb *Satureja montana* Winter Savory are similar, with Winter Savory being a little bitter to Summer Savory's slight sweetness. • Summer Savory is a popular culinary herb in Eastern Europe and in Canada, where it is used like Sage is in other parts of the world. In Bulgaria, the three spices on the table are salt, pepper, and Summer Savory. • Summer Savory is also used in the classic blend known as *herbes de Provence*. • The ancient Romans used Summer Savory to make their favorite love potions. The sensual reputation of Summer Savory was such that monasteries were absolutely forbidden to grow it because the monks could fall under its alluring spell and become sexually corrupted by it.

No. 348

Satureja montana

Winter Savory
Mountain Savory

✴ **SYMBOLIC MEANING**
Interest.

🌀 **POSSIBLE POWERS**
Air element; Anti-flatulent; Antiseptic; Diminishes sexual desire; Mercury; Seasoning herb.

☾ **FOLKLORE AND FACTS**
The slightly bitter-tasting Winter Savory was used by the ancient Greeks and Romans at least 2,000 years ago. • Winter Savory is occasionally planted with Bean plants to fend off bean weevil seed beetles and prevent them damaging the plants. • While Summer Savory is thought to be an aphrodisiac, Winter Savory is thought to have the exact opposite effect on the libido.

No. 349

Secale cereale

Cereal Rye
Rye

✴ **SYMBOLIC MEANINGS**
Apostasy; Condemnation; Dealings with the Devil; Disgust; Earth element; Mockery; Sardonicism; Trickery.

🌀 **POSSIBLE POWERS**
Black magick; Bondage; Devilry; Earth element; Feminine energy; Love; Sorcery; Venus.

☾ **FOLKLORE AND FACTS**
The edible parts of the Cereal Rye plant are the grain seeds that are ground into flour for baked goods, as well as for the main ingredient in the distillation of "rye whiskey." • Fine Cereal Rye flour mixed with iron oxide and linseed oil then cooked will produce the traditional iconic Swedish falu red paint that was originally used on homes and barns until around the early part of the nineteenth century. • Feed Cereal Rye bread to ensure love. • A Cereal Rye cracker is often used as a substitute for a communion-style host in some alternative-religion rituals.

S

No. 350
Sechium edule 🍶

Chayote
Chocho | Choko | Christophene | Güisquil

✳ SYMBOLIC MEANING
Testicle.

🌀 POSSIBLE POWERS
Health; Masculine energy; Sexuality; Zombie transformation.

☾ FOLKLORE AND FACTS
The fruit of the Chayote plant is mild-tasting and can be eaten raw and unpeeled, but it is most often prepared like a summer squash by boiling then mashing, or frying, baking, or pickling for use as side dishes or as an ingredient in recipes for salads, soups, stews, stir-fries, sautés, curries, casseroles, and even desserts. The shoots and leaves are also edible when young once they've been cooked. The tuber is also edible and can be prepared like a yam. • Once every seven years a zombie can be returned to life for nine days by feeding it Chayote. After nine days it will die or become a zombie all over again.

No. 351
Selenicereus undatus

Dragonfruit
Belle of the Night | Night-blooming Cereus | Pitahaya | Queen of the Night | Red Pitahaya | Strawberry Pear

✳ SYMBOLIC MEANINGS
Beauty under the moon's light; Moonlit beauty; Transient beauty.

🌀 POSSIBLE POWERS
Dragon magic; Protection.

☾ FOLKLORE AND FACTS
The fruit of the beautiful night-blooming Dragonfruit plant is edible. • An enormous hedge of Dragonfruit was planted in Honolulu in 1836 at the Punahou School by a woman by the name of "Mrs. Bingham." It is believed that this long hedge is the mother of nearly all the Dragonfruit plants in Hawaii, which were started from cuttings taken from it. • The fruit pulp's texture is similar to kiwifruit, with black crunchy seeds that are brewed as a tea or used in alcoholic beverages.

No. 352
Senegalia senegal ☠🍶

Gum Arabic
Acacia Gum | Arabic Gum | Cape Gum | Egyptian Thorn | Gum Arabic Tree | Gum Senegal Tree | Hashab Gum

✳ SYMBOLIC MEANING
Platonic love.

🌀 POSSIBLE POWERS
Air element; Artemis; Masculine energy; Money; Osiris; Platonic love; Protection; Psychic powers; Purification; Purifies evil or negativity; Ra; Spiritual enhancement; Spirituality; Sun; Wards off evil.

☾ FOLKLORE AND FACTS
The term "gum Arabic" dates back to when it was used in the Middle East, from around the ninth century. The highest quality of the Gum Arabic resin is from Sudan. The thick, gummy sap is harvested by cutting slashes into a

branch, stripping out the bark in the wound, then waiting several weeks for the resinous gum to collect in the gash and harden. • Among its many uses, Gum Arabic acts as a binder, thickening agent, stabilizer, or emulsifier in the manufacturing of certain food products, confections, and beverage syrups. • Because it is water-soluble, Gum Arabic is a valuable binder used for watercolor paints. • Gum Arabic is used to anoint and consecrate all the accoutrements used in carrying out magical rituals of all types.

No. 353
Sesamum indicum

Sesame
Benne | Sesemt

✳ SYMBOLIC MEANINGS
Purge; Reveal.

🌀 POSSIBLE POWERS
Aphrodisiac; Attracts love; Conception; Finds hidden treasure; Fire element; Lust; Masculine energy; Money; Opens a locked door; Protection; Reveals a secret path; Success in business; Sun.

☾ FOLKLORE AND FACTS
One of the oldest crops in the world that was cultivated for use as a cooking oil is Sesame. It can grow in harsh conditions and in very poor soils that cannot support other types of crops. • The nutty flavored seeds are used as an ingredient or as a topping for many types of baked goods. A Caribbean Sesame seed and sugar confection is shaped into a bar and enjoyed like peanut-brittle candy. • Ground Sesame seeds make the tahini that is a necessary ingredient in the iconic mashed chickpea spread that is known as hummus. • Every month, put fresh Sesame seeds in a small open jar in the house to draw money to it.

No. 354
Sinapis alba

White Mustard
Field Mustard | Mustard Plant | Wild Mustard

✳ SYMBOLIC MEANINGS
Charity; Indifference.

🌱 COMPONENT MEANINGS
Seed: Good luck charm; Indifference; Visible faith.

🌀 POSSIBLE POWERS
Banishes negativity; Ending relationships; Endings; Fertility; Fire element; Mars; Mental clarity or power; Protection.

☾ FOLKLORE AND FACTS
The *Sinapis alba* White Mustard plant is cultivated for its seeds, which provide the mustard element to the yellow mustard recipe commonly used in the USA as a condiment on the zingy iconic hot dog and the hot soft pretzel. The White Mustard leaves can be harvested before the plant blooms to be prepared and cooked as a leafy green vegetable or added to soups. • The first time White Mustard's vivid yellow mustard appeared drizzled along the length of a hotdog was at the St. Louis World's Fair in 1904. • Carry White Mustard seed in a red cloth pouch to increase your mental powers. • Bury White Mustard seeds under or near your doorstep to keep supernatural beings from coming into your home.

No. 355

Siraitia grosvenorii 🪔

Monkfruit

Luohan Guo

✹ **SYMBOLIC MEANING**
Sweeter.

🌀 **POSSIBLE POWERS**
Healing; Health; Sweeten.

☾ **FOLKLORE AND FACTS**
The pulp of the edible fruit of the *Siraitia grosvenorii* Monkfruit plant is eaten fresh, while the rind can be used to brew an herbal tea. The sweet juice is used as a sweetener, or another common way is drying the fruit and using it for a sweetener that is many times stronger than cane sugar. After the fruit has dried, the thin rind becomes very brittle and is easily removed, leaving the dried pulp intact.

No. 356

Sisymbrium officinale 🪔

Singer's Plant

Hedge Mustard

✹ **SYMBOLIC MEANINGS**
Cool; Smooth.

🌀 **POSSIBLE POWERS**
Fire element; Healing; Mars.

☾ **FOLKLORE AND FACTS**
The Singer's Plant is also known as Hedge Mustard in Great Britain and Northern Europe, where it is cultivated for its leaves, which are then prepared as a leafy green vegetable or added to soups. The seeds are ground into a paste condiment familiar in European markets. • The ancient Greeks once believed that Singer's Plant was not only a medicine for sore throats, but also an antidote for every poison. Alas, it was not quite as healing as that.

No. 357

Smilax ornata ☠ 🪔

Sarsaparilla

Honduran Sarsaparilla | Jamaican Sarsaparilla |
Sweet Sarsaparilla

✹ **SYMBOLIC MEANINGS**
Loveliness; Lovely; Mythology.

🌀 **POSSIBLE POWERS**
Fire element; Jupiter; Love;
Masculine energy; Money.

☾ **FOLKLORE AND FACTS**
The young shoots of the Sarsaparilla plant can be eaten raw or cooked like Asparagus. The berries can also be eaten raw or made into jam and jelly. Sarsaparilla root can be prepared like a root vegetable and boiled, stewed, roasted, or added to soups and stews. The root is also dried, then ground into flour. The root is also the primary ingredient in the old-fashioned traditional recipe for the beverage known as "root beer."

No. 358

Smyrnium olusatrum 🪔

Alexanders

Alisanders | Horse Parsley

✹ **SYMBOLIC MEANINGS**
Manly; Repels; Warrior.

🌀 **POSSIBLE POWERS**
Air element; Earth element;
Mars; Masculine energy;
Mercury; Protection against
the enemy.

☾ **FOLKLORE AND FACTS**
All parts of the Alexanders plant are edible. Its flavor is between Parsley and Celery, with the seeds having a peppery spicy taste. As late as the eighteenth century, Alexanders was an ingredient in soups and stews and known as a "pottage herb." In Alexander the Great's time, Alexanders was a very popular herb that was consumed as a vegetable and used in many different dishes. Roman soldiers fancied all parts of the Alexanders plant so much that they would carry the plant along with them wherever they traveled.

S

No. 359
Solanum lycopersicum 🕱 ⚗

Tomato

Cherry Tomato | Golden Apple | Love Apple | *Lycopersicon esculentum* var. *cerasiforme* | Plum Tomato | *Solanum lycopersicum* var. 'Plum' | Tomate | Tomatl

☀ SYMBOLIC MEANINGS
Contrariness; Fussy.

✹ POSSIBLE POWERS
Aphrodisiac; Feminine energy; Love; Love spells; Prosperity; Protection; Venus; Water element.

☾ FOLKLORE AND FACTS
With the exception of the ripe fruit, all other plant parts are toxic on *Solanum lycopersicum* Tomato, *Solanum lycopersicum* var. 'Plum' Plum Tomato, and *Lycopersicon esculentum* var. *cerasiforme* Cherry Tomato. Unripe green Tomatoes are toxic unless they are thoroughly cooked. Tomatoes will continue to ripen once they have been removed from the vine. • Although the Tomato is botanically a fruit, culinarily it has been fully embraced as a vegetable. • Tomatoes are eaten fresh, stewed, sautéed, and fried. • The Tomato is the base ingredient in Italian marinara sauce. • Although first considered to be poisonous, Tomatoes were enjoyed in Italy at least as far back as the 1500s. • Nearly a century later, the Tomato was introduced and eaten fearlessly in England, where it had also been believed to be poisonous. The Tomato was introduced to other countries and quickly adopted into their cuisines. Fried green Tomatoes, for example, is a dish that started in the southern USA. • It is believed by some that a large fruit of the Tomato placed on the mantle in a home will bring prosperity. • Tomatoes growing in the garden will scare away evil. • The Tomato's common name of Love Apple was not coined lightly. It may or may not be the fruit of human love, but it surely represents the love of the Tomato itself. • When a pet encounters a skunk in the worst kind of way, a time-tested method for de-skunking the poor animal is a generous washing using plenty of Tomato juice.

No. 360
Solanum melongena 🕱 ⚗

Eggplant

Aubergine | Brinjal | Common Aubergine | Dwarf Aubergine | Guinea Squash | Snake Aubergine

☀ SYMBOLIC MEANINGS
Government; Office holder; Phallus.

✹ POSSIBLE POWERS
Earth element; Healing; Health; Jupiter; Love; Luck; Masculine energy; Prosperity; Protection; Sex; Virility; Wealth; Wishes for higher status.

☾ FOLKLORE AND FACTS
Eggplant is a food that is either loved and enjoyed whenever possible, or entirely disliked and persistently avoided. • The edible part of the *Solanum melongena* Eggplant plant is the ripe cooked fruit that is botanically a berry. As a member of the nightshade family, the Eggplant stems, leaves, and roots are toxic. The uncooked berry is also toxic. • Most Eggplant cultivars produce a dark purple skin, but there are also reddish-purple-, yellow-, green-, and white-skinned Eggplants. Eggplant can be baked, barbecued, sautéed, steamed, fried, mashed, roasted, stewed, curried, stuffed, and pickled for use in dishes in several international cuisines. • According to thirteenth-century Italian folktales, the Eggplant could cause insanity. • The Eggplant still grows wild in India.

S

No. 361

Solanum tuberosum ☠ ⚗

Potato

Irish Potato | Potatta | Purple Potato | Red Potato | Russet Potato | Spud | Taters | Tatties | White Potato | Yukon Potato

✹ SYMBOLIC MEANINGS
Beneficence; Benevolence; Prodigality.

⟐ POSSIBLE POWERS
Earth element; Feminine energy; Healing; Image magic; Moon.

☾ FOLKLORE AND FACTS
Potatoes were first cultivated by the Incas around 3000 BCE and have since been a vital food crop around the world for all cultures. Nearly every culture in every country enjoys a popular dish made from Potatoes. • Every part of the Potato plant that is green is poisonous, including that found on the tuber itself. • Potatoes are most commonly a beige to tan flesh color, but can also be yellow, gold, red, purple, and even blue. • The most globally popular ways of enjoying a cooked potato are deep-frying it, baking it whole, peeling and sautéing it until tender, or peeling then boiling in salted water until the Potato is tender enough to mash. The Potato is also an ingredient in baked goods. Potatoes are highly adaptable. They can be prepared alone or with other ingredients and seasoned to taste. • It was believed by some that if you carried a very small Potato in your pocket, it would protect you against gout, warts, and rheumatism. It would cure a toothache or a cold if you had one. Your pocket Potato would also protect you from contracting a cold if you carried the tuber all winter long. And, if that pocket Potato happened to be a stolen tuber, it would also cure existing rheumatism.

No. 362

Solidago odora ⚗

Sweet Goldenrod

Anise-scented Goldenrod | Blue Mountain Tea | European Goldenrod | Fragrant Goldenrod | Golden Rod | Goldenrod | Missouri Goldenrod | Sweet-scented Goldenrod

✹ SYMBOLIC MEANINGS
Be cautious; Encouragement; Good fortune; Good luck; Precaution; Strength; Success; Treasure.

⟐ POSSIBLE POWERS
Air element; Divination; Feminine energy; Fire element; Luck; Mars; Money; Prosperity; Venus.

☾ FOLKLORE AND FACTS
The flowers and the crushed leaves of Sweet Goldenrod can be brewed into teas. • Witches frequently used Sweet Goldenrod in their potions. • It was believed that by wearing a sprig of Sweet Goldenrod one day, your future love will appear to you on the next day. • It was believed by some that Sweet Goldenrod can be utilized as a simple divining device by holding flowered stems in the hand. The stems may nod in the direction of the lost or hidden object, perhaps even toward treasure. • If Sweet Goldenrod suddenly grows near a door at your house in a place where it did not once grow before, expect an abundance of good fortune for the entire household.

S

No. 363

Sorbus aucuparia ☠ ⚗

European Rowan

Rowan

☀ SYMBOLIC MEANINGS

Balance; Connection; Courage; Harmony; Mystery;
Prudence; Transformation; With me you are safe.

🌀 POSSIBLE POWERS

Abundance; Communication with the spirit world; Defiance;
Determination; Divination; Fends off malicious witchcraft;
Fends off malicious fairy magic; Fertility; Fire element;
Healing; Inner strength; Intuition; Love; Lucky; Masculine
energy; Power; Prosperity; Protection; Psychic power;
Resilience; Strength when facing an adversity; Success; Sun;
Thor; Visions; Wards off evil or sorcery; Wisdom.

☾ FOLKLORE AND FACTS

The berries of the European Rowan tree are plentiful and
edible once they have been frozen in the first frost, then
cooked. European Rowan berries are used to make jellies,

jams, syrup, chutney, wine, liqueur, and tea. • To the ancient
Celts, the European Rowan tree is believed to be the most
powerful of all trees and is the Tree of Life; any that grow
near a stone circle will be the most potent of all. • Carry
European Rowan wood to increase psychic powers. • It is
believed that European Rowan is sacred to Thor, God of
Lightning, and that lightning will only rarely ever strike
it. • An effective divining rod can be made using a forked
European Rowan branch. • In Europe, for hundreds of years
protective crosses have been made from European Rowan
twigs that have been tied together with red thread and then
carried. • European Rowan branches near a house
can often be found pinned to grow over doorways in order
to ward off evil and sorcery from entering the dwelling.
• The European Rowan is the tree of the Queen of the
Fairies. • The European Rowan is closely associated with the
spirit world, offering its protection when journeying there.
• European Rowan wood is the traditional wood of choice
to use for carving a set of divination runes. • A European
Rowan wood magic wand can bring about success when
used for divination, healing, and aiding psychic power.
• On the day of the winter solstice and again on the summer
solstice, branches of European Rowan were often placed
across the door and window lintels to bring good fortune to
the home. • A European Rowan tree grows in most of the
oldest Welsh churchyards as a defense against evil spirits.
• The Druids planted circles of European Rowan around
their encampments to offer protection against the dark
powers that threatened all within them. • During the winter
solstice, the sparkly frost on the clustered branches of the
European Rowan tree can sometimes give the illusion of
twinkling stars.

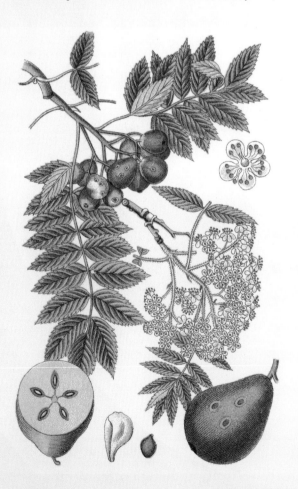

S

No. 364
Sorbus domestica ⚱

Service Tree

Sorb | Sorb Tree | True Service Tree | Whitty Pear

✸ **SYMBOLIC MEANINGS**
Harmony; Prudence.

🌀 **POSSIBLE POWERS**
Healing; Love; Prosperity.

🌙 **FOLKLORE AND FACTS**
The fruit of the long-living *Sorbus domestica* Service Tree resembles an Apple, but as it is extremely tart with a somewhat grainy pulp, it tastes nothing like one. The fruit is edible, but more pleasant to eat when it becomes a bit overripe. Then it can be used to make jam, juiced to make a fruit cider beverage, or distilled into a brandy. • Plato used the metaphor of a halved Service Tree fruit to explain the halving of the original humans by Zeus, originating the concept of "twin flames" whom Plato claimed originally had four arms, four legs, two faces on one head, and two separate sets of genitalia. • Service Trees can live up to 400 years.

No. 365
Sorghum vulgare ⚱

Sorghum

Durra | Great Millet | Jowar | Milho | Milo | Sorghum Bicolor

✸ **SYMBOLIC MEANING**
Parts of one's own self.

🌀 **POSSIBLE POWERS**
Earth element; Energy; Health; Power; Promotion; Reconciliation; Sustenance.

🌙 **FOLKLORE AND FACTS**
The nutritious, drought-tolerant Sorghum plant originated in Africa around 8000 BCE to then be globally cultivated in tropical and subtropical areas. It is the fifth most important cereal grain after rice, wheat, corn, and barley. The Sorghum plant can grow as tall as corn and will produce gluten-free grain. Sorghum whole grains and flour are used to make staples such as daily consumed flatbreads, porridges, and granola, and is added to soups and casseroles. It is also made into a sweet syrup, Sorghum molasses, which is used as a sugar substitute in some dishes, and can also be used as an ingredient for marinades, dressings, dips, a drizzle for fruit or vegetable dishes, or in cocktails. Sorghum is also commonly fermented to be a beer as well as a liquor. Grains are popped like popcorn or prepared like a rice dish. • Fermented Sorghum juice has been extracted from stalks to be converted into ethanol and be used as a biofuel. • Dried Sorghum stalks have also been used to make brooms.

No. 366

Spinacia oleracea 🜨

Spinach

Chieftain of Leafy Greens | Common Spinach | Espinafre

☀ **SYMBOLIC MEANINGS**
Power; Strength.

🌀 **POSSIBLE POWERS**
Earth element; Jupiter;
Powerfulness.

☾ **FOLKLORE AND FACTS**
Spinach has been
consumed for over 2,000
years. It was introduced into
Europe sometime in the fourteenth century.
• The leaves and stems of the Spinach plant are highly
nutritious, edible, leafy green vegetables that are enjoyed
raw, sautéed, steamed, boiled, and even juiced. • The
nautical cartoon character Popeye the Sailor Man,
introduced in 1932, claimed Spinach was responsible for
his bulging arm muscles and strength. • Dreaming about
Spinach could mean a subconscious feeling of repression due
to a sense of dread at being forced against your will to do
something that would be good to do.

No. 367

Spiraea ulmaria 🜨

Meadowsweet

Bridewort | Dollof | Lady of the Meadow | Meadow Queen | Meadow Sweet | Meadow-wort |
Meadwort | Pride of the Meadow | Queen of the Meadow

☀ **SYMBOLIC MEANINGS**
Usefulness; Uselessness.

🌀 **POSSIBLE POWERS**
Air element; Divination;
Happiness; Jupiter; Love;
Masculine energy; Peace.

☾ **FOLKLORE AND FACTS**
Meadowsweet is edible and
used to flavor wines, beers,
and vinegars. It is also added
to jams to season them with
a hint of an almond-like flavor.
• Meadowsweet was the preferred
floor-strewing herb of Queen Elizabeth
I of England. • Dried Meadowsweet flowers can be added
to potpourri blends. • A black vegetable dye can be

created from Meadowsweet roots. • In Wales, there was
found archeological evidence of Meadowsweet along with
cremated remains that date back to the Bronze Age.

No. 368

Spondias purpurea ☠ 🜨

Jocote

Hog Plum | Purple Mombin | Red Mombin | Sineguela

☀ **SYMBOLIC MEANINGS**
Privation; Sour fruit.

🌀 **POSSIBLE POWERS**
Healthy; Healing.

☾ **FOLKLORE AND FACTS**
Jocote fruit is edible raw and high in vitamin C when it
is fully ripe and soft. The fruit will ripen to a red, be very
sweet, and taste like a cross between the plum and mango.
• The pulp can be mashed and used in beverages and
cocktails, as well as cooked down to make a syrup that is
enjoyed as a topping for ice cream. • Boiled fruits can also be
dried for later use in dessert recipes and curries. • Underripe
fruits are very tart and can be pickled along with the flower
buds or made into spicy sauces. • The young leaves can be
cooked and eaten as a leafy vegetable.

S

Stellaria media

Chickweed

Satin Flower | Star Weed | Starwort

✹ **SYMBOLIC MEANINGS**
Cheerfulness in old age;
Welcome to a stranger.

✺ **POSSIBLE POWERS**
Encourage all manners
of good to enter; Feminine energy;
Moon; Protection; Protection against ghosts; Protection
against witches; Repels a hex; Repels all manners of evil;
Water element.

☾ **FOLKLORE AND FACTS**
The leaves of Chickweed are nutritious and edible, cooked
as a leafy green vegetable. Tender new leaves are sometimes
added to salads and eaten raw. Chickweed is a necessary
ingredient in a symbolic Japanese spring festival dish known
as *nanakusa-no-sekku*. • The small Chickweed flowers
are white and star-shaped. It appears to be that all the
Pennsylvania Dutch "hex symbols" that look like flowers are,
in fact, stylized Chickweed blossoms. • Prior to the steady
emigration of people moving from England, Chickweed was
virtually unknown in North America until it was introduced
into the newly planted English gardens in the New World.

Stevia rebaudiana ⚗

Stevia

Candyleaf | Sugarleaf | Sweetleaf

✹ **SYMBOLIC MEANINGS**
Sweet herb; Sweet leaf;
Sweet treat.

✺ **POSSIBLE POWER**
Sweeten.

☾ **FOLKLORE AND FACTS**
The extremely sweet leaves
of the Stevia plant have
been used for the purpose of
sweetening tea in Brazil and
Paraguay for hundreds of years.
The Guaraní people of South
America used Stevia 1,500 years
ago. • Starting in Japan in the early
1970s, awareness of Stevia as a natural alternative sweetener
to cane sugar steadily increased until it was readily available
around the world. Sweetening extracts obtained from the
Stevia plant's leaves are widely available as a liquid or as
powdered crystals.

No. 371
Syzygium aromaticum ⚱
Clove
Cengkih

✴ SYMBOLIC MEANINGS
Dignity; Lasting friendship; Love; Money; Restraint.

🌀 POSSIBLE POWERS
Aphrodisiac; Abundance; Advancement; Conscious will;
Energy; Exorcism; Fire element; Friendship; Growth;
Healing; Joy; Jupiter; Leadership; Life; Light; Love; Masculine
energy; Mental clarity; Money; Natural power; Protection;
Purification; Success.

☾ FOLKLORE AND FACTS
The seventeenth-century trade wars between European
nations and the Maluku Islands of Indonesia inspired
the planting of Clove trees wherever in the world they
would grow. • A Clove is the edible dried flower bud of
the *Syzygium aromaticum* tree. Clove is used as a fragrant
culinary seasoning in cooking with meats, curries, and
fruits as well as in baking in the cuisines of India, East Asia,
Africa, the Middle East, Peru, the Mediterranean, and North
America. A little bit of the intensely flavored and scented
Clove goes a long way. • Worn or carried tucked in a pocket,
the magical properties and fragrance of a whole Clove will
attract the opposite sex as well as comfort someone who
has suffered an emotional loss and is bereaved. • If Clove is
burned as an incense, it will stop people gossiping, attract
riches, drive away hostility, turn away negative energies,
and produce positive spiritual energy. All the while it will
also purify wherever the fragrance goes. • Clove essential oil
mixed in a spray bottle of distilled water can make a good
cleaner for the home when there is illness. • A time-honored
home remedy found in the spice cabinet is a whole
Clove to chew on to offer some relief from the
pain of a toothache.
• During the winter holiday
celebrations, the aromatherapy
of the warm, spicy fragrance of
essential Clove oil can bring
the nature of the holidays into
the home.

No. 372
Syzygium jambos
Rose Apple
Chom Pu | Cloud Apple | Malabar Plum

✴ SYMBOLIC MEANING
The Golden Fruit
of Immortality.

🌀 POSSIBLE POWERS
Calmness;
No aggression;
No combat; Peacefulness;
Peace of mind.

☾ FOLKLORE AND FACTS
Looking so much like a Guava, the fruit of the
Syzygium jambos Rose Apple tree is very often mistaken
for one. There the similarity stops, as the Rose Apple fruit
contains one or two seeds within a somewhat hollow cavity
of the fruit, while the Guava snugly holds dozens of them
in its pulp. A ripe Rose Apple fruit is often determined
by shaking it. When you hear a rattle, you know it is ripe
enough to eat its fragrant pulp raw or to use as an ingredient
in Chinese cuisine. • It is believed that the Rose Apple is the
Golden Fruit of Immortality and that the Buddha received
enlightenment under the tree. • The Rose Apple flowers are
fanciful tasseled tufts, while the blossom end of the fruit looks
like a crown.

S

No. 373

Tagetes patula ☠ ⚗

French Marigold

Marigold Flower

☀ SYMBOLIC MEANINGS

Creativity; Grief; Jealousy;
Passion; Spreading; Storm;
Uneasiness.

🌀 POSSIBLE POWERS

Amorousness; Colorize;
Dream magic; Evil thoughts; Fire
element; Helps with seeing fairies;
Legal matters; Love charms; Masculine
energy; Prediction; Prophetic dreams;
Protection; Psychic power; Rebirth;
Sleep; Sun.

☾ FOLKLORE AND FACTS

French Marigold is considered one of the most sacred
herbs of India, with the flower heads commonly strung into
garlands and used in temples and at weddings. • French
Marigold is occasionally added to the feed of home-farmed
chickens to intensify the color of the yolks and to cast
a yellow tint over the chicken skin. • In the Republic
of Georgia's cuisine, dried powdered French Marigold
petals are used as a favorite seasoning, and are included in
a seasoning blend known as *khmeli suneli*. • The Welsh
believed that French Marigold could be used to predict
stormy weather if the flowers did not open in the morning.
• French Marigold essential oil is often used as an insect
repellent, most especially against bedbugs. • Make, then
wear or carry a sachet of French Marigold petals with a Bay
Laurel leaf to quiet gossip being passed around about you.

No. 374

Tamarindus indica ⚗

Tamarind

Ma-Kham | Tamarandi | Tambran

☀ SYMBOLIC MEANINGS

Love; Romance; Sex.

🌀 POSSIBLE POWERS

Attracts negative energy; Bad luck; Feminine energy; Ghosts;
Healing; Love; Protection; Saturn; Sex magic; Water element.

☾ FOLKLORE AND FACTS

Tamarind was referenced in Marco Polo's writings. • The
pulp of a ripe Tamarind fruit is edible, tart, and sweeter as
it ripens. It is widely used after it has been processed into a
paste that is used in chutneys and sauces, added as a savory
component in meat dishes, made into sweets, and added
as a flavoring in baked goods, as well as being transformed
into a beverage, a stew, or a soup. • Make, then carry a pink
and red sachet of Tamarind seeds to attract romantic love.
• Hindu legend tells that the Tamarind tree symbolizes the
wife of the creator, Brahma. • Tamarind was believed to
attract ghosts. • Some people believe that a house should
never be built anywhere near a Tamarind tree because ghosts
congregate around the tree and it pulls negative energy
and evil spirits towards it. • Tamarind wood is used for the
making of common useful household objects such as mortars
and pestles, or for the artistic carving of small boxes all the
way to large cabinets. • The Tamarind fruit can also be used
as a metal polish for brass, copper, and bronze.

No. 375

Tanacetum balsamita ⚗

Costmary

Alecost | Balsam Herb | Bible Leaf | Mint Geranium

☀ SYMBOLIC MEANINGS

Gentility; Virtue.

🌀 POSSIBLE POWERS

Holy reference; Peace in the
home; Protection at sea.

☾ FOLKLORE AND FACTS

The silvery, fragrant
Costmary leaf is used to
season a salad for a lemony-
minty flavor or to season
chicken and sausage. It
gained its common name
of Alecost because it is
sometimes used to flavor ale.
• Costmary was used in medieval times as a place marker in
Bibles. • Carry a Costmary amulet if traveling by sea.

No. 376
Taraxacum officinale

Dandelion

Blowball | Common Dandelion | Dent de Lion | Swine Snout | Swine's Snout | Yellow Gowan

✺ SYMBOLIC MEANINGS
Coquetry; Faithfulness; Happiness; Oracle; Prosperity; Wishing; Wishing for love.

✺ POSSIBLE POWERS
Air element; Calling spirits; Depart; Divination; Jupiter; Love's oracle; Masculine energy; Moon; Oracle; Purification; Rustic oracle; Spirit magic; Water element; Wish magic; Wishes come true; Wishing.

✺ FOLKLORE AND FACTS
Prehistoric gatherers included Dandelion in their foraging. Fossilized Dandelion from the Pliocene Epoch has been found in Southern Russia. • Prior to the steady emigration of people moving from England, Dandelion was virtually unknown in North America until it was introduced into the newly planted English gardens in the New World. • The Dandelion plant's leaf, stem, flower, and roots are edible. Young leaves are eaten fresh in salads. The older leaves can be sautéed or added to soups and stews, or brewed as a tea. The flowers are made into wine. Dandelion root is one of the ingredients in root beer. • Bury a Dandelion seed ball in the northwest corner of your house to bring desirable winds. • A curious divination is that, if you blow the seeds off a Dandelion seed ball, you will supposedly live for as many years as there are seeds that remain on the stem head. Also, each of the Dandelion seeds blown off grants a wish. • To send a message to your loved one, visualize the message then blow on the fluffy Dandelion seed ball in his or her direction. • Dandelion pollen provides the first food for bees in the spring. • The natural latex that a Dandelion excretes has many of the same properties as those obtained from a Rubber Tree. In that respect, there has been a great deal of interest in the different ways the Dandelion sap can be developed.

No. 377
Tetragonia tetragonioides

New Zealand Spinach

Botany Bay Spinach | Cook's Cabbage | Kōkihi

✺ SYMBOLIC MEANING
Positive experiences.

✺ POSSIBLE POWERS
Earth element; Good luck; Health; Longevity; Jupiter.

✺ FOLKLORE AND FACTS
Growing well in salty soil in coastal locations, the New Zealand Spinach plant leaves are edible after blanching then cooking. The leaves have a flavor and texture similar to spinach and are cooked in the same manner by sautéing, as well as adding them to casseroles, soups, and stews. • For 200 years after botanist explorer Joseph Banks delivered its seeds to Kew Gardens, New Zealand Spinach was the only vegetable from New Zealand and Australia that was cultivated in England.

No. 378
Theobroma cacao ☠ ⚗

Cacao

Cacahuatl | Cocoa | Cocoa Tree | Food of the Gods

✺ SYMBOLIC MEANINGS
Food of the gods; Love; Sensual.

✺ POSSIBLE POWERS
Aphrodisiac; the Arts; Attracts love; Attraction; Awakens creativity; Awakens the inner self; Beauty; Clarify thoughts; Develops creativity; Enhances energy; Friendship; Gifts; Harmony; Healing; Healthy; Joy; Love; Meditation; Opening the heart; Peace; Peacefulness; Pleasures; Sensuality; Vibrancy; Wisdom.

✺ FOLKLORE AND FACTS
Long before there was an effort to transform the *Theobroma cacao* Cacao into what is known and loved as "chocolate," the Cacao beans were used in religious, cultural, and magical ancient Maya and Aztec ceremonial rituals. According to mythology, the Maya deity, the Plumed Serpent, gave Cacao to the Maya. The discovery that there was something edible inside of the Cacao pod on the Cacao tree was made by

T

indigenous people who lived deep in the tropical rainforests in Central America over 2,000 years ago. God bless them for their curiosity. • Processing a Cacao bean requires multiple steps, which include fermentation, roasting, and grinding. The fatty cocoa butter is extracted and used in cosmetics. Unsweetened, dried, powdered Cacao is a flavoring known as "cocoa powder," which holds the potential for an endless variety of desserts and treats of all kinds, chocolate baked delicacies, pastries, glossy frostings, puddings, silky, mouthwatering confections, sweet beverages, fragrant liqueurs, and the comfort of a cup of hot cocoa topped with slowly melting marshmellows. • In some areas of Mexico, such as the Yucatán, Cacao beans were used as currency until as recently as the late 1800s. • What is known as "white chocolate" contains cocoa butter but no cocoa.
• When feeling down and needing a lift, eat chocolate.

No. 379
Theobroma grandiflorum
Cupuaçu
Copoasu | Cupuassu | Cupuazú

❋ SYMBOLIC MEANING
Food for the gods.

✿ POSSIBLE POWERS
Health; Moisturizing.

☙ FOLKLORE AND FACTS
Although it is difficult to determine, the fruit of the tropical *Theobroma grandiflorum* Cupuaçu tree is roughly calculated to be ripe and ready to eat raw approximately 117 days after fruit begins to form on the tree. It has a creamy, custard-like pulp that has a fragrance like pineapple-chocolate. The flavor of the Cupuaçu fruit is a reminiscent blend of pear, banana, passion fruit, and melon. Cupuaçu seeds will produce "Cupuaçu butter," which is considered to be a white chocolate that is used to make confections and desserts. The pulp is used in smoothies and to make ice cream. • The Cupuaçu butter is also a moisturizing ingredient in some cosmetic products.

No. 380
Thymus vulgaris
Thyme
Common Thyme | English Wild Thyme | Garden Thyme | Lemon Thyme | *Thymus × citriodorus*

❋ SYMBOLIC MEANINGS
Action; Activity; Affection; Bravery; Courage; Daring; Death; Elegance; Energy; Ensures restful sleep; Happiness; Healing; Health; Love; Psychic power; Purification; Restful sleep; Sleep; Spontaneous emotion; Strength; Swift movement; Thriftiness.

✿ POSSIBLE POWERS
Ability to see fairies; Aphrodisiac; the Arts; Attracts love; Attraction; Beauty; Courage; Feminine energy; Friendship; Gifts; Harmony; Healing; Health; Irresistibility; Joy; Love; Pleasure; Protection; Psychic power; Purification; Sensuality; Sleep; Venus; Water element.

☙ FOLKLORE AND FACTS
As a common ingredient in *herbes de Provence* as well as the bundle of flavoring herbs known as a *bouquet garni*, Thyme has been used to flavor meats, fish, vegetables, soups, stews, cheese, and liqueurs. Fresh Thyme sprigs will last no more than a week unless the leaves are stripped off the stem to be either dried or frozen in an ice cube until needed.
• Because Thyme was a symbol of bravery and courage in medieval times, it was common for knights on their way to the Crusades to carry a scarf or wear a tunic that had the image of a sprig of Thyme embroidered upon it by their fair lady. • In ancient Greece, Thyme was burned as an incense to purify the temples. • It was once thought that if a woman were to tuck a sprig of Thyme in her hair, it would render her irresistible. • Thyme is thought to provide a home for fairies and a pleasant place for them to be able to dance. Wear a sprig of Thyme to be able to see fairies. Be sure to plant Thyme in a garden that is intended to please the fairies.
• It is believed that it is possible to cleanse yourself of all the ills and sorrows of the past every spring by taking a purifying bath that has had crushed Thyme and Sweet Marjoram leaves added to the water until it is utterly fragrant.

No. 381
Trachyspermum ammi ☠

Ajwain
Ajowan | Ajowan Caraway | Carom Seed | Thymol Seeds

✹ **SYMBOLIC MEANING**
Truthful communication.

🌀 **POSSIBLE POWERS**
Harmony; Healing; Protection.

☾ **FOLKLORE AND FACTS**
The edible Ajwain plant's fruit is often mistaken for a seed. To allow the flavor and aroma to develop, the raw Ajwain fruit is commonly dry roasted or fried in a clarified butter such as ghee before being used to flavor Indian cuisine. • In Afghanistan, Ajwain is used to sprinkle over bread, much like caraway, sesame, or poppy seeds. • Make, then carry a sachet of Ajwain leaf and fruit to eject negative energy. • Ajwain can be added to a healing spell to increase the healing energy. • Carry a sachet of Ajwain to remove bad luck and the lingering negative energy of a past illness. • Carry a sachet of Ajwain to encourage the truth in a conversation of any kind.

No. 382
Trifolium incarnatum ☠ ⚗

Italian Clover
Crimson Clover

✹ **SYMBOLIC MEANINGS**
Domestic virtue; Fertility; Revenge.

🌀 **POSSIBLE POWERS**
Air element; Blessing domestic animals; Consecration; Exorcism; Fidelity; Good luck; Luck; Masculine energy; Mercury; Money; Protection; Removes a negative spirit; Success.

☾ **FOLKLORE AND FACTS**
Italian Clover seeds can be sprouted and added to dishes such as salads, sandwiches, and soups. • Make, then carry or wear a boutonnière or sachet of Italian Clover to positively assist with financial arrangements of any kind. • Sprinkle an infusion of rainwater, natural spring water, or distilled water and Italian Clover around the home to remove negative spirits.

No. 383
Trigonella foenum-graecum ☠☙

Fenugreek
Bockhornsklöver | Methi | Vendayam

☀ SYMBOLIC MEANINGS
Growth; Transformation;
Youth.

✺ POSSIBLE POWERS
Air element; Apollo; Masculine energy;
Mercury; Money; Prosperity; Wealth.

☾ FOLKLORE AND FACTS
Fenugreek leaves and seeds are edible and used to flavor
curries and other dishes, such as soups, stews, and frittatas.
The seeds are sometimes boiled to make a drink that is
popular in Egypt in coffee shops. Sprouted seeds and
leaves are used in salads. They are also made into a relish
that is used as a condiment as well as ceremonially during
Rosh Hashanah, where it is consumed during the first or
second meal of the Jewish New Year. • One easy way to
bring money into the house fund is to add Fenugreek seeds
to the water you mop the floors with. • Fenugreek was
once believed to have the magical power of being able to
transform an old man back into a young man.

No. 384
Triticum aestivum ☙

Common Wheat
Bread Wheat | Dinkle Wheat | Durum Wheat |
Einkorn | Spelt Wheat | *Triticum durum* | *Triticum
monococcum* | *Triticum spelta* |
Wheat | Wheatgrass

☀ SYMBOLIC MEANINGS
Friendliness; Prosperity;
Riches; Wealth; You
will be rich.

✺ POSSIBLE POWERS
Ceres; Earth element; Feminine energy;
Fertility; Money; Venus.

☾ FOLKLORE AND FACTS
Common Wheat was cultivated approximately
12,000 years ago in Western Asia. It is one of the
three primary cereal crops in the world, the other
two being rice and corn. • The edible parts of the
Common Wheat plants are the seed grains which
are also known as "wheat berries." After harvesting, the
grain is separated from the hull or "chaff." The resulting
berries are available as a complete whole grain, or, more
commonly, after milling them into various grinds of Wheat
flours. Common Wheat is a hard Wheat flour that is most
commonly milled for bread-making. Durum Wheat is also
a hard Wheat that is known as Pasta or Macaroni Wheat,
as it is milled for making pasta, pizza dough, and couscous.
All-purpose flour is a combination of hard and soft wheats
suitable for general baking, while Cake flour is milled from
soft Wheat to be much finer and as silky as cornstarch.
• Carry or wear a stem of Common Wheat as a boutonnière
or in a sachet to encourage fertility. • A bundle of fruited
Wheat stems placed in a prominent place near the entrance
of the home attracts money.

T

No. 385

Tropaeolum majus

Garden Nasturtium

Indian Cress | Monks Cress | Nasturtium

✴ SYMBOLIC MEANINGS

Charity; Conquest; Maternal love; Paternal love; Patriotism; Resignation; Splendor; Victory in battle; Warlike trophy.

🌀 POSSIBLE POWERS

Enlightenment; Fire element; Healing; Karma awareness; Knowledge; Mars; Moon; Protection; Psychic sight; Reincarnation; Study; Sun; Uncrossing; Water element.

☾ FOLKLORE AND FACTS

A native of both South and Central America, the fragrant Garden Nasturtium flowers are the warm colors of a hot summer, growing in both bush and trailing forms with blossoms that are cream, apricot, salmon, yellow, yellow-orange, orange, red-orange, and red. The flowers are edible with a pleasantly peppery taste, as are the leaves, which can be sautéed or stir-fried, used as a garnish, or added to a special-occasion salad. • Interestingly, an optical illusion of a flash may occur at dusk with vivid orange Garden Nasturtium flowers that contrast against the green of the surrounding leaves. • Make a sachet of Garden Nasturtium with a flower and a leaf to carry or tuck under a pillow when attempting to investigate one's own reincarnation into the current lifetime, as well as attempting to determine and consider what might be the karma that needs resolution.

No. 386

Tuber melanosporum

Black Truffle

Black Diamond | French Black Truffle | French Truffle | Périgord Truffle | Summer Truffle | *Tuber magnatum* | White Truffle

✴ SYMBOLIC MEANINGS

Luxury; Refinement.

🌀 POSSIBLE POWERS

Aphrodisiac; Decadence; Love; Love magic; Lust; Luxury; Sensuality; Sex; True love magic; Venus; Water element.

☾ FOLKLORE AND FACTS

The edible Black Truffle may be found between November and April, optimally in parts of France, although also in Spain and Italy where it naturally develops in the ground. • Grown to be close to the size of a potato, it has a pungent earthiness to its aroma. • The Black Truffle is extremely difficult to find because of its strict growing requirements. A particular spot could be perfect in every possible way and still fail to support its growth. • The primary reason the Black Truffle is the most expensive food in the world is because five days after it is harvested it will spoil. • Depending on the recipe, Truffles are shaved or grated to top a dish after or during cooking. The unique, rich, earthy fragrance of the Black Truffle intensifies when it is heated, unlike the White Truffle, which becomes milder and is best used uncooked. • The extremely high price that the Black Truffle commands makes it a target for counterfeiting. A DNA genetic test was devised to definitively identify genuine Truffles. • Nowadays, rather than employing the skills of a traditional male truffle hog, truffle hunters are using highly trained dogs to sniff out these tasty and highly valuable *Fungi* treasures. A truffle hog can locate a Black Truffle by using its superb sense of smell, natural rooting behavior, and the very powerful sex hormone of androstenol to his advantage. A well-trained truffle dog is less likely to try to devour the truffle it has found. Holding back an intensely determined pig takes some doing. However, a Black Truffle located by the lusting pig will be a much, *much* more powerful herb, ideally suited for mutually enjoyed love magic. Even so, any Black Truffle will be magical, whether dried and powdered, or preserved in an oil.

No. 387

Typha latifolia ☠

Cattail

Broadleaf Cattail | Bullrush | Bulrush | Cat Tail | Common Cattail | Cumbungi | Reedmace

☀ SYMBOLIC MEANINGS

Docility; Independence; Indiscretion; Peace; Prosperity.

🌀 POSSIBLE POWERS

Aphrodisiac; Attracts love; Fire element; Insect repellent;
Lust; Mars; Masculine energy.

☾ FOLKLORE AND FACTS

In Europe, Cattail grain residue was found on grinding
stones to indicate that it was eaten 30,000 years ago.
• Nearly all parts of the Cattail can be processed in one way
or another and eaten. The shoots, rhizome, developing spike,
and the pollen are all edible. Which part of the plant that is
edible is dependent on which phase of growth the plant is
in during its growing season and how the plant is prepared.
Survivalists in the bush depend on Cattail for sustenance.
• A woman who wants to enjoy sex but does not already
like it at all should carry a Cattail with her at
all times as a charm to help promote her
future pleasure. • Put a Cattail under the
mattress on both sides of the bed
to encourage a positive loving
sexual experience. • A lit Cattail
punk will smolder for a long
while, and its smoke is useful in
keeping flying insects away.

No. 388

Umbellularia californica ☠ ⚗

California Bay Laurel

California Bay | California Laurel | Headache Tree | Myrtlewood Tree | Sō-ē'-bā

✴ SYMBOLIC MEANINGS

Agitation; Ambition; Ambitious; Beware; Danger.

🌀 POSSIBLE POWERS

Banishing; Learning who is against you; Power; Power to overcome enemies; Stirring up agitation.

☽ FOLKLORE AND FACTS

The leaf of the more intensely pungent California Bay Laurel is used to flavor soups, stews, and casseroles in the same way as a spicier *Laurus nobilis* Bay Leaf. However, it is the inner pit of the fruit that is sought out, as it will easily split in half, and can be roasted to a dark brown color that will indicate it is ready to be eaten whole or ground into a powder. As a powder, it resembles and somewhat tastes like cocoa powder. It can then be made into a beverage or used in cooking as a flavoring ingredient. • The fine-grained hard California Bay Laurel wood is a known tonewood that is also known as Myrtlewood, and it is used to make the backs and the sides of acoustic guitars. • In North Bend, Oregon, coins that were made from California Bay Laurel wooden discs were printed during a banking emergency in 1933 when the only bank in town, the First National, was forced to temporarily close down. The bank printed coins to pay their employees, with the promise of redeeming them as soon as possible, which did occur after a few months. However, many people kept their wooden coins as keepsakes. Those coins are still considered legal tender in North Bend. One full set is preserved in a collection held by the Chase Manhattan Bank in New York City.

No. 389

Urtica dioica ☠ ⚗

Stinging Nettle

American Stinging Nettle | Burning Nettle | Common Nettle | Jaggy Nettle

✴ SYMBOLIC MEANINGS

Cruelty; Slander.

🌀 POSSIBLE POWERS

Ambition; the Arts; Attitude; Attraction; Beauty; Clear thinking; Exorcism; Fire element; Friendship gifts; Harmony; Healing; Higher understanding; Joy; Logic; Love; Lust; Manifestation in material form; Mars; Masculine energy; Pleasures; Protection; Sensuality; Spiritual concepts; Thor; Thought processes.

☽ FOLKLORE AND FACTS

Before the plants start to flower, the properly prepared and cooked young leaves of the *Urtica dioica* Stinging Nettle plant are edible and high in vitamins A and C. They have a cucumber-like, Spinach flavor. The carefully prepared leaves are sometimes used in cheesemaking to wrap the pressed curd when making Cornish Yarg. Prepared Stinging Nettle leaves can also be used in a soup common to parts of Northern and Eastern Europe. In Greece, prepared leaves are used as a filling for a dish that is similar to spinach *spanakopita*, called *hortopita*. • Carry Stinging Nettle in a pouch to remove a curse and send it back to its creator.

U

No. 390

Vaccinium cyanococcus ⚱

Blueberry

Blåbær | Blaeberry | Highbush Blueberry | Lowbush Blueberry |
Ōhelo Wild Blueberry | Wild Blueberry

☀ SYMBOLIC MEANINGS

Belonging to Pele; Prayer;
Treachery; Treason.

✳ POSSIBLE POWERS

Applying knowledge;
Astral plane; Breaks
a hex; Colorize;
Controlling
lower principles; Curse
breaking; Dream magic;
Finding lost objects;
Luck; Overcoming evil;
Protection; Protection against
psychic attack; Regeneration;
Removing depression; Sensuality;
Uncovering secrets; Victory.

☾ FOLKLORE AND FACTS

The edible part of the Blueberry bush is
the berry, which can be eaten fresh, picked out
of hand, or used to make syrups, jams, sauces, and
fillings for pies and pastries. The berries are also added to
cereals and batters for cakes, breads, muffins, and pancakes.
The berries are distilled to make Blueberry wine and liqueur.
• If feeling under the power of a psychic attack, make and
eat a Blueberry pie to repel the attack from the inside out.
• A few Blueberries under the front doormat will keep evil,
unpleasant people, and negative entities from entering the
house. • Make a sachet of Blueberry leaves to wear or carry
to bring luck, fend off evil, and break curses and hexes.
• The wild Blueberry variety in Hawaii known as Ōhelo was
considered by ancient Hawaiians to be so sacred that they
would toss some berries into a volcano as an offering to the
goddess Pele before eating any of them, for fear of dreadful
consequences.

No. 391

Vaccinium macrocarpon ⚱

Cranberry

American Cranberry | Bog Cranberry | Common Cranberry | Cranberry Plant |
Large Cranberry | Small Cranberry | Swamp Cranberry

☀ SYMBOLIC MEANINGS

Love; Love relationship;
Sexual life; Sexual
romance; Sexuality.

✳ POSSIBLE POWERS

Celebration; Cure for
heartache; Mars; Restores
energy; Water element.

☾ FOLKLORE AND FACTS

The fruit berries of the *Vaccinium macrocarpon* Cranberry
plant are available fresh in season. Otherwise, they can be
found dried, canned, or as a juice year round. Cranberries
are cooked, added as an ingredient in baking, and used as
pastry fillings and jams. The juice is used in cocktails and
for liqueurs. Harvesting Cranberries is done in a way unlike
any other fruit. Approximately ninety percent of North
American Cranberry harvesting involves flooding the
bed or "bog" with around eight inches of water above the
ripe-fruited plants. A water wheel harvester moves through
the beds to remove the fruit from the plants. Floating
Cranberries are coaxed to a corner of the bed where they are
removed. • A cookbook from 1683 made the first mention
of Cranberry juice. A cookbook from 1667 has a recipe for
Cranberry sauce that the Pilgrims devised while in North
America. Annually, there is a conversation comparing
"whole berry" Cranberry sauce to the "jellied" type, as there
are avid lifelong fans of either or even both. • Cranberry
something or other is commonly found on Thanksgiving and
Christmas feast tables all across the United States, Canada,
and the United Kingdom. • Cranberry garlands made by
stringing hundreds of the hard round red berries with a
needle onto a long sturdy string is a traditional Christmas
decoration. • To restore depleted energy, place a bowl of
Cranberries under the bed while recuperating from an
illness. • Cranberry juice is a common home-remedy for
bladder irritation issues.

No. 392

Vaccinium myrtillus 🐚

Bilberry

Black-Hearts | Blaeberry | Blue Whortleberry | Common Bilberry | European Blueberry |
Hurtleberry | Myrtle Blueberry | Whinberry | Whortleberry | Winberry

✸ SYMBOLIC MEANINGS
Treachery; Treason.

🌀 POSSIBLE POWERS
Curse-breaking; Dream magic; Hex breaking; Luck;
Protection.

☾ FOLKLORE AND FACTS
The edible parts of the Bilberry bush are the dark blue and
often very nearly purple-black berries that grow singly or
in pairs as opposed to the clusters of Blueberries. A Bilberry
is softer and much juicier than a Blueberry, and much more
versatile. The Bilberries are sweetened to fill donuts and
other pastries, and are used in desserts more generally. They
can be used to make jams, pie fillings, or added to muffins
and pancakes. They are juiced to make frozen sorbet and
liqueurs such as Romanian *Afinată*. There is even a popular
Nordic Bilberry soup that is eaten either cold or hot called
Blåbärssoppa. • There is a four-couple jig with well-defined
dance steps that is known as
the "Whortleberry." • A sachet of
Bilberry leaves will bring luck,
fend off evil, and break curses
and hexes if carried.

No. 393

Vaccinium parvifolium

Huckleberry

Red Huckleberry

✸ SYMBOLIC MEANINGS
Faith; Simple leisures.

🌀 POSSIBLE POWERS
Breaks a hex; Dream magic; Feminine energy; Luck;
Protection; Venus; Water element.

☾ FOLKLORE AND FACTS
Due to the close resemblance between a salmon egg and the
edible fresh Huckleberry, many Native American tribes in
North America discovered that the berries make very good
fishing bait. • Huckleberries are used for making jams, pastry
fillings, puddings, confections, teas, soups, and syrups.

No. 394
Vaccinium vitis-idaea ⚗

Lingonberry
Cowberry | Mountain Cranberry

☀ SYMBOLIC MEANING
Nature's gift.

✺ POSSIBLE POWERS
Feminine energy; Healing; Health; Luck; Protection; Venus; Water element.

☾ FOLKLORE AND FACTS
Found in the wild, the Lingonberry plant is also commercially grown in the Pacific Northwest and other northern areas where this highly cold-tolerant berry plant thrives, never to lose its leaves in the winter. The tartly sour berries are edible and quite highly nutritious, as well as extremely beneficial medicinally. Lingonberries can be eaten raw or prepared as a side dish. They are also used to make jam, juice, and syrup. They can be added to smoothies, brewed as a tea, and cooked down to be used as a pie or pastry filling. They are also added to baked goods.
• Lingonberry sauce is a favorite with roast reindeer, elk, wild game, and poultry. It is also a favorite topping for pancakes, especially Potato pancakes. The syrup as well as the juice is used in cocktails and can also be made into wine, liqueur, or used as a flavoring for vodka. In Russia, the Lingonberry is used to make a drink known simply as "Lingonberry water." • In 1745, Empress Elizabeth of Russia decreed that Lingonberry plants were to be planted everywhere on the grounds of the Peterhof Palace in Saint Petersburg.

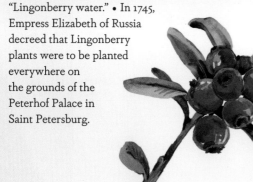

No. 395
Vanilla planifolia ⚗

Vanilla Orchid
Bourbon Vanilla | Flat-leaved Vanilla | Madagascar Vanilla | Orchid Bean | Tlilxochitl | Vanilla | West Indian Vanilla

☀ SYMBOLIC MEANINGS
Elegance; Innocence; Purity.

✺ POSSIBLE POWERS
Aphrodisiac; Attracts love; Energy; Feminine energy; Love; Lust; Mental clarity or power; Venus; Water element.

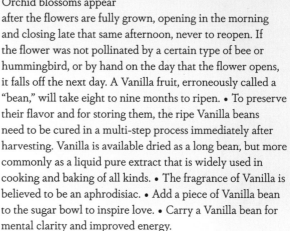

☾ FOLKLORE AND FACTS
Vanilla plantifolia Vanilla Orchid blossoms appear after the flowers are fully grown, opening in the morning and closing late that same afternoon, never to reopen. If the flower was not pollinated by a certain type of bee or hummingbird, or by hand on the day that the flower opens, it falls off the next day. A Vanilla fruit, erroneously called a "bean," will take eight to nine months to ripen. • To preserve their flavor and for storing them, the ripe Vanilla beans need to be cured in a multi-step process immediately after harvesting. Vanilla is available dried as a long bean, but more commonly as a liquid pure extract that is widely used in cooking and baking of all kinds. • The fragrance of Vanilla is believed to be an aphrodisiac. • Add a piece of Vanilla bean to the sugar bowl to inspire love. • Carry a Vanilla bean for mental clarity and improved energy.

No. 396
Vicia faba ☠ 🝕

Fava Bean
Broad Bean | Faba Bean | Härkäpapu

✳ **SYMBOLIC MEANINGS**
I cling to thee; Shyness;
Vice.

🌀 **POSSIBLE POWER**
Good luck.

🌙 **FOLKLORE AND FACTS**
Carbonized evidence of Fava Beans has been
found in various sites in Syria, Turkey, Bulgaria, Hungary,
and Slovakia, dating as far back as the Neolithic Period.
The Fava Bean has been part of eastern Mediterranean diets
since at least 6000 BCE. Fava Beans are usually eaten when
young with the outer seed coat needing to be removed before
eating. Afterwards, they can then be steamed, boiled, roasted,
puréed, or dried for later use or ground into a flour. Fried
Fava Beans are often salted and eaten as a snack. Mashed or
puréed beans are seasoned and used as is or made into dips
or spreads. Then they are used in a wide variety of dishes all
around the world, such as soups, stews, casseroles, desserts,
stir-fries, and snack foods. Young leaves can also be cooked
and eaten, or added to soups and stews. • Planting Fava Beans
at night or on a Good Friday is considered to bring good luck.
• The ancient followers of Pythagoras were forbidden by
their beliefs to look at, speak of, or eat a Fava Bean.

No. 397
Vigna angularis

Adzuki Bean
Aduki Bean | Azuki Bean | Red Chori

✳ **SYMBOLIC MEANINGS**
Revelation of love;
Romantic longing.

🌀 **POSSIBLE POWER**
Love.

🌙 **FOLKLORE AND FACTS**
Adzuki Bean has been a part of diets across the Asian
continent for thousands of years. The edible parts of the
Vigna angularis Adzuki Bean plant are the seeds. Although
some Adzuki Bean varieties produce a mottled bean or beans
that are black, gray, or white, most varieties produce easily
recognizable red-colored beans. The beans are available
fresh, dried, sprouted, and as a paste, which is favored in East

Asia. The paste is made by boiling the beans with sugar and
is then used in many different Chinese, Japanese, and Korean
dishes as a sweet ingredient, sweet filling, or topping. Adzuki
Bean paste is the main ingredient in a popular regional treat
in Hawaii when topped with shaved ice. In Japan, Adzuki
Beans are prepared and served with Rice for celebration
meals of all kinds. • The Chinese have used the beautiful,
deep-red Adzuki Beans as love tokens.

No. 398
Vigna radiata 🝕

Mung Bean
Green Gram | Moong | Monggo Mudga | Munggo

✳ **SYMBOLIC MEANING**
Misunderstood.

🌀 **POSSIBLE POWERS**
Health; Resilience.

🌙 **FOLKLORE AND FACTS**
The soaked then thoroughly cooked seed of the *Vigna
radiata* Mung plant is edible and is a common ingredient
in Chinese and Middle Eastern cuisine, either in savory or
sweet dishes. Mung Beans are served whole, mashed, or
macerated into a tasty paste that is used as an ingredient or
as a filling for cakes, pastries, dumplings, and pancakes. After
first soaking them, Mung Beans are easily sprouted at home
and can be used in salads and sandwiches. The beans can also
be sautéed or added to soups, stews, and casseroles.

No. 399

Vigna unguiculata ☠ ⚗

Black-Eyed Pea

Alasandalu | Black-Eyed Bean | Kacang Tunggak |
Lobia | Lobiya | Purple Hull Pea

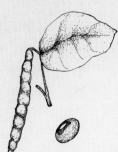

✹ SYMBOLIC MEANINGS
Good luck; Prosperity.

🌀 POSSIBLE POWERS
Good luck; Prosperity; Venus;
Water element.

☾ FOLKLORE AND FACTS
The Black-Eyed Pea plant is
grown all around the world. The *Vigna unguiculata* Black-
Eyed Pea plant's pea-sized beans within the pods, produced
after flowering, are the edible legumes. The color of the
distinctive "eye" on the bean can be black, pink, brown, red,
or green. The freshly hulled Black-Eyed Pea will be green,
turning a pale beige color when it is dried. Black-Eyed Peas
need to be thoroughly cooked until they are tender before
eating them. In the 1960s, in the Southern United States,
the Black-Eyed Pea was considered "soul food" and the
earthiness of this comfort food has made it a more popular
ingredient in a wide variety of flavorful dishes, hearty soups,
and filling stews ever since. Black-Eyed Peas are often
prepared along with salty bacon, ham, hog jowls, or other
pork cuts that fully enhance and elevate the cooked flavor
of the beans. • In most of the Southern United States of
America, wishing for a good new year while eating three
Black-Eyed Peas on New Year's Day is an annual tradition.
One for luck. One for fortune. One for romance.

No. 400

Viola odorata ⚗

Violet

Banafsha | Blue Violet | Common Violet | English Violet |
Garden Violet | Purple Violet | Sweet Violet

✹ SYMBOLIC MEANINGS
Faithfulness; Lesbian love; Lesbian
romance; Modesty.

🌀 POSSIBLE POWERS
Aphrodite; the Arts;
Attraction; Beauty;
Feminine energy; Friendship;
Gifts; Harmony; Healing; Joy;
Love; Luck; Lust; Peace; Pleasure;
Protection; Romance; Sappho;
Sensuality; Venus; Water element;
Wishing.

☾ FOLKLORE AND FACTS
The edible part of the Violet plant is the blossom, which
can be dried and used in brewing an herbal tea. The flower
can also be transformed into a cake and pastry decoration
by lightly painting all sides of the petals with whipped egg
whites before completely sprinkling over a full covering of
finely ground granulated cane sugar, then setting it aside to
fully dry. • Carry a Violet to provide protection against a
wicked spirit. • Carry a Violet for good luck. • It is believed
that if you pick the very first Violet you find in the spring,
you can make a wish on it and the wish will come true.
• The Violet represents both Aphrodite and Sappho. • In
many parts of the world, it is the Violet that is the most
closely associated with love on Valentine's Day and is often
exchanged between lovers who are aware of the close accord
between the Violet and a heart. • The Violet was a common
ingredient in Celtic love potions because the individual
petals are heart-shaped and were thought to be able to cure
a broken heart. • There is a superstition that if a Violet is
picked while still wet with dew, there will be a death of a
loved one and continuous weeping until the next Full Moon.
• Wear or carry a Violet to attract romantic love. • To bring
love into your life, plant Violets in the garden in the shape of
a heart. If they grow, so will love.

No. 401
Vitellaria paradoxa

Shea Butter Tree
Karité | Shea Tree | Shi Tree | Vitellaria

❋ **SYMBOLIC MEANING**
Butter seed.

🌀 **POSSIBLE POWERS**
Condition; Healing; Lubricate; Smooth; Soften.

☾ **FOLKLORE AND FACTS**
An edible, thick, fatty, rich emollient or "butter" is extracted from the seed kernel of the *Vitellaria paradoxa* Shea Butter Tree's plum-like fruit and is used in several African pastries and confections. Even though the smooth fat is sometimes used in cooking, especially baking, this emollient is most often jarred as a specific cosmetic skin softener, and is also potentially blended with a myriad of other ingredients intended for cosmetic products that would not be edible at all.

No. 402
Vitis labrusca 🥣

Fox Grape
Catawba Grape | Concord Grape | Delaware Grape | Isabella Grape

❋ **SYMBOLIC MEANINGS**
Blessings; Celebration; Faith; Fertility; Initiation; Life; Transformation.

🌀 **POSSIBLE POWERS**
Abundance; Blessings; Bacchus; Colorize; Dionysus; Feminine energy; Fertility; Garden magic; Hathor; Mental clarity or power; Money; Moon; Mystical transformation; Water element.

☾ **FOLKLORE AND FACTS**
The pendulous, hanging Fox Grape fruit is edible fresh when ripe. Its strong, recognizably "grape" fragrance and flavor are what the early American settlers who emigrated from Europe knew and enjoyed enough to propagate and cultivate wherever it would grow. Able to withstand weather extremes, unlike *Vitis vinifera* varieties, the Fox Grape can be found growing all along the east coast of North America, from the state of Georgia up through Nova Scotia. The significant difference between the *Vitis vinifera* Grape and the *Vitis labrusca* Fox Grape is that the Fox Grape's skins will slip right off rather than crushing the pulp, as is the case with *Vitis vinifera* fruits. Fox Grapes, such as the Concord Grape, have intensely fragrant fruit that is edible and enjoyed as fresh table grapes, as well as being the most common type of grape that is used for commercial, as well as homemade, jam and jelly. • The flavor of grape jam or jelly on a peanut butter sandwich is an indelible embedded childhood memory for most Americans. The juice is a commercially available beverage and is also used in syrups that are favorites for flavoring confections, sorbets, syrups, and gelatins.
• The Fox Grape is a favorite for making homemade wines, as well as being the fruit that is used to make kosher sacramental wine. The Catawba and Delaware varieties are a pink grape, while the Isabella is a very deep, dark purple that is very close to looking black.

No. 403

Vitis vinifera ⚗

Grape

Common Grape Vine | Muscadine Grape | Mustang Grape | *Vitis rotundifolia*

✷ SYMBOLIC MEANINGS

Blessings; Celebration; Charity; Faith needed for growth or to prosper; Fertility; Initiation; Intemperance; Joy; Kindness; Life; Meekness; Mental power; Money; Pleasure; Rural felicity; Transformation.

✺ POSSIBLE POWERS

Abundance; Colorize; Dionysus; Feminine energy; Fertility; Garden magic; Hathor; Mental clarity or power; Money; Moon; Mystical transformation; Water element.

☾ FOLKLORE AND FACTS

Wild Grapes have been harvested since Neolithic times. Grape pip seeds have been found that date back to 6000 BCE. • The edible parts of the *Vitis vinifera* Grape plant are the ripe fruit that grow in pendulous bunches, as well as the prepared and cooked leaves. There are nearly 10,000 varieties of *Vitis vinifera*, with only a select few being cultivated for wine and fresh table use. The majority of familiar wines worldwide are made using *Vitis vinifera* fruit. • Grapes are dried to produce raisins. • The *Vitis rotundifolia* Muscadine Grape grows wild in the southeast and south-central parts of the United States. Muscadine Grapes are used to make jelly, juice, and homemade wine. • Paint pictures of grapevines with fruiting Grapes on garden walls to promote fertility. • Grapes are grown everywhere in the world except in the Arctic regions. • Since ancient times, nearly every culture that knew of the Grape regarded it as sacred. • In the Bible, Jesus turns jugs of water into fine Grape wine while attending a wedding in Cana with his mother. It was the first tangible miraculous act that Jesus manifested.

No. 404

Wasabia japonica

Wasabi

Japanese Horseradish

✱ SYMBOLIC MEANING
Pungent awakening.

❋ POSSIBLE POWERS
Fire element; Flavoring;
Healing; Health; Mars.

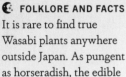

☾ FOLKLORE AND FACTS
It is rare to find true
Wasabi plants anywhere
outside Japan. As pungent
as horseradish, the edible
Wasabi root is ground into a light-green paste for use as a
condiment for Asian dishes, most particularly for sushi.
• Due to the mass appeal of sushi and the condiment Wasabi
that lends itself to it so well, it has been difficult to keep up
the cultivation of Wasabi plants to meet the demand for this
culinary herb. As a consequence, an extremely common
condiment substitute blend of horseradish, mustard, and
a starch such as rice flour is mixed with some green food
coloring. This is packaged in a container labeled "wasabi" to
be commercially offered to the insatiable sushi-devouring
public of the Western Hemisphere. There is most likely no
actual Wasabi plant added to be part of the mix. The fake
Wasabi tastes somewhat similar, but it will burn hotter and
longer than true Wasabi. • Beyond Japan, true Wasabi paste
is usually only found at very high-end Japanese-style sushi
restaurants or high-end specialty stores. • The difference
between fake and true Wasabi is that the fake is creamy
smooth, while true Wasabi has a grated, gritty mouth feel.
True Wasabi is served freshly and finely grated. The fake
version is prepared from the aforementioned powder.

No. 405

Ximenia americana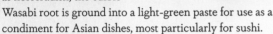

Hog Plum

Yellow Mombin

✱ SYMBOLIC MEANING
Retain.

❋ POSSIBLE POWERS
Venus; Water element.

☾ FOLKLORE AND FACTS
The fruit of the *Ximenia
americana* Hog Plum is
edible when ripe, juicy, and can
be eaten raw, but it is more often used
to make jam, juice, liqueurs, and a type
of beer. The fruit and the flower buds are sometimes pickled
in vinegar or also used in curries. The seed is large and its
kernel is pressed to produce an oil that is used as a butter
substitute in recipes and as an ingredient in cosmetics. The
nuts are purgative and the leaves are toxic unless they are
young and have been thoroughly cooked. Even then, they
should not be consumed in any large quantity. • Hog Plum
flowers smell like lilacs.

No. 406

Xylopia aethiopica

Grains of Selim

African Grains of Selim | Guinea Pepper

✱ SYMBOLIC MEANING
Bitter wood.

❋ POSSIBLE POWER
Purification.

☾ FOLKLORE AND FACTS
During the Middle Ages the seeds were used in Europe as
another type of pepper. In Africa, the fruit is used in water
for purification. • The dried aromatic edible seeds of the
Xylopia aethiopica Guinea Pepper tree are known as Grains
of Selim and are used as a seasoning to flavor food or soups.
In Senegal the fruit is used to flavor a spiritual coffee drink
widely known as "café Touba."

WX
YZ

No. 407

Yucca gigantea ☠ ⚒

Yucca

Adam's Needle | Adam's Needle and Thread |
Blue-Stem Yucca | Ghosts in the Graveyard |
Giant Yucca | Spineless Yucca |
Soft-Tip Yucca | Yucca Cane

✳ SYMBOLIC MEANINGS

Best friends; a Friend in need.

✺ POSSIBLE POWERS

Fire element; Hex removal;
Loyalty; Mars; Masculine energy;
New opportunities; Protection;
Purification; Purity; Transmutation.

☾ FOLKLORE AND FACTS

The flower petals of the *Yucca gigantea* Yucca are commonly eaten in Central America after first blanching, then sautéing them. • Yucca is found in some rural Midwestern American graveyards. When they are blooming, the flowers appear to be floating apparitions or ghosts. • Yucca fibers twisted into a cross then placed in the center of the home will protect the house from evil. • It was believed by some that if a person jumps through a loop of twisted Yucca fibers, he will magically transmute into an animal.

No. 408

Zanthoxylum piperitum ☠ ⚒

Szechuan Pepper

Chinese Pepper | Japanese Pepper | Japanese Pepper Tree | Japanese Prickly-Ash |
Mala Pepper | Sichuan Pepper

✳ SYMBOLIC MEANING

Numbing.

✺ POSSIBLE POWERS

Fire element; Flavoring; Healing; Mars; Masculine energy;
Numbing spiciness.

☾ FOLKLORE AND FACTS

The dried lemony-tasting Szechuan Pepper berry is a common seasoning in Chinese cuisine, but it is not actually a pepper. Szechuan Pepper is one of the main ingredients in the Japanese multi-spice blend known as *shichimi togarashi* and can also be found in Chinese five-spice powder. Szechuan Pepper leaves a tingly sensation in the mouth that can be followed by a sense of numbness.

No. 409

Zea mays ⚒

Corn

Blue Corn | Maize | Mealie | Mielie | Red Corn | Sweet Corn

✳ SYMBOLIC MEANINGS

Abundance; Quarrel; Riches.

⚘ COMPONENT MEANINGS

Broken: Quarrel.
Ear: Delicacy.

✺ POSSIBLE POWERS

Divination; Earth element; Feminine energy;
Growth; Increase; Luck; Protection; Venus.

☾ FOLKLORE AND FACTS

The edible parts of the tall-growing Corn plant are the seed kernels that develop on the "cob." • Corn is, in one way or another, a primary ingredient in the diets of many millions of people who enjoy it boiled, steamed, grilled, sautéed, creamed, fried, baked, added to soups, stews, and casseroles, distilled into liquors, as well as dried then popped in hot oil. • Cornstarch, which is also known as cornflour, is obtained from the *Zea mays* Corn kernel for use as a thickener for soups and sauces. Cornstarch is also used to make Corn syrup. • The Corn Mother is the goddess of fertility and plenty revered by Native American tribes in North America. Ancient North Americans would toss Corn pollen into the air in an attempt to call down the rain. Due to the sacred nature of Corn, it is believed by many that it is wrong to waste any of it with so many impoverished people in the world. • The early Mayans of Guatemala and the Navajo of the southwestern USA believed that it was Corn that created the first human beings. The Hopi offered Corn at every religious ritual to honor the Corn Mother. Corn has been, and still is, a mainstay of human survival, most especially in Mexico, for at least 10,000 years. In many other parts of the world, Corn has become a staple food in a great many international cuisines. • Some believe that to place an ear of Corn in an infant's cradle will protect the baby from negative energies and forces. • A bundle of Corn husks over a mirror will bring good luck into the house. • To increase the level and intensity of spirituality in the home, put Blue Corn on a place of importance, be it on the front door, upon a home altar or on the dining room table. • Place an ear of Red Corn in each of the four corners of the home for added protection. • Cornstarch is used medicinally when mixed with a liquid for a paste poultice, or as a talcum substitute for use as a body powder, particularly for babies. Cornstarch is also used as an anti-stick powder for latex gloves, condoms, and other plastic products.

No. 410
Zingiber officinale 🏺
Ginger
Ginger Root | Gingerroot

✳ SYMBOLIC MEANINGS
Aromatic; Comforting; Diversity; Pleasant;
Safe; Strength; Unlimited wealth;
Warming; Wealth.

🌀 POSSIBLE POWERS
Abundance; Accidents; Advancement;
Aggression; Anger; Breaks a hex;
Carnal desire; Conflict; Conscious
will; Energy; Fire element; Friendship;
Growth; Healing; Health; Joy;
Leadership; Legal matters; Life;
Light; Love; Lust; Machinery;
Mars; Masculine energy; Money;
Natural power; Power; Protection;
Psychic power; Rock music; Strength;
Struggle; Success; War.

🌜 FOLKLORE AND FACTS
The edible part of the Ginger
plant is the root, which is
available fresh, jarred, candied,
as a paste, and dried and ground
into a powder as a flavoring
for cooking, baking, candy, and
beverages. • Carry a sachet of Ginger
to foster your psychic abilities. • Put
Ginger into a leather pouch with silver
coins, then carry it in a pocket or purse
to bring in more money. • To promote
lust, sprinkle Ginger around the home.
• When Ginger ale, Ginger candy, and
Ginger tea fail to soothe a flustered
belly as well as one hopes for,
the one first-aid remedy that
usually works better for
almost any kind of irritated
digestion issues is just one
capsule of powdered Gingerroot
with a glass of water or milk.

No. 411
Zizania palustris
Wild Rice
American Wild Rice | Canada Rice |
Northern Wild Rice | Water Oats

✳ SYMBOLIC MEANING
Special spirit.

🌀 POSSIBLE POWERS
Air element; Sun.

🌜 FOLKLORE AND FACTS
Wild Rice is a sacred waterborne
plant to many Native Americans tribes. The
ripe edible seeds are harvested by canoe. The exposed heads
of the plants are bent over the open canoe and given a shake
to release the seeds as the boat slowly glides through the
growth in the shallow water. • The commercial cultivation
of the nutritious, high-protein Wild Rice in North America
began in the 1950s. • Many of the Native American cultures
in the Great Lakes region consider Wild Rice a sacred gift
from the Creator, as it was an important crop that was
valuable enough to use for trade with tribes that were unable
to gather the grain for themselves.

No. 412
Ziziphus mauritiana 🏺
Indian Jujube
Chinese Date

✳ SYMBOLIC MEANING
Bear.

🌀 POSSIBLE POWERS
Air element; Calming; Fertility;
Healthy; Induces sleep; Prosperity;
Relaxes the mind; Sun; Wealth.

🌜 FOLKLORE AND FACTS
Crisp and somewhat juicy, the ripe Indian Jujube fruit is
edible and exceptionally high in vitamin C. It resembles an
Apple with a pit that contains two seeds. The fruit can be
eaten raw or stewed, used in beverages, and pickled.

WX
YZ

CULINARY
FINDS
AROUND
the WORLD

Food has always been an integral part of the daily lives of human beings. In the beginning, people simply wandered around, gathering whatever edible bit of anything they could find. They would put it into their mouths, chew, swallow, then look for something else to eat. Living from hand-to-mouth, gathering, was all they knew. Many of these Gatherers survived long enough on their meager but tasty findings to experience the most profound discovery of all human history: fire.

Once there was fire, there then rose up some clever someone who might have thought, "Hmm, I need something sharp." So, with a rock and a piece of flint, some practice, and more time than they may have calculated, sharp knives were fashioned for the entire clan. All things considered, they were good enough, because with a versatile tool such as their new knives, the people could become productive hunters. The Hunters did their best to find any who-knows-what they could stalk, kill, dismember, then put on the end of a stick to poke into their precious fire. That cooked food was exceptionally tasty must have been an epiphany.

Fire-cooked food advanced eating into the future of deliberately prepared foods when somewhere along the timeline of our existence another brilliant someone was inspired to deliberately mix what was gathered with what was hunted. That mix was then placed into or onto something that could withstand fire, before *everything* was put into the fire to cook together. What resulted must have been an extraordinary, life-altering concept, because deliberate cooking ignited the imaginations of hungry people. It seems that from that profound moment onward, preparing all kinds of food, cooked or otherwise, became something worth fussing over.

People were no longer simply eating to stay alive; they were creating exciting new ways of making foods increasingly interesting, enjoyably delicious, and much longer-lasting. Preservation of foods became a point to consider and perfect, making it possible to save a growing list of ingredients for longer and much later. Even the edibility of prepared foods could be extended beyond when they would usually spoil. From way back then to now, that has not changed.

The idea of actually making particular foods repeatedly, because they were good the first time and worth preparing again, was one of the best things we humans ever did for ourselves. Every culture in the entire world has foods with styles that became known as cuisines. Recipes for dishes have been created, adopted, adapted, and shared again and again. This is because people sure do love to eat. There are uncountable growing numbers of interested people, all over the world, who not only enjoy their own cuisine but also that of other cultures.

We are a world of people with delicious foods with unique flavors that really are more alike than radically different. That our foods have symbolic meanings and possible powers is no surprise. For a very long time, we have imbued our foods with our energies while these ingredients have helped us survive, be hospitable, care for our families, and express our love. We have simply enjoyed preparing them and learning more about them, too. We have been innovative. We have generously shared recipes. Many of us have been very curious and have willingly tried new foods that we had never heard of before. And the greatest power of all is that the flavors of our foods reinforce our innate memories, easily connecting us all to the past, the present, and far into the future.

01

Alcoholic Beverages

Absinthe | Ale | Baijiu | Beer | Bourbon | Brandy | Champagne | Cider | Cocktail | Commandaria | Distilled Spirits | Fermented Tea | Gin | Hootch | Irish Coffee | Madeira | Marsala | Mead | Moonshine | Port | Pulque | Rice Wine | Rum | Scotch | Sherry | Shōchū | Shrub | Tequila | Vermouth | Vin Santo | Vodka | Whisky | Wine | Wine Cooler

✳ **SYMBOLIC MEANINGS** Class; Corruption; Destitution; Time out; Wealth.
🌀 **POSSIBLE POWERS** Calming; Festivity; Fun; Obliteration; Recreation;
Social interaction; Spontaneity; Tension reduction; Time off.
💀 **PLEASANT DREAMING** A dream about spilling alcohol on someone hints of truth
on the verge of being revealed.

🌙 FOLKLORE AND FACTS

Fermented or distilled, alcoholic beverages have been around since the Stone Age, with archeological evidence of deliberately fermented drinks found as residue in ancient jugs. Commandaria is a sweet Grecian dessert wine that dates back to 800 BCE in ancient Cypress and is made by fermenting sun-dried grapes. Its name originated during the crusades in the twelfth century. Commandaria is still produced and is considered to be the oldest-known wine that has a distinctive name.

Home-brewed ale, beer, mead, hard cider, or wine is not uncommon and is legal in all but a few countries. On the other hand, distillation of alcoholic spirits at home is illegal in most countries, or only permitted with a special license. The potential for fires and explosions during processing what is known as "moonshine" or "hootch" cannot be overstated.

Wine and beer are commonly used ingredients in many dishes, such as in Coq au Vin, Chicken Marsala, Beer-boiled Bratwursts, or a saturating glaze for a Rum Cake. The flamboyantly presented flambé dishes of ignited spirits is not something that is often done outside of a fine-dining restaurant, where for visual drama the lighting is performed at table-side.

When alcohol is used as an ingredient, even after cooking, some will remain in the food. How much depends on several factors relating to the alcohol, the temperature, the cooking time, other ingredients, and even the size of the pan! The quantity of the remaining alcohol can vary widely between approximately five and ninety-five percent.

It takes less than a splash of alcohol to make a non-alcoholic beverage alcoholic. The common minimum amount used in a cocktail or tossed back clean in the tiny "shot" or "jigger" glass measures out to be barely over 44 milliliters, which is just about 1.5 fluid ounces. The pour size of alcohol in the United States is 1.25 fluid ounces for it to be considered an "alcoholic serving." Even so, one shot of 150 proof rum will have considerably more of a kick than a shot of 80 proof rum.

In 1862, the first book dedicated to making cocktails was written by Jerry Thomas, an American bartender who is considered the "father of American mixology." Cocktails with many different ingredients, interesting catchy names, and showy garnishes have long since become the pride of any bartender. There are multiple cocktail recipes dedicated to every known spirit, with more to surely come.

02

Aspic & Gelatin

Aspic Gelée | Bavarian Cream | Gelatin | Gelatin Salad | Hladetina | Holodetz | Huspenina | Jelled Consommé | Jell-O® | Jello Salad | Jokpyeon | Kholodets | Meat Jelly | Mujuji | Muzhuzhi | Panna Cotta | Piftie | Pihtije | Pivtija | Pork Jelly | Qaris | Rog In 't Zuur | Sanyaa Khunna | Sky | Studen | Ta Khaa | Thit Nau Dông | Žolca

✹ **SYMBOLIC MEANINGS** Coldness; Congeal; Encase; Flexible; Have fun; Jiggle; Like a jewel; Wiggle; Wobble.
🌀 **POSSIBLE POWERS** Encasement; Flexibility; Fun; Protection.
💀 **PLEASANT DREAMING** A dream about gelatin is a hint to exercise flexibility to work in different circumstances.

🌜 **FOLKLORE AND FACTS**
In the Middle Ages, cooks recognized that when thick meat broth cools, it congeals. A dense jelly formed over the cooked meats and prevented them from spoiling for a little longer than usual. Once this concept caught on, preparing a broth to specifically create a thick- or thin-coating jelly became deliberate. Making aspic from scratch is time-consuming. The right kinds of animal parts are required, which are cartilage, bones, and skin. These need to be gently simmered long enough to enrich the stock with collagen and proteins to enhance solidification when it cools.

In the nineteenth century, the famed French chef Marie-Antoine Carême perfected the art of aspic making. His carefully arranged molded aspics with food suspended in quivery gelatin were gourmet showpieces to behold. Carême's spectacular gourmet aspics graced Napoleon Bonaparte's imperial dining tables. Other royals and aristocrats followed suit, requesting that their own chefs produce elegant and often outrageous savory jellied arrangements of meats, fish, vegetables, mushrooms, and anything else a creative chef could artistically arrange in a mold.

Other countries around the world have incorporated aspic and glazed foods into their cuisines. Romania, Korea, Nepal, Denmark, Belgium, England, and the USA all have at least one. Some dishes are delicate. Others sliceable. Some are completely inedible, only on the table as a fantastical decoration.

In the USA before 1904, old-fashioned aspics were out. Molded gelatin took on a new life when Jell-O® was marketed. Aimed at children and their mothers, the jiggling, light-reflecting delicacies were enticingly pretty and delicious. Home cooks as well as restaurant chefs went out of their way to successfully bring back the idea of jellied creations as strawberry or raspberry flavored, sweet, molded desserts. Other flavors included citrusy orange or lemon flavored molded salads of suspended grapes, banana slices, strawberries, sliced cucumbers, slivered almonds, and anything they could think of that would look attractively arranged with the intent to please the eye first. The product itself was an enormous success. Jell-O® is still a favorite of the young and old.

The spiked "Jell-O® Shot" was invented in the 1950s by Tom Lehrer as a way to sneak alcohol into a military base Christmas party. Once word got around about the intriguing concept of a quivery, congealed, homemade party cocktail, well, the rest is party-going history. All in all, you can expect the unexpected with aspic.

Bacon

American Bacon | Back Bacon | Beef Bacon | Collar Bacon | Cottage Bacon | English Bacon | French Bacon | Hungarian Bacon | Jowl Bacon | Lardons | Pancetta | Polish Bacon | Russian Bacon | Salo | Side Bacon | Smoked Bacon | Speck | Streaky Bacon | Szalonna

✳ **SYMBOLIC MEANINGS** Endurance; Satisfaction.
🌀 **POSSIBLE POWERS** Abundance; Blessings; Economic Power; Fertility; Fortune; Good luck; Honoring; Infinite power; Naïve but honest; Prosperity; Sharing; Sincerity; Sociable; Sustenance; Tolerance.
☾ **PLEASANT DREAMING** To dream of someone with clean hands eating bacon with you is a good omen.

☾ FOLKLORE AND FACTS

There are many different types of bacon that have lovers obsessed with their particular flavors. There are websites dedicated to bacon that are followed by bacon lovers from all around the world. American bacon fans think this meat should be the national food.

The highly identifiable flavor of bacon can make or break a recipe. Too little may not be enough. Too much could overpower and ruin the flavor of the other, more important flavor components. Just enough can elevate a recipe to a higher, saltier taste level in a good way. How much to add is discovered by following a trusted recipe or by trial and error.

Aside from being an ingredient in any dish, bacon is at the top of the larding choices when adding fat before cooking a lean cut of meat. Bacon fat is rendered and conserved as refrigerated bacon lard, to be used as a cooking fat for foods other than bacon, most particularly with American Southern-style cuisine.

A few traditional farm-style methods of transforming fatty meat into bacon is by utilizing the immense power of salt, many hours of slow hardwood smoking, lengthy boiling, or weeks to months of drying while curing it in cold air. Back bacon is leaner than side bacon. Pork is the most common meat used to create bacon because all cuts of pork preserve well. However, other meats or poultry can be used to resemble the presentation of bacon, such as with turkey bacon, which is either made into a cured slab or cut into slices or "rashers."

Bacon can differ greatly from country to country, or even from region to region, depending on the preferences expressed by the bacon-loving people. American bacon is cut from fatty pork belly and is usually fried or baked to be crispy. English bacon is cut from the leaner pork loin and may be browned but not crisped. Bacon is a favorite food in South Korea where it is uncured, thick-cut pork belly called *samgyupsal*, which means "three-layered meat."

Other types of bacon may also be cut from the loin or fat back to then be seasoned with various spices before curing or smoking it to offer a different flavor. All bacon styles are offered as a slab or sliced either thickly or thinly. Any bacon is used in cooking as either a fat, a meaty side dish, a significant ingredient, or a flavoring for use in soups or stews.

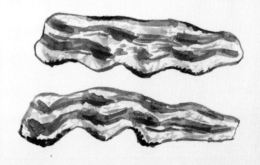

04

Batter &
Other Yeast-Raised Breads

Bagel | Batter Bread | Brioche | Challah | Cornbread | Cracker | French Bread | Italian Bread | Multigrain Bread | No-knead Bread | Potato Bread |
Pumpernickel | Rye | Soda Bread | Sourdough | Swedish Limpa | White Bread | Whole Wheat Bread

☀ **SYMBOLIC MEANINGS** Four seasons; Rebirth of the Sun; Unity.
🌀 **POSSIBLE POWERS** Blessings; Fertility; Love; Luck; Money; Prosperity;
Protection; Psychic awareness; Spirituality.
💀 **PLEASANT DREAMING** A dream about loaves of bread hints at frugality.

☾ FOLKLORE AND FACTS

The earliest bread that was made was an unleavened flatbread. Residues at different archeological sites in Europe date back to 30,000 years ago to indicate bread was made from cattails and ferns. In the Middle East, evidence of breads raised using airborne yeast spores dates back 14,500 years. Sumerians baked actual leavened bread around 6000 BCE, a technique that the Egyptians acquired close to 3000 BCE, when they began to deliberately add yeast to the flour. Before long, daily bread was a staple food in the Middle East, Egypt, Greece, and Rome. Then it went onward from there, continuously around the world until bread was made a part of nearly every meal, every day.

For yeast-raised breads, yeast is added to the combination of basic ingredients, which are flour, salt, and water. Kneaded or un-kneaded, the mixture is left to rise at least once before baking. Batter breads replace yeast with baking powder, baking soda, or cream of tartar. The batter is beaten well, placed into its baking pan, then encouraged to rise at a warm room temperature. The techniques and process for making sourdough bread begin with a starter or leaven that is known as the "mother," or "sponge," which is a mixture of flour and water that is encouraged to ferment for use in making the bread.

Sourdough starter can be continually fed to keep it alive for raising future loaves.

Gluten allows for elasticity and a spongy dough. Gluten-free bread recipes replace wheat flour with gluten-free flours such as amaranth, arrowroot, buckwheat, corn, flax, rice, soy, potato, bean, millet, quinoa, rice, sorghum, tapioca, or teff.

Bread is served warm, at room temperature, or toasted. It can be covered over with vegetables or meats, such as with chipped beef or beans on toast. It is used as an ingredient, such as for a stuffing inside of meats or vegetables, or added to bind and expand the bulk of other ingredients, as for a casserole or meatloaf. Stale bread can be made into croutons or breadcrumbs.

Breads made with bleached flour have diminished energy. An energy symbol can be cut into the bread's dough before baking. The possible powers of the grains used will be carried into bread. Be aware that bread loaves left upside-down will attract negative energy. When moving house, before moving anything else in, carry in salt and a loaf of bread. This act intends to bring good luck into the new home and fend off hunger from ever entering into it.

Beer & Ale

Barley Beer | Barley Wine | Belgian Ale | Brown Ale | Burton Ale | Cask Ale | Golden Ale | Handle | India Pale Ale | Middy | Mild Ale | Old Ale | Pale Ale | Pot | Schooner | Scotch Ale | Sorghum Beer | Spice Ale | Stout | Ten | Wheat Beer

✸ **SYMBOLIC MEANINGS** Down to earth; Friendship; Laid back; Loyalty; Unpretentiousness; Virtues of ordinary life.

🌀 **POSSIBLE POWERS** Addiction; Anxiety reduction; Bonding; Drunkenness; Euphoria; Gathering; Purification; Sociability; Violence.

🔮 **PLEASANT DREAMING** To dream of drinking ale is a positive omen that hints there will be good times to come.

☾ FOLKLORE AND FACTS

The use of wheat and barley to create beer and ale is believed to have been discovered by women fermenting bread as far back as Neolithic times. Barley beer offerings were frequently made to various gods during the times of the ancient Babylonians, Egyptians, and Sumerians. There is archeological proof that beer existed as far back as 13,000 years ago. Hammurabi's Code listed laws referencing beer. Stone tablets written in the Sumerian language that date back to 2800 BCE refer to nineteen different kinds of beer relating to that time period. In Egypt, the first public bar is believed to have existed around 1913 BCE. The Egyptian goddess Hathor is given the credit for creating drunkenness.

Originally, ale was a type of beer that was brewed without hops. Instead, it was brewed from grains, and, during the medieval period, ale-brewing was a common task for women known as "alewives," who routinely made ale in their homes for both their household's use or for profit. Ale was considered nutritious because it was safer to drink than the water for all people, including children. It was common for people to consume an average of a gallon of ale per day. An ingredient known as "small beer" was used to provide just enough alcohol to be a preservative in ale mixtures without contributing to drunkenness.

After water and tea, beer is the third most commonly consumed beverage in the world. Beer was first made using a mixture of choice cereal grains, which were most commonly wheat, barley, rice, and corn. Nowadays, hops is added for flavor and some bitterness, while brewer's yeast is used to promote the fermentation process. The primary ingredient in any beer is water, which affects the overall flavor. Other flavors for beer may include herbs and fruits. The further distillation of beer will result in a liqueur resembling whiskey.

There are many types of beer, with some regions having their own special brews. Most of the earliest beer breweries began in monasteries because there were hops growing nearby. Craft-brewed beer has promoted an increase in public micro-breweries and home-brewing. Home-brewing beer can be a rewarding hobby.

To prevent bad dreams, ancient Egyptians soaked leaves of select herbs in beer then rubbed them onto the dreamer's face. Add beer to a tub of bathwater to purify body, mind, and soul.

Biscuit Cookies

Animal Crackers | Bar Cookie | Biscotti | Biscuit | Brownie | Chocolate Chip Cookie | Digestive Biscuit | Drop Cookie | Filled Cookie | Florentine Cookie | Fortune Cookie | Gingersnap | Italian Cookie | Jam-filled Cookie | Macaroon | Madeleine | Molded Cookie | Moravian Gingersnap | No-bake Cookie | Pierniczki | Pizzelle | Pressed Cookie | Refrigerator Cookie | Rolled Cookie | Sandwich Cookie | Shortbread | Springerle | Spritzgebäck | Sugar Cookies | Wafer

✹ **SYMBOLIC MEANING** Precious small gift.
🌀 **POSSIBLE POWERS** Delight; Happiness; Satisfaction.
🔮 **PLEASANT DREAMING** A dream about a cookie hints that the dreamer is seeking appreciation.

☾ FOLKLORE AND FACTS

Since the advent of baking, biscuits have existed, originating in the seventh century in Persia. The sweet biscuits familiar to the world are also known as "cookies" in the United States.

Cookies are typically small enough for a child to hold. They are usually, but not always, baked. The most common cookie batter is a combination of butter, sugar, flour, eggs, baking soda, salt, and flavoring such as vanilla extract. They can be shaped into balls or extruded from a cookie press. They are most usually flattened from being dropped off a teaspoon or small scoop to drift outward into rounds from the heat while baking. They are also often rolled out to a defined thickness before being cut out with cookie cutters into identifiable shapes, such as the iconic Gingerbread Man. Baked cookies are often left as they appear coming out of the oven. In many other cases, they are simply or elaborately decorated with colored, firm-drying royal icing.

The softness or firmness of a cookie depends on how long it is baked, with some that are very thin and left to dry until they are hard enough to hear a snap when broken in half. They can also be thick and cake-like. They can be baked as a large, cake-like cookie with the intention of cutting it to create individual cookie servings, such as it is with a brownie. A cookie can also be made into an *extremely* large cookie that is decorated with a personalized message written with icing. In addition to birthday greetings, a few of the most common messages are, "Congratulations," Good Luck," and "I Love You." There are other messages that are humorous, with some being utterly rude.

Fortune cookies are fun and easy to make at home, but they are not rooted in ancient Chinese divination. They originated in 1920s California to advertise a Chinese restaurant. Even so, they are akin to an ancient Roman divination known as "aleuromancy," where messages were written on small pieces of paper to put in doughy balls made with flour and water. From an array, a person would select a ball to discover a fortune within it.

There are a great many different recipes for cookies, with variations for each of them. Dependable cookie recipes are cherished. Those that have been handwritten on index cards or that take up a precious page in a homemade cookbook are often butter-stained with loving fingerprints.

Bitters

✺ **SYMBOLIC MEANING** Bitterness.
🌀 **POSSIBLE POWERS** Digestive relief; Flavor.
💀 **PLEASANT DREAMING** To taste bitters in a dream, the dreamer may open a door to possibility.

☾ **FOLKLORE AND FACTS**

Bitters are intense infusions of specific herbs in alcohol. They were originally sold as popular medicines that were used as cure-alls for digestive issues, as well as a long list of other related and completely unrelated maladies.

The practice of using alcohol to intensely infuse herbs can be traced back to the ancient Egyptians, who used wine to make the first aromatic bitters by infusing medicinal herbs, barks, and roots.

Most brands of bitters that are still being used in the twenty-first century date back to the fifteenth and sixteenth centuries. One of the earliest recipes for bitters was in an 1864 cookbook titled *The English and Australian Cookery Book*, which calls for the infusion to be made with sherry.

The science of natural digestive bitters is that when one is uncomfortable after a meal and suffering from bloating, indigestion, heartburn, and gas, the bitters stimulate the taste receptors on the tongue, which in turn stimulate nerves that stimulate the digestive juices such as stomach acid, bile, and enzymes. This naturally helps digestion. Digestive bitters might taste somewhat like medicine, but they make the enjoyment of having just eaten a fabulous meal considerably less distracted by discomfort. A small amount of the flavored bitters liqueur itself is intended to be sipped after eating to aid in the digestion of a heavy meal.

The non-digestive bitters are used to flavor cocktails. Celery bitters blend well with a martini or gin and tonic, as well as tomato juice-based cocktails like a Bloody Mary. Chocolate bitters are rich-tasting and blend well with dark alcohols like rum or bourbon. Citrus bitters were originally infused with orange, but there are now other citruses such as lemon or grapefruit. Orange bitters are often further infused with the addition of warm spices like cinnamon, caraway seeds, cardamom, or coriander boosting the flavor. Floral bitters have infused ingredients such as dandelion, hibiscus, lavender, and jasmine that work well with vodka. Fruit bitters can be any infused ripe fruit, with the highly flavorful peach or apple to perk up summer cocktails. Herbal bitters with mint tend to be among the most favored. Spiced bitters mix well with dark liquors such as bourbon or rum cocktails to stand up to the extra spiciness of such herbs as ginger or seasoning blends like Jamaican jerk.

A few drops of the versatile non-digestive bitters can be a flavorful enhancement when added to some cooked foods. Bitters can be used in cookies and cakes, coffee and cocoa, on grilled steaks, in marinades, and added to soups and sauces.

Cakes

Angel Food | Babà al Rum | Basbousa | Battenburg | Baumkuchen | Bee Sting | Black Forest | Bûche de Noël | Butter Cake | Carrot Cake | Castella | Cheesecake |
Chiffon | Christmas Cake | Devil's Food Cake | Donauwelle | Dumpcake | Dundee Cake | Fruitcake | Genoa Cake | Icebox Cake | Madeira Cake | Mawa Cake | Poundcake |
Prinzregententorte | Red Velvet | Simnel Cake | Spice Cake | Stollen | Tiramisu | Tres Leches Cake | Upside-down Cake | Vetkoek Fat Cake | Victoria Sponge | Yellow Cake

✹ **SYMBOLIC MEANINGS** Appreciation; Celebration; Commemoration; Love.
🌀 **POSSIBLE POWERS** Love; Luck; Prosperity.
☗ **PLEASANT DREAMING** A dream about getting a cake hints at personal happiness.

☾ FOLKLORE AND FACTS

The baking of a cake is more science than art. The presentation of some decorated cakes has elevated them to become artistically astounding, so that, in some extraordinary instances, they seem to defy gravity. Although extreme cake creation is relatively modern, sweet cakes have been baked as offerings for gods and goddesses for thousands of years.

The ancient Babylonians baked fertility festival cakes shaped like male and female genitalia to give as offerings to the goddess Ishtar. A Roman honey cake recipe written in Latin dates to 900 CE. Since medieval times, the rich fruit and marzipan "simnel cake" has been a popular Easter offering in England. Simnel cake is decorated with eleven balls of marzipan, which symbolize eleven of the twelve apostles. In ancient Europe, cakes were made in the form of people, which were offered instead of actual human sacrifices. It was the Greeks who baked monthly round sweet cakes to the goddess Artemis, which were offered topped with burning candles, a practice carried over to birthday cakes, with the candles extinguished by the celebrant while making a birthday wish.

The wedding cake is a highly significant cake that is, by design, more than a centerpiece on a table. In ancient Rome, crumbs from a special honey-sweetened cake were sprinkled over a bride's head to wish fertility upon her. Those present at the nuptials carried pieces of that cake home to bring that luck with them. In Victorian England, pieces of another's

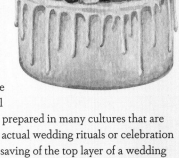

wedding cake were placed under the pillows of unmarried women with the hope that they would dream of a future husband. Special cakes have been prepared in many cultures that are intended for the actual wedding rituals or celebration afterwards. The saving of the top layer of a wedding cake to eat on the first anniversary is a contemporary practice that originated with the invention of the home deep-freezer. Prior to that, brides would save a piece of the cake, tucked away somewhere in the house, believing that as long as it was retained, she would retain her husband's love.

In 1796, cupcakes were originally baked in teacups. Cupcakes became more popular when they began to be prepared in plain or decorative fluted papers set into the cups of muffin tins. Cupcakes can be enjoyed plain, although they are more often simply frosted. The cupcake is elevated to a level of higher appreciation when it has been interestingly decorated to delight the eye as well as taste delicious.

09

Candy

Barley Sugar | Bonbon | Brittle | Bubble Gum | Butterscotch Drop | Candy Button | Candy Corn | Caramel | Chikki | Churchkhela | Cinnamon Drop | Cotton Candy | Divinity | Dodol | Fizzy Candy | Fruit Leather | Fudge | Gumball | Gumdrop | Gummie | Halvah | Jawbreaker | Jellybean | Jordan Almond | Licorice | Lokum | Lollipop | Marshmallow | Nonpareil | Nougat | Pastille | Peen Tong | Peppermint Drop | Ptasie Mleczko | Ribbon Candy | Rock Candy | Salmiakki | Saltwater Taffy | Sponge Candy | Sprinkles | Tameletjie | Toffee | Turkish Delight

✳ **SYMBOLIC MEANINGS** Goodness; Pleasure; Rewards; Temptation.
🌀 **POSSIBLE POWERS** Divination; Happiness; Love; Pleasure; Rewards; Sweetness; Wellbeing.
☾ **PLEASANT DREAMING** A dream about eating cotton candy hints at a pleasurable excursion to come.

☾ FOLKLORE AND FACTS

In the Middle Ages, ingredients such as nuts, aniseed, or pieces of ginger were dipped into molten sugar then hardened. These were put on banquet tables as a digestive aid. In England and France, working with sugar was starting to be taken seriously. Crystalized sugar was still known as "rock" candy, a luxurious treat enjoyed by rich Europeans. When rock candy began to appear in the USA in the eighteenth century it was still a luxurious treat.

By the nineteenth century, hard candy began to be more widely made, known, and enjoyed by the people who could afford a few small pieces. Both hard and soft types of candy, bar candy, and chewing gum became better known and available treats.

In the USA, before and after WWII, commercial candy making increased, and became commonly sold by the piece priced at an affordable penny. A penny was not exactly easy to come by at that time. Children who found their hand wrapped tightly around a precious penny headed straight to the nearest shop that sold their favorite candy. A rock-hard jawbreaker or a piece of bubble gum was long-lasting. The Tootsie Roll® was also considered to be energizing and was included with food rations because it would stay fresh for a long time.

Giving candy on Halloween night began as a means to appease ghosts with sweets. Candy has been used as an offering to deities in various parts of the world. A special candy known as *zaotang*

has a complicated recipe and is only made for the Chinese Kitchen God Festival. Traditional red-and-white-striped peppermint candy canes were originally shaped by hand, with the canes considered to represent Saint Nicholas's staff, closely associating them with Christmas. Small, egg-shaped jellybeans were invented in the late 1800s. Made in a variety of colors and flavors, jellybeans became forevermore associated with Easter. Small heart-shaped lozenges printed with messages such as "love me" and "be mine" are treats openly shared between people of all ages on Valentine's Day.

When sugar began to be frowned upon and urged to be avoided for various health reasons, sugar-free candies were developed, widely marketed and accepted as a viable alternative to fill the voids that would be left without candy. One way or another, candy is here to stay.

10

Casseroles

American Chop Suey | American Goulash | Bobotie | Baeckeoffe | Baked Ziti | California Tamale Casserole | Chicken-Cashew Casserole | Chicken Divan | Chicken Parmesan | Chili Mac | Cottage Pie | Eggplant Parmesan | Fish Casserole | Flygande Jakob | Funeral Potatoes | Gratin Dauphinois | Green Bean Casserole | Hawaiian Chicken | Imelletty Perunalaatikko | Janssons Frestelse | Johnny Marzetti Casserole | Kaalilaatikko | Kiampong | King Ranch Chicken | Krupenik | Kugelis | Lanttulaatikko | Lasagna | Macaroni and Cheese | Makaroni Schotel | Maqluba | Mirza Ghassemi | Mom's More Casserole | Moussaka | Pan Haggerty | Panaculty | Parmigiana | Pastelón | Pastitsada | Pastitsio | Potato Chip Casserole | Potatoes au Gratin | Rakott Krumpli | Rappie Pie | Shepherd's Pie | Shrimp De Jonghe | Spaghetti Casserole | Strata | Sweet Potato Casserole | Tamal de Olla | Tamale Pie | Tater Tot Casserole | Tepsi Baytinijan | Triple Bean Bake | Tuna Noodle Casserole | Turkey Tetrazzini | Undhiyu

✳ **SYMBOLIC MEANINGS** Efficient; One dish for all; Substantial.
🌀 **POSSIBLE POWERS** Community; Economy; Efficiency; Frugality; Togetherness; Unity.
☕ **PLEASANT DREAMING** To dream of a full, untouched casserole hints of
a substantial new love coming into one's life.

☾ FOLKLORE AND FACTS

A casserole is commonly known as a combination of ingredients mixed together or layered in one heat-safe vessel before baking it, then serving it in that same vessel to be shared by all at the table. Casseroles have been a regular item on the human menu in every culture and cuisine around the entire world for thousands of years. Nearly every edible ingredient has the potential for being included in a casserole dish, whether there are many complementary ingredients in one dish or only a few.

In the USA during the 1950s, the casserole became increasingly popular. Casserole cooking was spurred on by food companies promoting their products as casserole ingredients. Free recipes were offered on the backs of cans, boxes, or in magazines. These recipes, and all the advertisements that supported them, promised deliciousness that was affordable and convenient. There would be enough food in one casserole dish to feed a family and, perhaps, be enough to stretch into two meals. All that for two or three suggested ingredients. Quick and easy, the only time that needed to be heeded was the time required for the casserole to bake in the oven. During those years, recipes were accumulated and shared. The dishes were prepared repeatedly. Among others, the Turkey Tetrazzini Casserole, Potato Chip

Casserole, and Tuna Noodle Casserole were regular family favorites. In the Midwest United States the beef, macaroni, and cheddar cheese Johnny Marzetti Casserole was regularly on the lunch menu in school cafeterias.

Typically, a casserole might contain a basic build. There is often a protein, such as meat, fish, shellfish, or cheese. There may be a starchy binder, such as potatoes, rice, noodles, or pasta. And there may be a liquid, such as broth, milk, cream, or a sauce. From thereon, anything goes, because nowadays even though most casseroles tend to be made following a trusted recipe, there is no set rule dictating what goes into one. Like a soup or a stew, a casserole is subject to experimentation, since that is how all of the favorite trusted casserole recipes began.

11

Cheese

Blue Cheese | Brie | Camembert | Cheddar | Cheese Curd | Chèvre | Cotija | Cottage Cheese | Cream Cheese | Edam | Emmentaler | Feta | Goat Cheese | Gorgonzola | Gouda | Gruyère | Halloumi | Limburger | Manchego | Mascarpone | Monterey Jack | Mozzarella | Neufchâtel | Parmigiano-Reggiano | Provolone | Pule | Ricotta | Romano | Roquefort | Stilton | Stinking Bishop | Swiss | Taleggio

☀ **SYMBOLIC MEANINGS** Creativity; Hard work.
🌀 **POSSIBLE POWERS** Abundance; Adhere; Beguile; Charm; Cures impotence;
Entice; Eternal life; Fertility; Health; Healthy; Satisfy; Seduce.
🌙 **PLEASANT DREAMING** To dream of eating cheese with wine hints of
positive changes in one's love life.

🌑 **FOLKLORE AND FACTS**

Cheese is an ancient food that has been a part of the human diet since long before there was a method of writing to convey that fact. The earliest guesstimate is that cheese originated around the time that sheep were first being domesticated, approximately 8,000 years ago. Archeological evidence of cheese-making by deliberately souring the milk to start the process dates back to Poland in 5500 BCE.

There are specific methods for making certain types of cheeses. With well over a thousand kinds of cheeses with as many different flavors, available in different shapes and sizes all over the world, cheese is a common food and important ingredient in every cuisine.

There are unusual cheeses made from the milk of camels, reindeer, and yaks. The most expensive cheese in the world is a Serbian cheese called pule. It takes over 6.5 gallons of Balkan donkey milk mixed with goat milk to make a little over two pounds of the rare pule cheese. Pule cheese demands up to $1,000 per pound.

Cheese is served on its own, with fruit, with breads, on breads, melted, used as a dip such as with fondue, shaved, grated, and sprinkled over finished dishes. It is a common ingredient on buffet tables and charcuterie boards. Cheese melted on a grilled cheese sandwich is utterly iconic, commencing with childhood through to old age. Love it or hate it,

cheese will be part of the human menu for all time to come.

Cheese is magical because milk is magically connected and revered as sustenance for life itself. The twelfth-century mystic and medicinally astute nun Hildegard von Bingen considered the making of cheese as a parallel to the miracle of life, and because of that, cheese possessed magical properties. Long before she made that observation to arrive at that conclusion, Artemidorus, who was a second-century magical diviner, considered that fortune-telling using the way cheese curds gathered during coagulation, which is much like reading tea leaves, was somewhat unreliable. Even so, curd reading, which was also known as "tyromancy," was a common practice for determining answers to questions of money, love, and death. Other forms of Middle Age divination were practiced by unmarried girls who would scratch symbols in pieces of cheese to ponder questions of love. They would wait to see which piece gathered mold or had a mouse nibble on it to determine an answer of yes or no.

12
Chocolate

✴ **SYMBOLIC MEANINGS** Courtship; Romantic love.
🌀 **POSSIBLE POWERS** Alertness; Aphrodisiac; Courting; Energizing; Gratification; Healing; Health; Love; Money; Mood elevation; Relaxation; Romance.
☸ **PLEASANT DREAMING** To eat chocolate in a dream hints of an unexpected love that includes passionate kisses.

☾ FOLKLORE AND FACTS

At the conclusion of his fourth visit to the Americas, Christopher Columbus introduced the cacao beans of Mexico to Spain. The bitter cocoa was unimpressive. The Spanish monks who knew of cocoa as a frothy, thick beverage changed this perspective by preparing it thinned with water, flavored with honey, vanilla, and a hint of hot pepper. Within one century the taste for cocoa quickly swept across Europe, because the fragrance, taste, and physical pleasure from drinking cocoa was tantalizing.

Cocoa was deemed to be healthy and healing. Then it was made much sweeter with cane sugar. It also was spiced with cinnamon and nutmeg instead of hot peppers. Milk was added to fortify or entirely replace the water. By 1662, Pope Alexander VII declared that drinking cocoa would not in any way break a religious fast. Anyone could drink it! So, they did.

It wasn't until the 1820s when the Dutch chemist, Coenraad Johannes van Houten, invented the Dutch processing method of making powdered cocoa in such a way that it could easily be mixed with water, and of course, milk. Van Houten and his father are believed to have also invented a machine called the "cocoa press" that could separate cocoa butter from roasted cacao beans. That was another step in the right direction for making chocolate cocoa powder easier to produce and less expensive to buy. It also opened a door to more possibilities, which included mass-producing cocoa powder and offering it to a wider range of consumers beyond those who were wealthy.

In 1847, in England, J.S. Fry & Sons made a thick paste of the pure cocoa liquor with cocoa butter and sugar pressed into molds to become the first chocolate bar. That inspired more improvements to make it easier to chew than the extremely hard chunk that it first was. When Rudolf Lindt invented the "conching" machine the potential of chocolate was transformative. Lindt's conching machine mixed the chocolate so well that it gave it a consistency that would allow a piece of smooth bar chocolate to melt in the mouth. At that point, another step, known as "tempering," needed to be developed, which allowed chocolate to be used to coat confections.

Finally, working with chocolate produced masters of the new culinary field known as "chocolatiers," who are dedicated to chocolate as a culinary art form. Talented, adept, imaginative chocolatiers continuously produce delectable gourmet treats from bite-sized chocolate pearls to enormous, fantastical, towering chocolate creations that provoke audible gasps of astonished wonder. And that is still just the beginning of what is yet to be.

13

Condiments

Aioli | Ajvar | Bacon Jam | Barbecue Sauce | Beer Jam | Cheese Sauce | Chili Sauce | Chimichurri | Chrain | Chutney | Clarified Butter | Clotted Cream | Cocktail Sauce | Compound Butter | Curry Sauce | Dijon Mustard | Doubanjiang | Drawn Butter | Duck Sauce | Fish Sauce | Fritessaus | Garlic Butter | Garum | Harissa | Hoisin Sauce | Honey | Horseradish | Hot Pepper Flakes | Hot Sauce | Jus | Ketchup | Malt Vinegar | Maple Butter | Maple Syrup | Marie Rose Sauce | Marinara | Mayonnaise | Mint Sauce | Mostarda | Mustard | Nacho Sauce | Nam Chim | Olive Oil | Pesto | Piccalilli | Pickle Relish | Pico de Gallo | Pindjur | Piri-Piri | Plum Sauce | Powdered Sugar | Prik Nam | Ranch Dressing | Remoulade | Romesco | Salsa | Sambal | Seasoned Butter | Sour Cream | Soy Sauce | Sriracha | Steak Sauce | Sweet and Sour Sauce | Tabasco Sauce | Tahini | Tapenade | Taramasalata | Tartar Sauce | Tentsuyu | Teriyaki Sauce | Thai Chili Paste | Thai Dipping Sauce | Tkemali | Tomato Sauce | Truffle Oil | Tzatziki | Worcestershire Sauce | Zhug

✸ **SYMBOLIC MEANING** Enhancement.
🌀 **POSSIBLE POWERS** Elevating flavor; Enhancing food.
☠ **PLEASANT DREAMING** To dream about relish is a hint that something is being done with great enjoyment when awake.

☾ FOLKLORE AND FACTS

Although the use of a condiment is objective in the sense that certain foods complement others, something such as ketchup for a French fry or mustard on a sausage is still subjective, and is an ingredient that is optional, to be added to a finished dish, at the table, by the person who will be eating it.

Condiments can be sorted into five generalized categories. The salts, the sugars, the pickled, the spicy hot, and the compounds—which are generally sauces. Salt is the oldest and earliest condiment used for adding more flavor to the food at the discretion of the diner. Salt is also present in a shaker on nearly every table.

There are thousands of condiment possibilities and combinations. Many are regionally known and appreciated. Others are discovered from first-hand culinary experiences after traveling far and wide. Or a condiment might be read about then tried when urged onto a taste by curiosity. A few condiments or many are adopted as favorites, based on deliciousness. Internet shopping has greatly contributed to expanding the availability and potential for new condiment options, limited only on how experimental someone may or may not be.

Dipping sauces have been used with finger foods for thousands of years. Dependent on specific recipes or randomly put together on whim and instinct, dipping sauces are usually quite loose in texture, enough so as to be able to coat or saturate the food that is dipped into it. The oldest dipping sauce known on record is believed to be a pungent, salty fish sauce made with a mixture of any combination of small-sized fish, like sardines or anchovies, mixed in with the intestines of larger fish. This concoction was then fermented in the sun for several months to ultimately transform it into what was known as *garum* and *liquamen*. Dating back to at least the fifth century BCE, it was a favorite dipping sauce and commonly used ingredient in ancient Greece and Rome.

14

Couscous & Rice

Algerian Couscous | Arborio Rice | Basmati Rice | Berkoukes | Black Rice | Brown Rice | Calrose Rice | Couscous | Israeli Couscous | Jasmine Rice | Lebanese Couscous | Long Grain White Rice | Moghrabieh | Moroccan Couscous | Parboiled Rice | Pearl Couscous | Red Cargo Rice | Sticky Rice | Sushi Rice | Tunisian Couscous | Valencia Rice | Wild Rice

✹ **SYMBOLIC MEANINGS** Abundance; Blessings; Celebration; Dependable; Family; Fertility; Fidelity; Salvation; Solidarity; Union.
🌀 **POSSIBLE POWERS** Celebrations; Close family; Companionship; Family; Fertility; Fidelity; Gives blessings; Healing; Health; Link between Earth and Heaven; Luck; Masculine energy; Money; Positive energy; Prosperity; Protection; Rain; Sharing; Success; Unification; Wealth.
🎧 **PLEASANT DREAMING** To dream about rice is a good omen that hints of much good luck.

☽ FOLKLORE AND FACTS

Couscous is a pasta-like staple of North African and Middle Eastern cuisines. Couscous originated in the Maghreb region of Northwest Africa. It is made from the hardest part of the durum wheat grain that has been sprinkled with water, and traditionally made by rolling the damp mix between the palms, over and over, to create tiny bits of the dough. It is an intensive labor of love to make couscous. It is a love that has been expressed for many consecutive generations, spanning thousands of years. Nowadays, that labor is bypassed by using packaged couscous.

Rather than being boiled, couscous is traditionally steamed in a double-tiered pot called a *couscoussier*. In some countries, couscous is also made with pearl millet or coarse farina. A fully dressed serving of couscous is the centerpiece of a family meal. A large platter piled with steamed, soft, fluffy couscous is topped or layered with seasoned fruits, meats, vegetables, nuts, and sauces, to be fragrantly inviting. Moroccan couscous is topped with a sauce flavored with spices along with caramelized onions and raisins. Algerian couscous is topped with chopped vegetables and lentils. Tunisian couscous has a spicy tomato broth that may include lamb or other meats such as beef or camel. Coastal communities make couscous that includes fish.

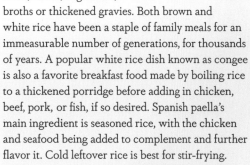

Rice is planted in earth beneath the water. Whether it has been prepared by steaming or boiling, rice is consumed plain, seasoned, or topped with other seasoned fruits, meats, vegetables, broths or thickened gravies. Both brown and white rice have been a staple of family meals for an immeasurable number of generations, for thousands of years. A popular white rice dish known as congee is also a favorite breakfast food made by boiling rice to a thickened porridge before adding in chicken, beef, pork, or fish, if so desired. Spanish paella's main ingredient is seasoned rice, with the chicken and seafood being added to complement and further flavor it. Cold leftover rice is best for stir-frying.

Couscous and rice have been the high-energy foods that have fended off starvation for millennia. Their delicious versatility has reached around the entire world. Couscous and rice have long ago proven their value in a multitude of ways in nearly every known cuisine.

15

Curry

Balti | Bhuna | Butter Chicken | Chinese Curry | Dal Makhani | Dhansak | Dopiaza | Green Curry | Indian Curry | Jalfrezi | Japanese Curry | Kaeng | Kaeng Kari | Kāre Raisu | Kāre Udon | Khichdi | Kofta | Korean Curry | Korma | Madras Curry | Pasanda | Pathia | Phaal | Red Curry | Roghan Josh | Sambar | Thai Curry | Tikka Masala | Vindaloo | Yellow Curry

☀ **SYMBOLIC MEANINGS** Rebirth; Renewal; Spiritual cleansing.
🌀 **POSSIBLE POWERS** Ambition; Enlightenment; Ingenuity; Intelligence; Sharpness; Spiritual renewal.
☗ **PLEASANT DREAMING** To dream of curry is a hint that enlightenment, perhaps spiritual in nature, will be part of an experience.

☾ FOLKLORE AND FACTS

In 2010, from the findings uncovered at an archeological site, a starch analysis was done on the remnants found in a 4,000-year-old cooking pot. What was discovered is the world's oldest-known Curry, which was a combination of sesame oil, cumin, ginger, eggplant, mango, turmeric, and sugarcane. So it is that currying foods with spices has been around for a very long time and will continue to be.

As heavily spiced foods began to branch out to surrounding lands, the styles of preparation and addition of different spices and ingredients expanded, adding in legumes, rice, coconut milk, chilies, lamb, chicken, yogurt, mint, poppyseeds, and pickled vegetables.

Some curries are wet, producing a sauce that can be served over or with rice or a flatbread such as naan. Others are dry and prepared like stir-fries. The four basic curry spices are coriander, cumin, red chili, and turmeric. Other fragrant and flavorful spices are added to produce the various unique flavor combinations that define three main regions, being curries of India, Thailand, and Japan.

Three internationally loved Indian curries are Tikka Masala, Madras Curry, and Butter Chicken. Thai curries are primarily simply known as Red, Yellow, and Green curries, with the hottest being Green and the most common being Red. Japanese curry, or *kāre*, is one of the most popular dishes in Japan. It is a little sweeter than either Indian or Thai curries and is made with a curry powder that includes many different dried spices mixed and ground together. *Kāre Raisu* is served over rice, while *Kāre Udon* is served over noodles.

In 1747, England was introduced to three Curry recipes for Indian Pilau in Hannah Glasse's cookbook, *The Art of Cookery Made Plain and Easy*. The spices were black pepper and coriander seeds. As time went by, more Curry recipes began to appear, calling for greater variety in the spicing and much more intense heat, which the British eventually recognized as being quite tame in relation to the original Indian recipes. Even so, nowadays that love for Curries and a desire to experience authentic preparations has made Curry lovers receptive to all possibilities, regardless of how searingly hot the authentic version of a dish might actually be. Curry is so much a part of British cuisine it is considered a national dish. The hottest of the British Curry dishes is "phaal," which does not have a parallel dish of its kind in India.

Dairy & Dairy Substitutes

Almond Milk | Butter | Buttermilk | Cashew Milk | Coconut Milk | Cottage Cheese | Cow's Milk | Cream | Goat's Milk | Half & Half | Heavy Cream | Ice Cream | Milk | Non-fat Dry Milk | Oat Milk | Powdered Milk | Rice Milk | Sour Cream | Soy Milk | Water Buffalo Milk | Whey | Whipping Cream | Whipped Cream | Yogurt

✹ **SYMBOLIC MEANINGS** Abundance; Eternal life; Fertility; Food of the gods; Innocence; Life itself; Maternity; Mother; Purity; Youth.
🌀 **POSSIBLE POWERS** Abundance; Fertility; Life; Maternal; Mothering; Nourishment; Nurturing; Promised land; Purification; Sustenance.
🔮 **PLEASANT DREAMING** To dream about milk in any way is a hint of good health and unexpected happiness to come.

🌙 FOLKLORE AND FACTS

Some religions or philosophical beliefs dictate the use or avoidance of dairy products on principle. There are also those who avoid dairy products for health reasons, or because of a basic dislike of them. All natural dairy products are among the most highly consumed foods in the entire world. There are hundreds of dairy products that are made and enjoyed around the globe, from full-fat heavy cream all the way through its many uses as yogurt, butter, cheese, and fat-free skim milk.

Plant beverages, extracted and processed to be milk substitutes, have taken the place of milk products in some ways. Ingredients such as coconut or nuts, including almonds and cashews, and seed grains such as oats or soy, are popular for producing drinkable milk substitutes that are usable in cooking or baking. Oat milk is economical and *extremely* easy to make at home using only rolled oats, water, a blender, and a strainer. Almond milk is a plant-based liquid that originated in the Middle East and dates back to the thirteenth century, when it was permitted as a substitute for cow's milk, as well as for meat-based broths during the fasting days of Christendom's Lent and Islam's Ramadan. During the Middle Ages, almond milk was popular among the upper classes in Europe.

Powdered milk products reduce the bulk and the weight of milk while extending its shelf-life until after it is reconstituted with water. The most widely available milk powder is non-fat dried milk. There are also powders for whole milk, cream, buttermilk, whey, and butter.

Learning how to bring raw milk to its safest full potential has been a challenge. Husbandry management of milk-producing animals began on home farms raising cows, goats, sheep, and animals found in the Middle East, such as camels. The pasteurization of milk by gently heating it to kill sickness-causing microbes in the raw milk was invented in 1864 by Louis Pasteur. In 1886 the German chemist Franz von Soxhlet suggested that milk sold to the public should first be pasteurized for food safety purposes. This sage advice was widely ignored until it slowly became recognized as a valid concern.

17

Dried Seasonings & Seasoning Blends

Adobo | Allspice | Anise | Annatto | Apple Pie Spice | Bahārāt | Basil | Bay Leaves | Caraway Seed | Cardamom | Cayenne | Celery Salt | Celery Seed | Chili Powder | Chinese Five Spice | Chives | Cilantro | Cinnamon | Cloves | Coriander | Cumin | Curry Powder | Dill Weed | Everything Bagel Seasoning | Fennel Seed | Flake Salt | Garam Masala | Garlic Powder | Garlic Salt | Ginger | Herbes de Provence | Italian Seasoning | Jerk Seasoning | Juniper Berries | Kosher Salt | Lemon Pepper | Mace | Marjoram | Mediterranean Sea Salt | Minced Onion | Mint | MSG | Mustard Powder | Nutmeg | Oregano | Panch Phoron | Pancha Phutana | Paprika | Parsley | Pepper | Pickling Spice | Poppyseed | Poultry Seasoning | Pumpkin Pie Spice | Ras el Hanout | Rosemary | Rosemary and Garlic Blend | Saffron | Sage | Salt | Sea Salt | Seafood Seasoning | Seasoned Salt | Sesame Seed | Shichimi | Star Anise | Taco Seasoning | Tandoori Masala | Tarragon | Thyme | Turmeric | Vadouvan | Za'atar

---

✸ **SYMBOLIC MEANING** Flavorful success.
🌀 **POSSIBLE POWERS** Happiness; Love; Peace; Prosperity; Protection; Purification.
☾ **PLEASANT DREAMING** To dream of smelling basil hints that many beautiful things will fill one's life and contribute to their happiness.

☾ FOLKLORE AND FACTS

Unseasoned food tastes somewhat bland. Seasonings flavor food and make them pleasurable to eat. There are several means of using oils and acids to improve the flavor and consistency of foods for both preservation and cooking. But it is the herbs and exotic spices that add those special touches and levels of flavor that can enhance, or can even utterly ruin, the flavor of the food. Just enough will elevate a dish to the degree of making it memorable. Too much or an incompatible seasoning combination can make a dish an inedible failure.

Since we, as a civilization, have congregated in cities far and wide, and we may or may not have the capacity to grow our own herbs and spices, or be near to where they can be readily available fresh-picked, dried seasonings can be an ongoing blessing when kept within reach in the kitchen. Whether we have grown and dried them ourselves, or resort to commercially packaged herbs and spices, there are several commonly used and depended-upon dried seasonings and seasoning blends offered for sale by reputable spice sellers and respected brands.

Salt is present in vast amounts in seawater and in salt mines where it has been extracted or mined since around 6000 BCE in Romania and China. It eventually became a valuable commodity for trade, first brought across the Mediterranean Sea to then be carried overland along specially built salt routes. The salt was carried onward via camel caravans to the traders along those routes, who would move it closer towards the ancient Hebrews, Greeks, Romans, Byzantines, Hittites, Egyptians, and the East Indians, who could not imagine their cuisine without it.

One Irish folk remedy includes salt in their cure for someone who is thought to have been "fairy-struck." It is believed by some that it is bad luck to lend salt. Spilling salt is considered bad luck, although immediately tossing some of it over the shoulder is the antidote that reverses this curse.

18

Dumplings

✹ **SYMBOLIC MEANINGS** Completeness; Family; Togetherness; Traditions.
🌀 **POSSIBLE POWERS** Family; Good luck; Spiritual connection; Teamwork.
🎧 **PLEASANT DREAMING** To dream of making dumplings hints at initiating a family get-together.

☾ FOLKLORE AND FACTS

A widely held belief is that dumplings were invented in the early third century in China by a doctor by the name of Zhang Zhongjing, as an effort to help warm his patients by eating steamed dough parcels he stuffed with herbs, chilies, and minced mutton. That makes a nice story, and it may be true. However, it seems that the idea to make a filled dumpling or simply drop dough by the spoonful into hot soup somehow made its way around the world on its own.

The method of following a river back to its source to find its origin works with trailing the back history of other foods, too. However, with the dumpling each trail reveals an entirely different and enlightening new source. It seems that it is via the dumpling that we humans are spiritually and cosmically connected.

Chinese dumplings are filled with meats, seafood, or vegetables, while the Italian ravioli includes cheese, sometimes with an added meat or vegetable. Polish pierogis are filled in ways similar to ravioli, but with more packed in. Like ravioli, they are filled, covered over with dough, and sealed all around before being boiled until they float. Pierogis are then browned in butter and topped with a dollop of sour cream. An empanada is made like a pierogi, but with savory spicy meat fillings that are then deep-fried or baked. Considering the size of a baked Cornish pasty, one may think "hand-pie" or "sandwich." However, examining its construction it looks like a much larger empanada. Before it is baked, it somewhat resembles a filled Chinese dumpling.

Soup dumplings that start out dried cook to a pasta-like consistency, while batter or herb-seasoned dough, such as the one found in many homemade stewed chicken and dumpling dishes, can be small doughy lumps or large fluffy pillows floating atop the stew. A Matzo ball is round like a ball. Potato gnocchi's soft dough uses both potatoes and egg before being rolled into a thick strand that is cut into segments to be boiled then served in a heap, buttered or covered over with a sauce. Fruits like apples can be wrapped with dumpling dough then baked to make a dessert dumpling. As part of dim sum, a platter presenting an array of differently prepared dumplings is a mouthwatering sight to behold.

Each of them, or most likely more, is a favorite dumpling of someone's. It is equally quite likely that every someone has at least one very favorite dumpling.

19

Edible Offal

Blood | Bones | Brain | Chitterlings | Gizzard | Head | Heart | Intestines | Kidney | Liver | Organ Meats | Pig's Feet | Pluck | Shin Bone | Stomach | Sweetbread | Tail | Testicle | Thymus | Tongue | Tripe | Variety Meats

SYMBOLIC MEANING Waste not, want not.
POSSIBLE POWERS Economize; Fends off starvation.
PLEASANT DREAMING To see liver in a dream implies something will be inherited.

FOLKLORE AND FACTS

What is considered to be edible offal is usually not muscle meat, which will take into consideration all of the other parts of a butchered animal. In some cultures, whether for religious reasons, dietary traditions, or outright laws forbidding it, none of the offal may be considered edible at all. In other cultures, some, if not all, parts might not only be considered edible within reason and right, but might also be a delicacy. Making something delicious out of something that might be thought to be waste is a commendable cooking art deserving of a written recipe, of which there are many.

Common edible offal is a part of most world cuisines, rising beyond novelty to the level of specialty foods that have become iconic by use and favor. Consider beef liver, which is a favorite when cooked with bacon and onions. The recipe for Jewish cuisine's chopped chicken liver may seem very homemade, but to those who enjoy it, it is also unquestionably gourmet. A sheep's stomach is a critical ingredient in the making of the ancient and ongoing traditional savory stuffed haggis. Cleaned and prepared pork and beef intestines are a preferred casing for a wide variety of sausages. Tripe, which is the lining of the stomach of hoofed farm animals, is a common ingredient in some Italian dishes and is a necessary ingredient in Philadelphia pepper pot stew. Kidney is an ingredient in the savory British steak and kidney pie. German pickled pigs' feet are popular in Poland and in many parts of the United States, too. Blood is used in the making of blood puddings, blood sausages, and black puddings. It is also a basic ingredient in some soups, such as the Polish favorite known as *czernina*, which wastes no part of a duck or goose in its making. Bones are used in soup preparation for their contribution to the broth and the making of stock. Animal hooves are used to make gelatin.

In the case of a goose, the controversial technique of force-feeding it to massively enlarge the size of its liver for *foie gras* is called "gavage." It originated in 2500 BCE when ancient Egyptians would force food into their geese and ducks to fatten them. Several countries have banned the production of *foie gras* due to the ethical concerns surrounding gavage.

Some edible offal is prepared in a wide variety of ways and have become popular enough to be culinary specialties. Edible offal is a type of food that one either tries and discovers they happen to like, or they will avidly avoid it all their livelong days. And so be it—that is just the way it is.

Eggs

Baked Egg | Boiled Egg | Century Egg | Chicken Egg | Coddled Egg | Deviled Egg | Duck Egg | Egg Salad | Fried Egg | Frittata | Goose Egg |
Hardboiled Egg | Omelet | Ostrich Egg | Poached Egg | Quail Egg | Quiche | Scotch Egg | Scrambled Egg | Soft-boiled Egg

✴ **SYMBOLIC MEANINGS** Birth; Fertility; Rebirth; Spring; The Miracle of Life.
🌀 **POSSIBLE POWERS** Cycle of Life; Life; Resurrection.
♟ **PLEASANT DREAMING** To eat an egg in a dream hints at a proposal of marriage,
an engagement, a long life, and much happiness.

🌙 FOLKLORE AND FACTS

Ever since early man first witnessed the hatching of an egg, it has been a symbol of new life. The ancient Egyptians gave it a position in their story of creation. The Romans included it in burial offerings and, like the Greeks, gave colored eggs as gifts to celebrate the Spring Equinox. As the symbol for new life initiated by the dawn of spring, the egg began to be so precious a symbol that it became a sacred object. The Chinese began intricately painting eggs as gifts 5,000 years ago. Colored, cute, or outright gorgeous decorated eggs are given as gifts. The association of the colored egg with the celebration of spring, rebirth, and Christianity is represented with the Pascal egg, which is better known as the "Easter egg."

Recipes for egg dishes can fill the pages of many books. Although eggs have been consumed raw in some recipes in the past, the danger of contracting salmonella is avoided by using dried eggs, pasteurized liquified eggs, or a lightly coddled egg in the recipe whenever possible.

To master cooking an egg is a high achievement. Each of the several styles for preparing an egg has specific requirements for the final result to be as expected. The lightest cooked egg is the coddled egg, which is most often prepared in a ramekin. It can be cooked barely at all and used as the egg element in a Caesar salad, which traditionally called for a raw egg in its dressing. An egg that is prepared coddled style can also be cooked almost through to the yolk and stand in perfectly for a ready-to-chop hard-boiled egg in an egg salad.

Once the cooking of a whole egg within its shell has been mastered in a saucepan of water on the cooktop or in the pressure cooker, it is possible to make perfect boiled eggs to suit, from the soft-boiled to the firm hard-boiled egg.

The milky liquid found after legume seeds have been cooked can be used as a substitute for egg whites. The liquid, aquafaba, is entirely capable of being whipped into a stiff meringue perfectly suitable as a topping for a pie or for use in any recipe requiring egg whites. It is believed that the aquafaba that originates with chickpeas or any of the white beans will produce the best quality. Aquafaba is suitable for use by anyone wanting to avoid eggs in their diet.

21

Fats & Oils

African Palm Oil | Avocado Oil | Babassu Oil | Bacon Fat | Butter | Canola Oil | Chicken Fat | Clarified Butter | Coconut Oil | Corn Oil | Duck Fat | Ghee | Grapeseed Oil | Lard | Margarine | Olive Oil | Peanut Oil | Pecan Oil | Safflower Oil | Schmaltz | Sesame Oil | Shortening | Suet | Sunflower Oil | Truffle Oil | Vegetable Oil | Vegetable Shortening | Walnut Oil

✹ **SYMBOLIC MEANING** Slippery.
🌀 **POSSIBLE POWERS** Flavoring; Frying; Health; Lubricate; Peace; Release; Sexuality; Softening; Spirituality.
🜍 **PLEASANT DREAMING** The appearance of lard in a dream hints that an increase in fortune is on the horizon.

☙ FOLKLORE AND FACTS

Originally, food was either consumed raw or roasted over an open fire. Eventually, it became apparent that the lack of a fat or an oil in a food accounted for its dryness or a basic lack of flavor. The fat made the food taste better and more tender. So, fat was deliberately added to the cooking process.

The fat was melted into a pan, food was added to it and frying became another new way of cooking. The fat could even be worked into grains or flour, then fried in the same way with more fat, or baked. Cooking became different; it became diverse. All it took was the fats and oils.

For thousands of years, the oil of choice was olive oil, which fulfills many of the needs for oil, unless the flavor of olive is less desired. Olive oil can be used for sautéing and salads better than almost anything. The solid fat of choice was "lard," which is rendered pig fat. Lard makes fried foods crispy and pastries extremely flaky. Eventually, when the health benefit of lard was questioned, it was pushed out in favor of butter.

When animal fats and butter were rationed in England and the United States during WWII, oleomargarine became the logical substitute. Although they may or may not stand up to the stellar reputation that lard once had, vegetable shortenings and other oils have since become intrinsically utilized in cooking, baking, and frying foods.

Peanut oil is known to withstand high-enough heat to stir-fry before it begins to smoke. Bacon fat is the fat of first choice for frying an egg in the southern United States. Thin sheets of suet are a vital ingredient in the making of some traditional steamed British puddings. Baking pans are commonly greased with a solid shortening or butter, then dusted with flour to encourage a smooth release of cakes from pan to platter. Rendered chicken fat is known as "schmaltz." In Jewish cuisine schmaltz is the golden standard that produces nearly every scrumptious dish that requires a fat. Chicken fat is also the perfect substitute for duck or goose fat. And, whether a luscious ripe avocado is enjoyed as a fruit or as a vegetable, as a buttery tasting oil it is as versatile as olive oil and can be used in all the same ways for sautéing and frying, and salad dressings too.

22

Flatbread

Bannock | Blini | Cecina | Chapati | Crêpe | Farinata | Focaccia | Fry Bread | Injera | Lavash | Matzah | Naan | Pancake | Pita | Roti | Socca | Tortilla | Waffle

✸ **SYMBOLIC MEANINGS** Bread of life; Daily bread.
🌀 **POSSIBLE POWERS** Luck; Money; Protection; Spirituality.
🜍 **PLEASANT DREAMING** To dream of serving or making pancakes is a hint
that one's spirit guide is with the dreamer.

☾ FOLKLORE AND FACTS

Flatbread dates back to 12,000 BCE. Every culture has several favorite types of flatbread; it is the most commonly consumed bread of any kind.

The most popular and widely enjoyed flatbread in all the Americas is the tortilla. The tortilla is prepared with flour and also with finely ground cornmeal, known as "masa." Homemade or store-bought, it is quite difficult to not be able to find a tortilla when one needs one.

Fry bread can be a masa flour type of handmade flatbread that, like the tortilla, is often topped with cooked ground meats, vegetables, cheese, and beans. Indian roti is another flatbread that is easily made at home in a frying pan on the stovetop. Naan is just as easy to make, but unlike roti uses yeast-raised dough.

In Northern Sweden, a common bakery is used to bake several families' *tunnbröd*, which is either a crisp or a soft flatbread made using a combination of flours that might include wheat, rye, and barley. Egyptian *eish merahrah* is a flatbread made using a combination of cornmeal blended with ground fenugreek seeds. Matzah is a Jewish unleavened cracker-like flatbread that is also kosher and eaten during Passover, when leavened bread is not permitted.

The familiar paper-thin French crêpe as well as the thicker hotcakes or griddlecakes, more commonly known as pancakes, are also types of flatbread that are made using a batter that includes eggs. Bubbly and browned pancakes denote luck in all parts of the world. They are, unarguably, "as flat as a pancake,"

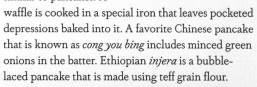

as the saying goes. Pancakes are a common food that is prepared in England for Shrove Tuesday, also known as "Pancake Day." A waffle also uses a batter similar to pancakes. A waffle is cooked in a special iron that leaves pocketed depressions baked into it. A favorite Chinese pancake that is known as *cong you bing* includes minced green onions in the batter. Ethiopian *injera* is a bubble-laced pancake that is made using teff grain flour.

There are so many types of flatbreads, made from numerous different longtime recipes, using just about every type of grain flour there is. Flatbreads are cooked on stovetops or hot stones, in electric ovens, clay ovens, or in cylinder-shaped tandoor ovens where they are baked pressed against the vertical hot walls. There are many recipes prepared by many different ways and means, that are all flat with varying degrees of puffiness to produce whatever it takes to make the delicious flatbreads that we use to wrap sandwiches, soak up soups and sauces, fold in toppings, or eat plain, buttered, or oiled.

23

Freshwater Fish & Crustaceans

Bluegill | Bream | Channel Catfish | Chinook Salmon | Coho Salmon | Common Carp | Crappie | Crayfish | Freshwater Drum | Mountain Whitefish | Muskellunge |
Northern Pike | Rainbow Trout | Silver Eel | Smallmouth Bass | Smallmouth Buffalo Fish | Smelt | Steelhead | Striped Bass | Sturgeon | Tilapia | Walleye |
White Bass | Widemouth Bass | Yellow Perch

✸ **SYMBOLIC MEANINGS** Birth; Fertility; Freedom; Higher self; Life; Rebirth; Salvation; Slippery when wet.
🌀 **POSSIBLE POWERS** Deeper awareness; Feelings; Love; Motives; Sea; Water magic.
♟ **PLEASANT DREAMING** To dream about crayfish is an indication of one's determination.

☾ FOLKLORE AND FACTS

Where there is a freshwater lake, stream, or river there will be someone fishing along its banks as there has been for thousands of years. As with saltwater fish, the fish and crustaceans of the freshwaters have long been as sacred as any other and have been offered to gods and other entities. The Native Americans discovered, early on, the power of fish. Many tribes considered them just as important for feeding a family as for fertilizing a field, utilizing freshwater fish and all the inedible fish parts to fertilize the cultivated crops they would plant in early spring.

Although salmon is spawned in freshwater streams and rivers to grow to adulthood in the ocean, where they are also fished, it is during their return to their spawning beds that they are in freshwater again and much more easily captured in the wild.

Archeological evidence of crayfish dates back at least thirty million years—if not older than that. Crayfish cannot abide polluted waters, so they are frequently farmed to provide ideal conditions for propagation and growth to their full size. Crayfish are considered a beloved freshwater crustacean delicacy in the southern United States as well as elsewhere in the world, where their farming adequately provides the thousands of tons of fresh crayfish that are consumed annually at "crayfish boil" picnics, and in restaurants that offer them on their menus during their season. Crayfish boils often include red potatoes and corn on the cob. Crayfish are also found in soups, stews, and the iconic Creole *étouffée*, which is a soupy, stew-like blend of crayfish meat cooked in a slightly roux-thickened sauce that is served over rice.

The eating of a whole boiled crayfish has a routine of its own that requires pulling off its head to suck out the insides, then the subsequent squeezing of the tail to press out the meat so it can be eaten. It takes practice and a desire to try it. Most people who dare will return to eat another and then another until all the cooked crayfish, potatoes, and corn on the cob are gone. Some will dare, then never try it again. Others will eat the meat from the tail and avoid the contents of the head entirely. Some will never dare try to eat one at all, and just eat the corn and potatoes. (And drink the beer.)

Frozen Treats

Baked Alaska | Frozen Custard | Frozen Lolly | Frozen Thrill | Frozen Yogurt | Gelato | Harlequin Ice Cream | Hawaiian Shave Ice | Ice Candy | Ice Cream | Ice Cream Cone | Ice Cream Sandwich | Ice Drop | Ice Gola | Ice Milk | Ice Pop | Italian Ice | Juice Bars | Pinachee Cream Ice | Pinachee Cream Ices | Plant-based Ice Milk | Pocchi Occhi | Semifreddo | Shave Ice | Sherbet | Snow Cone | Sorbet | Spumoni | Water Ice | Yum Yum

---

☀ **SYMBOLIC MEANING** Refreshing pleasure.
🌀 **POSSIBLE POWERS** Delight; Love; Refreshment; Soothing; Spirituality.
🎧 **PLEASANT DREAMING** To see children eating ice cream in a dream signifies happiness and prosperity.

☾ FOLKLORE AND FACTS

Somewhere along the way through ancient history the credit for the invention of ice cream was first given to Alexander the Great. He wanted a favorite jellied concoction that was known as *macedoine* to be chilled in snow.

Although it was a rarity, before there was even refrigeration, there was a thick, icy cold form of ice cream in the USA. It became better known and more frequently enjoyed after a refrigeration device was invented, known as the ice cream churn, which froze the custard mixture using ice harvested in the winter and rock salt as freezing agents while hand-churning the mixture in a container within the device. By the time dependable cold storage was widely available, between the ice cream churn and the ability to keep the firmed cream custard to be enjoyed a little longer, frozen desserts of all kinds became a common dish in almost any household.

Regardless of the final result, there are specific powers that can be attributed to specific flavors as well as embellishing ingredients that may be added. For example, blueberry offers protection. Vanilla, cherries, and strawberries are all about romance and love. Chocolate is a romantic aphrodisiac but also attracts money. The coffee flavor invites conscious thoughts. Pecan will draw in money, and gain or ensure current employment. Peppermint flavors are purifying and healing. Neapolitan ice cream's triple layers represent a loving appreciation of and desire for money. Peach invites love, good health, happiness, and increased wisdom. (Fresh, ripe, peach home-churned ice cream is also one of the most delicious ice cream flavors one can ever possibly eat.)

The ice cream sandwich is a globally enjoyed frozen treat. The generous scoop or cut block of ice cream in this treat tends to be vanilla or the three-flavored Neapolitan's vanilla-chocolate-strawberry. The sturdy thick biscuits, cookies, wafers, or even sweetened bread rolls enclosing it are what may differ from country to country.

One of the most popular frozen treats in the entire world are the various types of frozen ice pops that are made by freezing fruit juices or flavored waters in a mold, whether specifically designed to be as such, or in an ice tray, or a paper cup. A frozen ice pop almost always includes a wooden spoon, stick, or tongue depressor frozen within to be used as a holder while it is eaten, most often by children, who will surely enjoy every sticky drip and lick.

Gravy & Sauce

Allemande | Au Jus | Béarnaise Sauce | Béchamel Sauce | Bolognese Sauce | Bread Sauce | Bretonne Sauce | Brown Gravy | Butter Sauce | Cambridge Sauce | Cheese Sauce | Chocolate Gravy | Citrus Sauce | Country Gravy | Cream Gravy | Egg Gravy | Espagnole Sauce | Fish Sauce | Garum Sauce | Giblet Gravy | Hollandaise Sauce | Marinara Sauce | Marsala Sauce | Milk Gravy | Mushroom Gravy | Mushroom Sauce | Onion Gravy | Pasta Sauce | Polonaise Sauce | Red-eye Gravy | Rich Man's Gravy | Sausage Gravy | Sawmill Gravy | Spaghetti Sauce | Vegetable Gravy | Velouté Sauce | Whisky Sauce | White Sauce | Wine Sauce

✹ **SYMBOLIC MEANINGS** Abundance; Smooth.
🌀 **POSSIBLE POWERS** Calm; Flavoring; Healing; Smoothing; Softening; Soothing.
🎑 **PLEASANT DREAMING** A dream about gravy is a hint that one will have all they need.

🌙 FOLKLORE AND FACTS

Requiring a liquid in their composition, sauces and gravies are vital basic elements in all global cuisines. Sauces have been a characteristic that has particularly defined classical French cuisine. Dating back to the Middle Ages, there are hundreds of sauces that have been developed over hundreds of years. The famous French chef Marie-Antoine Carême began creating original sauces and adding more onto a list that he began in the early part of the nineteenth century. He included most of them in his educational cookbook, *The Art of French Cuisine in the 19th Century*. In his opinion, there were four "mother sauces" from which all others could be created. Allemande is thickened with egg yolks, heavy cream, and lemon. Béchamel is traditionally made from a roux of flour, a fat, and milk. Velouté is made with a roux and a light stock or broth. The last is Espagnole, which is the basic brown sauce made from drippings and roux thinned with milk, stock, or broth.

The Espagnole sauce is also known as brown sauce or brown gravy and is commonly served over meat, cooked potatoes, noodles, biscuits, or rice. A gravy known as Red-eye gravy is made with ham drippings in a frying pan that is first deglazed with coffee before lightly thickening it. Red-eye gravy is served over biscuits or grits and is a staple in the southern United States. Béchamel sauce is the same as white sauce, white gravy, or country gravy. It can be made using drippings from poultry, or butter mixed with flour then thinned with milk. White gravy is regularly served over chicken fried steak. Add cooked, crumbled pork breakfast sausage to a white country gravy and it is transformed into Sausage gravy that is delicious over biscuits or waffles. Velouté is a favorite on seafood and poultry and as a base for such sauces as the Allemande when a small amount of lemon juice, egg yolks, and cream are added.

Meat is not required to make either a sauce or a gravy. Vegetable gravy is made starting with boiled or roasted vegetables. A chocolate gravy served over breakfast biscuits is a winter favorite on Christmas morning in the Ozark and Appalachian Mountain communities of the United States.

Meats & Poultry

Alligator Tail | Bear | Beefalo | Bison | Boar | Buffalo | Camel | Capon | Caribou | Chicken | Deer | Duck | Elk | Goat | Goose | Horse | Lamb | Moose | Partridge | Pheasant | Pig Pork | Pigeon | Quail | Rabbit | Reindeer | Sheep | Turkey | Yak

✴ **SYMBOLIC MEANINGS** Affluence; Comfort; Christian love; Parental love; Strength; Virility.
🌀 **POSSIBLE POWERS** Balance; Comforting; Fends off hunger; Harmony; Lucky; Protection; Self-sacrifice; Spiritual love; Survival; Wish magic.
💀 **PLEASANT DREAMING** Dreaming of cooked meat hints at getting what one is striving for.

☾ FOLKLORE AND FACTS

Humans have hunted, trapped, or raised animals and birds to be butchered, prepared, cooked, and eaten since prehistoric times and the discovery of fire. Far apart and entirely separate from any ancient ritualistic purposes, the methods used for preparing meat and poultry involve careful butchering and various preparations prior to cooking. Once seasoning was discovered to be enhancing enough to elevate the flavor of the different meats, eating cooked meats became a way of life for many people, then as it is today.

Nowadays, meats are roasted, baked, boiled, broiled, sautéed, fricasseed, and fried in every manner that utilizes time-honored cooking techniques in the home or professional kitchen. Grilling and smoking meats is a common outdoor activity in the United States, United Kingdom, Australia, Argentina, and South Africa. Using open fire, hot coals, and wood smoke to make meats succulent awakens one's inner cave person.

There is no end to the love of barbecuing once the result impresses *anyone*. If the results are less than ideal—being too tough, too dry, or nearly incinerated—the desire to improve grabs a tight hold and kicks into high gear. Improvement can logically be expected. Grilling delicious barbecued meat is rightfully a proud accomplishment. Any style of barbecue is something that can be hungrily anticipated.

A simple grill or hibachi and some charcoal does an outstanding job with steaks, chops, burgers, sausages, ribs, pieces of chicken, fish, and skewered shish kebab. However, a combination grill with a smoker is a giant leap upwards into a new realm of possibilities, grilling all the usual favorites *plus* slow-smoking mouthwatering cuts like brisket, roast, and turkey.

The fork-shaped bone found in the thorax of birds is the "furcula," which is also known as the "wishbone." Wishes made on a wishbone go back to medieval times, when a dried wishbone was used to divine predictions regarding upcoming winter and spring weather, political campaigns, and such. Long after that, starting in the seventeenth century, the bone began to be used to divine general wishes, with two people involved in the divination holding onto each of the two ends, gently tugging on the bone until it snaps into two parts. Whoever is holding the larger part is granted the wish.

Although omnivore creatures other than edible birds are not commonly consumed, dogs, cats, guinea pigs, dolphins, and whales are still eaten in some parts of the world by people who consider them to be a food.

27

Non-Alcoholic Beverages

Aguas Frescas | Arabic Coffee | Arnold Palmer Iced Tea | Atole | Ayran | Bottled Water | Boza | Bubble Tea | Café au Lait | Caffè Americano | Cappuccino | Carbonated Soda | Chai Tea | Champurrado | Chocolate Milk | Chocolate Soda | Cider | Club Soda | Coffee | Cola | Columbian Coffee | Cortado | Cream Soda | Egg Cream | Eiskaffee | English Breakfast Tea | Espresso | Filtered Water | Fizzy Water | Flat White | Flavored Tonic Water | Frappé | Fruit Juice | Galāo | Ginger Ale | Ginger Beer | Green Coffee | Herbal Tea | Hong Kong-style Milk Tea | Horchata | Hot Cocoa | Ice Tea | Instant Coffee | Ipoh White Coffee | Julmust | Kefir | Kombucha Tea | Kona Coffee | Lassi | Lemonade | Licuado | Limeade | Macchiato | Maghrebi Mint Tea | Matcha | Mate | Mocktail | Moroccan Mint Tea | Orange Juice | Phosphate Soda | Pu'er | Punch | Reconstituted Fruit Drinks | Ristretto | Rooibos Tea | Root Beer | Ryazhenka | Salep | Sekanjabin | Shake | Shrub | Slushy | Smoothie | Soft Drinks | South Indian Coffee | Sparkling Water | Spritzer | Sweet Tea | Switchel | Thai Iced Tea | Turkish Coffee | Viennese Coffee | Vietnamese Coffee | Water | Wiener Melange

✺ **SYMBOLIC MEANING** Temperance.
🌀 **POSSIBLE POWERS** Healing; Hydrating; Refreshing; Relaxing; Thirst-quenching.
♟ **PLEASANT DREAMING** A dream about drinking water hints that a very
good thing is on the brink of happening.

☾ FOLKLORE AND FACTS

In the USA, the non-alcoholic beverage became known as the "temperance" drink when, from 1920 to 1933, Prohibition spawned mocktails such as the "Shirley Temple," named after the famous child star of the time. At any rate, non-alcoholic beverages are, as may have been guessed, any drinks made without alcohol. Beverages that are easily attainable have much to do with the community, because we will purchase what we find in shops nearby. Perceived value also plays a part. There was a time in the fifteenth century when a Turkish woman was entirely within her right to divorce her husband if he was not providing her with enough coffee to satisfy her expectations.

One of the most popular non-alcoholic beverages is homemade lemonade, which is also called "cloudy lemonade." It is best known sweetened with sugar and served cold, though it can also be served hot and sweetened with honey as a cold remedy. It is the beverage of childhood lemonade stands set up on sidewalks in front of suburban homes in the summer. Pink lemonade is colored with a splash of purple grape juice or a few drops of red food coloring. In the UK, South Africa, Australia, and Ireland, carbonated clear lemonade is the most commonly enjoyed version.

Fifty to seventy-five percent of the human body is water. Humans lose a portion of that throughout the day at varying rates, depending on their activity. What is lost needs to be replenished, so one of the things that humans require in order to survive is water. The simple glass of clean drinkable water is all that is absolutely needed to sustain human life—filtered tap water, if preferred or if outright necessary. Squeeze in a squirt of lemon juice for a bit of zing if that is desired. Clean water is clearing, hydrating, cleansing, and an overall healthy necessity for the entire body to be able to sustain and heal itself.

28
Noodles

☀ **SYMBOLIC MEANINGS** Happiness; Long life.
🌀 **POSSIBLE POWERS** Good wishes; Happiness; Health; Longevity; Luck.
🎧 **PLEASANT DREAMING** To stir-fry noodles in a dream hints that
considering one's own personal needs is a necessity.

☾ FOLKLORE AND FACTS

In 2005, a bowl with remnants of noodles dating back 4,000 years ago was found at an archeological dig, the earliest evidence of there being such a food. Noodles are made from unleavened dough. Stretched out, then folded to be stretched repeatedly is one way to multiply the strands. The dough can be thinly rolled out then cut into ribbon-like noodles from wide to very fine with a sharp knife. Extruding the dough through a machine is another method used to create noodles.

From their origin in China, noodles began appearing in every known cuisine. They are served alone, buttered or oiled, flavored with herbs, coated with gravies, sautéed, stir-fried, baked, added to soups, or covered over with sauces that are as thick as a stew. Thick or thin, noodles have most often been made with wheat flours, or buckwheat, such as the Japanese soba noodles.

Egg noodles are the favorite in chicken noodle soup and as a bed for thick goulash. Spätzle is a type of German noodle that has a dumpling-like characteristic when they are made at home by rubbing the dough between the palms and letting the clumpy bits fall into the boiling water or hot soup to cook. Cellophane noodles are made from mung beans or potato starch and are translucent when cooked. Thick or extremely thin rice noodles are a favorite in many dishes from East, Southeast, and South Asia, such as Thailand's "pad Thai."

When the versatile dried, instant noodle packet was created in 1958 by Japanese inventor Momofuku Ando, a noodle revolution began to wrap around the world. Considered to be one of the greatest Japanese inventions, instant noodles are currently sold in twenty-one countries. Available in different flavors, the pre-seasoned, "just add hot water" packet or cup is affordable, convenient, and quick to make. Their affordability made instant noodles an iconic frugal salvation for hungry people on the lowest of low-income days. In the USA they are referred to as "instant ramen" noodles. Most often eaten as is, other ingredients can also be added, such as a soft-boiled egg, sliced scallions, pieces of meat or fish, or extra vegetables. In more complex recipes they have been used as the main ingredient in noodle salads, noodle casseroles, and noodle-based desserts.

Since noodles are symbolic of a long life, it is considered to be unlucky to cut up a noodle's strand. To eat a long noodle on the Lunar New Year brings very good luck for the upcoming year.

Pasta

Acini di Pepe | Agnolini | Agnolotti | Alphabet Pasta | Anelli | Anellini | Barbine | Bavette | Bigoli | Bucatini | Busiate | Calamarata | Campanelle | Cannelloni | Capellini | Cappelletti | Casarecce | Cascatelli | Casoncelli | Casunziei | Cavatappi | Cavatelli | Cencioni | Chifferi | Conchiglie | Conchigliette | Conchiglioni | Corzetti | Culurgiones | Egg Barley | Fagottini | Farfalle | Farfalline | Fedelini | Ferrazzuoli | Festoni | Fettuccine | Fideos | Fileja | Filini | Fiori | Florentine | Fregula | Fusilli | Garganelli | Gemelli | Gnocchi | Lagane | Lanterne | Lasagna | Lasagnotte | Linguine | Lorighittas | Lumache | Lumaconi | Macaroni | Mafalde | Mafaldine | Malloreddus | Maltagliati | Mandala | Mezzelune | Orecchiette | Orzo | Paccheri | Pappardelle | Passatelli | Pastina | Penne | Pici | Pipe Rigate | Pizzoccheri | Ptitim | Radiatori | Ravioli | Rigatoni | Rotelle | Scialatelli | Sedani | Spaghetti | Spaghettini | Spaghettoni | Stringozzi | Strozzapreti | Tagliatelle | Taglierini | Tortelli | Tortellini | Tortelloni | Tortiglioni | Trenette | Trofie | Vermicelli | Ziti

✻ **SYMBOLIC MEANINGS** Always and forever; Family; Life; Tradition; Union.
🌀 **POSSIBLE POWERS** Communication; Creativity; Health; Protection; Psychic powers; Romance.
🜚 **PLEASANT DREAMING** To dream about macaroni hints that a stranger will enter one's life.

☾ FOLKLORE AND FACTS

Does it really matter who invented pasta? Pasta is still with us, since back when it made its first appearance around the fourth century BCE. That is thousands of years ago. Does it really matter whether or not Marco Polo's travels to the Far East gave him the opportunity to obtain the recipe for Kublai Khan's grandmother's noodles, then to bring it home with him to Italy in the late 1200s? That is most likely a myth because the appearance of pasta in Italy dates to sixteen years *before* Marco Polo returned to Italy from China. Pasta more likely originated in the Middle East. At any rate, one way or another, pasta gloriously appeared in Italy around the start of the 1300s and has been there ever since, to then make its way all around the world.

Pasta is such a simple mixture of raw eggs, flour, and a sprinkle of salt. Mix it. Knead it. Shape it all into any one of the 310 different shapes that are called by one of over a thousand different names. Flour them to keep them from sticking back together while they briefly air dry. Boil a big pot of water that is as salty as the sea. Drop the pasta in. Time them to cook until they are *al dente*, which means "to the tooth." Overcooking will make it mushy. Drain it. There are *so many* possible choices to dress a bowl of naked pasta, such as a marinara gravy, a buttery sauce, or herbed olive oil. Shave on a little Parmesan cheese. A little more than that! There. *Perfetto*. "*Mangia*! Eat!"

Every pasta shape is a delight, but the long, noodle-shaped spaghetti is the most familiar. It is no surprise that the world's beloved spaghetti, with or without meatballs, is the number one best-known and most-consumed pasta in the world. Maybe it is the way it can be easily twirled off the plate around the tines of the fork to bring up to the mouth. Once the technique is learned it is never forgotten. There is something magical about that.

Pickled Foods

Asparagus Pickle | Beet Eggs | Beetroot Pickle | Bread and Butter Pickles | Carrot Pickle | Cauliflower Pickles | Ceviche | Chinese Pickles | Chow-Chow | Cinnamon Pickles | Cornichons | Cucumber Pickle | Dill Pickles | Dongchimi | Fukujinzuke | Garlic Pickle | Genuine Dill | Gherkin Pickles | Green Chili Pickle | Green Tomato Pickles | Half-Sour Pickles | Hungarian-style Pickles | Indian Pickle | Kimchi | Kosher Dill Pickles | Lady's Finger | Lemon Pickle | Lime Pickle | No-salt Sweet Pickle | Onion Pickle | Overnight Dill | Pa Kimchi | Pào Cài | Pepperoncini | Piccalilli | Pickled Banana Peppers | Pickled Eggs | Pickled Green Beans | Pickled Herring | Pickled Hot Cherry Peppers | Pickled Jalapeños | Pickled Nozawana | Pickled Okra | Pickled Pearl Onions | Pickled Peppers | Pickled Pigs' Feet | Pickled Shallots | Pickled Watermelon Rind | Polish Pickles | Radish Pickle | Raw Mango Pickle | Red Chili Sweet Pickle | Refrigerator Pickles | Sauerkraut | Sour Pickles | Sweet Hot Pickle | Sweet Pickles | Takuan | Turşu

✹ **SYMBOLIC MEANINGS** Independence; Permanency.
🌀 **POSSIBLE POWERS** Love; Preservation; Purification; Unyielding.
🜂 **PLEASANT DREAMING** Seeing a pickle in a dream hints that there is a need
to consider being more carefree.

☾ FOLKLORE AND FACTS

The method of safely preserving a wide variety of foods to last a long time by processing them in a salty brine or white vinegar is known as pickling. There is archeological evidence of pickled cucumbers that dates back to 2030 BCE in the northern regions of Iraq. Although pickling will ultimately change the taste and texture of whatever food is treated in this manner, the taste has been pleasantly acceptable for many thousands of years. As long as a food can complement salty sourness, it can be pickled. There is a legend that Cleopatra favored eating pickles of any kind because she was informed they were beautifying.

There are unlimited possibilities with pickles. The most common are sweet or sour dill pickled cucumbers, pearl onions, cauliflower florets, eggplant, carrots, herring, shellfish (also known as ceviche), and a pickled mixture of vegetables with spices known as chutney. Other foods are less commonly found in a grocery store, but at nearly every county fair are pickled watermelon rind, okra, green beans, corn, and garlic cloves. The Pennsylvania Dutch delicacy of peeled hardboiled eggs pickled with sliced beets and onions turn the egg white a bright rosy pink that reaches all the way through to the yolk. Pickled peppers and chilies of every kind are found everywhere, with the most commonly available being pickled hot cherry peppers and pickled jalapeño pepper slices. The fermented pickled foods such as sauerkraut and Korean kimchi are not only delicious but also quite healthy, because they introduce natural probiotics into the digestive system as any fermented food will.

In other parts of the world seasoned meats and local fruits such as mango, papaya, and pineapple are commonly pickled. Pickled ginger is so common that it has made its way across the sea to every continent as a tasty condiment found on sushi platters. In Burma, even tea leaves are pickled! The list of foods and their combinations that might make a tasty pickle is inexhaustible.

31

Pizza

Beach Pizza | California-style Pizza | Chicago-style Pizza | Detroit-style Pizza | Fugazza | Greek Pizza | Hawaiian Pizza | Iranian Pizza | Italian Tomato Pie | Mexican Pizza |
Neapolitan Pizza | New Haven-style Pizza | New Jersey Tomato Pie | New York-style Pizza | Pan Pizza | Pizza al Taglio | Pizza Cake | Pizza Capricciosa | Pizza Margherita |
Pizza Marinara | Pizza Pugliese | Quattro Formaggi | Sardenara | Seafood Pizza | Sicilian Pizza | St. Louis-style Pizza | Stuffed Crust Pizza | Taco Pizza | White Pizza

✹ **SYMBOLIC MEANINGS** Life is good; Passion; Survival; Vitality.
🌀 **POSSIBLE POWERS** Energy absorption; Grounding; Harmony; Lust; Perfection;
Prosperity; Protection; Repels psychic attack.
🔑 **PLEASANT DREAMING** To see pizza in a dream indicates that relevant current choices
should undergo a thorough rethinking.

☙ FOLKLORE AND FACTS

The first time the word "pizza" was documented was in Southern Italy sometime around 997 CE. It wasn't until the late eighteenth century that pizza, as we have come to know it, originated in Naples, Italy. Neapolitan pizza is quite specific, to the degree it is legally certified and has a protection status. It is simply a flatbread crust, olive oil, sliced tomato, sliced buffalo mozzarella, and leaf basil. Delectable simplicity.

From that simple beginning, a craze for pizza grew beyond Italy to the far corners of the Earth. Pizzerias appeared in every city. A reputation for greatness depended on a pizza's chewiness, thickness or thinness of the crust, the overall flavor of the sauce, the quantity and melt of the mozzarella cheese, and the quality of the toppings. Pizza toppings are subjectively selected combinations of any cheese with pepperoni, anchovies, black olives, hot peppers, sliced meatballs, sweet sausage, mushrooms, ham, and more—even the bane of traditional pizza makers that is known as pineapple.

What is known as a Chicago-style pizza is a deep-dish pizza that is more like a crust container with a higher, thicker edge that holds in a thick layer of ingredients that bake together. A New York-style pizza has a crust that is thin and flexible enough to fold. A Sicilian-style pizza has a thicker crust, is made rectangular rather than a tossed circle, and sometimes will not even include a cheese topping.

The *quattro formaggi* or four-cheese pizza uses four local cheeses whenever possible. A calzone is a turnover made from flattened pizza dough filled with ricotta and mozzarella cheese, perhaps some meat or vegetables, before folding it over, sealing it all around the open edges, then baking it. There are personal pan-style pizzas. Pizzas wrapped within an egg roll. Pizzas made on English muffins. There is pizza something or another everywhere we look.

Nutritious and filling, with the capacity to cover all food groups atop one large piece of yeast-raised flatbread, a pizza is one of the most social foods a group can enjoy. Pizza is commonly the centerpiece of many tables where friends and families gather to celebrate or simply satisfy their hunger with a favorite pizza along with a cold beverage. Life is good.

Plant-based Foods and Proteins

Fruit | Grain | Legumes | Meat Substitute | Nuts | Seeds | Texturized Vegetable Protein | TVP | Vegan Food | Vegetable | Vegetarian Food

✹ **SYMBOLIC MEANINGS** Earthy; Freshness.
🌀 **POSSIBLE POWERS** Gaia; Health.
♉ **PLEASANT DREAMING** A dream about eating vegetables is a hint that mental or spiritual food is needed to renew one's energy.

🌙 **FOLKLORE AND FACTS**

Plant-based foods are primarily fruits, vegetables, grains, legumes, nuts, and seeds. In the Middle Ages, Wednesdays, Fridays, and Saturdays were fasting days for the average Christian when they could not consume animal products. No eggs, dairy, or meat, as they were from creatures on Noah's Ark during the Great Flood. (But because sea creatures lived in water, they were exempt from this weekly restriction.) Eventually the strict fasting was by personal choice for many, more often. In the following centuries, the most difficult replacement has been for meat itself. Sure, one could enjoy a luscious Veggie Burger made of lentils, quinoa, vegetable bits, and spices. They were loved as they still are and will continue to be. But Veggie Burgers are not the perfect faux protein to imitate actual Hamburgers.

The challenges in creating a plant-based meat alternative are its taste, moisture, and texture. In 1967 scientists in Buckinghamshire, England, discovered a high-protein fungus called *Fusarium venenatum* growing in the soil. It is now grown in fermentation vats filled with a growing medium that has been inoculated with the *Fusarium venenatum* culture, while fed with glucose syrup. It is used to make texturized vegetable protein (TVP), which is a meat substitute flavored to taste like beef or chicken. It is then shaped into familiar meat-style shapes like sausages, patties, and cutlets, with some including soy proteins as well.

Other plant-based proteins include Tempeh and Tofu, both made from soybeans. Tofu, or compressed soy bean curd, has a neutral taste but it can also be smoked, as well as flavored by other ingredients in a dish. Tempeh is also concentrated into a sliceable cake form that is flavor adaptable as well as higher in protein and fiber than Tofu. Seitan, another prominent plant-based protein, is also known as "wheat meat." It is made from wheat that has had the starch rinsed away from the dough, leaving only the gluten behind. The gluten is compressed, sliceable, and made into meat-like proteins that are much like those made from *Fusarium venenatum*. Seitan is mildly flavored and able to take on other flavors to become such a thing as a meatless "Buffalo chicken wing" or a highly adaptable protein in any curry dish.

Hummus and baba ganoush are creamy Lebanese spreads made from nutritious chickpeas or eggplant, respectively. A falafel is another chickpea-based dish of a ball-shaped, deep-fried fritter that can be used in a sandwich. Ratatouille is a colorful, thick, all-vegetable French ragout of eggplant, sweet peppers, tomatoes, onions, and herbs. There are two popular vegan home-made cakes, one chocolate and one vanilla, that do not include eggs, milk, or butter in the recipes and are receptive to different variations.

Salads & Salad Dressings

Ambrosia | Antipasto | Balsamic Vinaigrette | Blue Cheese Dressing | Boiled Dressing | Bok l'Hong | Caesar Salad Dressing | Chinese Chicken Salad | Chopped Salad |
Cobb Salad | Coleslaw | Crab Louie | French Dressing | Fruit Salad | Garden Salad | Ginger Dressing | Greek Salad | Green Goddess Dressing | Italian Dressing |
Louis Dressing | Macaroni Salad | Mayfair Salad Dressing | Oil and Vinegar | Passionfruit Seed Dressing | Peanut Sauce | Pesto Salad | Potato Salad | Ranch Dressing |
Remoulade | Russian Dressing | Salad Cream Sauce | Salad Dressing | Salade Niçoise | Seven-layer Salad | Tahini Sauce | Thousand Island Dressing |
Tossed Salad | Vinaigrette | Wafu Dressing | Western Salad Dressing

---

✳ **SYMBOLIC MEANING** Be all that can be.
🌀 **POSSIBLE POWERS** Good luck; Pleasure; Protection.
💀 **PLEASANT DREAMING** A dream about dressing a salad hints that one's life needs
to be lifted up morally or spiritually.

🌙 FOLKLORE AND FACTS

As early as the first century, ancient Romans and Greeks would drizzle olive oil and wine vinegar over their platters of raw torn greens and chopped vegetables before sprinkling their favorite herbs over them.

Although salad dressings were a known ingredient, they didn't become popular until the 1920s, to become more so as time went by. This is because it became obvious that although a salad can be as simple as one leafy green in a bowl, in order to make it enjoyable to eat, a salad of any quantity or composition *needs* some type of sauce.

There are many types of salads, incorporating a wide variety of greens and vegetables from a spinach leaf to a boiled potato, but it is the dressing that pulls everything together. From a simple vinaigrette to a creamy seasoned boiled dressing, without these tasty, moist sauces the salad would not be much more than ingredients to add to a soup or be food for a rabbit.

A salad can be a spontaneous composition or based on a specific recipe. Overall, there are several types of salads, ranging from Tossed Green salads to what is known as a "bound" salad, such as Potato salad or Macaroni salad. There are specifically arranged salads such as Niçoise, Chef, Caesar, or Cobb salads. Some are based on the protein that might be found in the bound salads, utilizing tuna, egg, or chicken. Fruit salads, such as the Ambrosia salad, are often blended with sweetened dressings made from a mixture of both whipped and sour cream.

One particular salad that may have originated in the American South and has become a favorite at potluck picnics is the Seven-layer salad, which has more variations than layers. The one constant is that it is topped with a sealing layer of a mayonnaise-based dressing before it is covered over and refrigerated overnight to allow the dressing's flavor to permeate throughout.

Whether a salad is served chilled or warm, as an appetizer or intended to be the entire meal itself, it is the salad dressing that is the element that unifies whatever combination is included, for it to be all that it can possibly be.

Saltwater Fish, Shellfish, Sushi & Poke

Abalone | Ahi Tuna | Alaska Pollock | Albacore Tuna | Anchovy | Angelfish | Atlantic Pomfret | Blue Crab | Bonito | Butterfish | Clam | Cockles | Cod | Conch | Coquina Clam | Crimson Jobfish | Dolphin Fish | Flounder | Fluke | Flying Fish | Gafftopsail Catfish | Grouper | Halibut | Hāpuka Grouper | Herring | John Dory | King Crab | Kingfish | Lobster | Langoustine | Mackerel | Mahi Mahi | Mako Shark | Monkfish | Mullet | Mussel | Ocean Perch | Octopus | Opakapaka | Orange Roughy | Oyster | Pink Snapper | Plaice | Porgy | Prawn | Quahog | Red Drum | Red Mullet | Red Snapper | Redfish | Rosefish | Sardine | Scallop | Scrod | Scup | Sea Trout | Sea Turtle | Sea Urchin | Sheepshead | Shrimp | Skate | Snapper | Sole | Sprat | Squid | Swordfish | Tilefish | Tuna | Weakfish | Whelk | Whiting | Yellow Tuna

✺ **SYMBOLIC MEANINGS** Good fortune; Harmony.
🌀 **POSSIBLE POWERS** Expand the ability to love; Love; Psychic awareness; Sea; Water magic.
♟ **PLEASANT DREAMING** To eat fish in a dream is a hint there will be good luck while gambling.

🌙 FOLKLORE AND FACTS

Mummified fish have been discovered in Egyptian tombs. Ancient Egyptians offered fish to their gods as well as to other entities. Because certain fish were associated with Osiris, Egyptian priests would not eat them. Ancient Babylonians would also not eat fish, because they were considered divine and worthy of worship. Ancient Romans and Greeks ate them, even though fish were considered sacred to the gods Neptune and Poseidon. The ancient goddesses of the Mediterranean all seem to have been associated, in one way or the other, with the sea and water in general.

Fish and shellfish are known to be easier to digest than meat. Poached, baked, roasted, grilled, and stewed, fish and shellfish are commonly enjoyed around the world as they have been for thousands of years. Traditionally, caviar is made by salting the fish eggs, or roe, from sturgeon. Commonly available now, caviar was once only for the richly served tables and savored as a fine aphrodisiac. Roe from fish such as salmon or trout are currently produced to be caviar substitutes.

Sushi has taken on a leaping worldwide surge of appreciation that is more akin to obsession than

merely love. There is a restaurant that serves well-prepared sushi in nearly every major city in the world. Fancy sushi is thinly sliced raw fish that is usually prepared with vinegar-seasoned sticky rice along with slivers of colorful vegetables such as cucumber, avocado, carrot, and radish. Sashimi are bite-sized cut pieces of the raw fish. Both are often garnished with pickled sliced ginger and served with wasabi and soy sauce as condiments. At any rate, sushi and sashimi are prepared by an accomplished sushi chef well trained in the skillful preparation and art of sushi.

Poke is a flavorful and succulent sashimi-like Hawaiian creation of well-seasoned raw fish pieces that are mixed in with tidbits of other ingredients such as green onion, chopped chili peppers, seaweed, soy sauce, and anything else that might be tasty, such as pieces of cucumber, avocado, mango, or a pickled something or other. And a hearty squeeze of fresh lime, of course!

Sandwiches

Avocado Toast | Bacon Butty | Bacon, Egg, and Cheese | Bacon, Lettuce, and Tomato | Bierock | Bocadillo | Burrito | Cheeseburger | Chivito | Choripán | Club | Corned Beef | Croque-Madame | Croque-Monsieur | Cuban | Egg Salad | Fischbrötchen | Francesinha | French Dip | Grilled Cheese | Ham and Cheese | Hamburger | Hoagie | Hotdog | Hot Roast Beef | Hot Roast Turkey | Italian Beef | Italian Sausage | Jambon-Beurre | Lobster Roll | Medianoche | Monte Cristo | Muffuletta | Panini | Pastrami on Rye | Pasty | Patty Melt | Peanut Butter and Jelly | Philly Cheesesteak | Reuben | Roast Beef | Roast Pork | Sabich | Sloppy Joe | Submarine | Taco | Tuna Melt | Tuna Salad | Turkey Club | Veggie Burger | Welsh Rarebit

---

✸ **SYMBOLIC MEANINGS** Layered; Stacked.

🌀 **POSSIBLE POWERS** Convenience; Grounding; Layering; Portability; Protection; Stacking.

🔔 **PLEASANT DREAMING** In a dream, eating a sandwich that has been cut in half or quarters hints that the dreamer prefers solving problems in smaller pieces.

☾ FOLKLORE AND FACTS

The idea of placing a filling in between two slices of bread dates back to the eighteenth century. Earlier than that, the use of a flatbread to wrap a filling within it dates back much further, to the ancient Middle East and Africa. Long credited to the fourth Earl of Sandwich, John Montagu, he promoted sandwiches by eating them as a means of keeping his hands from getting food-soiled when doing paperwork or playing cards.

There are countless popular types of sandwiches—stacked and covered, or open-face—and it seems there are a few in particular that have grown beyond being favorites to become iconic. However, the most widely available sandwich of all is the Hamburger. Although no ham is involved, the basic hamburger is one thick or thin, cooked, circular patty of seasoned ground meat that is presented between a split soft bun. The most popular meat used is beef, followed by chicken. Topping any burger with cheese transforms it into a Cheeseburger. Without the top half of the bun, the burger is known as another favorite, called the Patty Melt. A Veggie Burger can be a mix of any non-meat protein mixed together with finely chopped vegetables, grains, or mashed legumes, and pressed into a round patty.

For American children and adults, the peanut butter and jelly sandwich on plain white bread has become a lifelong comfort food. So has the simple grilled cheese sandwich that has been a favorite since the Great Depression. Tuna fish salad, Egg salad, and Ham salad sandwiches are popular.

The Philly cheesesteak is a grilled shaved steak, onion, and cheese sandwich served on a buttered baguette. A Croque-Madame is a grilled or baked ham and cheese sandwich topped with a fried egg. A Bacon sandwich in England is also known as a Bacon Butty. In the USA, lettuce and tomato are added and served on toasted bread as the Bacon, lettuce, and tomato sandwich. The sliced deli meats and cheese-laden sandwich served on a long baguette is the hoagie, grinder, or submarine sandwich, of which some are so long they can be cut apart to feed a crowd at a party.

Sausage

Beef Sausage | Blood Sausage | Bologna | Bratwurst | Breakfast Sausage | Chicken Sausage | Chipolata | Chorizo | Cipollata | Country Sausage | Cumberland Sausage | Cured Sausage | Fresh Sausage | Frankfurter | Hot Dog | Hotdog | Italian Sausage | Kielbasa | Knockwurst | Liver Sausage | Liverwurst | Lucania | Oxford Sausage | Pork Sausage | Pork and Apple Sausage | Raw Sausage | Salami | Salsiccia | Salsiccia Fresca | Smoked Sausage | Sobrassada | Tomato Sausage | Vegan Sausage | Vegetarian Hot Dog | Venison Sausage | Weißwurst

✴ **SYMBOLIC MEANINGS** Economy; Frugal.
🌀 **POSSIBLE POWERS** Frugality; Phallic; Sexuality; Storage; Sustenance.
🔮 **PLEASANT DREAMING** To make sausage in a dream hints at success in multiple ventures.

☾ FOLKLORE AND FACTS

Stone tablets that date as far back to ancient Mesopotamia mention the preparation of sausage. It also appears in Chinese writings from 589 BCE. The ancient Greeks and Romans popularized it. In the *De Re Coquinaria*, which was compiled in the first century BCE, sausages were described as a common ancient Roman dish that was eaten with porridge and as an ingredient in other dishes. A favorite smoked sausage of the time, called *Lucania*, is still made today.

Before long, in every country in the entire world, sausages of all kinds were being made, increasingly based on recipes that were developed to consistently enhance the flavors. Many recipes have been handed down through families. In the case of commercially-made sausage the recipes are retained as highly protected company secrets.

Sausage is a product rooted in economy, made up of bits and pieces of meat left over from butchered animals. The meat pieces are minced or ground, well-seasoned, and mixed together with or without grain added. The prepared mixture can remain loose, or it can be forced into an edible natural casing of either cleaned pork intestines or edible artificial cellulose. The casing can also be inedible plastic for large sausages intended to be thinly sliced, like bologna. The resulting sausage is then either cooked fresh, is refrigerated, or is cured in various ways from heavily salting it, smoking, drying, or pickling it to store for use at a much later date.

The main countries that produce fermented dry-cured salami are Italy, France, Hungary, Germany, Spain, and the United States. Pepperoni is also cured in the same way. Pepperoni is the number one favorite topping requested on a pizza. Salami and pepperoni are both traditionally made with beef or pork.

Available loose or in links, fresh breakfast sausage or country sausage is a favorite in the United States. It is usually made of pork, although turkey and chicken mixtures can also be found. Breakfast sausage is available either loose or in small casings. The loose version is favored when making sausage gravy to serve over biscuits.

The links of sweet, mild, or hot spicy fresh pork sausage with fennel is known as "Italian sausage" in the USA. It is a favorite sausage for bun sandwiches at events and fairs. In Italy, it is called *salsiccia fresca*.

The hot dog is a link-style sausage made using mildly seasoned beef, beef with pork, or chicken with turkey. A vegetarian version is also produced. The hot dog can be sold loose, individually or as a long, segmented link, but it is more often sold wrapped in packages of eight. The hot dog is a favorite choice for bun sandwiches sold by street vendors and at sports games.

Soups & Chowders

Alphabet Soup | Bab Leves | Bean Soup | Borscht | Broccoli Cheese Soup | Bún Bò Huế | Butternut Squash Soup | Cabbage Soup | Caldo Verde | Cauliflower Soup | Chicken Noodle | Clam Chowder | Corn Chowder | Cullen Skink | Fiskesuppe | Gazpacho | Gumbo | Hot and Sour Soup | Khao Soi | Khichdi | Kulajda | Lanzhou Noodle Soup | Leberknödelsuppe | Liver Dumpling Soup | Lobster Bisque | Matzo Ball Soup | Minestrone | Miso Soup | Mulligatawny Soup | Niu Rou Mian | Pappa al Pomodoro | Pasta e Fazool | Pea Soup | Phở | Pumpkin Soup | Ramen | Rasam | Soba Noodle Soup | Sopa de Tortilla | Split Pea Soup | Thai Noodle Soup | Tom Yum | Tomato Soup | Tortilla Soup | Udon Noodle Soup | Vegetable Soup | Wonton Soup | Yaka Mein

☀ **SYMBOLIC MEANINGS** Comfort; Good news.
🌀 **POSSIBLE POWERS** Economy; Frugality; Health; Nutrition; Sustenance.
☙ **PLEASANT DREAMING** To make broth in a dream hints that one will have power over one's own fate as well as that of others.

☾ FOLKLORE AND FACTS

Soup has been feeding people for thousands of years. Although commonly-available waterproof vessels capable of holding water to boil are only around 5,000 years old, in China, traces have been found of boiled soup cooked in clay pottery vessels dating back to 20,000 BCE. There are cookbooks from the 1700s that include several recipes for soup.

In 1897, the Campbell Soup Company's chemist, John T. Dorrance, invented and perfected the first shelf-stable canned condensed soup. The first flavor offered was Beefsteak Tomato. Canned condensed soup made its way onto market shelves as a convenience product that quickly caught on. Canned soup continues to be popular and available, ready to heat and eat.

Dried soup was first developed in the late 1700s by cooking highly seasoned meat down to become a thick mass that could then be dried, stored, and reconstituted at a much later date. Currently, drying is done to an absolutely dried powder that can include a blend of dried vegetables with noodles, barley, or rice. Just put the mix in a pot, add water, heat it on the stove or microwave it and it is ready to eat in minutes.

Soup can be no more than a clear delicate broth or it can be thick and nearly stew-like. It can be fruity and served as a sweet dessert. It can also be chilled as a salad, or so hot it needs to be cooled with steady puffs of breath before bringing the spoon close enough to touch the lips. Soup can be served from a wide-mouth thermos at one's work desk or on the go. Or it can be ladled into the finest porcelain bowl made specifically for that purpose on a fine dining table set for an elegant supper. In France, a full formal meal almost always starts with soup. On a lunch table in the USA, soup is most often the main course to be enjoyed with a sandwich or a salad. At any rate, soup is diverse, nutritious, economical, and incredibly easy to make from scratch, starting with a big pot of cold water.

38

Steamed, Boiled, & Baked Puddings

Asida | Black Pudding | Blood Pudding | Bread Pudding | Bubur Pulut Hitam | Butterscotch Pudding | Capirotada | Chocolate Pudding | Clootie Dumpling | Crab Pudding | Corn Pudding | Couscous Pudding | Crème Brûlée | Figgy Pudding | Flan | Flourless Chocolate Cake | Haggis | Halwa Pudding | Indian Corn Pudding | Kheer | Mousse Cake | Pastel de Jaiba | Popover | Railway Cake | Raisin Duff | Saxon Pudding | Scrapple | Spotted Dick | Steak and Kidney Pie | Sticky Toffee Pudding | Summer Pudding | Vanilla Pudding | Yorkshire Pudding

☀ **SYMBOLIC MEANING** Unity.
🌀 **POSSIBLE POWERS** Economy; Nutrition; Tradition.
🔔 **PLEASANT DREAMING** A dream about pudding hints that one is noticing how genuinely good something is.

☾ FOLKLORE AND FACTS

A tenth-century cookbook in Arabic included a recipe for a cooked, doughy sweet pudding with honey. Since then, the development of sweet or savory, steamed, boiled, or baked puddings has spanned outward to the world. Recipes for puddings can be found in every cuisine.

With regard to savory puddings, many are made in ways similar to sausages, such as with bits of sheep meat mixed with oatmeal, onion, and spices for the pudding known as haggis. Haggis is traditionally served as a main course with potatoes and a glass of whisky on special occasions in Scotland. Although haggis produced in the USA is allowed to be sold in the country, authentic haggis has been banned from importation since 1971. Blood pudding or black sausage is believed to be the oldest type of sausage there is. Savory Pennsylvania Dutch-style scrapple is bits of seasoned pork mixed with cornmeal, cooled in a loaf shape, sliced, then fried till toasty brown. Other savory puddings may begin as a batter before being poured into a pan then baked, such as cornmeal spoon bread and Yorkshire pudding. Others are baked within a thick crust like a pie.

Dessert puddings are similar to cake in many ways. A favorite baked sweet pudding is bread pudding, which has a cake-like consistency. Another is rice pudding, which does not. Two popular cake-like steamed puddings are sticky toffee pudding and Christmas plum pudding. With regard to the Christmas pudding tradition, these puddings are most often a bit boozy with charms hidden within that, upon finding, divine a special luck for the coming year. For example, a silver coin for success, a wishbone for good luck, a thimble for thriftiness, an anchor for safety, and a ring to foretell a marriage engagement.

Boiled puddings are often milk-based, thickened with cornstarch, flavored with chocolate or vanilla, then cooked until creamy before chilling. Egg-based custards, such as crème brûlée, are also cooked before chilling. Chilled crème brûlée is sprinkled over the top with sugar that is flame-caramelized to create a crackable candy-like crust.

Bag puddings, such as the figgy pudding, the Canadian *poutchine au sac*, and the Scottish clootie dumpling, hold a mix of flour, raisins, nuts, sugar, and spices. They are boiled and simmered for hours before being lifted out of the water to dry in an oven.

With all the differences in preparation and final outcome, is it any wonder there is genuine confusion about what *exactly* a pudding is?

39

Stew

Adobo | Beef Bourguignon | Beef Stew | Bigos | Bouillabaisse | Brunswick Stew | Bunny Chow | Cabbage Stew | Chicken Paprikash | Chili Con Carne | Cioppino | Coq au Vin | Dal | Étouffée | Gumbo | Hungarian Goulash | Irish Stew | Korma | Lobster Stew | Mulligan Stew | Mushroom Stew | Oyster Stew | Philadelphia Pepper Pot | Pot Roast | Ragout | Ratatouille

✹ **SYMBOLIC MEANING** Hearty comfort.
🌀 **POSSIBLE POWERS** Economy; Frugality; Health; Nutrition; Sustenance.
🔦 **PLEASANT DREAMING** To dream of a stew is a hint that there is a good idea with sustaining potential and longevity that is worth looking into.

🌍 FOLKLORE AND FACTS

Before there were soups, there were stews. Similar to a soup, a stew has less liquid in the end, will cook longer on a lower heat, and be thick enough to eat most of it with a fork. In a fourth-century BCE document, it was discovered that in the beginning stews were cooked over fire within entire sacrificial animals that had been opened before having water and other ingredients added into the carcass. There is also evidence uncovered in archeological digs that indigenous tribes in the Amazon cooked stews held in tortoise shells. Stew is known to have been prepared in Japan dating back to 14,000 BCE, cooked in vessels that would hold *some* liquid, although not as much as necessary for simmering a broth-rich soup.

Many stews are exalted to the degree of being iconic. One of the most widely known is Irish Stew's simple mix of mutton, potatoes, and onions. The French Bœuf Bourguignon is beef chunks simmered in a burgundy wine sauce with mushrooms, onions, and carrots that is seasoned with bacon and garlic. (Coq au Vin changes out the beef for chicken and the burgundy for cognac or brandy.)

One of the most commonly made stews in the USA is the regionally diverse Chili Con Carne, which is a spicy tomato-saucy stew with meat and beans. Or, without beans. Or, without the meat. Or, without the tomatoes! One thing is for certain: there are a chockful of opinions about Chili Con Carne. Should it be served plain or over rice, corn chips, or spaghetti

noodles? Should it be topped with grated cheddar, pico de gallo, a dollop of sour cream, or some fresh lime? Should it be mild or fiercely hot?

Throughout human history, stewing has been a method of preparing a hearty meal of meats or fish with other vegetables and added grains. There have also been stews created entirely of vegetables or legumes that have consistently resulted in tender flavorful foods in a thick sauce-like broth. Since then, quite simple to very specific and sophisticated recipes have been developed. They involve using a wide variety of ingredients that can range from being lusciously appealing or mouthwatering just looking at it, all the way down to looking at a bowl full of a curious mix to seriously wonder, "What in the world can that possibly be?"

40

Sweet & Savory Pastries

Alexander Torte | Baklava | Banbury Cake | Blackburn Cake | Cannoli | Chorley Cake | Cinnamon Bun | Cream Pie | Cream Puff | Crocetta of Caltanissetta | Donut | Eccles Cake | Éclair | Fruit Pie | Hot Cross Bun | Linzer Torte | Mooncake | Palmier | Petit Four | Pilipit | Pionono | Pirozhki | Pot Pie | Profiterole | Rugelach | Runeberg Torte | Rustic Open Crust Pie | Steak and Kidney Pie | Strudel

☀ **SYMBOLIC MEANINGS** Delight; Indulgence; Pleasure.
🌀 **POSSIBLE POWERS** Delight; Fulfillment; Passion; Pleasure; Satisfaction; Sweetening.
🍐 **PLEASANT DREAMING** A dream about seeing but not eating pastry hints that
success can be attained with patience.

☾ FOLKLORE AND FACTS

In ancient Egypt when pastry was new, it was an actual paste of flour and water smeared entirely around meat before it was baked. Later, the ancient Greeks, Romans, and Phoenicians developed the pastry known as "phyllo-style." The dough is very thin and layered many times, as with baklava. The ancient Egyptians introduced the meat pot pies we have been enjoying for thousands of years. A recipe for a chicken pot pie was deciphered on a stone tablet that dates back earlier than 2000 BCE. They also made the first sweet pie, which had a covered crust and was filled with spiced honey.

Around 1000, "shortcrust-style" pastry was developed, which is achieved by working a fat such as lard or butter into the flour to create a fine, meal-like consistency, adding a small amount of cold liquid such as water or milk, then rolling or patting it out.

The tart appeared when medieval pie-making became fairly common. The tarts originally held meats, but soon also had fruit or custard fillings. Unlike a tender pie crust, a tart can have a firm-enough crust to stand on its own without aid of the pan it was baked in.

By the middle of the sixteenth century, pastry recipes began passing from hand-to-hand around all of Europe and far beyond, with adjustments and adaptations galore. In 1540, the invention of choux pastry dough made it possible to form shapes that expanded when baked, which left a hollow within that could be filled with meat pastes, thickened creams, and custards.

In the early nineteenth century, adjustments to the original choux recipe were made by the renowned French chef Marie-Antoine Carême. That recipe is basically the same still used for profiteroles, which are also known as cream puffs. The dessert known as a croquembouche is a scrumptious-looking tower of filled puffs that is served in France and Italy for special celebrations. When pastry reached China, new and intriguing rice-flour pastries were developed with sweet bean paste, fruit, or meat fillings.

Wherever the concept of a pastry went, new ways of making them emerged, were adjusted, adapted, and shared. It is still that way today. Fantastical, beautiful, and extraordinarily delicious creations can be found in bakeries and on restaurant dessert carts to tempt us to eat more than just one.

41

Tea

✹ **SYMBOLIC MEANINGS** Clearness; Comfort; Heritage; Hospitality; Joy; Purity; Respect; Reverence; Sophistication; Tranquility; Truthfulness.

🌀 **POSSIBLE POWERS** Awareness of beauty; Hospitality; Identity; Present in the moment; Social politeness; Spiritual satisfaction; Zen.

🜨 **PLEASANT DREAMING** A dream about drinking tea is a hint that you will be in the company of pleasant people.

☾ FOLKLORE AND FACTS

Dating back to ancient China in the 2000s BCE, tea has long been enjoyed both hot and ice cold, plain or sweetened with sugar or honey, with milk or cream or a slice of lemon. Whether brewed with strained loose leaves or by using a pre-made teabag, whether drunk for medicinal reasons or purely for pleasure, black tea or other herbal teas are a universal beverage.

Steeping Black Tea longer than a maximum of five minutes makes the tea bitter. This over-steeping is referred to as "stewing." The three most common ways to prepare a cup of steeped Black Tea is plain, adding sugar with milk, or adding sugar with fresh lemon. In the American South, highly sweetened iced Black Tea is known as "sweet tea" with or without lemon or other flavors added, such as peach, raspberry, or mint.

Masala chai is one of the oldest beverages in history. Its spiced flavor is a staple of India, as well as of many other South Asian countries. Its recipe changes somewhat depending on which family, village, city, or country it is brewed in. Because of those differences, the taste of Masala chai will bring back a specific memory of place and time, events, and people. All across India, chai vendors can be found ladling out the tea into glasses from simmering pots where the hot Assam tea has been fragrantly flavored with cardamom, orange, ginger, black pepper, salt, and sugar. Some people like it sweeter, spicier, or with milk.

The enjoyment of tea has been tightly tied into world cultures via well-established social traditions that, in most cases, date back hundreds of years. The English "afternoon tea" evolved from its beginning during the Victorian era when the Duchess of Bedford, Anna Maria Russell, requested a pot of tea along with some light snacks in the late afternoon. Invitations were extended to her royal friends. The "high tea" initiated with working class people would enjoy their tea after work with heartier foods. In the twentieth century, a new late morning country-wide tea-time with snacks became known as "elevenses."

In Japan, a traditional tea ceremony is ritualistic and deeply rooted in the Zen Buddhist appreciation of harmony, purity, respect, and tranquility. Matcha, which is powdered green tea, or Sencha, which is a leaf green tea, is traditionally offered in a garden room setting where the furnishings, each piece of equipment, and each step has been specifically selected and choreographed. A formal ceremony can last up to four hours.

A hot cup of tea has been the go-to cure-all for nearly every sudden impairment, small or great—whether it's lightheadedness, swooning, sadness, or a gloomily slumping spirit—for hundreds, perhaps thousands of years. Who knows? Maybe even millions of years.

42

Vinegars

Apple Cider Vinegar | Apricot Vinegar | Balsamic Vinegar | Beer Vinegar | Cane Sugar Vinegar | Champagne Vinegar | Chinkiang Vinegar | Malt Vinegar |
Raisin Vinegar | Raspberry Vinegar | Red Wine Vinegar | Rice Vinegar | Sherry Vinegar | White Vinegar | White Wine Vinegar

✳ **SYMBOLIC MEANINGS** Calming; Curing; Restorative.
⊚ **POSSIBLE POWERS** Calm; Health cure; Preservation; Protection; Purification.
♟ **PLEASANT DREAMING** To dream of red wine vinegar hints entirely of romance.

☾ FOLKLORE AND FACTS

In wine-making and cider-making, when alcoholic fermentations extend beyond the intended degree, the mixture will begin to sour intensely, becoming undrinkable. *That* is vinegar.

Vinegar is one of the most useful ingredients in cooking. It will provide a preservative acid for pickling. It will be a complementary balance to oil for a salad dressing. Misted on raw meat then salted and seasoned prior to roasting, the vinegar will pull the salt and the flavors of other surface seasonings deeper within.

Once fermentation of vinegar reaches the point where it is actually vinegar, it becomes shelf-stable, never to require refrigeration as long as the container's lid is on tight and it is kept in a cool, dark place away from heat. After a while, there may be sedimentation settling at the bottom of the container. This will not affect the vinegar, although the sedimentation can be poured through a paper coffee filter to remove it.

Distilled from apples, apple cider vinegar has gained a medicinal reputation. It is also delicious in salad dressings and chutneys. Distilled from grain, white vinegar is indispensable in pickling and can be a household cleaner. The milder red and white wine vinegars are favorites in vinaigrettes or reductions. White wine vinegar can also be used in pickling. Rice vinegar is distilled from rice wine. It is a little sweeter than the red or the white vinegars, and can be used in pickling and marinades. Malt vinegar is distilled from barley and is a condiment for fish or drizzled over vegetables, most especially over deep-fried potatoes.

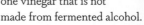

Balsamic vinegar is a dark, concentrated vinegar that has a unique zesty flavor with a touch of sweetness to it. It is the one vinegar that is not made from fermented alcohol. All balsamic vinegar is meticulously brewed, using specific types of wine-worthy grapes, which are most usually the Italian Lambrusco and Trebbiano. The vinegar is made applying wine-making methods associated with the finest wines. Balsamic vinegar brewing is taken very seriously. It is an excellent finishing and drizzling vinegar for sweet or savory dishes, as well as fruit. Balsamic vinegar becomes increasingly better as it ages. The older it is, the more expensive it will become. Balsamic vinegar has been sold in auctions to exceptionally high bids.

Three small bowls of apple cider vinegar placed in the home can be used to remove negative energy. A few drops of it in a glass of water can be consumed as a purification for body, mind, and spirit to balance the emotions.

Worldly Street Food

Arepas | Babbouche | Bakso | Bánh Mi | Barbadian Flying Fish | Beef Noodle Soup | Belgian Waffle | Boxty | Bubble Tea | Bunny Chow | Burek | Canadian Poutine | Cannoli Siciliani | Ceviche | Char Kway Teow | Cheburek | Chili Cheese Dog | Choripán | Conch Salad | Coxinha | Currywurst | Döner Kebab | Empanadas | Espetada | Falafel | Fish and Chips | Fondue Fuul | Gado-Gado | Gelato | Grilled Cheese | Guarapo | Hainanese Chicken Rice | Halo-Halo | Halv Special | Hotdog | Italian Sausage | Jerk Chicken | Jianbing | Khachapuri | Lahmacun | Llauchas | Mahjouba | Martabak | Meat Pie | Mititei | Mote Con Huesillo | Pad Tai | Pierogi | Pljeskavica | Poffertjes | Pommes Frites | Rendang | Samosa | Satay | Scotch Pies | Shave Ice | Shawarma | Smørrebrød | Som Tam | Souvlaki | Tacos | Tsukune Yakitori | Tteokbokki | Viennese Sausage | Yaroa

✸ **SYMBOLIC MEANINGS** Accessible; Nearby; Too good to ignore.
🌀 **POSSIBLE POWERS** Accessibility; Experimentation; Instant feedback; Interaction; Satisfy hunger.
🜨 **PLEASANT DREAMING** To dream about street food hints at being involved in a strong partnership.

☕ FOLKLORE AND FACTS

The ancient Greeks discovered there were vendors in Alexandria, Egypt, who were frying and selling fish on the street. That inspired some ancient Greek people to start frying and selling fish on the street, too. Archeologists uncovered an ancient street food counter in Pompeii with remnants of 2,000-year-old food and wine in terracotta jars. In ancient Rome, the average person was relatively poor and lived in dwellings that did not have access to cooking facilities. When craving hot food, they would often make way to one of the many food stalls that were nearby. An affordable favorite back then was chickpea soup with bread. Later, in the fourteenth century, fritters and lamb kebabs were sold by vendors on the streets of Cairo. Street food has been around for a while, and for good reasons, too: street food is the food of the people.

Some of the most delicious, most innovative, and difficult tastes to duplicate are found in foods sold away from conventional restaurants. The best "places" are those where the food is prepared by someone who really does know what they are doing. That reveals itself when the foods look enticing. The aromas are alluring. And they taste delicious.

Street food can be prepared and served from a card table under an umbrella or a long table under a tent, at a booth in an open market, from a food truck, a pushcart, or anywhere else someone can effectively make or even simply reheat their specially prepared foods. Their customers are the hungry people who are actually on the street, wandering around an outdoor market, on their way to or from school, or at work needing to grab something for lunch from a traveling food truck before it drives off to park elsewhere in town.

There are some booths that are relatively stable and have endured for years along lanes that are filled with other booths selling other street foods. The fragrance of the street is a blend of cooking smells that lure the hungry from one direction to another, inspiring a leisurely, lingering walk-along to taste several different foods along the way.

44

Worldwide Comfort Foods

Aglio e Olio | Bacon Sandwich | Banana Pudding | Bangers and Mash | Beans on Toast | Biriyani | Cereal with Milk | Chicken and Dumplings | Chicken Noodle Soup | Chicken Pot Pie with Mashed Potatoes | Chocolate | Cinnamon Toast | Cookies and Milk | Fish and Chips | Fries | Grilled Cheese | Hot Cocoa with Marshmallow | Ice Cream | Khichdi | Lassi | Macaroni 'n' Cheese | Matzo Ball Soup | Okayu | Pizza | Popcorn | Potato Chips | Ramen | Rice Porridge | Scrambled Eggs | Shepherd's Pie | Stew | Toad in the Hole | Tomato Soup and Crackers | Tortellini | Welsh Rarebit on Toast | Yogurt with Honey | Zosui

✺ **SYMBOLIC MEANINGS** Peace of mind; Soothing comfort.
🌀 **POSSIBLE POWERS** Calm; Centering; Connection with family; Good memories; Love; Mood-boosting; Peace of mind; Positivity; Stress relief.
🎧 **PLEASANT DREAMING** To dream of eating comfort foods is a hint that one feels a need for comforting.

☾ FOLKLORE AND FACTS

There are foods that trigger tastes that we have memorized. Those tastes and those particular foods are closely connected to very good memories. They are reminiscent of people, places, or things that made us happy once upon a time. We connect them to calm, inner peace, happiness, jubilant fun, special occasions, or a love of food, through food, and with food. Comfort food is just that: comforting. And sometimes we need the comforting more than almost anything else.

Comfort foods are typically, but not exclusively, high in fat or sugar, dense with energy, and may be low in nutrition. So *they* say. When one is in need of some dependable comforting with a food, that is the time when one least cares about its nutritional value or another's opinion. In a time of high stress, which can be emotionally, physically, and psychologically damaging to one's self, that stress triggers the desire for the comfort of one of our particular special feel-good foods. Once that happens, one's only thought is: I need it. Right now!

A food that tastes particularly good, and that we know was satisfying the last time we ate it, can trigger a quick rush of feel-good dopamine into our brain. The dopamine relieves our stress, inputs warm feelings, is pleasurable, and induces good memories. Dopamine helps us love ourselves even when we feel that nobody loves us back. Comfort food feels best when we really need comforting the most.

Feeling good feels so good! It's as if we have been given a big hug by the ice cream we are still digging into. We genuinely needed that surreal hug. It feels like it is coming from deep within. We begin to see things a bit clearer. Suddenly, an option pops into our head like a cork emerging up from down in deep water. We tuck a few tentative plans into the back of our mind to consider later. We ready ourselves to move onward to face the unpredictable future with a positive, healthier outlook. If there were tears, we dry them. Even so, we may still take another spoonful or two of ice cream or eat another slice of pizza. Just because it *feels* so good.

WORKS CONSULTED

———— ❖ ————

Acamovic, T, C.S. Stewart, and T.W Pennycott, Eds., *Poisonous Plants and Related Toxins* (Cabi, 2004)

Alexander, Courtney, "Berries as Symbol and in Folklore," https://cpb-us-e1.wpmucdn.com/blogs.cornell.edu/dist/0/7265/files/2016/12/berryfolklore-2ljztoq.pdf

Ancient Wisdom Foundation, "Herbs: A-Z List: The Medicinal, Spiritual and Magical Uses," https://www. ancient-wisdom.com/herbsaz.htm

Arndt, Alice, "The Flavors of Arabia," https://archive.aramcoworld.com/issue/198802/the.flavors.of.arabia.htm

Arrowsmith, Nancy, Calantirniel, et al, *Llewellyn's 2010 Herbal Almanac* (Llewellyn Publications, 2010)

Bailey, L.H., Ethel Zoe Bailey, Staff of Liberty Hyde Bailey Hortotorium, and David Bates, *Hortus Third: A Concise Dictionary of Plants Cultivated in the United States and Canada* (Macmillan, 1976)

Barrow, Mandy, "Primary Homework Help: The Romans: What Did The Romans Eat?" https://www.primaryhomeworkhelp.co.uk/romans/food.html

Bathroom Readers' Institute, *Uncle John's New & Improved Briefs: Fast Facts, Terse Trivia & Astute Articles* (St. Martin's Press, 1988)

Baynes, Thomas Spencer, Day Otis Kellogg, and William Robertson Smith, *The Encyclopedia Britannica* (Encyclopaedia Britannica, 1897)

Behind the Name, "The Etymology and History of First Names," https://www.behindthename.com

Bender, David A., *A Dictionary of Food and Nutrition, 4th Edition* (Oxford University Press, 2013)

Beyerl, Paul, *A Compendium of Herbal Magick* (Phoenix Publishing Inc., 1998)

Biodiversity Heritage Library, https://www. biodiversitylibrary.org

Blanchan, Neltje, *Wildflowers Worth Knowing* (Doubleday, 1917)

Bremness, Lesley, *Herbs* (Dorling-Kindersley Smithsonian Handbooks, 1994)

Brickell, Christopher, *The Royal Horticultural Society A–Z Encyclopedia of Garden Plants* (Dorling Kindersley Publishers Ltd, 1996)

Buhner, Stephen Harrod and Brooke Medicine Eagle, *Sacred Plant Medicine: The Wisdom in Native American Herbalism* (Bear & Company, 2006)

California Department of Food & Agriculture, https://www.cdfa.ca.gov

Coats, Alice M. and John L. Creech, *Garden Shrubs and Their Histories* (Simon & Schuster, 1992)

Connolly, Matt, "Timeline: A Short and Sweet History of Fake Meat," https://www.motherjones.com/environment/2013/12/history-fake-meat

Coombes, Allen J., *The Collingridge Dictionary of Plant Names* (Hamlyn, 1985)

Cornell University Library, "Online Exhibitions: Chocolate: Food of the Gods," https://exhibits.library.cornell.edu/chocolate-food-of-the-gods/feature/theobroma-cacao-food-of-the-gods

Culpepper, Nicholas, M.D., *The Complete Herbal* (A. Cross, 1652)

Cunningham, Scott, *Cunningham's Encyclopedia of Magical Herbs* (Llewellyn Publications, 1985)

Cunningham, Scott, *Cunningham's Encyclopedia of Wicca in the Kitchen* (Llewellyn Publications, 1990)

Cunningham, Scott, *Magical Herbalism: The Secret Craft of the Wise* (Llewellyn's Practical Magick, 1986)

Cunningham, Scott, *The Magic in Food: Legends, Lore, & Spellwork* (Llewellyn Publications, 1991)

Delaware Valley Unit of the Herb Society of America, https://www.delvalherbs.org

Dobelis, Inge N., *Magic and Medicine of Plants* (Reader's Digest, 1986)

Dosti, Rose, "Casseroles–Main courses for baby boomers in the 1950's," https://www.latimes.com/archives/la-xpm-1989-03-02-fo-0-story.html

Dream Glossary, https://www.dreamglossary.com

Duke, James A., Peggy-Ann K. Duke, and Judith L. duCellie, *Duke's Handbook of Medicinal Plants of the Bible* (CRC Press, 2007)

eFloras.org, https://www.efloras.org

Encyclopedia, https://encyclopedia.com

Fairchild Tropical Botanic Garden, https://www. fairchildgarden.org

FDA Poison Plant Data Base, https://www.fda.gov/food/science-research-food/fda-poisonous-plant-database

Fielding, Robert O., *Spices: Their Histories* (The Trade Register, 1910)

Folkard, Richard Jr., *Plant Lore, Legends, and Lyrics: Embracing Myths, Traditions, Superstitions, and Folk-Lore of the Plant Kingdom* (R. Folkard and Son, 1884)

Francis, Rose, *The Wild Flower Key: A Guide to Plant Identification in the Field* (Frederick Warne & Co., 1981)

Frost, Natasha, "How Medieval Chefs Tackled Meat-Free Days," https://www.atlasobscura.com/articles/mock-medieval-foods

Gardening Channel, "List of Herbs from A to Z," https://www.gardeningchannel.com/list-of-herbs-from-a-to-z/

Garland, Sarah, *The Complete Book of Herbs and Spices* (Viking Press, 1979)

Gordon, Barbara, "No Worries, the Alcohol Burns Off During Cooking–But, Does It Really?" https://www.isu.edu/news/2019-fall/no-worries-the-alcohol-burns-off-during-cookingbut-does-it-really.html

Grieve, Maud, A Modern Herbal online, https://botanical.com

Harvard University Herbaria & Libraries, https://kiki.huh, harvard.edu/databases/botanist_index.html

Hazlitt, William Carew, and John Brand, *Faiths and Folklore and Facts: A Dictionary* (Charles Scribner's Sons, 1905)

Heiss, Mary Lou and Robert J. Heiss, *The Story of Tea* (Ten Speed Press, 2007)

History.com Editors, "History of Chocolate," https://www.history.com/topics/ancient-americas/history-of-chocolate

Hohman, John George, *Pow-Wows or The Long Lost Friend: A Collection of Mysterious and Invaluable Arts and Remedies* (Self-published, 1820)

Howard, Michael, *Traditional Folk Remedies: A Comprehensive Herbal* (Century, 1987)

Huang, Rennica, "Tea Traditions around the World," https://sites.duke.edu/thewellianmag/2021/04/13/tea-traditions-around-the-world

Hutchens, Alma R., *Indian Herbalogy of North America: The Definitive Guide to Native Medicinal Plants and Their Uses* (Shambhala, 1991)

Ildrewe, Miss, *The Language of Flowers* (De Vries, Ibarra, 1865)

Ingram, John, *The Language of Flowers, or Flora Symbolica* (Frederick Warne and Company, 1897)

Jackson, Ellie, Clarck Drieshen, and Calum Cockburn, "Great Medieval Bake Off: Lent Edition," https://blogs.bl.uk/digitisedmanuscripts/2021/03/bake-off-lent.html

Jones, Tony, "Everyday spirituality: baking bread," https://www.minnpost.com/minnesota-blog-cabin/2012/07/everyday-spirituality-baking-bread

Keightley, Thomas, *The Fairy Mythology: Illustrative of the Romance and Superstition of Various Countries* (George Bell & Sons, 1892)

Kepler, Angela Kay, *Hawaiian Heritage Plants* (University of Hawaii Press, 1998)

Kew Royal Botanic Gardens, "Plants of the World Online," https://wcsp.science.kew.org/home.do

Kew Royal Botanic Gardens, "World Checklist of Selected Plant Families," https://plantsoftheworldonline.org

Koehler, Jeff, "Couscous: A Symbol of Harmony In Northwest Africa, A Region Of Clashes," https://www.npr.org/sections/thesalt/2019/06/27/735429939/couscous-a-symbol-of-harmony-in-northwest-africa-a-region-of-clashes

Kubala, Jillian, "Whole-Foods, Plant-Based Diet: A Detailed Beginner's Guide," https://www.healthline.com/nutrition/plant-based-diet-guide#overview

Lad, Vasant K., *Ayurveda: The Science of Self-Healing* (Lotus Press, 1985)

Lust, John, *The Herb Book: The Most Complete Catalog of Herbs Ever Published* (Bantam Books, 1979)

Mah, Sue, "New & Trends: The Science of Comfort Foods," https://nutritionfornonnutritionists.com/2020/05/the-science-of-comfort-foods/

McCormick & Company, Importers and Grinders of Spices, *Spices: A Text-Book For Teachers* (McCormick & Co., 1915)

McGuffin, Michael, *American Herbal Products Association's Botanical Safety Handbook* (American Herbal Products Association, 2013)

Medieval Cookery, https://www.medievalcookery.com

Miller, Gustavus Hindman, *10,000 Dreams Interpreted: An Illustrated Guide to Unlocking the Secrets of Your Dreamlife* (Metro Books, 2001)

Moscoso, Carlos G., "West Indian Cherry–Richest Known Source of Natural Vitamin C," https://www.jstor.org/stable/4287902

National Capital Poison Center Poison Control, "Poisonous and Non-Poisonous Plants," https://www.poison.org/articles/plant#poisonousplants

Nations Online, "Chinese Customs: Food Symbolism," https://www.nationsonline.org/oneworld/Chinese_Customs/food_symbolism.htm

Natural Medicinal Herbs, https://www.naturalmedicinalherbs.net/herbs/natural/

Northcote, Lady Rosalind, *The Book of Herbs*, (Turnbull & Spears, 1903)

Ody, Penelope, *The Complete Medicinal Herbal* (Dorling Kindersley, 1993)

Okakura, Kakuzo, *The Book of Tea* (Fox, Duffield & Company, 1906)

Petre, Alina, "What is Tofu, and Is It Good For You?" https://www.healthline.com/nutrition/what-is-tofu

Pickle Packers International, "Pickle Primer: A Glossary Of Pickles And Pickled Peppers," https://www.ilovepickles.org/pickle-facts/definitions-2/pickle-primer-a-glossary-of-pickles-and-pickled-peppers/

Plants for a Future, https://pfaf.org

Radeska, Tijana, "The Necessity of Coffee: In 16th Century Constantinople, Not Providing Your Wife With Enough Coffee Was Grounds For Divorce," https://www.thevintagenews.com/2017/09/07/the-necessity-of-coffee-in-16th-century-constantinople-not-providing-your-wife-with-enough-coffee-was-grounds-for-divorce/

Ricketts, Colin, "What Did the Romans Eat? Cuisine of the Ancient Romans," https://www.historyhit.com/what-did-the-romans-eat-food-and-drink-in-ancient-times/

Rohde, Eleanour Sinclair, *The Old English Herbals* (Longmans, Green and Co., 1922)

Rupp, Rebecca, "The Bitter Truth About Olives," https://www.nationalgeographic.com/culture/article/olives--the-bitter-truth

Science Direct, https://www.sciencedirect.com

Sietsema, Robert, "The Offal-Eaters Handbook: Untangling the Myths of Organ Meats," https://www.eater.com/2015/6/16/8786663/offal-organ-meat-handbook-cuts-sweetbreads-tripe-gizzard

Simonetti, Gaultiero and Stanley Schuler, ed., *Simon & Schuster's Guide to Herbs and Spices* (Simon & Schuster, 1990)

Simons, Frederick J., *Plants of Life, Plants of Death* (University of Wisconsin Press, 1998)

Tan, Rachel, "Technique Thursdays: Aspic," https://guide.michelin.com/us/en/california/article/dining-in/aspic-food-technique-how-to

Taste Atlas, https://www.tasteatlas.com

Theoi Project, "Flora 1: Plants of Greek Myth," https://www.theoi.com/Flora1.html

Thiselton-Dyer, T.F., *The Folk-Lore of Plants* (1889)

Tisserand, Robert B. *The Art of Aromatherapy: The Healing and Beautifying Properties of the Essential Oils of Flowers and Herbs*, (Healing Arts Press, 1978)

Tsapovsky, Flora, "Are We Ready for an Aspic Comeback?," https://www.foodandwine.com/travel/restaurants/aspic-comeback-restaurants

University of California, "Safe and Poisonous Garden Plants," https://ucanr.edu/sites/poisonous_safe_plants/

University of Rochester Medical Center, "A Guide To Common Medicinal Herbs," https://www.urmc.rochester.edu/encyclopedia/content

U.S. Forest Service, "Plants of Mind and Spirit," https://www.fs.fed.us/wildflowers/ethnobotany/Mind_and_Spirit/index.shtml

USDA (United States Department of Agriculture) Natural Resources Conservation Service, https://www.nrcs.usda.gov/wps/portal/nrcs/site/national/home

Valnet, Jean, *The Practice of Aromatherapy*, translated from French by Robin Campbell and Libby Houston (Random House, 1982; Vermilion, 2011)

Vaughan, John, and Catherine Geissler, *The New Oxford Book of Food Plants* (Oxford University Press, 2009)

Vaughan, J.G. and P.A. Judd, *The New Oxford Book of Health Foods* (Oxford University Press, 2003)

Will, Melissa J., "25 Fruits That Ripen After Picking (and Those That Don't)," https://empressofdirt.net/fruits-ripen-after-picking/

Worthington, Tara, "The Chai Story: A History of India's Most-Loved Drink," https://passionpassport.com/chai-tea-history/

ACKNOWLEDGMENTS

I have greatly appreciated my beloved daughter Melanie's enormous encouragement and excitement while I was researching this intriguing subject and writing this book. Melanie has had a lifelong fascination with food that has made her a fabulous cook, an exquisite baker, and a tantalizing candy maker. For her, the art of food has been a tangible expression of her love for her family and friends. As a language, the food that she has prepared and presented is saying, "I love you. Enjoy!" That is something that I find completely delightful. Melanie has been an inspiration to her entire family, because they all enjoy cooking and sharing their love and appreciation for family and friends in the same ways.

I would like to dedicate this book to my three little great-granddaughters, Daphne, Maggie, and Ruby. They all love to eat. I expect that they will be just as receptive to the same inspiration while watching and helping their parents and grandparents preparing, cooking, and presenting the food they make. They, too, will learn from them that food is a tangible expression of their love for their family and friends. Yes, food definitely means love. There is no secret about that. Food is a language that speaks of love in every language on Earth.

Special thanks to Wellfleet Press and all things Quarto Publishing Group USA. Everyone I have worked with has been outstanding and encouraging. A million and one thanks to Wellfleet's Editor, Elizabeth You, for her much appreciated guidance. Thank you to Quarto's brilliant Publisher, Rage Kindelsperger, and wonderful Managing Editor, Cara Donaldson, for their overall vision and ongoing encouragement. Thank you to my Copyeditor, Helena Caldon, for her careful attention to the text. Thank you to Creative Director, Laura Drew, and the entire Art Team for skillfully creating such a beautiful book. You are all amazing people. I wish you all the very best in every way imaginable.

To my dear friend Robert, who I dearly adore. God bless you always. I owe you a pie.

Thank you to God for his blessings and for an endless ongoing list of seriously good reasons.

To all of the Food Loving and Plant Loving People of the World: look up, look down, look all around. Peace and love to you all.

ABOUT
THE AUTHOR

Spring, summer, and autumn container gardening on a small apartment's balcony is all the more appreciated during the short growing season in the Enchanted Mountains of Western New York State, where eclectic artist and writer S. Theresa Dietz makes her home. Her fascination with all things magical and mysterious, along with a deep abiding love of trees, plants, and flowers motivates her to continue learning more about them.

PHOTO CREDITS

LIST OF
CULINARY HERBS

No. 049   Achiote *Bixa orellana*

No. 075   Ají Cito Pepper *Capsicum baccatum*

No. 381   Ajwain *Trachyspermum ammi*

No. 358   Alexanders *Smyrnium olusatrum*

No. 290   Allspice *Pimenta dioica*

No. 025   Angelica *Angelica archangelica*

No. 291   Anise *Pimpinella anisum*

No. 235   Arrowroot *Maranta arundinacea*

No. 165   Asafoetida *Ferula assa-foetida*

No. 262   Basil *Ocimum basilicum*

No. 208   Bay Laurel *Laurus nobilis*

No. 243   Bee Balm *Monarda didyma*

No. 107   Bergamot Orange *Citrus bergamia*

No. 106   Bitter Orange *Citrus × aurantium*

No. 260   Black Cumin *Nigella sativa*

No. 055   Black Mustard *Brassica nigra*

No. 294   Black Pepper *Piper nigrum*

No. 386   Black Truffle *Tuber melanosporum*

No. 200   Black Walnut *Juglans nigra*

No. 051   Borage *Borago officinalis*

No. 052   Brown Mustard *Brassica juncea*

No. 345   Burnet *Sanguisorba minor*

No. 124   Calamint *Clinopodium menthifolium*

No. 073   Caper *Capparis spinosa*

No. 082   Caraway *Carum carvi*

No. 158   Cardamom *Elettaria cardamomum*

No. 153   Carrot *Daucus carota* subsp. *sativus*

No. 029   Celeriac *Apium graveolens* var. *rapaceum*

No. 028   Celery *Apium graveolens* var. *graveolens*

No. 027   Chervil *Anthriscus cerefolium*

No. 100   Chicory *Cichorium intybus*

No. 074   Chili Peppers *Capsicum annuum*

No. 015   Chives *Allium schoenoprasum*

No. 102   Cinnamon *Cinnamomum verum*

No. 114   Citron *Citrus medica*

No. 371   Clove *Syzygium aromaticum*

No. 012   Common Onion *Allium cepa*

No. 335   Common Sorrel *Rumex acetosa*

No. 133   Coriander *Coriandrum sativum*

No. 375   Costmary *Tanacetum balsamita*

No. 293   Cubeb *Piper cubeba*

No. 147   Cumin *Cuminum cyminum*

No. 248   Curry Leaf Tree *Murraya koenigii*

No. 024   Dill *Anethum graveolens*

No. 096   Edible Chrysanthemum *Chrysanthemum coronarium*

No. 209   English Lavender *Lavandula angustifolia*

No. 013   Everlasting Onion *Allium fistulosum*

No. 383   Fenugreek *Trigonella foenum-graecum*

No. 338   French Sorrel *Rumex scutatus*

No. 014   Garlic *Allium sativum*

No. 017   Garlic Chives *Allium tuberosum*

No. 410   Ginger *Zingiber officinale*

No. 005   Grains of Paradise *Aframomum melegueta*

No. 115   Grapefruit *Citrus × paradisi*

No. 033   Horseradish *Armoracia rusticana*

No. 076   Hot Pepper *Capsicum chinense*

No. 196   Hyssop *Hyssopus officinalis*

No. 202   Juniper *Juniperus communis*

No. 118   Kabosu Papeda *Citrus sphaerocarpa*

No. 105   Key Lime *Citrus × aurantiifolia*

No. 004   Korarima *Aframomum corrorima*

No. 220   Koseret *Lippia abyssinica*

No. 010   Leek *Allium ampeloprasum* var. *ampeloprasum*

No. 111   Lemon *Citrus × limon*

No. 240   Lemon Balm *Melissa officinalis*

No. 018   Lemon Verbena *Aloysia citrodora*

No. 151   Lemongrass *Cymbopogon citratus*

No. 180   Licorice *Glycyrrhiza glabra*

No. 214   Lovage *Levisticum officinale*

No. 109	Makrut Lime *Citrus hystrix*		No. 347	Summer Savory *Satureja hortensis*
No. 116	Mandarin Orange *Citrus × reticulata*		No. 257	Sweet Cicely *Myrrhis odorata*
No. 268	Marjoram *Origanum majorana*		No. 168	Sweet Fennel *Foeniculum vulgare*
No. 255	Nutmeg *Myristica fragrans*		No. 117	Sweet Orange *Citrus × sinensis*
No. 275	Opium Poppy *Papaver somniferum*		No. 408	Szechuan Pepper *Zanthoxylum piperitum*
No. 269	Oregano *Origanum vulgare*		No. 077	Tabasco Pepper *Capsicum frutescens* var. *tabasco*
No. 282	Parsley *Petroselinum crispum*		No. 034	Tarragon *Artemisia dracunculus*
No. 241	Peppermint *Mentha × piperita*		No. 263	Thai Basil *Ocimum basilicum* var. *thyrsiflora*
No. 110	Persian Lime *Citrus × latifolia*		No. 380	Thyme *Thymus vulgaris*
No. 314	Pomegranate *Punica granatum*		No. 148	Turmeric *Curcuma longa*
No. 113	Pomelo *Citrus maxima*		No. 395	Vanilla Orchid *Vanilla planifolia*
No. 016	Rocambole *Allium scorodoprasum*		No. 404	Wasabi *Wasabia japonica*
No. 078	Rocoto Pepper *Capsicum pubescens*		No. 259	Watercress *Nasturtium officinale*
No. 343	Rosemary *Salvia rosmarinus*		No. 354	White Mustard *Sinapis alba*
No. 137	Saffron *Crocus sativus*		No. 348	Winter Savory *Satureja montana*
No. 342	Sage *Salvia officinalis*			
No. 353	Sesame *Sesamum indicum*			
No. 011	Shallot *Allium ascalonicum*			
No. 280	Shiso *Perilla frutescens* var. *crispa*			
No. 242	Spearmint *Mentha spicata*			
No. 198	Star Anise *Illicium verum*			
No. 119	Sudachi *Citrus sudachi*			
No. 325	Sumac *Rhus coriaria*			

Index of
COMMON FOOD NAMES

Index of
CULINARY FINDS
AROUND THE WORLD

Items in this section begin on page 192

Index of
COMMON FOOD
MEANINGS

ALSO AVAILABLE

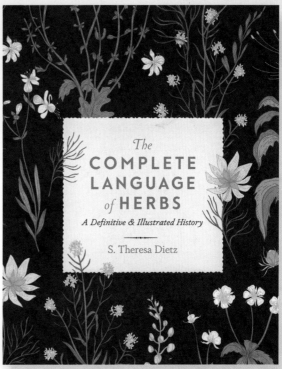

THE COMPLETE LANGUAGE OF FLOWERS
ISBN: 978-157715-190-6

THE COMPLETE LANGUAGE OF HERBS
ISBN: 978-157715-282-8